TRIUMPH BY NAME - TRIUMPH BY NATURE.
The Sidescreen TR Compendium.

By Bill Piggott.

DALTON WATSON

FINE BOOKS

TRIUMPH BY NAME - TRIUMPH BY NATURE
The Sidescreen TR Compendium
by Bill Piggott

First published in 1995

ISBN 1-85443-107-2

c 1995 Bill Piggott & Dalton Watson Fine Books

British Library Cataloguing in Publication Data:-
A CIP catalogue record for this book is available from the British Library

Designed by David G Styles
Published by Dalton Watson Fine Books,
P. O. Box 2, Belton, Loughborough LE12 9UW, England.

A catalogue of other titles in the Dalton Watson Fine Books range is available upon receipt at the above address of a C5-sized stamped addressed envelope.

TRIUMPH BY NAME - TRIUMPH BY NATURE

CONTENTS:

TRIUMPH BY NAME - TRIUMPH BY NATURE

ACKNOWLEDGMENTS:

I wish to thank the following people and organisations for their help, be it direct or indirect, with the preparation and production of this book. I hope I have managed to record everybody's name, but may I apologise in advance should there be omissions. Any such omissions are not due to a lack of intent, simply a failure of administration on my part!

GENERAL ACKNOWLEDGEMENTS

John Ames, "Autocar" magazine, "Autosport" magazine, A.R.A. Barree, E. Batte, Birmingham City Libraries, Adam Blackaby, Tom Blackburn, Brian Blackwell, Stuart Bladon, British Motor Industry Heritage Trust, David Boreham, "Brooklands Books", Peter Buckles, David Burrows, Peter Cathie, Graham Cheetham, Brian Chislett, Peter Clarke, Roger Clarke, Anders Clausager, John and Evelyn Cook, Peter Cooper, Ian Cornish, Peter Cox, The Earl of Elgin and Kincardine Kt, John and Caroline Edmonds, Don Elliott, Mike Ellis, Liz English, Ian Evans, Express Newspapers PLC, Roger Ferris, Mary Fraser (nee Walker), Ian Gibson, J.W. Godsell, Rosy Good, Geoffrey Goodall, Peter Gorrie, Ian Griffiths, Ian Hall, Graham Hallett, Vic Hammond, Haymarket Publishing Ltd, Mike Hazlewood, Glen Hewett, Eddie Holden, Nigel Holmes, Francois van Hoof, John Hopwood, T.R. Householder, Paul Howell, Terry Hurrell, T. Kerr Baillie, Dave King, J.H. King, Jon Korbin, Richard Larter, L.A.T. Photographic Ltd, Raymond Laird, Jon Laver, Barry Leavens, Martin Lodawer, Jim Lowry, Geoff and Sheila Mansfield, Barrie March, Mike and Jan May, "Motor" magazine, "Motorsport" magazine, Ken Munford, National Motor Museum Beaulieu, Fred Nicklin, T.A. (Bill) Parkes, Trevor Parker, Jan Pearce, Philip Peerboom, Brian Pugh, Alec Pringle, T.J. de Putron, Ken Rawson, Joe Richards, Ken Richardson, Paul Richardson, Peter Rix, Alan Robinson, Graham Robson, Joel Rosen, John Saunders, Roger Seal, Chris Sergison, David Siegle-Morris, Terry and Val Simpson, Bob and Ginny Soden, Julian Stephens, Dr David Styles, The T.R. Register and its Staff, Darryl Uprichard, John Waddington, John Wallwork, Harry Webster, Nick Webster, Tony Wemyss, Robert West, Lawrence West, Nigel Wiggins, Keith Wigglesworth, Peter Wigglesworth, Bob Woodley, J. Woolverton.

I would also like to thank both Tricia Butler and Helen Vassallo for typing my untidy manuscripts so ably, and also Karen Nadin for all her help and support, both with proof reading and generally.

PICTURE ACKNOWLEDGEMENTS

The photographs reproduced in this volume have been drawn from many sources, mainly from the 1950's but some are more modern. The source credited is generally that which provided me with the particular photograph, for in many such cases, the original photographer's name is unknown. This is particularly so in the case of pictures extracted from 1950's magazines. If however the original photographer's name is recorded, then I have credited him as appropriate. Many photographs have been taken from private collections where the original print is firmly fixed in an album, thus preventing access to the reverse and to any details thereon. In such cases, I have again credited the actual source providing the photograph. If I have breached anyone's copyright in so doing, I wish to say that this was not my intention; it is however frequently very difficult to establish copyright when dealing with old photographs extracted from many sources. I hope that all reasonable steps have been taken to establish ownership, but I apologise in advanace to anyone whose copyright has been inadvertently breached. Where no acknowledgement is given for a particular illustration, it is from the Author's own collection or on rare occasions a photograph actually taken by him.

W. G. P.

FOREWORD
by Ken Richardson

This is Bill Piggott's third book on TR sports cars, the development of which I had overall responsibility for in the 1950's. I have enjoyed his previous books, and it is clear that Bill has a considerable historical knowledge of the subject. I have however, I hope, been able to fill in some gaps and also to set the record straight as regards my time at Standard-Triumph, for not all of the previously published writings accord with my memories of the actual events!

Following the development of the first TR2 from the unsatisfactory 20TS prototype, it was evident that we had a car of considerable competition potential on our hands, and a Competitions Department was established under my direction. The production TR2s and 3s were an instant success with the public, and became a firm favourite as club rally cars. We enjoyed many successes on the International Rally scene throughout the Fifties, and it was and still remains a source of great pride to my team and myself that these TRs were considered the cars to beat in International Competition. This was achieved by constant development, hard work and attention to detail by all of us in the Competition Department, including the mechanics, who were a marvellous bunch of lads. They should share in the credit for the successes we achieved as a team, together with our drivers and navigators. I regularly meet up with members of the old team to talk over past times, and looking back nearly forty years, I can say that I thoroughly enjoyed my involvement with the early TRs. It is with great pleasure that I witness the interest that these cars continue to generate today.

I am regularly invited to attend TR Club meetings in various parts of the world including the Annual Vintage Triumph Register Convention in America; I never fail to be impressed by the first class restoration work and the beautiful condition of TRs I have seen on both sides of the Atlantic. The enthusiasm of the owners of these cars, together with books like Bill Piggott's will keep alive and reinforce the "TR spirit", and I commend them to you on behalf of myself and all in our old team. Ultimately, however, there is only one real way to enjoy a sidescreen TR and that is by driving it hard and fast. Long may it be possible to do so!

Ken Richardson,
April 1995

I NTRODUCTION

As Registrar of the TR Register, and an enthusiastic TR driver for many years, I was particularly gratified to be given this opportunity to write this, my third book on the subject. In addition to my own previous work, there are at least six other books dealing specifically with Triumph TR sports cars, so the reader might well be forgiven for thinking that the subject has been already fully chronicled, and that there remained nothing further either new or useful to say. Both I and my publisher David Styles of Dalton Watson think this not to be the case, and I hope that those interested enough to study the contents will come to a similar conclusion. I have tried not to duplicate previously published material, and to concentrate on aspects of the subject that have not been covered in detail before, using much original material and new research.

This book is specifically about TR2/3/3A/3Bs, cars built between 1953 and 1962. I shall refer to these cars generically as "sidescreen" TRs. not because I particularly like the term, but because it forms a useful shorthand way of distinguishing these earlier TRs from the more sophisticated, yet arguably less overtly sporting, later cars. The use of the term "Sidescreen TRs" seems to have become accepted within the TR clubs and by the Classic Car press over the years, and despite trying, I find that I am unable to better it! Similarly, the term "TR3A" should be read as including also the "TR3B" model, unless the contrary is stated or the context dictates otherwise. Although there have been many TR books, the only previous one exclusively devoted to sidescreen TRs is my own "Superprofile", published in 1987 and now out of print. That was of necessity a slim and basic volume, some aspects of which I now take the opportunity to amplify in this present book. Another point to make is that throughout this book, the words "The Company", "Works", and "Factory", should be read as synonyms for Standard-Triumph's plants in Coventry where the cars were built.

To avoid any misrepresentation, let me state what this book is not; it is not a guide to the purchase or restoration of sidescreen TRs, nor is it an "originality" guide. It is a "TR Companion", a book drawn as far as possible from contemporary sources, from interviews with people who owned and competed with the cars in the 1950's and 1960's, from archive material and from largely contemporary photographs, many previously unpublished, together with some that appeared in the motoring magazines of the time but that are new to a 1990's readership. Concerning the photographs, I apologise that in some cases the quality is not as good as it might be, but many of the negatives are now lost, and we have had to 'scan' the pictures electronically from contemporary printed sources. The only alternative would have been not to use them, which would have been a pity. Where known, I have given attributions and acknowledged copyright, but again, in many cases it has not proved possible to uncover this information. A considerable number of photographs used were stuck into albums with no access to any details on their reverse, and similarly, some photographs have come from the collections accumulated by the TR Register over the years, where the details of whence they emanated are either not recorded or are lost. May I therefore apologise in advance to anyone whose copyright or photograph is either not or is mistakenly acknowledged; I and my publisher have striven as far as possible to get things correct, but it has not been easy. A further point concerns the comparative lack of TR3A photographs as compared with the earlier cars. Presumably because by the late 1950's the TR was no longer "big news", far fewer TR pictures were published than had been the case in the mid 1950's, and so inevitably there are not as many TR3A pictures for me to draw on today; I hope that this will not detract from anyone's enjoyment of this book.

The book is, I hope, a collection of items of interest to the sidescreen TR owner and the non-owning enthusiast, assembled here for the first time in one place, and it is also a digest of many of the fascinating and sometimes arcane items I have collected by virtue of my position as sidescreen TR Registrar of the TR Register for the past 15 years. It is a parallel and, I hope, complementary volume to the TR2/3/3A/B section of my "Original TR" book, and it includes many items that were not appropriate to that book devoted as it was to vehicle originality, but which I felt would nevertheless intrigue those with an affection for these rugged, sporting cars. By the same token, I have striven to avoid any overlap with my previous books, although a small measure of repetition is inevitable when dealing with such a specific subject as one model of one make of a particular sporting car! There is also a certain amount of unavoidable overlap and minor duplication within the individual chapters in this book, for it has been difficult at times to know where to place chapter divisions. I hope that in such cases that the reader will bear with me, and consider it better that a certain fact be repeated rather than that it be omitted entirely!

I have been very fortunate in being able to interview Ken Richardson for this book, Ken having also kindly written the Foreword. As is well known, Ken Richardson was employed by Sir John Black of The Standard-Triumph Company to refine the prototype Triumph sports car of 1952 into the record breaking, production TR2 of 1953/4, and he was also a racing and test driver of considerable skill, having been employed by both the ERA and BRM racing car concerns. Now a sprightly octogenarian, Ken retains a remarkably clear and concise memory of the events surrounding the creation of the sidescreen TRs, even though more than 40 years have elapsed. My interview provided him with a welcome opportunity to amplify and clarify some previously published details and misconceptions surrounding the creation of the TR2 and Ken's part in this process, and I feel this chapter will be both interesting and illuminating to all TR enthusiasts. I am aware that some of the details as recalled by Ken conflict with other accounts; all I can say to this, however, is that Ken Richardson was there!

Although I have been able to "unearth" many long-forgotten items and aspects of TR lore, I have come to the conclusion it will never be possible to answer all questions concerning sidescreen TRs satisfactorily, particularly in relation to the manufacturing process and production details. Many of the personalities involved have now died, and comprehensive records were not necessarily kept, and even where they were, they have not always survived. The cars had a designed life of between 10 and 15 years, and that was a long time in the rust-prone 1950's. Can one blame the people concerned with TRs then for not foreseeing that forty years later the exact point at which the split steering column was introduced on the TR3A would be a matter of considerable moment?

Nevertheless, despite the impossiblity of being comprehensive, I trust that all enthusiasts for the sidescreen TRs in particular and classic sporting cars in general will find reading this book as enjoyable as I have found compiling it!

Bill Piggott
Nottingham
June 1995

The three Works Rally TR2s from 1954 are posed at the Coventry Factory, accompanied by some of the mechanics who built them. The date is probably mid-1954, prior to the cars being driven "in anger" in a major event..

The late Paul Good corners hard in his TR2 at Prescott Hill Climb in the early 1980s, always one of his favourite venues (Rosy Good).

This book is dedicated to the memory of two great TR enthusiasts; firstly Paul Good, co-founder of the Chiltern Group of the TR Register, and secondly Virginia ("Ginny") Soden, Editor of the TR Register's "TR action" magazine from 1982 to 1993.

DALTON WATSON

FINE BOOKS

CHAPTER ONE:

On Fore-runners and Prototypes

This chapter is not intended to be a history of the development of the post-war Triumph Sports cars from the 1800 and 2000 Roadsters, through the 20X "Bullet" prototypes, for that has been covered thoroughly elsewhere in several Standard-Triumph books. Rather it is a pot-pourri of other information that has come my way, much of it I hope not previously published, and all of it relating to the development of the TR and the various prototypes built. Nor, I should add, do I propose to deal with either the factory racing cars or the Works rally cars, for again, these have been well chronicled previously.

It has been said, and it has also been denied, that the true ancestor of the TR was the Special built up by Ken Rawlings from Standard-Triumph parts in the late 1940's. Clearly this was not in any way a Works sponsored effort, but information I have gathered leads me to believe that this car may have had somewhat more influence on subsequent events at Standard-Triumphs - i.e. the birth of the TR - than has previously been allowed. Certainly this car, christened "Buttercup", and registered JOX 7, was a successful and influential device, both on the road and in the trials competitions for which it was principally designed. Its builder was an employee at P J Evans Ltd, who were the Standard-Triumph distributors for the Birmingham area, and consequently access to parts was not the problem that it would have been for "outsiders" at that time of post-war shortages. "Buttercup" had a Standard Eight chassis and suspension, a Standard Twelve axle and a Vanguard engine and gearbox, clothed in a one-off, light alloy trials-type body. Being of light weight and comparatively low geared, it was not surprising that the torque of the Vanguard engine caused it to perform

well. Now it is said that the then Managing Director of P J Evans Ltd was a firm friend of Standard-Triumph boss Sir John Black, and that "PJs" had been involved with the testing of several Standard-Triumph prototypes.

It has also been suggested to me, though not in any way proven, that Sir John Black was involved with "Buttercup" on a personal level "behind the scenes", unknown to others back at Coventry. That Black was trying hard to produce a successful sports car is of course well known, so it does seem possible that he could have had a "secret" involvement in the project.

When interviewed many years later however, Black's assistant Alick Dick (who replaced him as Managing Director) insisted that neither he nor Sir John had any involvement with Buttercup nor indeed any knowledge of it. Maybe Sir John kept it so quiet that even his right hand man did not know! The use of a Vanguard engine in this sports car was suggested to have been a clandestine way of testing its suitability for a true sports car. After all, this engine was going to appear before long in the Morgan Plus Four (and Black was, at that time ,trying to buy the Morgan company) and in addition he had in mind its eventual use in his own sports car should the Morgan purchase prove abortive.

Even for someone working at a Standard-Triumph distributors as Rawlings did, the obtaining of a new Vanguard engine in 1949 would have been no easy matter; there was evidently at the time a four year waiting list for the cars, and a one year wait for a spare engine! (It is said that Morgans only got their engines because Black was interested in the firm.) Thus, if Sir John were personally involved with the "Buttercup" project, parts supply problems would disappear, the car could be built and evaluated rapidly and Black would have a "back-door" way of testing his engine without any odium falling on him or the Company were it to fail in this application. Although this story has come to me on what I consider to be good authority, it may or may not be correct, though I must say that it seems quite likely, and accords with Sir John Black's known propensity for "behind the scenes" wheeler-dealing!

Whatever the true situation, Rawlings' special soon became very well known in sporting circles, and would have inevitably come to the wider attention of the Standard-Triumph board. It seems impossible to believe that they were not influenced by its success when initial plans were afoot to produce what became the 20TS prototype; after all, the 20TS was as much a Standard Triumph "parts-bin special" based on an existing chassis frame as Buttercup had been, and the temptation for the company to say "We could do that!" would have been overwhelming!

Moving on to the first true TRs, I have gleaned various bits of information concerning the prototypes. I've already said that this is not a technical history of these cars, but new information has come to light and is related here and in Chapter Three, in the course of my interview with Ken Richardson. Much mystery surrounds the creation of the 20TS prototype (often erroneously referred to as the TR1), which is surprising, as it was built little over forty years ago and several of the participants are still with us. However, each seems to have a memory of those events at variance with the others; for instance, there is controversy over whether the running 20TS prototype was broken up, or was "converted" into one of the TR2 prototypes, and if so, which one? If indeed such a conversion occurred, then MVC 575 (the "Jabbeke" record car) seems to have the better claim to be the scion of the 20TS. Its present owner certainly thinks that it was built incorporating major parts from the 20TS.

Another dispute concerns which TR2 prototype was the first TR2 actually shown to the public - at the Geneva Motor Show between 5th and 15th March 1953. The car concerned (with no registration number) was flown there rather than driven. Photographs show it to have had wheels finished in a darker colour than the bodywork, and darker than those on the "Jabbeke" car MVC 575. My own view is that the "Geneva" car was MWK 950, although its present owner disputes this and believes MVC 575 was the car flown to Switzerland. Of the two, MWK was registered first, and a photocopy of its logbook in my possession shows that it was first registered in Coventry by the Standard Triumph Motor Co on 23rd January 1953, chassis no X508, fitted originally with experimental engine number X571E, although this was later replaced by

production engine number TS31E. The colour was said to be "blue", though the Ice Blue shade in which both prototypes were finished was in reality a light green! MVC 575 was first registered on 31st March 1953, chassis number X519 with engine number X569E, but both cars probably ran on Company "trade" plates prior to being road-registered. Both were left hand drive, though prior to sale by the company, both were converted to right hand drive. By courtesy of the present owner of MVC 575, I have obtained copies of an invoice by which it was sold in October 1956, and also of a letter written by Standards shortly thereafter to Mr Hedger, who bought it from Welbeck Motors Limited after the Company sold it off. The car was referred to as "the first TR2 built", which may or may not be true, whilst it is also said that the car was "updated" prior to sale.

In addition to those modifications mentioned, it had also been given wire wheels and the post-1954 "short" doors which incorporated outer sill panels. The statement that: "it has more recently been fitted with the standard 3.7 axle" is intriguing, and implies that it must either have been fitted earlier with the 3.89 ratio as fitted to the 20TS prototype (did it do the Jabbeke runs with this ratio, one wonders ?) or alternatively, as the car was a "mobile test bed", maybe it was used in 1955/6 to test the forthcoming 4.1 axle ratio? Despite the statement that it was fitted prior to sale with a "production engine and gearbox", the later owners confirm that the original experimental engine stamped X569E was still in the car - although possibly only the cylinder block (which is the part that carries the number) was used, the engine internals having being updated? Certainly, the engine was to TR3 specification by the time of sale.

Surprisingly, MVC 575 has only had two further owners since its sale by Standard-Triumphs via Welbeck Motors to Mr Hedger. The first, who was known to Mr Hedger was Graham Hallett, an early TR Register Member, who acquired the car around 1969/70, and who wrote of his experiences in an early copy of the TR Register magazine. He recalled first seeing the car in the mid 1960's "when a very glamorous lady harpsichordist whom I knew used to roar up to rehearsals in it" - possibly this was Mrs Hedger, and how, one speculates, did she get a harpsichord into a TR2? Although he heard stories at the time that this was no ordinary TR2, Hallett did not realise quite how special it was. He expressed an interest in acquiring the car should the Hedgers ever wish to sell, which at the time they did not.

Some years passed, Graham Hallett restored a TD MG instead, and then out of the blue received a phone call from John Hedger to say that he was probably going to scrap MVC 575 because it had been damaged in a minor accident, and was pretty rusty as well, but before he did, did Hallett still

A rare photograph showing the bodywork of the "20X" Bullet prototype under manufacture. The complication (and expense) of this structure, as compared with the TR's bodywork, can be seen (DG Styles collection)

Ken Rawlings' competition special "Buttercup" showed what could be done when the Standard Vanguard engine was fitted into a sporting car.

This shot shows the 20TS body awaiting mounting on to its chassis. (National Motor Museum)

A rare head-on view of the 20TS prototype taken in 1952. The separate sidelights on the wings can clearly be seen, as can the prototype badge. Despite its poor photographic quality, this view is sufficiently unusual to justify inclusion here.

On the right is an October 1952 advertisement for the 20TS prototype, looking even less appealing in this artist's impression than it did in the metal.

Below: It's late 1952 and Sir John Black is seen at the wheel of the running 20TS prototype. The unappealing rear end is clearly demonstrated in this photograph, which is said to have been taken in the USA, at the premises of the Willys Overland Corporation in Ohio. Whilst demonstrating this car in the USA, Sir John presumably kept quiet about developments back in Coventry that were leading to the TR2 (TR Register Archive).

want the car? Most certainly Hallett did, and dropping everything, he rushed to the owner's house expecting to find an absolute wreck - instead, the car was licenced, insured and mobile! They charged off over the Berkshire downs "Blasting past everything in sight in a way never experienced in a MG 'T' type, and with the steering pulling ferociously to the left, a legacy from the accident." Whilst being given this rapid and hairy test-drive, Hallett was told for the first time the details of the car's pedigree, and simply could not believe his luck! He was then entertained to tea, whereupon the owner produced paperwork to support the car's claimed history and a very minor sum of money changed hands - "a virtual gift" as he described it in his article.

The suspension was soon "straightened out" and a vehicle test passed (with one rear damper link actually missing!), then Graham Hallett took to the road in the "Jabbeke" TR2, using it through the spring and summer of 1970. In fact he and the car attended the second ever TR Register meeting held at Hopcroft's Holt Inn between Banbury and Oxford in April 1970 and by coincidence, Ken Richardson himself was there as an invited guest speaker. Ken was thus reunited with the car and even confirmed that the faded bluish-green paint was as the original.

The TR was entered in many MG Car Club events and driving tests during the period, causing much mirth because of its shabby condition, and it was also used as an everyday workhorse, covering several thousand miles very rapidly. The owner says that although his MG handled better (the TR feeling unsafe at high speed - well, it **was** worn out!), the TR was fantastic fun and a brute of a sports car. He admitted to seeing 4700 RPM in overdrive top one day on the M1 motorway whilst being provoked by a Jaguar XJ6. By my calculations, this equates to 115 mph, so it can't have been that unsafe at high speed! On Sunday 14th June 1970, Graham Hallett used MVC575 in the Autotest that formed part of the Standard Register's rally at Woburn Abbey, and very fortunately a photograph of the car competing in this event was taken by Trevor Parker, and by his kindness is reproduced.

After a thrilling summer charging around, hood down, in this historic but disreputable device, Graham Hallett decided that the time had come to take it off the road for a much needed rebuild, and the car was stripped down. During this process, many "one-off" details of its build came to light - for instance, there was a lot of crude wooden framework supporting the body, particularly under the front bulkhead. The spare wheel carrier was 2 inches shallower than normal, and thus whilst a disc wheel would fit, a wire wheel would not, so that when the works had converted it to wires, they had built a special spare wheel carrier mounted on the bootlid - a similar pattern was used by one or two of the Works rally TR2s. The "chicken-wire" grille was still fitted, as

was the unique badge (taken from the 20TS possibly?). Although the "Jabbeke" rear wheel spats were not in situ, one original rear wing came with the car, and this still had the spat mounting points attached.

Despite his initial enthusiasm, Graham Hallett eventually found himself unable to complete the rebuild of this historic TR, and reluctantly had to offer it for sale. The Author recalls seeing it advertised in the motoring press in the 1970's still in it's dismantled condition, and wishing that he could produce the wherewithal to acquire it! Although it was nearly sold to the USA, in fact MVC 575 passed into the hands of a TR Register member who still has it to this day, although as yet it has not been seen back on the road. The same fortunate gentleman also owns the sister car MWK 950. This TR has had a more chequered history than the "Jabbeke" car as its logbook reveals, for it has had at least six owners since a replacement logbook was issued in 1967, with a minimum of four more prior to that following its initial sale by the Company. Although I have not been able to establish exactly when this sale was, I feel sure that it was prior to the sale of MVC 575 in 1956 - it seems unlikely that the Company would have wanted two "mobile test beds", and the lure of several hundred pounds at a time when second hand TRs, even prototype ones, were in short supply would have been too much to resist!

As with MVC 575, MWK 950 was only just saved from scrapping in the early 1970's, and again this tale was recounted in an early TR Register magazine by Mrs Pam Gouldstone. She, with her husband, was running a TR4 and a TR3A at the time (1973/74) and purchased a scruffy, rusty TR2 very cheaply, the idea being to use it for spares. Very fortunately, they studied the log book of this car, and realised that it was registered several months prior to the date of the "Jabbeke" record run of MVC 575 in May 1953, and that it must therefore be a very early TR indeed. By an equally fortunate coincidence, they lived at the time in the same vicinity as the then Secretary and Registrar of the TR Register, Alan Robinson, and he realised that this car was something very special, and thus it was saved from scrapping. As with Graham Hallett, so the Gouldstones resolved to rebuild their historic car, but again it was not to be, and the dismantled MWK 950 passed to the same owner as MVC 575.

The real "mystery" TR is the third prototype car, and the first right-hand drive TR2, chassis number X516 and registered ORW 666. I cannot establish exactly when this car was first registered, but clearly the 'O' series of Coventry registration plates post-dates the 'M' series, so it must have been later in 1953 than the first two cars. However, the chassis number of X516 is actually **prior** to the X519 number of the Jabbeke car, so one must assume that it was built in around April 1953, although presumably not registerd until the Autumn of

Above: probably the TR's first public appearance at a motor sporting event was on 20th September 1953 at Prescott Hill Climb. The "Jabbeke" car, MVC 575, was paraded, but not competed, by Ken Richardson, seen here touring up the hill. Although by this date, the car had acquired full road equipment, the aerodynamic rear spats were still fitted, as was the unique front badge (TR Register Archive). The poster reproduced on the left needs no caption.

The "Jabbeke" record car, MVC 575, seen here in its run-down state in 1971 at a Standard-Triumph rally at Woburn Abbey. Owner Graham Hallett tries his hand at the Gymkhana, whilst behind him can be seen Valerie Simpson who, with her husband Terry, founded the TR Register in 1970. This is the only photograph of the car to come to light in its later days (Trevor Parker).

1953. ORW 600 and ORW 868 were both production TR2s registered in October/November 1953, so clearly ORW 666 must have been registered at around the same time. ORW 666 was fitted originally with engine number X582E, although as no details survive as to the ultimate fate of this car, one can only speculate as to whether this engine stayed with it. The few surviving photographs show it with wire wheels, the first TR thus equipped, and non-standard front overriders, which looked suspiciously like those fitted to the 20TS prototype! According to the June 1954 edition of the Standard-Triumph Review, ORW 666 was at the formal opening of the Motor Industry's new test track at MIRA near Nuneaton in May 1954. This car was back at MIRA again in July 1954, driven by Ken Richardson himself, this time attending the Mechanical Institute's open day. The car appears in the photograph to have been finished in white, with black hood and sidescreens, and to have the production type TR2 grille, rather than the "mesh" type on MVC 575.

Although ORW 666 was the first right hand drive TR2, it seems to have been used (and photographed?) by the company far less than it's two sister left hand drive cars. Not only that, but following the end of 1954, I can find no further reference to it in any of the Standard-Triumph paperwork I have examined, and no direct evidence that it was even sold off, although presumably it must have been as the Company always needed the money such sales generated. Ken Richardson, when interviewed, had only a hazy recollection of this car, and nobody else I spoke to had any idea what happened to it. However, as part of the research for this book, I submitted a list of registration numbers borne by notable TRs to the Driver and Vehicle Licensing Centre at Swansea, to see which of them were still "live" numbers on the DVLC computer. Very surprisingly, the number ORW 666 is still recorded with them as being "live", so maybe this third prototype TR also still exists somewhere, presumably in the hands of someone who wishes to remain anonymous, for the continued existence of the car has never been known to the TR Register.

It is of course quite possible that this registration number was transferred away from this TR many years ago and put onto a "modern" car in a "cherished" transfer arrangement. Just because the number is "live" doesn't necessaril;y mean that the TR that (formerly?) carried that number also exists, though it is an intriguing thought that it might - which would mean that all 3 prototypes survive. In view of the hard life such cars endure, this would be nothing short of amazing. However, until someone comes forward to produce ORW 666, I shall remain somewhat sceptical. The DVLC will not of course reveal details of vehicles on their computer, nor will they reveal the owner's whereabouts, not even in the interests of historical research, so at this point the search for the 3rd prototype TR2 must rest.

Whilst the three cars dealt with here are the genuine proto-

One of the very few known photographs of the third prototype TR2 ORW 666. It is seen in mid-1954 at an open day held at the Motor Industry Research Association's test track near Nuneaton. The car was the first TR to carry wire wheels and to have right-hand steering: it also had some unusual front over-riders fitted, possibly similar to those on the 20TS prototype (TR Register Archive).

This unique photograph shows the first production TR (TS1-LO) in use in Montreal, Canada, in the autumn of 1953. It reached Canada to be shown at the Canadian Motor Show and was thereafter used for about a year by the man seen with it. He was CDS Phillips, at that time head of Standard Motor Company (Canada) Limited. Note the very small hood rear window and that, as can just be discerned, the car is fitted with rear wheel spats (TR Register Archive).

type TR2s, it is also arguable that the first two "production" TRs, TS1 (LO) and TS2 were prototypes of a sort. They were certainly not true production cars, rather what would be termed today "pre-production" vehicles, built by hand to see that all the various bits fitted and that there was at least a sporting chance of a production line running reasonably smoothly. In addition, these two cars were assembled at Banner Lane in the Experimental department. I understand that although Mulliners were, by July 1953, in a position to supply the finished TR bodies, (as they did throughout the production run) those first two bodies were also built up in the Experimental shop. That of TS1 at least was largely made in aluminium (for ease of hand working, presumably) as its first private owner later confirmed. Both TS1 and TS2 were finished in Pearl White with Geranium hoods and interiors. TS1 was left hand drive and built with overdrive, whereas TS2 was right hand drive with standard transmission. Both cars were built up alongside each other, and the finishing date was stated to be 22nd July 1953. The left hand drive car was immediately sent to Toronto for display at the Canadian Motor Show, so surprisingly, the first TR into North America went not to the USA but to Canada. The other car was destined for the Dublin Motor Show in Ireland, and both cars remained in these countries once they had been exhibited.

Although the records do not specifically state which engines were fitted to these cars, the owner of TS1 confirms that it still has its (presumably original) engine no. TS3E. Circumstantial evidence points to TS2 having had engine no. TS2E, and I have heard that one of the very earliest engines (maybe TS1E?) was fitted to the prototype Swallow Doretti. Engine TS4E went to Morgans for the prototype TR engined "Plus Four" so I've been told, and thereafter engine numbers vary rarely coincided with car numbers (see Chapter 2). Once more, against all the odds, both these first production cars have survived, so it is quite possible that all the first 5 TR2's built are still with us! Present owners confirm that, like the prototypes, TS1 and TS2 differ in detail from the production cars, a fair amount of wooden framing being utilised within the bodywork. A contemporary photograph of TS1 shows it to have had a very small rear window in the hood, and also that it was fitted with rear wheel spats, as indeed were MVC 575 and MWK 950 at various times. TS1 was used following display by Mr C D S Phillips, who was the then president of the Canadian arm of Standard-Triumph, and it is he who is standing by the car in the photograph reproduced in these pages. He ran the car as personal transport until 1955, when it was sold to a Mr Tom MacKenzie, who kept it for around a year. He sold it because of its non-standard aluminium body panels, for he was concerned as to the likely high cost of repairs should the car suffer damage. It then passed to a gentleman who raced it in production car events, finally resurfacing after various vicissitudes in the USA where it is in good hands and currently being restored.

TS2 was registered for use in the Republic of Ireland under the number IR 6360, on 25th March 1954 by the County Offaly licensing authorities. Presumably between the Dublin Motor Show and its registration it was used as a showroom exhibit, and run, if necessary, on trade plates. Little is known of its history up until the early 1970's, although it would appear to have been raced, as when it was registered with the TR Register in August 1972, it had various non-standard items fitted, such as a roll-over bar, wide wheels and a small, side-filling petrol tank. At that time, it was in the ownership of Thomas Brown of Bangor in Northern Ireland, but had been re-registered as 773 EWO. In the 1950's/60's, when a vehicle was permanently imported into the United Kingdom from the Republic of Ireland, it was re-registered, and 773 EWO was issued in mid-1962 by the old Monmouthshire County Council. Thus, TS2 must have been imported from Eire into Britain sometime between 1954 and 1962, losing its original registration number in the process. It must then have been taken back to the island of Ireland after 1962, though as it went to Northern Ireland, it kept its Monmouthshire number, as it was still within the United Kingdom. It passed into Mr Brown's ownership, and when, around 1975, he wished to part with it, he telephoned the Author in response to a "wanted" advertisement in "Exchange and Mart" magazine seeking to buy a very early TR2. Although they do not come much earlier than TS2, to my regret I did not buy the car (I can't now recall why!) although it did in any event shortly thereafter come to England and was purchased by an enthusiast living in the Midlands who has a long term restoration in progress.

The first true batch of production TRs were TS3, TS4 and TS5, built at Canley between the 10th and 14th of August 1953. All were left hand drive, the first being finished in Geranium, the second in White and the third in Ice Blue, and all three were immediately dispatched to California, where they became the first of tens of thousands of TRs of all types to grace the USA.

Seen at the 1953 Earls Court Motor Show, in London, was this "Jabbeke" replica, believed to be TS 19 - (SP) LO, the so-called "Speed Model" TR2. As can be seen, no front bumper was fitted and the metal tonneau cover is in place, together with rear wheel spats ("Autosport").

Very fortunately, one of the surviving factory documents is the original Register of all the prototype and experimental Standard and Triumph cars and vans built in the period between 1948 and about 1974. Each vehicle, or in some cases part of a vehicle listed, is given an 'X' (for experimental) number; the date and the original number are listed as is the type, and there is usually an explanatory note in the "Remarks" column. I say "part of a vehicle" for when a major component was to be modified, the prototype of such

modification was also allocated a number - for instance, X570 was a TR3 rear axle incorporating modified brakes, and thus not all the numbers from X481 to X864 actually represent cars. Having studied this document in some detail, I will extract those 'X' numbers that appear relevant to the sidescreen TR series as follows (the words in brackets in the Remarks column are author's notes and are not part of the original record):

NO	TYPE	DATE	ENGINE	REMARKS
X505	20TS prototype	1952	-	3.889 axle ratio - 1st prototype.
X508	20TS Triumph Sports	1954	X571E	3rd prototype, RHD, MWK 950, Hardtop - Ice Blue (note that the car is dated 1954, which is clearly wrong, and is described as the "3rd prototype", even though it is numerically the second car built - note that like the next two cars, it is also still called a "20 TS" even though they were all TR2s. X508 was built LHD, though later converted to RHD).
X509	20TS Triumph Sports	1952	-	Rear axle only. (This is not a car, being merely an axle - described as "2nd prototype" and as being of 3.889 to 1 ratio.)
X516	20TS Triumph Sports	1953	X582E	1st prototype, Right hand drive, ORW 666
X519	20TS Triumph Sports	1953	X569E	3rd prototype, left hand drive, pale blue/red, MVC 575 (Note: although MWK 950 was commonly described as "Ice Blue", this car was called "pale blue" though it was in fact the production Ice Blue - "Red" presumably refers to the upholstery. Again it is incorrectly called "3rd Prototype".
X544	20TR2 Sports	1955		Rear Axle only 9/41 (Note: This low ratio axle was presumably fitted to a production TR for evaluation purposes - a further handwritten note implies that a 10/41 4.1 to 1 ratio was also later produced under cover of this same 'X' number.
X545	20TR2 Sports	1955		Rear Axle only 10/43, 4.3 Ratio fitted to TR2 per Richardson for experimental work (Note: the mention of Ken Richardson's name is interesting - presumably he requested that this 4.3 axle be built - possibly for rally work - it is too low for most racing circuits, even in conjunction with overdrive). Incidentally, the 4.3 axle ratio did eventually appear fitted to some of the Triumph Italias.
X549	20TR2 Sports	1955		Rear Axle only (no further details given)
X550	20TR2 Sports	1955		Special Axle shaft Mark 3 type diff gears and pinion. (Presumably these were updated halfshafts made to try to cure the TR2's known propensity for breaking halfshafts under hard usage - the reference to "Mark 3" may refer to the 'phase 3' Standard Vanguard?).
X551) X552)	20 TR2 Sports	1955		Axles only - 4.1 ratio "for Alpine Rally" (note - this must have been the first serious use of the 4.1 axle destined to go into production as an optional item.)
X556	20TR3	1955		Rear Axle only. Girling, 10 x 2 1/4" Brakes. (note - this is the first mention both of Girling brakes and of 'TR3' - it also shows how much trouble was being experienced with rear axles, the Achilles Heel of the TR2 and early TR3, that so many 'X' numbers related to axles - see the following eight numbers!).

NO	TYPE	DATE	ENGINE	REMARKS
X569)				
X570)				
X571)			(All various rear axle prototypes, utilising differing
X572) All 20 TR3		1956		combinations of Lockheed and Girling brakes incorporating
X573)				varying modifications.)
X574)				
X575)				
X576)				
X592	20TR4	1957	X667E	1st prototype, independent rear suspension. (note - The Register really **does** say TR4 - possibly the plan in 1957 was that the TR4 should be a TR3 with an independent rear end? A photograph of this independent rear suspension shows it to be a relatively crude system. A car bearing this chassis no. was later registered YDU 208 and sold off by the factory, although by this time it had conventional suspension. It has survived and is owned by a TR Register member).

The somewhat crude first attempt at independent rear suspension by the Standard-Triumph engineers still utilised the old cart springs! It was, not surprisingly, unsuccessful and was abandoned in around 1957 (Graham Robson).

| X598 | 20TR3 Sports TVC819 | 1957 | TS17870E | Broken up - Production built - from E.C.2324 and future. (note - This car had a production engine fitted and was road registered, and yet was listed as "broken up", whereas most prototypes were rebuilt and sold off - one wonders what the arcane note "Production Built" meant? - "E.C." stands for "Engineering Change", but I cannot find out exactly what E.C. 2324 was.) |

NO	TYPE		DATE	ENGINE	REMARKS
X605	20TR3A Sports		1957		Sold, 1st prototype, RH Steering, overdrive, disc wheels, Canley Built. (note - Again, the Register states TR3**A**, despite the factory's refusal to use this designation! Although quoted as sold, no record of a registration number is given. One can only presume this was possibly a TR3 with the prototype TR3A front, and also the various other TR3A modifications. Such a prototype must have existed, so maybe X605 was it? Or it might have been the Coventry developed (as opposed to Italian) potential TR3 replacement worked on in the 1956/57 period, and eventually rejected in favour of Michelotti's "Zest" ideas. It will be observed that there seems to be no TR3 prototype listed, at the time of the change from the TR2 - maybe the updating experiments were simply carried out on a production TR2?)
X614	20TR3 Sports	WDU 708	1957	X693E	Production Built Chassis, Italian Body. (This was the 'Zest' prototype - the first fruits of the co-operation between Standard Triumph and Michelotti's Italian design firm. A standard TR3 chassis was used, clothed in what was in effect an early prototype of the TR4 body. This car was sold off in the early 1960's)
X620	20TR3 Sports		1958		Fitted with Borg-Warner Transmission . Sales dept. Market Rasen (This may be evidence that an automatic transmission TR3A was built, with a Borg-Warner gearbox. One assumes that as usual it was re-converted to a standard gearbox prior to being sold off, in the Lincolnshire area judging from the note).
X627 - X628 - X629 -		XHP 938) XHP 939) XHP 940)			The three 1959 twin-cam engined Le Mans TR3S cars code-named "ZUPA". The Prototype register is not forthcoming on these cars, other than to note "broken up" - As is now known, this was not strictly true. These cars were dismantled following their largely unsuccessful foray to Le Mans, but the engines, adapted chassis and many other mechanical parts were believed to have been used for the later Le Mans cars and for other experimental work, and one at least of the fibreglass bodies has survived, for the author has inspected it! An intriguing puzzle is also provided by a TR3A logbook of which I have a copy. It relates to a car first registered on 6th May 1961 as 1414 RW (a Coventry issued plate.) The engine number is given as TS50365E, a 1959 engine, but the chassis number is given quite clearly as X627, i.e. the "broken-up" Le Mans car XHP 938! One can only speculate as to how this occurred, but a certain amount of "factory subterfuge" looks likely. Maybe some dodge to avoid purchase tax by "allocating" an old chassis number - who knows? At all events, I cannot believe that the TR3A 1414 RW was anything to do with the Le Mans cars, although the logbook shown to me was stamped "built-up vehicle". Rather it was probably an amalgam of TR parts collected together in 1961 to form a roadgoing car around a pre-

NO	TYPE		DATE	ENGINE	REMARKS
					existing chassis number known by then not to be in use else where! As previously recounted, the factory was extremely short of funds in early 1961, just prior to the Leyland takeover, so no doubt the several hundred pounds thereby created were most welcome. Such practices have caused headaches for historians 30 years later - and grief for owners who thought their TR was more special than turned out to be the case! It has recently been suggested that four, rather than three, of these TR3S cars were built, but I have so far seen no evidence of that.
X635	TR3		"Frame Only"		For Italian body. (note - no further details are given of this chassis frame - did it have an engine, for instance? Possibly it was used by Michelotti for further work on the TR3 replace-ment, or alternatively it might have been the chassis used for the prototype Triumph Italia made by Vignale in Italy).
X637	TR3		1959		"Retooled body, production built" Sold to Genner and Foreman Inc. (Renumbered as TS63010). Jersey City, October 1959. (note - the above implies that this was the prototype TR3A built with the retooled (post 60,000) bodyshell - presumably as an exercise to ensure that all would be well for series production to start. As can be seen, it was sold to the USA, and numbered in the normal TR3A series - TS63010 was, I assume, the next available commission number, for the timing at October 1959 is about right. Why, though, did this 'X' car merit renumbering in the production series whereas 1414RW/X627 mentioned above did not?).
X644	Sports YKV259		1959	X676E 20X	1st prototype
X645	Sports YKV260 (both code-named ZOOM)		1959	X775E 20X	2nd prototype (These were the two "Zoom" prototypes, fitted with detuned, road going versions of the Twin Cam racing 20X engine. These cars were in many ways like the production TR4 to look at, particularly at the rear, though the frontal treatment was different. They had wheelbases six inches longer than nor-mal, to accommodate the longer 20X engine. The track was also wider than on the TR3A, as indeed it was on the TR4 when it appeared. One at least of these cars survives, both having been sold off. Although not strictly "sidescreen" TRs, they are included for the sake of completeness).
X654	926HP	20X	1960	X809E)	(These were the four Le Mans racing TRSs used in the 1960/
X655	927HP	20X	1960	X734E)	1961 races, with some success. Their history has been well
X656	928HP	20X	1960	X737E)	detailed previously. However, the Prototype Register reveals
X657	929HP	20X	1960	X785E)	the following notes: "X654: sold to our American Company between December 1962 and January 1963" - as to X655, "available for collection from experimental dept, 14/1/63" and as to X657, "available for collection from experimental dept, 14/1/65". Nothing is said about X656, and I feel sure that the 1965 date mentioned for X657 is a misprint for 1963. All four cars did in fact go to the USA when sold off, although one at least has returned permanently).

The final sidescreen TR prototypes to be found on the Register are the TR3 "Betas" and the following detail appears in view of the considerable confusion that has arisen, and still arises, between these cars and the production TR3B:

There are 3 TR3 Betas listed in the Prototype Register and I extract below the given information as it appears.

NO	TYPE		DATE	ENGINE	REMARKS
X660	Beta - LHD		1960	CT3E -	"2nd prototype, experimental built, Joseph Lucas". "Vehicle being prepared for sale, 1/12/64".
X662	Beta Chassis LHD		1960		"Beta LHD to Italy. Cancelled chassis scrapped January 1st 1962 per Mr J Lloyd"
X693	TR3B	917HP	1962	X776E	"On loan to Burgess Products. Increased width of track front and rear with TR3 body modified to suit".

As regards X660, this was originally left hand drive, and it had a very early TR4 engine, CT3E. At one stage in its career, it is believed to have been painted blue, but it has spent most of its life red and has become known as "Red Beta". The car was used by the factory for experimental purposes for some years, and then in about 1963, it was lent to Joseph Lucas and Co. for development work. When in 1964 it was no longer required, Standard-Triumph's sold it off to a gentleman in the Kidsgrove area of Staffordshire, and it was registered as AVT 413C. It had not been previously registered, as far as I can ascertain. The original engine, CT3E, which had been extended experimentally to 2.5 litres, went with it, although it was later removed and used in Stock Car Racing! At some stage, it is thought to have had a twin-cam 20X engine installed, but neither this nor the CT3E engine is now with the car. AVT 413C was used as a rapid road car for some years, but suffered from a fire in the early 1970's, and was taken out of use and stored. It changed hands in around 1980 and survives in a private collection in reasonably original form.

X662 was clearly stated to have been scrapped - whether it actually went to Italy as the note says and why is unclear; maybe the (TR4 type) chassis was to be used for further evaluation by Michelotti? Presumably it was scrapped: I have never heard anything to contradict this. Neither is it known if X662 was ever bodied - probably not. I suspect that it would have been sold off to raise much needed cash had it been so.

X693, like X660, also still exists and indeed turned up unexpectedly at one of the TR Register's major events at Malvern in the mid 1980's, when it was offered for sale! It was registered as 917HP, a number which it retains, and it has always been known as the "Black Beta". Interestingly, it was not built until 1962 after the introduction of the TR4, whereas X660 and X662 date from 1960. The reason for this I believe to be that there were two wholly separate periods during which Standard Triumph's were considering introducing the Beta as a production car, and for two separate reasons. In

the 1960 period, when the expense of tooling up for the TR4 was proving irksome and the company was all but bankrupt, a frantic search was on to find a much cheaper way of introducing a revised TR rather than spending all that money on the TR4 bodyshell. One such way was to utilise the proposed TR4 mechanical and chassis arrangements, but to employ a modified TR3A body to clothe them. Thus the Beta was born, although ultimately as we know the TR4 did proceed as planned in 1961, thus quickly making the Beta irrelevant. However, nearly two years later, the North American market clamoured for the re-introduction of a revised, sidescreen TR3A style TR, to run in parallel with the then newly introduced TR4. Therefore the Beta idea was revived, and 917HP/X693 was created as a potential way of solving these difficulties. Again as it turned out, this route was abandoned, and the TR3B, not the TR3 Beta, was produced, as I shall shortly relate. As can be seen from the extract above, the Prototype Register actually calls X693 a 'TR3B' rather than a 'TR3 Beta', which causes more confusion, and lends weight to my contention that the revived Beta idea was by 1962 being seriously considered for the USA market.

I shall attempt to clarify exactly what a TR3 'Beta' prototype consisted of, and how it differed from the 1962 production TR3B. The Beta was built on a TR4 style chassis, that is one having a 3 inch wider track both front and rear than did the TR3A, and also with the wider, strengthened front chassis rails that were seen on the TR4. It had rack and pinion steering, and was initially fitted with the 2138cc TR4 type engine and all-synchromesh gearbox. The body, as can be seen from the photographs, was widened to cover the wider track by the simple expedient of making the four wings more bulbous, the central section remaining virtually standard TR3A. The body/chassis were not lengthened as per the TR3S 1959 Le Mans cars, as has sometimes been suggested. A different front grille was fitted, and the front sidelights were mounted on the front wings rather than in the grille. Rear quarter bumpers were fitted, at least on the Black Beta, presumably with the USA market in mind. Those who have driven a TR3 Beta appear unanimously to agree that it was an impressive

A head-on view of the TR3 Beta emphasises the bulbous front wings covering the wider-track front wheels. Note the repositioned side lights, the revised grille and that the car is left hand drive (TR Register Archive).

This three-quarter rear view of the TR3 Beta demonstrates the wrap-around bumpers, together with the wider wings. The car has a distinctly chunky, purposeful look (TR Register Archive).

car, faster and more sure footed than the TR3A, and with lighter, more direct steering. In retrospect, it seems a pity that the reintroduced TR3B was **not** built to Beta specification, but one assumes that retooling costs would have been involved (for wings, grille etc), whereas use of the TR3A bodyshell obviated this, the old tooling simply being dusted off and re-employed.

To turn to the production TR3B, this was assembled for Triumphs by theirsubsidiary the Forward Radiator Company, for the Canley plant was not able to accommodate this TR3A

phoenix now that the TR4 was proceeding rapidly. Triumph's North American dealerships requested the reintroduction of the TR3A in 1962 for several reasons; firstly, it was simply cheaper to build, and thus cheaper to sell, than the more complex TR4. Secondly, too few TR4s were coming off the production lines to satisfy USA demand, leaving some North American dealerships with nothing to sell and thirdly, it was felt that a 'sidescreen', cut-away door, traditional sports car would appeal to a somewhat different market than did the more sophisticated TR4. It would better please the competition minded owner, and thus TR market penetration as a whole would be improved. To an extent, this must have been true, for not every sale of a TR3B would have jeopardised the sale of a TR4, and vice versa, and I would venture to suggest that at the end of the TR3B's availability a couple of thousand more TRs had been sold than would otherwise have been the case had Triumph's not acceded to their USA dealers' requests. There were two batches of TR3B's, the 'TSF' series, numbered from 1 to 530, and the TCF series, numbered from 1 to 2804. All were left hand drive, and almost all went to North America or to North American servicemen. I say almost all, for a few chassis were used for bodying in Italy as Triumph Italias. No TR3Bs had rack and pinion steering, nor did they have the wide-track chassis. The 'TCF' cars did have the TR4 2138cc engine and improved gearbox, but otherwise, all TR3Bs were exactly as per the last TR3As. The 'TSF' cars still had the 1991 cc engine and non-synchromesh first gear. All TR3Bs were built in 1962, although some were not sold until well into 1963, by which time the TR4 had already been on sale for more than 18 months!

I hope that by the foregoing I have been able to clear up the TR3B/Beta confusion; however, where there is still some doubt is with the 'Betas' themselves. We have seen that only three such appear on the Prototype list, two finished cars and one (probable) chassis unit. However, there have been persistent rumours that more Betas **were** actually built, two "unofficial" cars said to have been built at the Canley works, one in the Experimental Department and one in the Competitions Department, plus possibly a further two left hand drive cars built (where?) as demonstrators for the North American market. One at least of these "unofficial" Betas (the competition department car) is claimed to have been fitted with the twin-cam 20X engine, which really would have made it a TR to be reckoned with! Whether

these cars existed I cannot verify, but it does seem quite possible - as to where they went if they did exist - well, maybe there is the ultimate sidescreen TR still waiting to be rediscovered somewhere!

Something that has occurred to me upon a detailed examination of the Prototype Register is that nowhere does there seem to be a record of a production TR3A being fitted with a roadgoing version of the 20X Twin Cam engine for development purposes. This is most surprising in that the 20X engine in de-tuned form **was** definitely considered for production and fitting to the TR3A. A specification book of such a car was produced, for the TR Register has a copy.

It has been said that, being somewhat longer than the normal engine, the 20X would not fit into the standard TR's engine bay, but this has turned out to be untrue - in fact, at least one twin-cam TR3A is known to have been built up unofficially in the 1960's, and ultimately the much longer 6 cylinder engine was used in the TR5, contained within a chassis of similar length to the TR3A. I find it very hard to believe that in 1959 or so the Works did not fit a twin cam motor into an ordinary TR, and yet no record of such a vehicle appears in the Register, and no 'X' number was allocated. Possibly one of the other 'X' cars was later used for just such an experiment and the records were not noted - at all events, if anyone reading this has further information, I would be pleased to hear from them.

Finally, for the sake of completeness the "Conrero" TR should be included in this chapter on prototypes, for it appears in the Prototype register and is a sidescreen TR descendant. The details as related in the Register are as follows:

NO	TYPE	DATE	ENGINE	REMARKS
X707	Triumph GT Saloon. Registered 3097VC	1962	X832E(20X)	(The "notes" column states "Conrero Le Mans, sold to our American Company Dec. 1962"). This car is now again back in Great Britain, in a very original state, and is owned by a TR Register member based near London.

CHAPTER TWO:

Numbering, Production & Sales

This chapter is not an attempt to catalogue accurately production changes, colours, delivery destinations and such matters - I would refer those interested to my earlier books where most of such detail as is available is set out. Rather I will attempt to deal with some aspects of sidescreen TR production that have not been covered previously, including information that I have been able to collect by virtue of my position as TR2/3/3A Registrar of the TR Register.

Clearly the best sources for production details are those contemporary factory records that have survived, and fortunately two almost complete sets of production records still exist. The British Motor Industry Heritage Trust hold on microfilm production details for TR2s, TR3s, TR3Bs and the majority of TR3As, though a gap exists between TS 62328 and TS 82125. However, they do have microfilm records of sales invoices for these "missing" TR3As which provide almost all the details that would have been on the absent production records. Unfortunately, the early microfilm has faded somewhat, especially that covering the TR2s, but Anders Clausager, the indefatigable Archivist at B.M.I.H.T. has become most adept at peering at scratched and faded celluloid, and full details can be provided on almost all sidescreen TRs. B.M.I.H.T. will provide TR owners with a certificate recording such details as are shown for a modest fee, and their Archive Section can be contacted at the splendid new Heritage Motor Centre and Museum at Gaydon in Warwickshire.

By serendipitous chance, a "hard" copy (as opposed to microfilm) set of sidescreen TR build details has also survived, still in the original files where they were placed upon being typed up at the end of each day's production! These records cover not only TRs, but also the other Standard and Triumph Cars of the 1945 - 1960's period. The TR Register has access to these records, but does not have custody of them. They start at TS1-LO and run right through to TS 82215, but for some reason the last 100 or so TR3As are not included, and there are no TR3B records at all. Delivery destinations are not given, and nor is the engine number of each individual car always listed, but otherwise the build specification is largely complete, although usually more detail is found on the TR3s and TR3As than on the TR2s, especially as regards the very earliest cars for which only basic information is recorded.

Both sets of records usually quote the six or seven figure bodyshell numbers, and neither lists the other number that also appears on the bodyshell, commencing with an "EB" prefix. Both the shell number and the "EB" number are stamped on brass plates screwed to the front bulkhead, just above the battery box; the shell number, possibly allocated by Mulliners who built the great majority of the shells, seems to be the one that interested the factory and hence it is recorded, whereas the "EB" number, which is usually slightly higher than the car's commission number, has an unknown function. In theory, it would be possible to trace a body to a particular commission number, but in practice, because both sets of records are arranged in commission number order and not in bodyshell number order, this would be difficult. Numbered bodyshells arrived in batches, and were not necessarily used on the production line in strict order of numbering, some also being used for spares, thus from a bodyshell number one could obtain a general idea, to within say a few hundred vehicles, of the car commission number to which that body was originally fitted, but to isolate it exactly could take hours of "trial and error" research!

Standard Register

**Extract from the production records of
The Standard Motor Company Limited.**

Commission No:	TS 31211 'O'
Type:	TR3
Building Date:	Wednesday, 14th May 1958. 10.30am–1pm
Body Shell No:	986584
Tyre Size:	550(Michelin X)
Body Colour:	Pearl White
Trim Colour & Type:	Black Leather
Hood/Side Curtains Colour:	Black/Black
Delivery Destination:	Hong Kong
Other Specifications and Equipment:	R M X Wire 'O' HT(Black) TC(Black) WW Soft Top Kit Aluminium Engine Sump
Special Notes:	Electric automatic aerial to be mounted on rear of car

for codes see reverse

An extract from TR production records, as provided to owners via the TR Register (TR Register)

Anders Clausager has recently found time to do some delving into these six or seven figure "Mulliner" body numbers, and he has kindly allowed me to draw on his findings.

Briefly, there appear to have been at least eight different series of bodyshell numbers, the individual sequences corresponding fairly accurately (but not so far identified exactly!) to a block of commission numbers. The series so far identified are as follows:-

First Group — Shell numbers 726001 to 728999 (approx) relate to commission numbers TS1 to TS3020 (approx) from July 1953 to August 1954.

Second Group — Shell numbers 773250 to 773750 (approx) relate to commission numbers TS3021 to TS3500 (approx) during the months of August and September 1954.

Third Group — Shell numbers 769751 to 773242 relate to commission numbers from TS3501 to TS7300 (approx) during the period from September 1954 to July 1955.

Fourth Group — Shell numbers 840631 to 848106 relate to commission numbers TS7301 to TS15500 (approx) during the period from July 1955 to January 1957.

Right: a very standard-looking early production model TR2 competes in a 1950s rally. Note the presence and position of the radio aerial on the front wing (NMM Beaulieu).

Below: A fascinating photograph taken in late 1956 at the premises of LF Dove Limited, the Standard-Triumph dealer in Wimbledon, South London. Doves set up what they called the "TR Centre", a specialist workshop dealing solely with TRs. Gearbox work seems to be the order of the day in this view ("Autosport").

Left: this interesting picture dates from April 1957 and shows the interior of Hunt's of Birmingham, specialist sports car dealers. It is one of the very few pictures to survive showing a brand new sidescreen TR on sale: the problems caused by fuel rationing and the Suez Crisis are evident in the notice on the TR, offering £100 off list price! One of the directors of Hunt's was keen TR2 rally driver Neville Jarrett, who had one of the earliest TR2s, OOK 2, which he used on the 1954 RAC Rally ("Autosport").

Fifth Group	Shell numbers 970816 to 986625 relate to commission numbers TS15501 to TS31300 (approx) during the period from January 1957 to May 1958.
Sixth Group	Shell numbers 1006420 to 1018067 relate to commission numbers TS31301 to TS43100 (approx) during the period from May 1958 to January 1959.
Seventh Group	Shell numbers 1048572 to 1066000 (and over?) relate to commission numbers from TS43101 to TS62327 (and over?) during the period January 1959 to November 1959 and presumably later.

At this point, as B.M.I.H.T. do not have production records for cars between TS62328 and TS82125, no accurate details can be presently assembled for bodyshells fitted to cars between these numbers, but it must be reasonable to assume that several further groups of bodyshell numbers were used. Some shell number records do exist - for instance, several 1960 cars in the TS70000's have shells in the 109XXXX series, and a final group is evidenced by the fact that the shell numbers of the very last TR3As (for which records **do** exist) come from a series that includes for instance 1103187 for TS82126. Anders Clausager draws attention to further two points, namely that no TR3As were built with commission numbers between TS47956 and TS50000 (inclusive), so this gap needs to be taken account of should one wish to reconcile bodyshell numbers with commission numbers, and also that it is possible that these six or seven figure body numbers were never issued to cars exported as C.K.D. (Completely Knocked Down) kits for local assembly. TR3B cars had body numbers in an entirely different sequence, these bodies being manufactured by Forward Radiators Ltd. Surprisingly, a new bodyshell number sequence was not commenced when the re-tooled bodyshell was introduced for the TR3A at commission number TS60001, despite this being by far the most major bodywork revision to occur during the whole sidescreen TR production run.

As mentioned earlier, although the "EB" body numbers appear to remain fairly consistently approximate to the commission numbers, they are little help in identifying vehicles as no records of them seem to have been maintained.

The three major mechanical components of each car also had numbers, each prefixed 'TS' (for "Triumph Sports" one assumes). Production Engines commenced their numbering at TS1E, the 'E' suffix being added to avoid confusion with the 'TS' commission numbers, but gearboxes and rear axles, which also carry 'TS' numbers, do not appear to have utilised suffixes. The actual number of each of these principal components approximated to, but was normally slightly higher than, the individual vehicle's commission number, presumably because of the manufacture of spare units. Although the engine number of the particular engine originally fitted to an individual car is usually recorded in each of the two existing sets of records, numbers for gearboxes and axles are not. Thus, provided a unit is original to that vehicle, one can gain a general idea of the age and commission number of an otherwise unidentifiable vehicle, but specific identification in this manner is usually impossible.

Detailed research into the build records of the first 1000 cars has shown that engines were on occasions used "out of sequence", but that normally engine numbers ran anything up to one hundred numbers higher than the relevant commission number. "Out of Sequence" use can probably be explained by particular engines having to be returned to the Engine Shop for fault rectification; for instance, TS815 was fitted with engine no TS899E, TS817 was fitted with engine no TS873E but TS816 was fitted with engine no TS163E, some months after this particular engine would have been built! So far, I have only found one instance of the commission and engine numbers being the same, in the case of TS961, fitted with engine TS961E.

I mentioned earlier the C.K.D. 'kit' cars dispatched from the factory to several overseas destinations for local assembly, and this is a convenient point to investigate these vehicles in more detail. As regards records, the B.M.I.H.T. records merely indicate that a particular commission number was a C.K.D. car, and the other set of production records do not even state this, the numbers simply being omitted from the sequence. Clearly a TR that was assembled locally from parts could have neither a factory build date nor a factory paint and trim specification, and consequently very few details can be provided for owners of such cars, often no more than an approximate date of the manufacture of the parts themselves. Some records of the local assembly plants may survive, but none such have been brought to my attention. The first "gap" in the records occurs between TS470 and TS475, six cars that are believed to have been CKD kits sent for assembly in Belgium. A further 6 TR2s, TS702 to TS707 followed them a few weeks later, and TS850-TS855 shortly thereafter. With help from Francois Van Hoof, the President of the Belgian TR Register, I have been able to learn more of the assembly of TRs in Belgium.

The Belgian car manufacturing concern named Imperia found that their factory had considerable spare capacity in

Right: an item that never reached production was these tiny child seats in the rear of a TR2. As this is an official photograph, one assumes that consideration was given to fitting them as an option. The "wicker" or "metric" trim is fitted to this car and shows up clearly in this photograph (TR Register Archive).

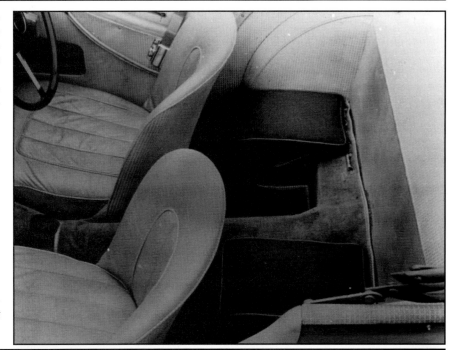

Below: an official photograph of a production long-door TR2, showing the neat hood-stick cover in place.

the early 1950's, and they were seeking new work. They therefore commenced assembly of Standard Vanguards from kits shipped from Coventry, and as this project proceeded well, the directors approached Standard's about the possibility of assembly work for 'kit' TRs as well as the Vanguards. Thus the "pilot" batches of TR2s referred to above were sent over and successfully assembled. The plant was situated at Nessonveaux, near Liege, and consequently all Nessonveaux built TRs had an 'N' suffix added to their commission number, in addition to the 'L' suffix already present to denote left hand drive. Some appear also to have had

an 'A' added as well, though the reason is unclear. Imperia continued to assemble TRs for several years, the resultant vehicles being in the main supplied to Holland and Germany, as well as to Belgium itself. In addition, the TR2 fixed head coupe known as the Francorchamps, of which 22 examples were built, was designed and assembled at Nessonveaux by Imperia. Surprisingly, not all TR cars sold in Belgium came from this plant, for it was possible to order a Coventry-built example direct from the main distributors!

Several hundred TR2s and TR3s were built up in Belgium,

On the left is one of the very rare (only 22 were built) TR2 "Francorchamps" fixed-head coupes, built in Belgium in 1954/55. This particular example was about to undergo a restoration. A surprisingly high proportion of these cars survive - more than half it is believed (TR Register Archive).

\Below: the rear script badge from the TR2 Francorchamps Coupe. Also seen is the standard TR2 central brake light, which doubled as a number plate illuminator and a third rear light, giving the TR a distinctive appearance when following it at night.

although Francois says that not that many TR3s were completed in the 1957 model year. An interesting peculiarity of some of the Nessonveaux TRs is that they have a manually controlled overdrive unit, with no solenoid being fitted. This works, via a Bowden cable, on all four forward gears, a mechanical locking device preventing overdrive being selected in reverse. Other production anomalies have been known to appear also, such as cars with commission numbers higher than TS4002 being fitted still with "long" doors, and cars whose numbers indicate that they should have been fitted with the vent lid in the scuttle not being so fitted. One must assume that batches of parts were therefore used up somewhat slowly, and also that the kits of parts held in stock were sometimes "intermingled", leading to such peculiarities. Additionally, Imperia TR2s were available in some special colours over and above the basic "Coventry" range, and so far Francois Van Hoof has identified light blue metallic, light green metallic, a solid grey as well as a metallic dark grey, pearl black and a dark red, verging on maroon. The Imperia plant also assembled Alfa Romeos, so he suggests that some of these at least may be Alfa colours.

Assembly of TRs at Nessonveaux continued until the 1958

model year, but Standard-Triumph had by then decided to open their own assembly plant, which was established in late 1958 at Mechilen, between Brussels and Antwerp. Here TR3As were assembled from Coventry sourced parts, these cars being distinguished by a 'B' prefix before the TS commission number - for instance, BTS 44285LO was built there in May 1959. This facility continued in use for many years, and TR4s, 4As, 5s and TR6s were all assembled at this plant.

The other most important country involved in local assembly of C.K.D. kits sent from Coventry was South Africa, and here I have been assisted by Graham Cheetham, The Registrar of the Triumph Sports Car Club of South Africa. Graham has reason to believe that about 1050 sidescreen TRs were assembled in South Africa, these being built up from CKD kits by the firm of Motor Assemblies of Durban. Of these, around 250 were TR2s. These South African TRs do have a "TS" commission number in the normal series, but have usually been allocated in addition a local commission number prefixed by 'TR', which has caused some confusion when some of these cars have recently been reimported into the UK! For instance, Graham's own TR2 is TS8330, but it also carries the local assembly number of TR151. From late TR3 production, the figure '8' is often added to the 'TS' prefix, so late TR3s and most TR3As assembled in South Africa have 'TS8' prefixes to their main numbers, as well as having the local 'TR' commission number! South African assembled cars do not carry bodyshell numbers evidently, and as a further confusion, some of the TR3As assembled there have an 'S' in front of their local number - as an example TS (8)33779 is locally numbered as STR1018.Assembly appears to have stopped with TS (8)33814 (STR1053) so the bulk of such cars were TR3s and early TR3As, TRs supplied thereafter either being shipped from the UK, or possibly being assembled in Rhodesia (Zimbabwe). Graham Cheetham confirms that there was indeed a CKD assembly plant in Rhodesia, although few details are known about it or for how long it operated. As was the case with Belgium, during the time that TRs were being locally assembled in South Africa, it was still possible to order a UK built car direct!

In addition to the countries already mentioned, it is possible that sidescreen TRs were also assembled elsewhere in the world on a small scale. I have heard rumours that a plant existed in some South American country, but have had no confirmation. Unfortunately, although the B.M.I.H.T. records do indicate which cars were CKD kits they do not indicate the country of destination in such cases. Also, it has always

surprised me that no local assembly apparently occurred in Australia, given that it was an English speaking, right hand drive, colonial market with high import tariffs on finished cars and with high transport costs in respect of complete vehicles. I have found details on two early TR3s, TS 8860 and TS 8871, both of which were sold in Australia, and both of which left Coventry as C.K.D. kits. However, as no delivery destinations are listed, this cannot be taken as proof of Australian assembly, although this must be a possibility. A further possibility is that some "partially" knocked-down TR kits were assembled in the Republic of Ireland: However, I have not yet seen any documentary evidence to support this.

Although they were not strictly CKD cars, mention should here be made of the 320 or so chassis that were sent to Italy to be bodied as Triumph Italias. These left Coventry for Italy as rolling chassis and mechanical units, complete save for the bodies and items of trim. A special suffix letter 'C' was added to the commission number, presumably indicating "chassis only". As virtually all of the Italias were left hand drive and also fitted with overdrive, the suffix designation of "LCO" in the records is an almost certain confirmation of an Italia.

As to other surviving original factory records, fortunately a

A rear three-quarter view of the elegant TR "Italia", built by Vignale in Italy on a virtually standard TR3A chassis. It was not marketed in the UK, although a handful of cars did see use in Britain. Something over 300 were made in all, the exact figure still being uncertain. The car photographed could be the prototype: this would seem to be an official Works picture, possibly taken at the Coventry plant. (TR Register Archive).

good number of Standard-Triumph's "Engineering Changes" books survive, and are held in the TR Register's archives. It is believed that these are unique, and whilst not every volume exists, the great majority appear to be extant. They are in effect bound up volumes of the specification details that surrounded each change in a production detail of the car, each such change being given an 'EC' number. Because these books contain such a huge amount of arcane and minute detail, no one has yet had time fully to research them, although all the more important specification changes have been extracted. In addition to the "EC" books, the TR Register also has some original factory records and specifications of some of the TR prototypes, including details of the "20X" twin-cam competition engines. Again, these are only of limited or historic interest in that few such cars survive, but it is encouraging to know that a considerable amount of written factory material weathered the great "clear-outs" of the 1970's British Leyland era and lived on into these more enlightened times. Some full scale drawings also exist, although the sheer size of these has posed storage problems over the years, and I believe some have been occasioned some damage. B.M.I.H.T. have not yet had either the time or the manpower available to sort and to catalogue all the historic material that they have inherited from the various constituent companies of the old British Motor Corporation/Leyland Empire, so it is possible that further unique TR related paperwork may yet come to light as facilities permit.

I will turn now from the written records of TR production to the actual production of the cars themselves.

As has been recorded previously, sidescreen TR production started very slowly in mid 1953, gathered momentum steadily but inexorably and climbed ever more rapidly until reaching a peak in late 1959/early 1960, whereupon it fell away dramatically almost to nothing in 1961, only to finish in 1962 on a more positive note when more than 3000 TR3Bs were built. There were of course some minor peaks and troughs during the 1953 to 1960 escalation in production, principally a trough in mid 1955 once initial home market demand had been satisfied and a further decrease during late 1956/early 1957 due to the Suez Crisis and its consequent fuel rationing, but regarded overall, the production and sale of the sidescreen TR became ever more successful until suddenly in 1961 the car began to look dated compared with new competitors. By this time the market had got wind of the impending and greatly revised TR4, which caused many potential buyers to eschew purchase of a TR3A in favour of waiting for a TR4.

Looking at TR manufacturing on an average daily basis, in the period from the start of production to the end of 1953 two cars were being produced approximately every day, which increased to an average of 8 cars per day in early 1954, the average throughout 1954 being nearly 16 cars each day, based on a six day working week. Saturday morning working was common throughout British industry in the 1950's, and factory records prove that cars were even sometimes produced in a special Saturday afternoon/evening shift at times of peak demand. Due presumably to the factors mentioned above and to the TR3 introduction, average daily production in 1955 fell to around 14 cars a day, although it returned to 17 cars a day by 1956, despite the Suez crisis.

From this point, the real climb in sales began, and in 1957 the average daily output rose to 34 cars, and rose again in 1958 to just over 50. By 1959 the figure had risen to 68 cars each working day, and the editorial in "Autosport" Magazine for 9th October 1959 was able to congratulate the Company on its phenomenal export success with the TR3A, stating that 11,000 of these cars had reached buyers in the USA in the preceeding six months!. Although the overall average figure for 1960 fell to 54 because of the steep drop towards the end of that year, this masks the fact that the best single quarter of all for sidescreen TR production appears to have been the first quarter of 1960. During this period almost 70 cars were leaving the production lines each working day, a phenomenal figure for an out-and-out sports car. As around 90% of these cars were being sold in North America, this presented the company with the logistical problem of how to get such numbers of vehicles across the Atlantic. Regular daily trains were run to take the TRs to the docks, whence on occasions entire ships were chartered to carry the vehicles to the USA, for with 350 or so TRs to be transported each week, an odd corner provided by a freight shipping service was no longer adequate! Home market cars were delivered in batches by transporter if enough were going to a particular area, and one-off orders were frequently taken under their own power by delivery drivers or even collected from the factory by assiduous owners, anxious to ensure that careful running-in took place, which it did not always do otherwise! Cars for European destinations were often consigned individually to the railways, and those for other continents than North America or Europe were either driven or transported to the appropriate docks and then consigned to ships. On occasions, they were crated for protection, but this had to be paid for as an extra by the ultimate purchaser and was thus not often done, hence many export TRs sustained damage during long voyages.

Let us now look at production and numbering anomalies. The more that one researches sidescreen TR history, the more apparent it becomes that all the "rules" were laid down to be broken, and that what were previously thought to have been definite specification change points were somewhat "flexible". I have space only to delve into a few such anomalies, and will start with probably the largest, the change point of TS60000 when the revised body pressings were introduced. It is said, and I have uncovered no evidence to contradict this, that by late 1959 the original body panel pressing tools were life-expired and that when new ones were substituted, the opportunity for revision and improvement was taken.

All the factory literature states that this change occurred at TS60000, i.e. from car no TS60001, but in recent years a number of owners of cars in the TS59XXX series have found that their vehicles had the later bodyshell and in several cases known continuous history proves these cars to be as originally built. For instance, TS59965L was built on 21st October 1959 with the post TS60000 body. TS59698L is likewise equipped, and several TR3As in the TS592XX series have also come to light sporting the later body. An extreme example is provided by TS59005, which was built with the revised bodyshell on the same day as TS60001! Upon consideration that this was the period when 60 or more cars were being produced each day, an "overlap" of 1000 or so cars represents a time period of under three weeks, so such anomalies are not altogether surprising; however, they do make a mockery of the factory issued publications, and must have caused grief to dealers, parts-storemen and owners alike over the years. That the "overlap" can work both ways appears to be evidenced by car no TS61426 built on 4th November 1959. Unusually, this car was fitted with an engine bearing a number some hundreds lower than the commission number, i.e. TS61014E, and more remarkable was the fitment of a body carrying the "EB" number of 57983, some three and a half thousand numbers lower than the commission number, and one of the pre-TS60000 bodies! Although little is known about the "EB" numbers, they are almost invariably slightly higher than the commission number, so this vehicle is indeed anomalous. Whilst researching, I came across a factory dealer information sheet from October 1959 which sets out what I feel ought to be the definitive list of the post TS60000 body changes, and I am quoting this verbatim, for there has been considerable debate in the past over the exact differences that appeared in these later TR3As.

The changes are listed as:-

1)   Modified body panels including a rear panel incorporating a wide rim on the inside of the boot opening and raised platforms for hinge mountings; the wide rim inside the boot cures any water leakage problems, and the raised hinge platforms on the boot and bonnet improve clearance between the body and bonnet and body and boot lid. The boot floor pressing is raised slightly to increase clearance in spare wheel tray for larger tyres.

2)   Standard body bolts be used on windscreen mounting so that once unbolted the screen lifts straight off instead of sliding back and forth as with the "Dzus" fasteners.

3)   A flat platform has been installed behind the seats on models without the occasional rear seat. This does not decrease luggage space and makes it much easier to carry small bags which were difficult to balance on the previous "well" and "tunnel" behind the seats. The petrol tank is slightly modified to take account of the new arrangements.

4)   A rheostat to be fitted for the dashboard panel lights to adjust the brightness of the instrument lighting.

5)   Ignition wiring modified by the use of the latest Lucas (should this have been Lucar?) snap connectors.

6)   New type rear view mirror.

7)   Separate keys to be fitted for ignition and doors, and for boot and glove compartment, to enable glove compartment to be opened whilst the car is running. (i.e. two different keys per car)

8)   Door bottoms modified so that the lower inner frame is rounded, not square (no reason given!).

From my own experience, I believe that the change in the colour of the flashing indicator warning lamp from amber to green also took place around this time, so it is just possible that the above list is not definitive, but I shall treat it as so until something better turns up, for it is an official Works publication.

Another TR anomaly concerns the "missing" 2044 cars that should have been numbered between TS47957 and TS50000 inclusive. As is well known, these cars appear never to have been built, for they are not mentioned in either set of production records, and nor is there any note that they were CKD vehicles. That they truly never existed is I think conclusively proved by the TR Register's records. In all my years as TR2/3/3A/3B Registrar, I have only once been asked to register details of a car within this number range, TS49221 and upon further enquiry, this turned out to be an error. Clearly therefore, any TR3A purporting to be numbered in this series has good claim to being a fake! The strange thing is, why did the Standard Triumph production controllers leave this gap? There were some minor specification changes at TS50001, e.g. the introduction of the revised starter motor, but nothing of sufficient moment such as to justify breaking off a previously continuous numerical series, leaving a confusing gap and then restarting at the next convenient large, round number! No-one I have interviewed has been able to explain this, nor explain why a similar numerical gap was not also left at the post TS60000 changes, which were much more significant. Such a gap here would have avoided the "overlap" anomalies already dealt with.

So far as is known, there are no other large gaps in the numerical sequence of 'TS' commission numbers, although as we have seen, some number blocks do not appear in the records when they were allocated to CKD cars assembled abroad. In such cases a TS number was reserved for the vehicle, even if, as in the case of some locally-assembled cars, this TS number did not actually appear on the vehicle. There are however a few cases of individual TS numbers appearing to be blank in both sets of records and where there is no mention of any C.K.D. build. In such cases, the particular car may truly never have been built. Instances of this that have come to light include numbers TS6577 and TS30102. I cannot believe that such individual vehicles can have been CKD cars, for these always seem to have been despatched in batches of a minimum of at least 5 cars, so maybe for some reason (a cancelled special order, possibly?) the car simply was not made.

Other instances occur of cars being built out of sequence, usually built later than their number would indicate, although TS900 was built a couple of weeks early! The most mysterious example of this practice so far to be discovered concerns TS7374, which should have been a TR2 from late July 1955. The records indicate however that it finally left the production line on the 11th November 1955, and as a TR3 not as a TR2! A note in the records states that "an engine modified to TR3 specifications" was to be fitted, and presumably the TR3 style grille was also utilised. Quite whether this vehicle had actually been built as a TR2, (either fully finished or only partially completed), and then later converted to a TR3, or whether it existed only as a "phantom" for 3 months, is impossible to ascertain.

The changeover from TR2 to TR3 production in September/October 1955 is proving to be a rich vein for production anomalies, such as TS8709 being the first TR3 constructed, five days earlier than TS8637, numerically the first TR3! Correspondence that I have had with several current owners of very early TR3s (i.e. those numbered below TS9000) shows that these cars are somtimes fitted with a commission plate on the bulkhead that states "20TR2" rather than the appropriate "20TR3". Presumably TS7374 mentioned above likewise had the wrong plate? As instances, one can cite TS8713, which has the correct "TR3" plate, whereas TS8757, ostensibly the later car, has had from new a "TR2" commission plate, despite being built as a TR3. One is thus led to believe that quite a number of late TR2s were converted into TR3s either during their build, or as fully fin-

ished cars. The relatively few changes required to update a late TR2 into a TR3 would have made this a viable proposition, for only the front grille, badge, bonnet and boot hinges together with the stainless steel wing piping would have needed attention from an external point of view, and the engine changes would have been simple to fit retrospectively. This suspicion is reinforced by a story that has come my way via a TR devotee of many years, Alec Pringle, allegedly from a factory apprentice at the time. Apparently there were in the late summer of 1955 several hundred TR2s, finished but unsold, parked at various points in and around Coventry. Although the car had been selling well during the previous months, rumours of the impending introduction of a "TR3" were rife in the rallying and enthusiast world, and were also being heard in the USA. This led to a sudden decline in sales, as keen types waited for the new model, the introduction of which was originally scheduled for 1956 - maybe they anticipated something more revolutionary than a new grille and bigger carburettors!

The Management apparently panicked at this sales problem, and promptly brought the TR3's introduction forward to the 1955 London Motor Show, despite the fact that not all parts needed to build the new car were on hand in sufficient quantities! Faced with a strong demand for the new TR3 upon its launch, and a field or two of unsold, but almost identical, TR2s, it would have been surprising had the Standard-Triumph management **not** then been tempted to "recycle" some of them into TR3s! I feel sure myself that this did happen, and that the "20TR2" commission plates are the outward and visible evidence of a bit of judicious "creative upgrading". Further corroboration that there were plenty of unsold TR2s on hand at the time of the TR3 launch is provided by the fact that the TR2 was listed alongside the TR3 as being still available new throughout the 1955/6 winter, it being priced at £50 less, and by the number of TR2s known to the TR Register which were not in fact registered until early 1956, as late as April that year in some cases. Delays in delivery of parts specific to the new "TR3" led to cars being only partially completed, to some TR2s being converted to TR3s, but not fully, and to the other anomalies - a real mix-up in fact which took months to sort out, and the aftermath of which puzzles today's owners.

The changeover from TR3s to TR3As in September/October 1957 provided the factory with little scope for a similar exercise, for the difference between the two cars were too great to have made conversion worthwhile, and in any event, by late 1957, with the Suez Crisis and petrol rationing over and the great success of the TR3 in rallying, sales were strong. However, one case of an anomaly relating to this changeover has come to light, that of car no TS22061. This car was built, for the UK market, in September 1957, and

A fascinating photograph taken in Mat 1960 at what is believed to be Cardiff Docks. The TR3As have arrived by train from Coventry for export to the USA. As was usual, wooden "buffers" have been added and bumpers, lights, hubcaps, hoods and sidescreens are stored in the footwells to save space and avoid damage. The Vauxhall Victors are not such exciting cargo! (NMM Beaulieu).

On the left, the badge says "TR2" yet the TR3 grille and surround are in place! This Works picture presumably shows a TR3 prototype fitted with the grille for evaluation (TR Register Archive).

On the right is an official Works shot of a wire-wheeled TR3, showing off the stainless steel wing beading introduced with that model. That the "tear-drop" boot-lock escutcheon plates continued on to TR3s is demonstrated by this photograph (TR Register Archive).

A TR3A looking particularly smart in white, with matching hardtop plus wire wheels, poses at an Earls Court Motor Show. This is also the car illustrated on the back of the jacket for this book.

A publicity shot showing a new TR3A with a well-dressed lady of the period. This was believed to be a Standard Motor Company (London) photograph, rather than one taken by the Coventry factory photographic department, hence the London registration (NMM Beaulieu)

was built as a TR3, not a TR3A. The present owner has confirmed with previous owners that it has always had the "small-mouth" grille, TR3 seats and other unmistakable features, yet TR3A production commenced at TS22014, nearly 50 cars earlier, with, so it has always been said, the entire first batch of TR3As going to the States. Indeed, the TR3A (or TR3, 1958 model, as the works preferred to call it) was not announced to the home market until January of 1958. A further such anomaly concerns TS 23671 L, which was apparently supplied new with the TR3-style bootlid having budget-locks and no external handle, even though it was made as a TR3A more than 1500 cars into TR3A production!

As a service to TR Register members, the club has, for many years, provided extracts from the factory build records for individual cars; on occasions, these too reveal production quirks, unusual or "one-off" colour schemes and other (presumably) particular requirements of the original owner. For instance, the following items amongst others have come to light in this way.

TS17008 was a TR3 built on 1st April 1957, but finished in Wedgewood Blue, a colour not standard until TR4 production. It was exported to Rhodesia and was fitted with Dunlop "Fort" tyres, presumably for colonial use on dirt roads, for the Dunlop "Fort" was a strong tyre more usually associated with heavyweight limousines and even lorries and buses - one wonders what the maximum speed rating was!

TS3897 should have had the original "long" doors fitted, as a pre TS4002 car; however, the production record states "fit new type doors" so clearly for some reason this car acted as a kind of short-door prototype, for this could hardly have been a special order, as the public would not yet have known of the availability of new doors and outer sills.

TS42647LO was a TR3A built on 19th January 1959, supplied new to West Germany. The build record specifically states "Fit wire wheels with hexagon nuts and appropriate spanner". This is the first evidence that I've seen that sidescreen cars were supplied new to certain Continental countries with "safety" nuts rather than "knock-offs", and as early as 1959. Thus present day owners of TR3As in those countries where knock-off hub nuts are not permitted can utilise hexagon nuts secure in the knowledge that these could have been original equipment. TS6087, built on 29th April 1955, has on its record the note "Fit Renown trim". I have not seen this elsewhere, and presumably it meant only the use of Triumph Renown type fabric - the Renown saloon bench seat would hardly be appropriate in a TR3!

TS5521, built on 17th February 1955, was finished in Geranium, almost a year after this exterior colour had theoretically ceased to be available, and the record gives the interior trim colour as "Stone Vynide". Now I have seen an official factory data sheet that states that "Stone" (believed to be a lightish fawn colour) trim was only available in Leather, yet here is clear evidence that such a colour could be supplied in vynide. The record for this particular car goes on to assert "fit sliding sidescreen windows and also red carpets", so clearly this was a special order vehicle, and a good example to prove that you could have what you wanted, at a cost and within reason, even outdated colour schemes! Further instances of "one-off" finishes in sidescreen TRs can be found elsewhere, but I would also mention TS 9304. a December 1955 TR3, finished in black, that was supplied with Geranium trim, thus proving that this availability of colour survived right up to the TR3.

Perhaps the most comprehensively equipped TR that I have yet seen a factory build record for is TS79052, built on 9th August 1960. This car, finished in Spa white, had the following extras new from the Works:- Red leather upholstery, heater, wire wheels, occasional rear seat, black hard top, black soft top kit, black tonneau cover, two speed wipers, 2.2 litre engine, aluminium engine sump, overdrive and a short front undershield, all of which must have increased its price by around 50% above that of a basic car!

Detailed examination of the build records between TS12500 and the "official" introduction point of disc brakes at TS13046 proves that there were quite a number of pre TS13046 TR3s that had disc brakes fitted from new, and also that the TS128XX series of cars seem to have been built prior to the TS127XX series. As an aside, a perusal of records has shown that a majority of sidescreen TRs going to North America had leather trim (as did all the first 150 TR2s built) whereas the great majority of home-market TRs had vynide; maybe the Americans simply had more money to spend!

The record for TR3A TS60152-0 states "a new type body, old type steering" in the 'notes' section. "New type body" is not surprising, but "old type steering" can surely only mean the one-piece column, replaced in production by the two-piece type more than a year earlier. The car also had the adjustable steering specified however, so maybe this had something to do with the note, despite the fact that adjustable steering was available with the two-piece column!

Perhaps the most arcane special direction I have yet found on a build record concerns car TS80000L, built 5th September 1960 for export to France. The notes state that "Ripault Resistive High Tension type cable" is to be fitted - why, one wonders? - was the Lucas item considered defective, and did the buyer arrange for a reel of Ripault cable to be especially sent to Coventry for the purpose? Space unfortunately precludes further examples, and no doubt other instances of the somewhat eccentric nature of sidescreen TR production will surface in times to come - it is a fascinating study where hard and fast rules seem to be broken!

I discovered recently from a TR3 in my possession that a brief summary of the build specification can sometimes be found chalked under the commission plate! Upon removing this for restoration, I found the chalked letters "R.M.H. NIL" to be clearly readable, this code indicating that the car was to be right hand drive, to home-build specification (i.e. UK supplied), to have Imperial calibrated instruments and to have no heater fitted. Such a code may not always be present, but if it is, it provides an interesting confirmation of the car's original specification.

As there were production anomalies, so there were delivery and numbering anomalies; I have uncovered a number of instances of cars whose build records indicate that they were earmarked for export markets in fact being delivered in the UK to home market specification, although not so far vice versa. Maybe pressure from the UK dealer network at times caused these diversions - certainly in the early TR2 days there are several instances of right hand drive TR2s supposedly built for various colonial destinations being diverted at the last minute to the home market, which had been starved of cars, especially sporting cars, for many years. As an example, John Schofield's car, TS82 and Coventry-registered as NHP222, which was stated to be an export to India, was in fact supplied in the UK as a demonstrator. My own TS210, supp.lied new in London in December 1953, nevertheless is listed as destined for Australia. As far as can be gathered, those cars earmarked for the USA did actually reach that country, where demand was insatiable once the first enthusiastic road tests were published and initial doubts about a sporting Triumph were overcome.

Upon looking through delivery statistics, I was struck by the lack of early cars going to Australia, which would have seemed an obvious market - just a couple of (presumably) demonstrators appear to have reached that country in 1954. However, one of my Australian correspondents has told me that new foreign cars carried penal import duties in Australia in the mid-1950's, and consequently cars were shipped in from Singapore and Malaya as ostensibly second hand when they were in fact new, and then resold on the Australian black market!. If this story is true it would also explain why a seemingly disproportionate number of TR2s went to Singapore and Malaya, which had formerly puzzled me. Thus one learns that factory records do not always give the true picture, a further discouragement from making categorical statements concerning sidescreen TRs!

Delivery destinations of home-market supplied cars make an interesting study; unfortunately, the receiving dealers names do not always appear on the records, although they are recorded in around 90% of cases. What is apparent is a geographical imbalance within the UK, with a far higher proportion of sidescreen TRs going to the Northern half of England than population distribution would seem to justify. Maybe this had something to do with the preponderance of rallies and rally-men in those parts - or was it just that the more financially prudent Northerners knew value for money when they saw it! Large numbers of sidescreen TRs, especially TR2s, went to North-West England, the Stockport (Manchester) based firm of Hollingdrakes taking an extraordinary number of cars, considerably more indeed than the Standard Motor Company's own London distribution depot, whereas the Birmingham distributors P.J. Evans & Co took relatively few, despite being based in the Kingdom's second largest city. J. Kaye & Co in Leeds took a large number, and the firm of Rossleigh Ltd, based in several of the Scottish cities, were also prominent. In fact more sidescreen TRs were supplied new in Scotland than either the population size or the climate would seem to warrant! South Eastern England seems to have taken disproportionately few, with hardly any appearing to go to East Anglia or Wales. The West Country counties however took a surprisingly large number,

and quite a few quickly found their way to both parts of Ireland. Although the vast size of the records means that no accurate statistics on deliveries have yet been compiled, random sampling indicates that these trends in distribution seem to have been broadly maintained through TR3A production, although the proportion of cars supplied to London and the home counties rose considerably towards the end of the TR3A's manufacturing run.

Numbering anomalies also occur, in addition to those already referred to and to those occasioned by "local" numbering and prefixing of CKD cars. For instance, there are well established instances of cars with commission numbers prefixed "EB" rather than "TS", leading to confusion with the "EB" body number. Such cars do have a number in the normal series, but for some undiscovered reason this different prefix. Some left hand drive cars have the letter 'D' preceding the normal 'L' suffix letter, and again, the significance of this additional letter is unknown. A further odd prefix that has been found is "FC" instead of "TS", car FC16838L being an example. It has been suggested that this, with the usual subtlety of Standard-Triumph codes, stood for "foreign construction", but if so, one wonders why all CKD cars did not sport such prefixes?

A further suggestion is that when the Factory sanctioned a full rebuild of a (presumably) accident-damaged car and a further warranty was issued - which evidently happened in certain overseas countries - then a new 'FC' commission plate incorporating the original number was issued, indicating "Factory Commissioned" or some such. As is well known, factory rebuilt engines carried the "FR" suffix, so it is not impossible that this 'FC' theory is accurate, but it remains highly unproven, despite the existence of more than one TR with a "FC" commission number. No doubt more such alphabetical and numerical anomalies exist, and I would be pleased to hear of any further properly-authenticated instances. I have referred elsewhere to the "speed" model TR2s, which had 'SP' incorporated into their commission numbers. This one might imagine was an abbreviation for 'speed', but I have been told that it may also have stood for "special project" indicating an experimental vehicle of some kind.

A more detailed look at the actual production process at Coventry is instructive; it has been said, and with some justification, that Standard-Triumphs were not so much motor car manufacturers as mere vehicle assemblers, for they utilised a high proportion of 'bought-out' parts and in addition some of the major assemblies that went into their cars came ready built by outside suppliers. Arguably, Standards manufactured a lower proportion of the finished vehicle than did any of the other major UK car plants of the time.

TR bodies came from Mulliners with floorpans fitted, and also apparently with the four wings loosely bolted into place, as was the bonnet, boot lid and doors. The front aprons were not initially fitted, as otherwise access to engines and radiators would be restricted. (But see later in this Chapter). The bodies also came with windscreens and seats loose inside. and with the upholstery, dash, instruments and trim already fitted. It goes without saying that they were also fully painted, and I have found details of the painting process to which each body was subjected. This official document dated 28th June 1955 is reproduced in full, both for information and to enable concours perfectionists to paint their own TR exactly as original! However, note the alarming lack of corrosion protection measures and the reference to "rusty parts" - on new bodies! - in view of this, it is surprising that we have any TRs left to enthuse over nearly 40 years later!

MULLINERS PAINT PROCEDURE

1. Front end comprising - Bulkhead, Wings, Apron and Valances, degreased and one coat red stoving synthetic primer applied to all surfaces inaccessible after assembly.

2. Rear End - Underbody degreased and brush coated with bituminous black paint.

3. Main Floor and Sills - Degreased and brush coated with bituminous black paint.

4. Sill Outer Panels - Degreased and brush coated with bituminous black paint (inner surfaces only).

5. A-Posts - Degreased and one-coat red stoving synthetic primer applied.

6. Inter-joint faces are covered with an approved welding primer. Clamped or bolted faces are primed before fixing.

7. Front and Rear wings are spaced out from the body prior to entry into paint shop to allow coverage on wings flanges and body surfaces.

After assembly of Body:

1. All parts which have been welded or metal loaded must be thoroughly washed with hot water to remove traces of welding or soldering fluxes.

2. Pretreat with Primer Surfacer or Deoxidine. Rusty parts scoured with wire wool, five minutes after application of Primer Surfacer or Deoxidine.

3. Thoroughly wash body with cold water, followed by a thorough wash with hot water.

4. Blow off and completely dry off at 200 F for fifteen minutes (minimum).

5. Cool for ten minutes, wipe with cellulose thinners.

6. Spray one coat Red Stoving Synthetic Primer (interior and exterior of body).

7. Stove at 180/200 F for 20-30 minutes.

8. Inspect, Ding and Rectify.

9. Spray two coats Red Stoving Synthetic filler. Exterior, Door Shuts and Apertures.

10. Stove at 260 F for 70-80 minutes. Final film thickness 0.001" minimum.

11. Face down using 240 papers, Exterior and Door Shuts and Apertures, completely dry off body at 180F for 20 minutes.

12. Spot in bare patches.

13. Spray one coat colour or recommended sealer.

14. Flash off.

15. Force dry 10 minutes. 160-180 F.

16. Ding if necessary. Stop up with stopper 2561. Face down stopper.

17. Two coats colour.

18. Flash off.

19. Flat with 320 paper by hand.

20. Spot in where necessary.

21. Final coats colour (two).

22. Flash off.

23. Force dry 20 minutes at 180 F. Final film thickness 0.003" minimum.

24. A bank of finished bodies should be built up of at least one days duration to enable any 'sinkage' to take place before polishing.

Photographs of the TR production lines are not common. This one was taken in early April 1954 and shows several virtually finished long-door TR2s. Note that the chromed headlamp rims are hung on the front bumper. The car in the foreground carries an "Export" label, despite being right hand drive, and was probably destined for Australia. these cars would be numberd circa TS1100 (TR Register Archive).

A batch of new TR2s leaves the factory in April 1954. The last car carries a set of whitewall tyres and, as might be expected, none has wire wheels. These were a rare fitment on TR2s, fewer than 10% of cars being thus equipped (TR Register Archive).

Having been finished as outlined, the bodies were conveyed to Standard's Canley assembly plant, where they were placed on a single conveyor production line to have wiring looms and various further small items fitted, this line moving at roughly one inch per second. The chassis came on a second line, set at right angles to the body line, and on this various minor chassis items such as brake pipes and fittings were added. Each time that a chassis reached the top of its line, both lines stopped temporarily, and a largely completed body was lifted by overhead crane off the body line, and placed onto a wheeled trolley. It was then pushed to encounter its chassis, the two being amalgamated and placed on a chain-conveyor running at the same speed of one inch per second, this conveyor set at about 18 inches above ground level. At this stage, the major mechanical

components had not yet been fitted it should be noted. (This changed later during the TR3A production run.) Upon this chain-conveyor line, one set of operatives fitted the rear axle, and simultaneously a second team bolted on the front suspension and brake units.

Engines arrived, already fitted with their gearboxes, on overhead hoists direct from the engine assembly shop, and were lowered into the cars. Cooling system components came next, following which front aprons and grilles could be fitted, together with lights, badges and minor trim items. Bumpers and overriders were however left off, and on export vehicles were placed loose in the otherwise finished car to reduce overall length and hence shipping costs. To obviate body damage, wooden boards were often fixed to the bumper brackets, bumpers being dealer-fitted. Wheels and weather equipment were added at a late stage, just prior to the largely completed vehicle coming off the line. Petrol, water and oil were then added, and the finished car was taken for a road test of between 10 and 20 miles, each car being driven over one of several, pre-determined routes. The test driver noted any problems, and upon return the car went to rectification bays where any mechanical problems were set right. While this was being done, bodywork inspectors gave the paint, panel-work and trim a thorough review, and again anything doubtful was set right. As a company, Standard-Triumph had a good reputation for build quality and standards of finish on their cars, and my interviews with original purchasers lead me to believe that they were well satisfied with the appearance of their TRs as delivered.

As to the sources of the principal components in a sidescreen TR, Sankey's produced most of the chassis frames (although Standards made the first fourteen hundred themselves and Rubery Owen made some of the later ones.) The braking systems were obtained from Lockheed or Girling as appropriate. Dunlop produced the wire wheels, and I understand that steel wheels had centres by Sankeys but with rims by Dunlop. Most major castings (both ferrous

A Factory photograph of a complete TR engine awaiting installation. The stencilled "TR3" can just be discerned on the crankcase, enabling the fitters to differentiate it from engines for other models (TR Register Archive).

An official photograph of a newly-built TR3 with hardtop, taken in the grounds of the Canley (Coventry) factory (TR Register Archive).

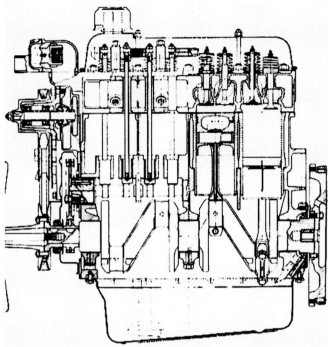

Fig. 1   Longitudinal view of Engine. For illustration purposes the sump oil filter has been omitted.

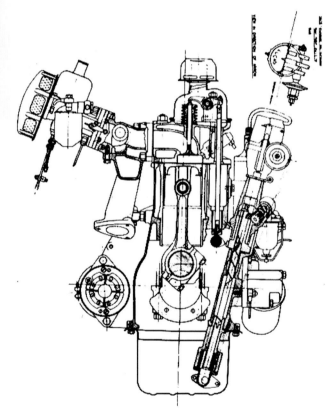

These two diagrams show the TR engine in profile and end sections (TR Register Archive).

and non-ferrous) were produced by the GKN group, Standard-Triumph not having appropriate facilities. Some castings, such as exhaust manifolds, were however produced by Qualcast, with Bean Industries also active in this field, and there may also have been other sources. Locks and chromework were for the most part manufactured by Wilmot-Breedon, who had a virtual monopoly at the time,

and the Coventry Hood and Trim Co. produced hoods, tonneaux and sidescreens for the first part of the car's production period. However, by 1957, Standards had installed a new trim shop, and took to making these items themselves. The stoneguards, wing beading and grilles came from Holyoake and Company, the windscreen from Worcester Windshields Ltd, hinges from the Bloxwich Lock and

Stamping Co, and badges either from Fattorini and Co or from Joseph Fray and Co.

Electrical equipment was almost exclusively Lucas, and the Coventry Radiator Co. and the Forward Radiator Co. (a Standard subsidiary) produced cooling system components. Final machining of some engine parts was done in the engine shop, as was all assembly, but the engines contained a considerable proportion of bought-out items, including fully machined crankshafts, pistons and liner sets (from B.H.B. Ltd or Hepolite) and also the camshafts. Cylinder heads were assembled by Standard Triumph, but the components were bought-in. Both TR and Standard Vanguard engines were assembled side by side on the same line, but those intended for the TRs were clearly marked to ensure that the correct cylinder heads and carburettors were fitted. They were also more accurately balanced in that the reciprocating components were more carefully matched than was the case for Vanguard engines.These latter were electrically motored in batches of 10 for around 20 minutes, but each individual TR engine was, after intial motoring, fired up and bench run on a dynomometer for upwards of an hour. Any engine which did not produce its designed power output was rejected, dismantled and demoted to "Vanguard" status if swift rectification did not prove possible. For the TR3/3A "high port" engines, the required power output on the bench was 74BHP at 3500 RPM. For the "low-port" TR2 engines, I have been fortunate to discover an original document detailing the exact procedure laid down for the bench testing of engines, and this is set out below. As can be seen, 73 BHP at 3500 was expected of these power units in controlled conditions, running without ancillaries. It will be observed therefore, that the factory went to some considerable trouble to ensure that the TR engines were worthy of the rugged sports cars to which they were fitted, the total individual engine test time being in excess of four hours.

TR.2. ENGINE TEST (PRODUCTION)

Dual Drive Running-in Stands.
Every Engine.

Description of Operation	Time (Mins)
Load engine on stand	8
Slave at 1000 r.p.m.	20
Change over	16
Fire at 1000 r.p.m.	20
Unload engine	8
	72

Brake Test. Engine fitted with aircleaner and dummy sump. Fan belt not fitted. Shop exhaust system. Room temperature taken and

B.H.P. corrected to 60 degrees F, 29.92 Hg

Every Engine.

Load engine	10
Run at 1000 r.p.m. light	15
Run at 1000 r.p.m. under load	10
Run at 1500 r.p.m. light	15
Run at 1500 r.p.m. under load	10
Run at 2000 r.p.m. light	10
Run at 2000 r.p.m. under load	5
Run at 3000 r.p.m. light	10
Run at 3000 r.p.m. under load	5
Run at 4000 r.p.m. light	10
Run at 4000 r.p.m. under load	5
	105 Mins

Allow engine to cool, adjust carburettors, take power readings at:-

1000 r.p.m. acceptable average B.H.P.	- 17)
1500 " " " "	- 29)
2000 " " " "	- 40)
2500 " " " "	- 52)
3000 " " " "	- 63)
3500 " " " "	- 73)
4000 " " " "	- 81)
(Take readings up and down)	
Unload engine	10
	180 mins

Total time - floor to floor (all engines)	252 mins.

Overdrive units came ready to fit from the sole manufacturers, Laycock de Normanville, but gearboxes were machined, gears were hardened and the boxes were fully assembled by Standard-Triumph. It is believed that Bean Industries Ltd produced the internals for the rear axle, the GKN group providing the casings, but the axles were finally assembled at Standard's old Banner Lane plant. Propellor Shafts came from Hardy Spicer, shock absorbers from Armstrongs, steering and front suspension components from Alford and Alder and the steering wheel itself and control head assembly were manufactured by Bluemels. Smiths Industries supplied the heater, certain cooling components and also the "Jaeger" brand name instruments. Dunlop cross-ply tyres of varying types were always original equipment unless a special order for Michelin "X" radials was received. The fitment of S.U. carburettors is in retrospect somewhat surprising, as the S.U. Company was wholly owned by the competing British Motor Corporation, makers of the TR's principal rivals, the Austin Healey and M.G.A. Incidentally, the reconditioning of TR engines and axles was contracted out by the Company

This works picture demonstrates boot handles that did not reach production - although something similar was available from accessory manufacturers. Twin reversing lights are also fitted to OKV 603 which, to judge from its "OKV" Coventry registration, was a long-door TR2 from May 1954 (TR Register Archive).

to Bean Industries, though they carried a Standard-Triumph Warranty.

Two exceptions to the general statement that Mulliners' main plant produced all the sidescreen TR bodies should be mentioned. Firstly, the first handful of production TR2s had Standard-Triumph assembled bodies, some of the panel-work being virtually hand made in aluminium. The second exception relates to the TR3Bs; the bodies for these were manufactured by the Forward Radiator Company Ltd as by 1962 Mulliners had assumed that no further sidescreen TR bodies would be required. They had turned therefore to other contracts (including TR4 bodies) and were not in a position again to take up TR body manufacture, this despite the fact that Mulliners had been a Standard-Triumph subsidiary company since 1958.

In fact, I understand that Forward Radiator Ltd not only built the TR3B bodies, but that they virtually assembled the whole car, Standard-Triumphs having utilised all their Canley assembly space for the TR4, demand for which was very high in 1962. However, Forward Radiator was, by this time, also a subsidiary of Standard, so the whole production was in effect still "in house", at least from an ownership and accounting point of view.

As can be seen from the foregoing details, in many ways it was true that Standard-Triumph were assemblers rather than manufacturers, as arguably only about half of the con-

tent of the car in value terms was manufactured within the Group. However, as anyone who has utilised Meccano will know, it's not just having the parts, it's what you do with them that counts, and the Company's contribution to the design, testing, assembly and overseeing of trouble-free production cannot be over emphasised. The quality and the reputation of the finished product was Standard-Triumph's responsibility alone; it was they who issued the guarantee and to them that the customer would return in the event of a problem, not to an individual component supplier.

A further insight into work at the Standard-Triumph plant was provided when I interviewed Peter Clarke. His memories of his time in the Competitions Department will be found in Chapter 4, but I also discussed with him his time on the production line, for he undertook a full five year apprenticeship with the company during the sidescreen TR production period.

Peter confirms that while the bodies did indeed arrive from Mulliners fully painted and with outer panels in place, a lot of hand fettling and finishing was required on the production line and in the rectification bays. He recalls that once the "split" type two-piece steering column was introduced in mid-1958, the bodies came with the front aprons already in place, for this type of steering could be fitted much more easily; indeed it was re-designed specifically to facilitate installation. This contrasts with the TR2 and TR3 production method, where as described earlier, the apron was fitted

A rare picture of the TR3 production line in early 1957. The car in the foreground sports whitewall tyres and thus is probably destined for the USA ("Motor Sport").

later. At around the same time of the change to the split-column, the engine, gearbox and other major components were fitted into the chassis prior to the body being fitted, the whole body being lowered into place onto the largely completed chassis. This method saved both time and money as compared with the arrangement described previously.

Peter Clarke also recalls that Standards made the seats rather than that these came from Milliners with the bodies, but I have received conflicting information on this point; the truth is probably that the factory made them at one period

(as they did the hoods etc.), but that they were externally supplied at other times. It is suggested that the extra-cost option leather trim items were usually factory made, but vinyl trim was more likely to be externally supplied. He remembers also the aluminium panels fitted on the early cars being handmade on a traditional wheeling machine, and that on some occasions, in the tinsmith's shop, this tool was pressed into service to rectify steel panelwork and even to manufacture items that were unaccountably missing from otherwise complete bodies where not to do so would hold production up! Some of the tinsmiths at the Company were

One of the few photographs available showing the TR3A production lines, probably dating from 1958 (TR Register Archive).

able to repair and rectify painted panelwork, without damage to the paintwork itself, a tribute to their skill and a worthwhile economy.

Peter mentions that stock control and parts ordering to keep the lines running smoothly was sometimes erratic, and it was not unusual to have a batch of cars finished except for one vital component. The main interest was, unsurprisingly, the keeping running of the production lines and no thought was taken of what we today might term "originality". This led to the apparent lack of "clear" changeovers when new parts were introduced, and Peter confirmed that this often occurred, despite what the parts manual says about change points! Rather than stop the production line, superseded components were utilised if necessary, sometimes some months after the supposed change-over!

Peter Clarke spent a considerable time on the engine production line in the Engine shop, and was trained to do each of the many different assembly and machining jobs involved. At the end of this period, he had to pass out by building two complete engines himself, both of which had to reach the target brake horse power figures - good training indeed for the TR restoration work that occupies him today! He spent a fair proportion of his apprenticeship at the Banner Lane plant, where the Engineering and Experimental (Competition) shops were originally located. This site was however later taken over by Ferguson's for tractor assembly, so Competitions and Experimental went to join the Service Department at the Allesley site in 1957, and Engineering went to the Fletchhampstead North plant. At Banner Lane there was no car assembly, but Standard 8 and 10 engines were built, together with (inter-alia) TR rear axles. Peter turned his hand to all these operations, but not unnaturally preferred work on the TRs, for this was the Company's flagship product, and the one of most interest to a teenager keen on motor sport. Peter recalls that just behind the Banner Lane works was a jet aircraft engine test house, which caused alarming noise and vibration when the engines were run up, making it not the most pleasant place in Coventry to work!

One of his most vivid memories of this period at Standard-Triumphs was the sad sight of rows of stored, unsold TR3As dumped around the perimeter of Bagington Airfield in Coventry in the winter of 1960/61, at the time when the Company's fortunes were at their lowest ebb. The economic recession of the time had all but killed the home market, and USA sales had slumped badly, partly because the 3A was now looking somewhat dated, and also because persistent rumours of an impending TR4 were abounding. As has been related elsewhere, only the Leyland takeover deal in early 1961 saved the Company's fortunes, and Peter con-

firms that this was greeted at the time by the ordinary workforce with both enthusiasm and profound relief - the Company's financial ills were well known in the area and large scale redundancies had been feared. Incidentally, whilst on the subject of stored TRs, Peter told me that at the end of the 1970's some brand new TR6s were discovered in one of British Leyland's Coventry compounds, having been stored for 5 or 6 years! They were evidently missing certain parts that strikes had prevented being fitted whilst they were being built, and having been stored they had been promptly forgotten! Having heard many stories of the things that went on within the British Leyland empire in the 1970's, I find this tale not in the least surprising, but one does wonder whether the cars were ever finished and how they were ultimately disposed of!

I took the opportunity of discussing the existence or otherwise of aluminium panelled TR3As with Peter. He confirmed that it would have been a relatively simple matter for Mulliners to press these panels as an alternative to steel to special order, and that he was sure that on occasions it was done for "Rally Replicas". Whether there were any Works rally TRs with aluminium bodies Peter cannot confirm from his own recollections, but another source has told me that one or more of the 1958 Works Rally TR3As had aluminium body panels fitted, at least for one or two events; presumably this was in contravention of the homologation regulations. While I have been unable to obtain any confirmation of this story, some TR3As with aluminium body panels **did** escape, as is related elsewhere, just to make the subject of the sidescreen TR history an even less exact science!

Lastly, I am able to deal briefly with a different aspect of the design and construction of the sidescreen TRs, for I was fortunate enough to meet Vic Hammond, a designer and stylist who worked at Standard-Triumphs during the period under review. Vic Hammond was born in Coventry and grew up with a keen interest in cars, and after studying at Coventry School of Art and working briefly on body jigs for the 18TR Triumph Roadster at the Canley factory, he went into the Styling and Design department at the Works in January 1946. This Styling department was an offshoot of the body design department under Walter Belgrove, and it consisted of just three people, Leslie Ireland, Vic and a Secretary. It was located at the Banner Lane site, and Vic recalls that his initial salary was Six Pounds 10 shillings a week. He was put to work doing detailed drawings of the grille and fascia for the Standard Vanguard. which was then evolving into its production form, but before long, Sir John Black, on one of his periodic tours of the factory, noticed this new face and enquired of Belgrove who he was. As a result, Vic Hammond commenced work on drawings for details of the Triumph Roadster, at the time Black's pet project. However, as is well known, although Sir John Black was happy with the Roadster in general terms, he wanted to produce something with more of a "sports car" feel, hopefully to compete with Jaguar's XK120. Thus, the design team, including Vic, was set to work on the "TRX", code number 22TR, the "silver bullet" roadster. This vehicle was designed and built in conjunction with Helliwells of Wolverhampton, an aircraft company used to working with aluminium to high specifications, and where Frank Rainbow who designed the Swallow Doretti was based. The "Bullet" body was styled by Belgrove, his sketches being passed to Vic Hammond who made up an orthographic layout for conversion to full size, enabling the prototypes to be built. Despite a lot of hard work by the team caused by this car's complexity, the project was eventually cancelled by Black once the prototypes had been built. Again, it was becoming obvious that it was not the MG and Jaguar beating sports car originally intended, and in any event, production costs would have been tremendous.

Vic recalls a day when Black came in unexpectedly and announced that what he really wanted was a "cheap and fast sports car based on the old Standard 8 chassis frame, and with a Vanguard engine" (one wonders whether "Buttercup" was in his thoughts again?). When Black wanted something, he wanted it yesterday, so work on other projects was immediately suspended, and Belgrove, Ireland, Hammond and others got down to designing the first TR, the 20TS prototype. Belgrove designed the first image for the 20TS, the full size layout being done by Ireland and Bert Haddock, who had been a draughtsman with Triumphs prior to the war. No clay models or mock-ups were used due to time pressure, for Black made it clear that the car must be at the 1952 London Motor Show. A wooden buck was made from the full sized drawing, and this buck was then panelled, the car being built in the Experimental shop at Banner Lane. Hammond worked on various smaller items that went to make up the complete car, including the unique "globe" badge only fitted to the prototype TRs. The windscreen was designed by Worcester Windshields, who manufactured it, Coventry Hood and Sidescreen Co Ltd providing the weather equipment. The chassis and wheels came from Rubery Owen and Mulliners provided the seats. As an aside, Vic told me that when the TR body was in full production at Mulliners later, Albert Lane, Mulliner's chief buyer at the time, told him that the price paid by Standards for a fully painted and trimmed sidescreen TR body was £60! Considering what a high proportion of the finished car the body represented, this seems a bargain, even allowing for inflation.

Leslie Ireland accompanied the 20TS to the Earls Court Motor Show and did duty on the Standard-Triumph stand, but Hammond confirms that none of the stylists were ever happy with the bob-tailed rear end of this car, due to lack of luggage space and poor visibility when reversing, and they realised that it would have to be changed. When the order came to rework the 20TS after the Show, Vic helped Leslie Ireland to redesign and redraw the rear of the car with an opening boot, including the incorporation of the clever spare wheel storage arrangements. The frontal styling was left largely unchanged, but its creator Belgrove designed the various "tidying-up" arrangements, such as the new bumpers and the moving of the sidelights. I enquired about the revised "shield" front badge that was to last in essence through to the TR3B. The shield itself was conceived by an outside consultancy, and Vic Hammond adapted their outline into the TR car badge, the prototype badges then being manufactured in vitreous enamel by Joseph Fray and Co.

An interesting story surrounds the creation of the hardtop, which was introduced at the end of 1954. In early 1954, when the production TR2 was at last up and running, Belgrove took it on his own initiative to sponsor a removable hardtop, to be manufactured in the then new glass fibre material. Vic recalls that the actual lines of the hardtop with its classic "wrap-round" rear window were Belgrove's with help from Jack Ward and Tim Younger. Evidently however, no mention of this project had been made to Ted Grinham, Director of Engineering, and the man to whom Belgrove and his department ultimately reported. Belgrove ensured that the model making was done discreetly, to avoid frustrations from those above. Tim Younger was superintendent of the body shop which made the first wooden model hardtop, and it was this that Grinham eventually spotted. Hammond is not alone amongst those I've spoken to when he relates that Grinham was not always a pleasant man with whom to deal, and as soon as he saw the prototype hardtop, Grinham flew into a rage and demanded that the project be scrapped, for he had sanctioned no such thing! Belgrove however knew a good thing when he saw one, and had the prototype top fitted to a car which was casually left parked by the Experimental shop. In his anger, Grinham telephoned Frank Higham in the Sales Department, but when the Sales Department people saw the car, they swiftly demanded that a run of 500 be made, Grinham's objections being overruled at a board meeting! Ultimately, many thousands of this top were sold, some to people who never removed it from their cars! The initial production runs were made in fibreglass, but evidently the workers were unused to handling this material, and didn't quite trust it from a personal safety point of view. At all events,, the outwardly identical hardtop was soon being pressed in steel such that the fibreglass ones are quite rare today.

The minor styling changes (including the new grille) that distinguished the TR3 from the TR2 were made by Leslie

The main factory administration block is seen as a background to Nancy Mitchell, posing with the Works TR3 prior to her driving it in the 1957 Mille Miglia. Unfortunately, she crashed the car in this event, happliy without damage to herself. It was, of course, the last Mille Miglia ("Motor Sport").

tIreland, whereas the TR3A restyling was more of a team effort. Vic Hammond was responsible for the minor changes at the rear, including the design of the "Triumph" badge, and also the "Triumph" lettering on the front apron; the recessed headlights and new, full-width grille were the work of Sid Gadsby, a man who had done extensive work on the Armstrong-Siddeley Sapphire. Walter Belgrove was not happy with the re-working of his classic TR2 frontal aspect into the "dollar-grin" TR3, but the USA market demanded a change. In fact, Belgrove left the company abruptly in late 1957, and Vic says that this was as a result of an argument with management on the Triumph stand at the 1957 Motor Show concerning the Standard Vanguard replacement. Belgrove turned to Hammond on the Stand and said, "Victor, load all my stuff into the car, I'm leaving!" and with that he went, leaving Vic both upset and astonished. Les Ireland himself had already left the company, and Ted Grinham asked Vic Hammond to take charge of the department, which he did. He, like the others, soon found that restrictive management policies, personality clashes with senior personnel and lack of development funds were putting a damper on the job, and so Vic too left after around 3 years, to join Volvo in Sweden. Additionally, at this time the company was employing the Italian Michelotti to restyle the range of cars, including the TR, so much of the in-house Styling and Design Department's work had been removed from them, which was somewhat dispiriting.

Vic continued to tell me fascinating inside stories concerning the senior management at the plant in the 1950's, including what he heard at the time of Sir John Black's ousting by the Board in the winter of 1953/54; however, maybe these are details better left unpublished at present!

CHAPTER THREE:

An Interview with Ken Richardson

Whilst researching this book, I was fortunate in being able to secure an interview with Ken Richardson, the man primarily responsible for the development of the prototype Triumph Sports car into a world beater in International events, and who was manager of Standard-Triumph's Competition Department from 1954-1961.

I had met Ken previously when he attended the TR Register's International Weekend at Peterborough in 1988, for as Registrar responsible for sidescreen TR's I was given the job of escorting him round the show and taking him to lunch. It occurred to me then that a proper interview with Ken could prove illuminating, and would enable him to make known his own memories both of the development of the TR2 and of his subsequent career at Triumphs. The clarity of his memory was most impressive, he being able to answer the most technical of questions fired at him by TR Register members that day without hesitation. Thus it was that, through the good offices of his son Paul, I was able to spend a day in April 1992 with both Ken and Paul at a pleasant country pub near Stamford in Lincolnshire, not far from Ken's home. I arrived with a carefully prepared list of questions, but after posing the first few, they were sufficient to jog Ken into a fascinating, day long series of reminisces that not only answered my prepared questions (and more that I had not thought to ask) but also provided a fascinating window onto those optimistic and relatively carefree days in the 1950s when, as viewed from the 1990s, everything seemed possible and the sun always shone!

What follows is a summary of the interview with Ken taken from my notes, and in many places Ken's own words have been quoted. We touched on subjects in random order,

dealing with them as they occurred to both Ken and myself so the reader is asked to bear with me if chronological order is sometimes eschewed. I thought it best however to write up the interview very much as it occurred, lest any spontaneity or nuances be lost. I hope that my day spent with Ken Richardson will prove interesting to TR enthusiasts - would that Ken could be persuaded to write at length about the whole of his long career in the motor industry, including his time as a racing and test driver - that would be a book for all motoring enthusiasts to savour! I should add that I am well aware that in many respects Ken Richardson's memories as set down here of the events surrounding the creation and conduct of the Triumph TRs and the Works Competition Department differ from some other published accounts, but Ken did however have the advantage of being there, and throughout the whole 1954 - 1961 period.

Richardson was born in 1911, at Bourne at Lincolnshire where his father had a wholesale/retail butchery business. Also in the town of Bourne was the ERA racing car company headed in the 1930's by Raymond Mays, a member of a wealthy local family of wool merchants. Ken had always been fascinated by high performance machines and engineering generally, and at the age of fourteen owned his first motor bike, a round tank BSA. After an engineering apprenticeship, he was invited by Peter Berthon and Raymond Mays to join the staff of ERA in 1933/4, where, time, he became chief mechanic, works test driver and reserve driver to Raymond Mays. Ken was not only involved with the development of the ERA racing car but became involved in several "one off" projects at ERA, including the "Raymond Mays" car, a high quality sporting saloon that was intended for production. The Raymond Mays cars, of which only a handful were ultimately built, utilised a production chassis frame

Back in the 1930s, Ken Richardson worked for English Racing Auto-mobiles, based in his home town of Bourne in Lincolnshire. Here, Ken (left) is seen working on Raymond Mays' 2-Litre ERA in the paddock at Shelsley Walsh hill climb course. Ken recalls that this car produced nearly 300bhp and twin rear wheels were fitted in an attmpt to transmit this power to the track (Ken Richardson).

Ken Richardson, in his capacity as test driver for British Racing Motors (BRM), is seen here practising for the Italian Grand Prix at monza in 1951. Note that the circuit is surfaced with cobblestones! (Ken Richardson).

Raymond Mays, head of British Racing Motors, poses in the new BRM V-16 Grand Prix car at Folkingham airfield in mid-1951, where much testing was carried out. Ken Richardson is seen on the extreme right and a youthful Tony Rudd is standing next to him (LAT Photographic).

manufactured by the Standard Motor Company in Coventry, which was much modified by Ken who built up the first chassis himself. This was his first contact with the firm destined to become his employers nearly 20 years later.

At the outbreak of the second world war, Ken volunteered for the RAF to become a fighter pilot, but was not accepted due to his specialist engineering knowledge and background. Instead he was seconded to work on top secret aero engine development for the Government, eventually to be transferred to Rolls Royce where he became involved with the first Whittle jet propulsion engine. It was during the war that Ken first met Ted Grinham who later became the Engineering Director of the Standard Motor Company.

Once peace arrived, Ken was again invited to join Raymond Mays, this time to be involved in the creation of the "national" racing car, the BRM V16. In the late 1940's many leading industrialists were persuaded to put up money to finance the creation of a world-beating racing car for Britain, a prestige product to trounce the Italian cars in Formula One and to be seen as a flagship for British industry. Ken insists that the major reason for the unreliability of the BRM V16 was the fact that major sponsors who promised a regular supply of essential parts simply did not come up with the goods. "We often waited months for new spares, and lost around a year of development time because of this problem. In fact, the inner half shafts that snapped on the start line at Silverstone on the first public outing of the V16 had suffered the stresses of over 2,000 miles of high speed testing, with myself at the wheel, prior to the race. These shafts, like many other parts, should have been regularly changed to avoid fatigue failure, but we had no others! Eventually, when we finally had a full stock of those specialised spares that we needed, the V16 proved very reliable. I drove the car on extended high speed tests on a great many occasions with no trouble; in fact one day Reg Parnell and I covered over 600 miles of non stop high speed testing at Folkingham Airdrome. The V16 ran perfectly and the only stops were for fuel". Ken went on to state that "to produce a first class racing machine of any type two essential ingredients are necessary if failure is to be avoided. The first is the constant supply of any replacement or modified spares needed, the second being the availability of many thousands of man hours to prove the mechanical integrity of the machine."

The amazing V16, two-stage supercharged BRM with its astounding exhaust note proved incredibly fast and fearsome whilst it held together. The 1500 cc engine developed over 500 BHP and the car was capable of over 200 MPH. Ken was the brave man appointed test driver to the team as well as carrying the onerous responsibility of being chief mechanic and reserve driver for races. Again there was a Standard-Triumph connection, for Standard's machined the blocks and cylinder heads for the BRM's V16 engine, and Walter Belgrove designed the Mark 1 BRM's cigar-shaped bodywork, Belgrove being Standard-Triumph's chief body stylist. Sir John Black was one of the industrialists backing the BRM project and he was of course Chairman of the Standard Motor Company at the time, both he and Ted Grinham visiting BRM at Bourne more than once during this period. This led to Sir John and Ken Richardson becoming acquainted well before the Triumph Sports project. Ken tells with wry amusement now the story of how the new BRM was to be demonstrated to all the industrialists who had backed it, including Sir John Black, at Folkingham airfield, not far from Bourne. Ken himself was at the wheel and after about fifteen high speed laps he was entering a bend at around 140 mph when the steering wheel came off in his hands, car and driver careering off the circuit into a field of sunflowers. The steering wheel was replaced and was additionally retained by a nut and bolt as well as by the quick release mechanism (which was not properly locked previously). Ken went out again and after three further laps again had steering failure, also at high speed, more sunflowers being felled! This second steering problem was due to a bolt coming loose in one of the steering column universal joints and jamming the steering solid. After this Ken decided he had had enough of the V16 for the day, ordering a complete inspection of the car while he tested a new E.R.A. engined sprint/hillclimb car, only to have a rear hub and wheel shear off at high speed and whistle past his ear! Such incidents all in one day give some insight into the hazardous life of a test driver involved with Grand Prix machines. Ken now bursts into laughter remembering his reply when Raymond Mays said to him, "What do you think we have accomplished today, Ken?" Ken's response was, "Well I don't know what you've done Ray, but I've harvested about half an acre of sunflowers and I've also found out for the first time that adrenalin is brown in colour!!".

Sir John Black and Ted Grinham had both been impressed with Ken's development work and vast engineering experience with high speed machinery of all types, and also with the fact that Ken was well known for his ability behind the wheel of a Grand Prix car. Sir John made a direct approach to Richardson asking him if he would join Standard-Triumph which, Ken emphasises, was before the 1952 Earls Court Motor Show at which the new Triumph Sports Car was first shown, and before Ken had even seen the car, let alone driven it!

Richardson recalls that Black's exact words to him were, "We have built a new sports car, and we would like you to join us to develop it as no-one here knows anything about sports cars."

Thus Ken joined the Standard Motor Company, his position to be Development Engineer with particular responsibility for the new sports car project. He was not shown the prototype at his interview, but Sir John gave him two tickets for the forthcoming October Motor Show and said the car would be on the stand, as indeed it was. Ken recalls now that his immediate reaction upon finally seeing the 20TS prototype which he had agreed to develop was, "My God, what have I done!"

However, he decided to leave final judgment on the new prototype until he had test driven the car, which took place two or three days later back at the Banner Lane factory in Coventry. The Company had organised a large press day, whereby the 20TS was shown to the world's motoring pressmen, who were all invited to drive the car. The car was the one that had been displayed at the Motor Show, and Ken finally drove it at about 3.30 in the afternoon, Sir John saying, "Take the car out Ken, and let me know what you think of it." Ken's road test involved a drive from the Banner Lane factory using some twisty, undulating roads that he knew, turning at a large roundabout on the Fletchamstead Highway. Short as this test drive may have been, it was enough to make Ken realise the true extent of the work he had let himself in for. Ken says that it was quite obvious that the chassis on the car was a complete "cobble-up", and was, he found out later, an amalgam of several previous attempts to produce a sports car chassis. He avers that on inspection of the chassis it was obvious that proper chassis design and essential stressing was non-existent. "In fact," Ken said, "the chassis was an absolute disgrace." That the car was indeed intended for production in its 20TS form, Ken has no doubt, for otherwise why announce it at the Motor Show, and why let the world press drive it a few days later? Ken insists that Sir John Black and Ted Grinham were both under the impression that their new car was ready for production "apart from minor modifications." This is further evidenced by the fact that the 20TS was already entered for the Geneva Motor show only a few months later in March of 1953. Ken states that this is why there was such a panic that winter; to produce the redesigned prototype TR2 in time for the Geneva Show.

Following his test drive, Ken went back to his new office at Banner Lane and began writing his report, but completion of this damning document was pre-empted by a phone call from Sir John who called him to his office. Ted Grinham was also present, and after Sir John had ordered a round of drinks from his butler came the question, "Well Ken, what do you think of the new car?" Richardson recalls saying, "You want the truth Sir John?" "Of course." was the reply. "Well I think your new prototype sports car is the most bloody awful car I've ever driven - it's not at all safe to drive

and will kill someone - in fact it ought to be scrapped." Needless to say the faces of Sir John and Ted took on a paler shade, and after a few seconds of contemplation Ken was asked to leave the office for a while. A few minutes later he was called back, and Sir John said "Both Ted and I have decided to take your criticism of the car seriously. What can be done to put this car right?" Ken recalls saying that the first job to be done was to have a new chassis designed and stressed properly, as the present chassis was totally useless. In addition, there would also have to be major modifications to increase the engine power, as the performance of the car was extremely disappointing.

Sir John then said "I am going to order the complete redesign of this car, but it is essential that we have the new car in time for the Geneva Motor Show - would it be possible to redesign and produce such a new car in about eight weeks, in time for that show?"

After due consideration Ken said that he felt that this would be possible, but only if all the best engineers and technicians in the Company, and any other staff needed, were put on to the project forthwith. As is now known, the redesign was indeed completed inside those eight weeks, which Ken stresses was a superb team effort by everyone involved.

The job demanded virtually solid day and night work for everyone on the team, during which proper meals were often missed. In addition to advising on several design aspects of the new car, Ken also had to consider what performance modifications were needed, which again involved him in his previous role of test driver, and thus he spent several days driving the Motor Show 20TS at the MIRA test circuit. This experience Ken did not enjoy for obvious reasons, but the 20TS was the only "sports car" available in which to test engine and transmission units, whilst work went on at the factory with the new chassis. The 20TS testing took place with the sole aim of establishing how best to improve engine performance and to identify areas where essential mechanical improvements and major changes had to be made. Ken remembered that later, whilst testing the first TR2, he once blew up six engines in one week, which apparently prompted some of the management to consider his dismissal, surely a case of "shooting the messenger."

At this stage Ken pointed out that Ted Grinham had very little enthusiasm for the TR project and had no interest in sports cars. He preferred to busy himself with the more traditional saloon projects. This, in Ken's opinion, had contributed to the lack of success of the 20TS prototype. However, Grinham's number two, Lewis Dawtrey worked enthusiastically on the TR2 project, as did Harry Webster and John Turnbull. Whilst the redesign was under way, it became obvious to Ken that Lewis Dawtrey was, in his opinion, the finest Design Engineer in the Company at that time. Ken insists that if more notice had been taken of Dawtrey in the first place, the 20TS would have had no major design problems. Richardson recalls that Lewis was a kind, gentle man who had an extremely deep knowledge of engines, chassis and suspension. Dawtrey's insight into what was needed to produce a real sports car played a major part in the success of the redesigned TR, Ken finding it a delight to work with him, as once the right solution to a problem was found, Lewis was always quick to implement it.

Walter Belgrove and his styling department went to work on the required body modifications in parallel with the engineering team, and the revised TR2 body turned out to be a model of sporting practicality, if not quite having the beauty and grace of the Austin Healey 100 or the XK 120.

At this point in the interview I asked Ken **exactly** what had been wrong with the 20TS prototype. His reply? "It shook like a jelly when cornering, and was generally unstable. The chassis was so weak that the suspension, such as it was, was rendered useless because of the chassis twist. The performance was extremely poor and valve bounce could be induced at ludicrously low revolutions. The all out maximum speed was about 78 mph, not even enough to see off the pre-war style 1 1/4 litre MG TD! Frankly," added Ken, "it was downright dangerous even in the hands of a skilled driver, let alone in those of a novice member of the public." He added that his own Standard Vanguard Phase One would outperform the 20TS as presented. Ken went on, "The windscreen was far too high and vibrated, air getting under the front hood rail causing the hood to billow and flap. The gearbox ratios were wrong, as was the steering ratio, and the brakes came on in a fashion that would better describe the engine firing order - it was an absolute shambles, plus the fact that there was very little room for right arm movement when steering the car, and visibility was limited both by a very low seating position and the spare wheel being sited on top of the tail. My original critical report on the car ran to three full pages!"

Richardson also recalls the shock waves that his condemnation of the car caused among the top brass at Standard's, who like both Sir John Black and Ted Grinham had evidently been led to believe that the 20TS really was almost ready for production as displayed at the Motor Show.

The story of how in those two months during the winter of 1952/3 the disastrous 20TS prototype was redesigned into the hugely successful TR2 has been chronicled previously, in particular in a very informative two part article that originally appeared in "The Autocar" magazine in 1955, and which has been reprinted more than once in recent years. At this point, I asked Ken for his recollections on a question that has puzzled TR historians for many years, namely, was only one 20TS built, and what happened to it? He is quite sure that there were two 20TS cars built. One was the car on the Motor Show stand in October 1952, being also the car that Ken and the press drove at the Banner Lane factory press release. The other was not fully finished and never ran, work on it being stopped when the extent of the problems became apparent. He recalls seeing two cars together both painted cream, with red seats and feels sure that the old legend of there being only one car is wrong.

As to what happened to them, again it has been said for many years that the 20TS was scrapped, but as I outlined in my "TR2/3/3A Superprofile" book, the present owner of MVC575, chassis no. X519, the "Jabbeke" car, has found tangible evidence during the dismantling and rebuilding of this car that it incorporated many 20TS parts, and Ken Richardson confirms this to be the case. He also believes that all usable parts from the second uncompleted 20TS were used on the first prototype TR2 MWK950 (chassis no. X508) which was, it isbelieved, the car shown to the public for the first time in March 1953 at the Geneva Motor Show, when the Triumph Sports was relaunched.

This car has a lower chassis number on the experimental list than the "Jabbeke" car MVC575, and thus can be presumed to have been built first, being finished and registered in January 1953 according to the factory prototype register. This accords with Ken Richardson's 8 week redesign period, which would have commenced in early November 1952 just after the Earls Court show closed. It seems therefore likely that the incomplete, non-running 20TS would have been dismantled first and then all usable parts built into MWK950. The complete 20TS car that the press drove was as stated previously initially used by Ken Richardson for engine development, and then presumably left complete until a second prototype TR2 was required, whereupon it was dismantled and all usable parts were built into MVC575. Ken cannot be categorical but seems to recall that after he had used it for testing, the completed 20TS was hidden from view under a dust sheet for some time whilst work went on on the first prototype TR2. He is certain that anything that could be re-used for the two prototype TR2's was indeed re-used, the 20TS cars thus not being scrapped as such. Money was short at Standard Triumphs, as ever, and the whole sports car project was being run on a tight budget; thus it is only logical, therefore, that as much as possible from the 20TS cars was made use of. Indeed, Ken clearly recalls the bodies being cut in half laterally behind the seats to enable the new TR2 type rear sections to be grafted on, the doors, front bulkhead and wings thus being "recycled", and he also remembers the dashboards being shortened and re-used. Both the two TR2 prototypes were finished in Ice Blue, both were originally left hand drive, and Ken is sure that one at least initially still had the 20TS type 9 inch front brakes fitted. Incidentally, although Ken Richardson has no recollection of the event, photographic evidence proves that Sir John Black took the completed 20TS to the USA towards the end of 1952 on a promotional tour. This would be whilst the redesign was going on, so one wonders whether Sir John kept silent on this point!

Referring again to the rapid redesign process, Ken elaborated on the subject of engine development, and I reproduce his own words "The engine of the first TR underwent a great deal of development, of course, but before any major surgery was undertaken there were several simple modifications that had to be made. The first necessity was to alleviate chronic valve bounce, which was cured by fitting double valve springs which were held in place by a collar and split collets. As was to be expected, as we increased the performance of the engine, major problems showed up, not the least of which was crank failure, which I had experienced many times during test sessions on the MIRA circuit. On inspection it was obvious to me that the fillet radii on the journals and pins (where failure was occurring) were far too small, which allowed stress cracks to develop and thus crank failure. After taking a look at several failed cranks under a magnifying glass, I also noticed ridges on several journals where the grinder had stopped in the area of the fillet radii where the finish should be perfectly smooth. This was a manufacturing fault. After talking things over with Lewis Dawtrey the fillet radii were increased, and he devised further crankshaft improvements and the necessary upgrading in quality control. I also recommended the use of Vandervell bearings".

I then went on to tax Ken on his recollections of the record breaking high speed runs at Jabbeke in Belgium, which did so much to dispel the press's initially cool response to the Triumph Sports and make doubters realise that the redesigned car was indeed something significant. One day in March 1953, just as the TR2 prototypes were achieving their final production form and gaining reliability, Sir John Black rang Ken Richardson to ask if he'd heard about the Rootes Groups's success with the Sunbeam-Talbot Alpine. This car had just achieved a 120 mph observed run driven by Sheila van Damm on the Jabbeke high speed road in Belgium, which was being claimed as both a Belgian and a ladies' production car record, although it has to be said that the standard Alpine would barely top 100 mph (I know, I owned one!). Thus the car concerned must have been "tweaked" in some way and certainly it carried some aerodynamic aids incorporated into the bodywork. Black asked

Ken straight out if he thought that the TR2 could beat this 120 mph run and Ken said "Yes, I'm sure we can with some fine tuning and some modifications to improve aerodynamics." He was then exhorted to pull out all the stops to ensure that the new Triumph exceeded this speed record at the earliest opportunity, by the end of May at the latest. Ken picked 5 or 6 of the most enthusiastic of the company's staff, overcoming difficulties with union demarkation regulations and the general lack of enthusiasm for working 'after hours'. Among those chosen was Kit Heathcote, who later became Ken's rallying co-driver and personal assistant. Sir John had also made it clear to Richardson that, should he succeed in beating the 120 mph barrier, it would be well worth his while in some as yet unspecified way!

MVC575 was chosen as the record attempt car, the other car still being used on promotional duties when the preparations started. The engine was producing 84 BHP net on the bench with reasonable reliability, and although he agrees that it was built up most carefully, Ken assured me that the engine was not super-tuned in any way and was no different to the engines fitted to the production TR2's once these started leaving the works from July 1953 onwards. How then, I enquired, was the ultimate speed of 125 mph achieved, having regard to the fact that a standard TR2 will barely top 110 mph, even when the windscreen is removed and a single aeroscreen is substituted? According to Ken, and the facts bear him out, the extra MPH needed to break the record were achieved solely by the aerodynamics and streamlining. A full aluminium undershield was fitted, as was a single aeroscreen and an aluminium, all enclosing tonneau cover, which Ken says very much restricted his elbow room, this not being important on the short record runs. Rear wheel spats and a stick-on front number plate further reduced drag. In addition, Ken recalls that he had no proper seat fitted, he merely sat on a cushion on the floor to keep him well down out of the airstream, and also that he had had some of the tread on the tyres skimmed off and the tyre pressures increased to sixty p.s.i. to reduce rolling resistance.

How, I asked, was he reasonably confident before the Jabbeke observed runs that 120 mph could be exceeded? The answer was because he'd already exceeded that figure in the car in England! The reader here must cast his or her mind back to the pre-motorway days of the early 1950's - yes, there was considerably less traffic than now, but on the other hand, there were only probably a handful of straight and fast roads in the Kingdom where 120 mph plus could be achieved in comparative safety. One such highway was the dead straight section of the Bicester to Oxford A421 road, and it was to this road that Ken and his little band came for several nights in April and May 1953, armed with a surveyor's chain to measure accurately an exact kilometre and mile.

Marker posts were erected, these secret trials taking place at around 3.30 am each morning. Lookouts were posted to hold back (unofficially) what little overnight lorry traffic then existed, and every night a little more speed would be conjured from the car by aerodynamic or mechanical fine tuning until Ken knew he could reach and hold 123 mph in a two-way run, as confirmed by stopwatches. After these small-hour sorties, the party would travel back to Coventry in time to embark on a full day's work! This involved more fine tuning by Ken (even before the war he was well known as an engine tuning ace and was an expert on carburation both on normally aspirated and on supercharged engines). Ken was also using MVC575 as his commuting car at this time, making constant notes concerning development and improvements. At this point in the interview, Ken's son Paul recalled how as a small boy he had sat on his father's knee, steering this TR2 at over 100 mph on the Newark to Grantham straight on the old A1 road. One wonders what Sir John Black would have said had he known!

Fortified by the knowledge that he at last possessed a serious sports car, Sir John Black made the arrangements both with the official observers and the Belgian authorities to have the high speed road at Jabbeke closed for a record attempt, and travel arrangements were also made. When Sir John rang Ken to tell him that the date selected was May 20th 1953, Richardson was aghast to learn that only one day's road closure had been booked, not three as he would have suggested. Supposing there was to be strong wind or rain, or some kind of mechanical problem - there would be no possibility of a second chance! Black in his autocratic fashion steam-rollered the objections, insisting that the booking had been made, time was of the essence and they would just have to go and hope for suitable conditions! The press had already been notified of the date so Ken and his team simply had to do their best! A charter Bristol Freighter aircraft was booked for Sunday 17th May, this plane transporting Ken, the car and mechanics, whereas Black, Dick, Grinham and sundry top brass and invitees flew over in the Company plane on the afternoon of Tuesday 19th May. The mechanics who were present were Messrs F. Smith, I Walton, W. Vickers, and R. Wilson, together with Mr T. Ward from Joseph Lucas & Co. and Mr T. Parkinson from Dunlops. In addition to Ken Richardson, Lewis Dawtrey and Harry Webster were also there, as was the Company's P.R. man, Mr I. Penrice.

The first trial run took place at 5.00 am on Monday 18th May, 123.5 mph being achieved. The road was **not** closed to the public, but was carrying little traffic at that time of day. Although another couple of trial runs took place, by the Tuesday evening the wind had got up to 25 mph, and there were grave doubts that the booked runs on the Wednesday

could take place. Fortunately for all, however, the wind had dropped overnight, and conditions at 6.00 am on Wednesday 20th May were perfect, still and clear, and a considerable crowd began to gather. Following his practice run, and knowing the results of his early morning tests in England, Ken Richardson had no real doubts that he could break the Sunbeam's record. After his first run that Wednesday, he instructed the mechanics to replace the plugs, check the transmission oil levels, change the engine oil and to leave the oil filter out until he had inspected it. He then went for a cup of tea with Sir John and Ted Grinham. On his return to the borrowed garage, to his horror, he found the car still on the ramp with engine oil plastered all over the underside of the chassis and undershield! In fact, when drained, the sump had contained virtually nothing! On inspection Ken spotted the problem; someone had drilled a hole in the undershield and extended the engine breather pipe through it, fitting on the end of the pipe a rear pointing elbow. Richardson immediately demanded in no uncertain terms to know who had ordered this unauthorised modification without reference to him. There was no answer. Ted Grinham then demanded the name of the offender, again to be met with silence. By now a furious Ted Grinham said to the assembled company that if the culprit did not own up within one minute everyone present apart from Richardson would be sacked and sent home. The perpetrator did then own up (even today Ken will not reveal this man's identity!). The culprit was informed by Sir John Black and Ted Grinham never to touch the car again, or any other car under Richardson's control. Ken confirmed that by extending the engine breather pipe through the undershield with a back facing elbow, the air pressure at maximum speed had caused a vacuum at the end of the pipe which had sucked all the oil out of the sump! The alteration was totally devoid of any sensible engineering principle and its only possible consequence was the potential destruction of the engine. Ken continued, "We had no spare engine with us and I could not detect any bearing damage, so once the breather pipe was put back to normal, we had to press on. Another consideration large in my mind at the time was the fact that if the oil had reached the rear tyres, I could have lost control of the car at maximum speed and careered onto the other side of the dual carriageway into any oncoming traffic".

The other side of the Jabbeke dual carriageway was open to normal traffic, but the record attempt side was closed for 6 miles with all entrances sealed and manned. A four mile run-in led to the timed mile, with a further mile to allow for slowing down.

It is now well known that the car performed up to expectations (except when a plug lead came off, though the car still achieved 104 mph on three cylinders!) A two-way run of

Ken Richardson speeds past one of the marker boards at 120mph during the Jabbeke high-speed run in May 1953. It can clearly be seen how low he must have been sitting - on a cushion on the floor, in fact! (Ken Richardson).

Following the high speed runs in "aerodynamic" trim, the Standard - Triumph mechanics are seen converting the TR2 to "Touring" specification to enable it to secure more records. The metal tonneau cover is seen in the foreground. The gendarmes look on with interest and a Standard Vanguard estate car does duty as a mobile workshop (Ken Richardson).

124.095 mph was achieved and officially confirmed as a World speed record over the measured mile for up to 2 litre production sports cars, allowing Standard-Triumph to make much of the whole event in subsequent publicity. Such a speed from what was genuinely almost a production vehicle really was something to shout about back in 1953 and Sir John Black was delighted. More runs were undertaken with the car in different guises, including some with the hood and sidescreens in position, when 114 mph was achieved, (Ken confirms that the full undershield remained in place throughout). Towards the end of these runs, Black asked Ken if he would take as a passenger a certain lady who was with the party, but Ken refused. This turned out to be just as well as during that subsequent run, a small bird hit the top of the windscreen whilst the car was travelling at over 100 mph. The lift-a-dot hood fastenings gave way, and the remains of the bird were forced at high speed into the cock-

pit, where Ken feels sure that they would have hit and possibly injured any passenger. The bird, he assured me, proved to be both a chaffinch and dead!

Despite this, Black then asked Ken to let one of the senior press men present drive the car. Again Ken refused, as by then he was sure that the big-end bearings were beginning to fail. He had noticed fluctuations on the oil pressure gauge, bearing damage probably having been occasioned by the lack of oil in the sump on the test run. Obviously this fact did not need to be revealed! He told Sir John that he would take the press man as a passenger, but with Ken driving, as he knew that by some judicious throttle work he could disguise any early symptoms of such bearing failure! The day was adjudged a great success and only those on the inside knew how close to disaster they had been at one stage. I asked Ken whether Sir John had honoured his promise to

Following the successful conclusion of the record runs at Jabbeke, Richardson holds up the deceased chaffinch at the point at which it hit the windscreen, as related in this Chapter. Sir John Black, among others, looks on, clearly pleased with the events of the day (Ken Richardson).

Sir John Black (left) and Alick Dick pose with Ken Richardson after the record runs. MVC 575 is now in "Touring" trim, although it can be seen that the under-shield is still in place, as are the wheel spats (Ken Richardson).

reward him should the record be taken. "Yes", was the reply, for immediately after the runs Black invited Ken to choose a house in Coventry into which to move his family, who were still living over in Bourne. The property chosen was No 4, Gibbet Hill Road, Coventry, a house which had formerly belonged to Sir William Lyons, Chairman of Jaguar. Ken confirmed that he always found Sir John Black a straightforward and very fair man with whom to deal, despite his reputation for being autocratic and sometimes erratic. "Sir John was a gentleman in my opinion," continued Ken, "and I got on with him extremely well."

Next I discussed with Ken the cars he used himself as road cars during his period with the company. In fact, even before he joined in late 1952 he was driving one of their products, and a very rare one at that. He had one of the 10 or so Triumph Mayflower Drophead Coupes built, a nicely made but somewhat slow and heavy little car, with a small sidevalve engine that did not lend itself to tuning. In fact, Ken has doubts that it would even have reached 60 mph! This car he swapped with Bobby Dickson, the Triumph dealer in the Carlisle area, for a Standard Vanguard. Dickson went on to drive TR2s in competition later, in particular the 1954 works supported Le Mans car OKV 777. As a senior member of staff Ken was entitled to a car, and had a succession of Vanguards, some tuned and incorporating TR2/3 parts. Being a family man, a four seater was essential, but he frequently drove TRs from the factory in addition and as mentioned earlier, he used the "Jabbeke" car MVC575 for a long period. "In Coventry," Ken continued, "there was a straight road about a mile long from the Fletchamstead Highway to the turn off into the road where I lived. It had about twenty yards' depth of grass verge on either side, so any cars emerging from the relatively few drives were easily spotted. Thus I used this road to test the Works cars on my way to and from home. Several of us involved with competition cars used this road for testing, including my next door neighbour "Soapy Sutton" who was a test driver at Jaguar's. You'd be amazed at the sundry experimental cars that were driven rapidly on that piece of road! It was particularly useful to me because I could run a TR to maximum speed, and if there was a convenient gap in the traffic as I neared my turn off, I could switch off, drift into my road and just reach the drive of my house where I could extract the plugs for inspection to check the top end carburation setting."

One particular TR3A that he recalls as being his personal car was WVC251, a sister TR3A to the four 1959/60 works rally team cars, WVC247 to WVC250, and built to the same rally specifications as those cars. Another TR he ran for a period as his personal car was OVC276, the 1954 Alpine and Mille Miglia car. On the question of which cars were left or right hand drive, Ken confirmed that he regularly had his cars' steering changed from one side to the other and then back again, depending simply upon where the next event was to take place; this of course explains the discrepancies that owners of ex-works TR's have found over the years, both in photographs and in fact. The truth is that many works TR's were both left and right hand drive! Ken also recalls that all his "personal" TR's had white tops, whether they were hard or soft tops.

At this point our conversation turned back to the redesign of

the 20TS car into the TR2, and Ken said that he wanted to dispel once and for all the notion that he single-handedly effected the transformation of a "lemon" into one of the greatest production sports cars ever made. Yes, he did condemn the 20TS as a "death trap" and recommend a chassis-up redesign. He also advised on design aspects of the new car, and was given overall responsibility for its development. Because of his experience, Ken also completed all the test driving himself. Ken again stressed that others should also get credit, in particular Lewis Dawtrey, someone who has never received the recognition he deserved. Ken also considers that Walter Belgrove did an excellent job in redesigning the body to be infinitely more practical than the 20TS style, yet also keeping tooling costs within the very severe price constraints laid down by the management. The chassis frame redesign was done largely by John Turnbull, this being a most important contribution to the success of the production TR and one which Ken says cannot be overemphasised. Again, he recalled that the transformation was a superb team effort, and that it is quite wrong to single out one particular person, as no one man could have achieved what was achieved in so little time.

Following the success of the Jabbeke runs and his own experience on the road, the considerable competition (and hence sales) potential of the car was becoming apparent, both to Richardson and to others at the company. Actual production was slow to build up for technical reasons ,however,and only 300 cars were built between the summer of 1953 and the end of the year. Ken appeared in the "Jabbeke" car MVC575 at the Prescott Hill climb in

Ken Richardson demonstrates to the press the high-speed capabilities of the then-new TR3 in hardtop form in the Winter of 1955/56. He is reputed to be travelling at a speed of 110mph, so the presence of a truck in the distance is somewhat surprising. RKV 335 was a hardworked demonstrator converted from a TR2 into a TR3 prototype (Ken Richardson).

September 1953, but he assures me that he was not competing, merely touring, and the photograph reproduced elsewhere in this book seems to confirm this. In fact, I have been unable to find any records of TRs being used in any form of serious motor sport in the UK during 1953, though it is probable that some were so used abroad. In fact only around 50 TRs reached the home market in 1953, and most of these were used as display and demonstrator vehicles in dealers' showrooms to obtain orders for cars for 1954 delivery. However, from January 1954 this situation changed rapidly as production cars came in to the eager hands of competition-minded individuals. The story of the car's sensational outright win driven by John Wallwork in the 1954 RAC Rally (held in March in those days) is well documented and is dealt with in more detail in Chapter Four. Ken confirmed that it was this win which prompted the Standard-Triumph management to form a Competitions Department with Ken at its head. During this period (from 1954 to 1957) the Competitions Department was an offshoot of the Experimental Department but from 1957 onwards, it became a part of the Service Department, under the aegis of one of the Sales Chiefs, Mike Whitfield. This latter arrangement suited Ken better, he and his department being virtually autonomous and subject to very little outside interference; additionally he received a wage rise with the move!

Concerning the actual cars used as Works competition cars, Ken confirmed that these were taken as finished cars straight from the production line and then dismantled and rebuilt, the Competitions Department having actually to purchase the cars using real money, taken from their annual budget! On this subject, he recalls that the budget was a mere £18,000 per annum, small in real terms even allowing for inflation, and desperately small when one takes account of the fact that the purchase cost of the cars themselves had to come out of it! Small wonder then, that the works drivers did not get paid salaries, merely their expenses. Contrast this with the situation at Abingdon, where Ken believes that the BMC Competitions Department had a budget of around £100,000 per annum, **and** did not have to pay for the cars used - hence they **could** afford to pay their drivers and consequently attracted some big names.

However, money or not, what counted was the cars themselves and their rally winning potential, and it was the TRs that won and that were the cars to beat in the mid to late 1950's, not the products of BMC. This situation only changed from 1959 when the Austin Healey 3000s came long, by which time the TR3As were reaching the end of their development having regard both to the funds available and the technology of the time.

The reader should bear in mind that, at the time the Triumph

Competition Department was formed in 1954, Ken had himself never been involved in rallying, coming very much from a racing background. When forming his team, it was made clear to Ken by the management that he must utilise personnel from within the factory rather than bringing in people from outside. To have done otherwise would have been to invite the occurrence of one of the motor industry's traditional demarkation disputes, and the management was not prepared to risk having 17,500 men on strike just so that Ken Richardson could pick the men he considered most suitable for the job in hand! Ken stresses however that the race mechanics in his department were chosen with great care, and were a credit both to his department and the Company.

At this point I asked Ken what it was like driving in International Rallies in those days. He replied "Well, although I had driven high powered racing machines on all of the European circuits over a twenty year period, I had never driven in a single rally before joining the Standard Motor Company. I had given serious consideration to hanging up my helmet for good because of family responsibilities, but it was not to be, due to the fact that I was so involved with the competition peformance of first TRs, and the fact that Sir John Black considered it necessary for me to drive in events because of my previous experience. The European International Rallies in those days had to be taken very seriously, especially those involving the high Alpine passes, which were little more than cart tracks, loose-surfaced, and often only the width of one car. One mistake on the majority of these passes could lead to car and driver disappearing over the unguarded side, with the only thing to look forward to being a three thousand feet drop! After considerable research on my part I decided I needed the best navigator available and luckily I found him from within the Company. Kit Heathcote was recommended to me, and at that time he was working for Lewis Dawtrey in the Experimental Department. I asked Lewis if he would mind if Kit joined my new Competition Department and although sorry to lose him, Lewis agreed to the transfer. Then I approached Kit who was very keen on the idea, and thus I had my navigator. Kit had been a pilot in the RAF, and one of his many qualities was a commitment to accuracy in anything he undertook, which appealed to me and was essential for a top rally nagivator. At this stage I would like to point out that in all the International Rallies that Kit and I competed in, he never once took me down a wrong road, and he proved to me on many occasions that he was indeed about the finest navigator around in those days. Kit also became my P.A. and was a tower of strength. When he decided to emigrate to Canada to take up a Government post in 1957 I resolved

The last outing for OVC 276 as a Works team car seems to have been the Liege-Rome-Liege Rally in August 1955, when Richardson & Heathcote brought it home into 5th place overall, winning its Class. Here, they are seen at a control (possibly the finish) looking distinctly cheerful. At the time of writing, OVC 276 has just emerged from a marathon rebuild, looking superb and as far as possible, to original specification (Ken Richardson).

to retire from competitive motoring, though I did still remain involved in test driving. I still meet Kit regularly and he remains one of my dearest friends."

As the history of which rallies and races Ken and his department competed in and how well they fared has been well chronicled previously, I did not discuss these matters further with him - suffice it to say that during the 1954 to 1960 period, under Richardson's expert leadership, the Standard-Triumph Competitions Department was amongst the world's most successful, using principally TRs plus the occasional tuned Standard Ten and Vanguard. Sales of the TR rose dramatically, inspired both by these successes and also by the car's general suitablility for amateur competitive events, as well as those at international level. One could be rallying on Saturday, racing on Sunday and going to work on the Monday, all in the same car, the rugged and versatile TR! The mangement at Standards had every reason to be pleased both with Ken Richardson's efforts on their behalf and with the transformation overseen by Ken on the original 20 TS Sports. Sir John Black certainly got his world-reknowned sports car, even though his departure from the Company coincided with the start of the car's most successful period.

It has often been stated that the Works TR's were very little if at all different from those that any member of the public could purchase "off the shelf." I brought this assertion up during my interview with him and Ken confirmed that it was indeed company policy that anyone with a cheque book could buy a replica of the then current Works rally cars, a situation very different to that which applies today at most car companies involved with competitive motoring. My own research has confirmed that several private owners did indeed purchase replicas of the latest specification rally TR3s and TR3As, these being built to order in the Competitions Department. However, taxed further on the point, Ken did inform me that there were one or two small mods made to his Works cars that did not necessarily reach private owners - for instance the 2138 cc TRs and the twin cams both had valves made of Nimonic 80 (both inlet and exhaust). I asked Ken to elaborate. "This was an extremely expensive nickel alloy with 80% nickel in its composition. It had a very high heat tolerance, and I decided to use it on the 2138cc engine as we had experienced early signs of valve burning during extensive high speed tests. I had had experience with Nimonic 80 when I was involved with the first experimental jet propulsion engines at the beginning of the war. Nimonic 80 was in fact chosen in preference to Hastelloy B, Stayblade, or Rex 748 for the turbine blades of Frank Whittle's reverse flow engine and for many years thereafter in a great many jet engines. I remember asking a great friend of mine, Geoffrey Clarke the Chairman of Valves Ltd of Coventry, if he would be prepared to make and supply me with several sets of TR Nimonic 80 valves at no charge. Geoff said "Of course, Ken. Send me the spec etc" which I did. However, Geoff was on the phone to me next day. "Good God, Ken, I didn't realise the cost of this material; do you know that the run of the mill production valve costs about three and sixpence (about 17p), and these Nimonic 80 valves will cost about four quid each?!!! Nevertheless, I got my valves!"

Richardson revealed that high pressure springs were also used in the overdrive units of rally TR's to ensure instant engagement under maximum power during rallies. The force with which these units operated was such that one needed to dip the clutch in normal, rather than "balls out" motoring, to avoid a mighty "clunk" racking the car. Factory cars also frequently had the overdrives wired to operate on first gear, as well as second, third and top, but Ken confirmed that using this facility significantly shortened the life of the unit. He also arranged for Lucas to incorporate a special overdrive switch in the gear lever knob whereby the overdrive was engaged by moving the knob up or down, another pioneering modification instigated by the TR team.

Asked about the unusual Apple Green colour applied to many of the earlier works rally TR3's and 3A's, Ken confirmed that he was instrumental in choosing this, with management approval. The colour was not particular to the Works cars, however, as it was a catalogued colour available on the Standard 8 and 10 ranges at the time. They felt that something different was needed, yet it was also felt that the basic colour should still be green, as it was the British national colour for competition cars. Black interiors were used on the Works cars, but with the added touch of white piping to the trim. In fact the Apple Green finish did appear for a brief period in the normal colour range for TRs, although it did not prove a popular option, despite its team car associations. The later TR3A works rally cars were red, I should add. As an aside, Ken assured me that the distinctive Geranium shade used on many early TR2's was always known as "nipple pink" within the factory!

I raised the question of the development of the suspension and its suitability for rally work, and Ken's reply that follows is set down in his own words:-

"I spent hundreds of hours discussing suspension and shock absorbers with Lewis Dawtrey, as well as engine modifications, and he would often come with me on road tests. One of the problems with the first TRs was that there was not quite enough suspension movement. On the International rallies the Alpine passes were tortuously rough on suspen-

sion, thus we had to employ relatively stiff spring and shocker settings to avoid the rear axle destroying the bump stops and crashing into the under-panels. This compromise necessitated me undertaking many hours of road and track testing to make sure the front and rear suspension settings were balanced to give optimum performance, and the springs and shockers for my cars were to be made to an exact rating to achieve this. It was during this period as I was sorting out suitable spring and shocker rates, that I came up against one of the problems associated with mass production in those days. With my previous experience of driving Grand Prix cars, I was particularly sensitive to handling changes, and I had noticed on production TRs that the handling could vary considerably from car to car. I decided to investigate as this

Ken Richardson discusses the new TR3As with his foreman in the Competitions Department, Ben Warwick. The TRs, which probably became the "WVC" teamcars, look to be brand new, seemingly just arrived from the production line. As described in this Chapter, they will be dismantled and carefully rebuilt, having various rally modifications incorporated in the process (Ken Richardson).

type of thing irritated me, besides being a warning that something might be wrong. I took about two dozen shock absorbers out of the bins on the assembly line and had their ratings tested. I found out that often the tolerance was ten percent either side of optimum. At worst this meant that the difference in shocker rating from say the off side front suspension to the near side rear, could be around 20 per cent. This state of affairs was of course no good, and had to be put right.

"Whilst we're on the subject of suspension, I well remember Ted Grinham asking me how the early Vanguard suspension could be improved, as the company had had several complaints of the suspension being too 'springy'. This problem had also been mentioned to me by several others including Frank Hyam who was in charge of Home Sales. Frank was a dear friend, who because of his practical interest in gastronomic delights weighed over 20 stone! He hated the early Vanguards as of the 'springy' phenomenon over rough roads often developed to such a pitch with Frank, because of his weight, that he took on the motion of a cork on rough water. He insisted that on several occasions he had nearly lost his breakfast due to the feeling of sea sickness that this phenomenon had caused him. Now I knew what the problem was because I had experienced it myself and had put it right on my own Vanguard, but I couldn't resist having some fun. I phoned Frank and said "I can cure the suspension problem in about fifteen minutes." The jungle telegraph went into operation and about half an hour later my office was like Clapham Junction and now included Sir John Black, Lewis Dawtrey, Ivor Penrice our public relations manager who had a marvellous sense of humour, Jack Croft from publicity and of course Ted Grinham and Frank Hyam, all curious to learn the technical details of how I intended to cure the problem.

"In the meantime I had had Frank's Vanguard taken into the shop, and the front seat exchanged for the one in my car-.. I said 'Your car's O.K. now Frank, go and give it a try! After his road test he came back to my office wearing a broad smile, and said "That's bloody incredible; the suspension is fantastic now, what have you done to it"? I said "I've had the front seat changed". My reply, seemingly unrelated to a suspension problem and essentially 'low-tech', caused Ivor Penrice to take to an uncontrollable laughing fit which was so contagious that everyone became convulsed, including Sir John and myself.

"The modified seat I had had made for my car was what we called in motor racing circles "Dead Beat" i.e. it contained no springs but was packed with a suitable material that would give firm but comfortable support without acting with a sprung frequency over bumps. I had experienced the effect of a heavily sprung seat at Brooklands in the early thir-

ties in an E.R.A., and it could be extremely dangerous; one often had to hang on to the steering wheel over bumpy sections to maintain a seated position and to retain sensitive foot contact with the accelerator pedal. This was one example of how motor racing can help in the development of production cars, and what fun the life of a development engineer can be sometimes".

A further departure from standard production specification for the Rally Cars was in the use of Nickel Steel for exhaust pipes and silencers, for added strength and durability. The famous hard top roof-mounted, swivelling spotlights Ken had made up specially by Lucas, and these rapidly set a fashion both for genuine rally cars and "boy racers" in the late 1950's. I asked about Weber carburettors and whether the Works cars had ever utilised these. Richardson recalls that Gatsonides tried a pair on his own car at one stage but they did not make sufficient difference over the normal SU's to be worth pursuing. Thus the works cars did not use Webers, which will I know come as a disappointment to those involved in the present day historic rally scene, some of whom have tried hard to have Webers homologated for use within present day regulations by maintaining that they were in regular use in the 1950's on TRs! Ken also recalled that three TR3As were built in his department with all-aluminium bodies, though he was unable to recall exactly which cars these were. Certainly I once met a TR Register member who claimed to have owned a car with an all aluminium body; I was sceptical at the time but it looks as though he may have been correct! (This subject is dealt with in some detail in Chapter 9).

I took the opportunity at this point in our discussions to enquire as to when the larger 2138cc engine was first used. Ken feels sure that this was in 1958 in time for the Alpine Rally. Ken initiated the 2138 engine to compete with the 2.6 Litre Healeys. He recalls, "We did not need any more top speed to beat the big Healeys but we did need more torque. This, in conjunction with overdrive on all four forward gears, would enable us to beat the Healeys on the Alpine passes, where the battle would be won or lost. I had tried to convince the management in 1957 that we needed a new and bigger engine but to no avail due to the cost, so I toyed with an economical way of increasing the torque of the existing TR engine, eventually organising the 2138cc engine off my own bat. Although the Standard Vanguard had had a 2088cc engine, utilising 85mm pistons, since its inception, these pistons were not strong enough for use in the TR. However, the plus 040" pistons used for reboring Vanguards gave 2138cc, as they were in effect 86mm in diameter". Ken of course knew that a considerable gain in torque would result from the use of such 86mm pistons in his Works TRs, and so, entirely unknown to management, he had four sets of specially strengthened 86mm pistons manufactured secretly by the firm of Specialloid. As he was unable to show these on his expense sheet, he persuaded the Managing Director of this firm, who was a friend of his from BRM days, to produce them without payment, on the understanding that if they proved successful, many further orders would follow. As the whole project was unauthorised, the completed prototype 2138cc engine could not even be run initially on the main factory's test bed, and thus Ken had the engine built privately in his department by his mechanics, and tested it himself on the road, finding the results most rewarding. Ken was proved right, because in the 1958 Alpine all the big Healeys were well beaten.

The larger capacity engine became standard wear for rally TRs, except of course if there was a 2 litre class limit, when the 1991 cc engine still had to be employed. By 1959 the 2138 cc capacity engine was a publicly listed option for the TR3A, and was specified by many competition-minded buyers. Its fitment endowed the car with more than enough performance to keep ahead of the Austin-Healey 100/6's and the twin-cam MGA's. Ken added that as far as he could recall, the team never had a major engine, gearbox or axle failure in rallying, although the TR3A used in the record attempt at Monza did eventually blow its engine up, albeit after 96 hours at racing speeds!

We then turned to the "Sabrina" twin-cam engine, and the reasons why it was not used in the rally cars and failed to reach production status. It is Ken Richardson's opinion that this engine was never in fact meant to be a production engine, and this is borne out by the complicated construction of the unit itself, which would not easily lend itself to production techniques. Ken's view is that it was built both as a publicity exercise, and also as a test bed for pressure die-casting of aluminium, a technique in its infancy in those days. He himself liked the engine but fought against using it in any of his rally cars as he felt it needed more development for rallying. He saw no point in impairing the TR's legendary reliability, this potential disadvantage being more than enough to outweigh the extra power produced. He recalls the engine as being both too heavy and very noisy in operation, too noisy in fact for a production vehicle, the valve gear being a particular culprit.

Three special racing TRs, all having this twin-cam motor, were entered for the Le Mans 24 hour race in 1959. The cars superficially looked like TR3As, but had fibreglass bodies and were six inches longer, incorporating many other modifications essential to racing. As is well known, none of the cars finished this race, although whilst running, one had been leading its class. It is here that Ken pointed out that he

had been adamant that fans should not be fitted to these cars, and had had several major rows with those senior engineers who had insisted that fans should be utilised. "This was yet another example of quite ridiculous interference by the same people with whom I had had constant battles, starting with the breather pipe fiasco on the "Jabbeke" car back in 1953," Ken recalls. "It was ludicrous to fit fans to cars at Le Mans as all the air required to cool the engine would be forced through the radiators by the high average speed, but in addition the fans would simply act as a drain on horse power. (The TR twin cams are believed to have been the only cars with fans that year at Le Mans). However, the most compelling reason for not fitting fans to the twin cams was that because of the design of the cars, which were essentially stretched TRs, the engine driven fans ran dangerously close to the radiators. I pointed out that should the engine or gearbox mounting rubbers soften due to the heat and/or braking loads, the engines would move forward under braking and the fans would puncture the radiators. I predicted to all concerned that if fans were fitted to our cars at Le Mans then the cars would not last, but I was overruled. I had even instructed one of my mechanics - George Hylands - to make engine movement restrictors for the cars an as insurance as well as having some extra strong engine mountings fitted, but even this was overruled. We couldn't believe it, and I made one last ditch effort to get the fans removed just before the race but to no avail. The race started and sure enough two of the cars went out with fans through their radiators! I had the fan removed from the third car regardless, and it went extremely well, eventually to retire whilst in seventh place overall when oil pump failure occurred two hours from the end of the race. Thus the first race for the twin cam TRs became a total disgrace to the Company. Everyone's hard work on the new cars was ruined by a minority who by their senior position implemented directives that only bore witness to their lack of both engineering common sense and knowledge of race preparation." Ken then showed me signed documentation confirming that the fitting of fans to these Le Mans twin cams was indeed not his idea and that nor was the problem "simple fan failure" as has been often reported. "After the race," Ken continued, "there were of course some red faces, but as usual, cover up stories were carefully put about by the instigators, who had developed extremely intricate desk side manners over the years, which not only preserved careers, but transferred the blame for their own mistakes to others. I think that the most laughable explanation was that "fans were fitted for development reasons and that the cars should be as near standard as possible to enhance public appeal." I remember pointing out at the time that the three TR's we entered for the 1955 Le Mans race did not have fans, and that in any event the twin cams were race prototypes and were never intended for production anyway."

Then I brought up the question of the 1960 Le Mans race, and Ken related the story. "The TR team's chances in that race were again scuppered, this time by a change being made to a tried and tested valve seat material. The valve seat "Brinell" (hardness) factor had been reduced by half, entirely unknown to me! Thus during the race the valves hammered into the by now soft valve seats and all valve clearances were lost . As a result, we lost power. Due to the drivers taking care not to tax the engines too much we did finish the race, but did not cover enough distance to be classified as finishers. When I found out about this valve seat modification, I was naturally furious. Not only was I not consulted but any modification to a well tried and tested part should obviously be evaluated before using it, especially in a race like Le Mans. I did, however, ensure that there was no interference with the preparation of the cars for the 1961 event, after yet another flaming row with the perpetrators and an in depth conversation with Alick Dick the Chairman, in which I detailed how inept alterations had ruined several events for us over the years, including a twelve hour race at Sebring, but that is another story!."

Following the great success of the team of 3 TR2's in the 1955 Le Mans race, I wondered why no Triumph team cars had been entered in 1956, 57 or 58. "Because I felt that we couldn't do any better," was Ken's quick reply, and indeed, given the almost standard production nature of the TR's being campaigned by the factory at that time, there is no doubt that he was right. To have continued to enter would merely have risked failure without any hope of better placings than the 1955 cars had achieved - the Le Mans race was, at that time, rapidly becoming more specialised and the regulations were moving inexorably against the standard production car. Ken pointed out at this stage that considerably more power could be obtained from the TR engine if race tuned, but right from Sir John Black's day the idea was that the competition cars should be raced and rallied virtually as they were supplied to the public, an idea that appealed both to Sir John, to Ken and to the management. Ken also pointed out that it should not be forgotten that the power of the TR engine had been increased from 75 BHP in the 20 TS to around 105 BHP in the 2138cc TR3A's, an increase of some 40%. This was no mean achievement bearing in mind that throughout this development the engine retained its mechanical reliability, both as a competition unit and also for everyday "stop-start" motoring. Race tuning an already heavily developed engine would have brought with it an element of unreliability that could have damaged the TR's reputation. Thus, when the factory next entered Le Mans in 1959, the cars used were more specialised, non-production vehicles. On the final attempt at Le Mans in 1961 further-developed versions of the 1960 special bodied cars were used, and Triumph's managed to secure the team prize with Ken

organising for all three cars to cross the line together. The leading Triumph finished ninth overall and the first two Triumphs over the line were the first two British cars to finish the race, a remarkable achievement for a team run on something of a shoestring! Ken felt that this was as well as the team was ever likely to do, especially having regard to the limited budget available, and looking back now, he feels that there probably would have been no Works TR team entry in 1962, even if the Competition Department had not been suddenly closed.

The full reasons behind the sudden termination of the Competition Department in July 1961 are still unclear. The Company had considerable financial troubles in the 1960/61 period, and had been taken over by Leyland Motors in a financial rescue operation in April 1961 following negotiations that had commenced at the end of the previous year.. Clearly if savings needed to be made, competitions was one obvious candidate, despite the department's considerable success over the years and its undoubted contribution to boosting sports car sales. The new owners lost little time in "rationalising" the Company, and Ken Richardson found his services dispensed with shortly after the successful Le Mans result; even the Chairman Alick Dick himself only lasted until the end of that September.

We concluded our day's discussion with me asking Ken for any recollections about the personalities and related anecdotes connected with his time as Competitions Manager. What, I asked, was his "hairiest" driving experience during his time at Standard-Triumphs? He replied, "All the major continental rallies in those days were hairy. This was essentially due to the narrow, unsurfaced Alpine passes that I referred to previously, tracks which were roughly hewn out of the sides of the mountains. If you add to these the obvious dangers of snow, sheet ice, freezing fog and the fact that the edges of these passes had no guard rails and often a two to three thousand foot sheer drop off the side, it will give you an idea of how wonderfully concentrated one's mind needed to become - and bear in mind also that often we had to average some forty eight miles an hour on the timed sections. I have spoken to Kit Heathcote my navigator/co driver many times since our Rally days, and we both agree that the Alpine was extremely "interesting" to say the least, but the most arduous and dangerous rally Kit and I ever took part in was the 1955 Liege-Rome-Liege in OVC 276. This rally was also the one on which we achieved our best result. We were newcomers to the Liege that year, and to give you an idea of what it was like, the rally took 98 hours, four days and four nights, of virtually non-stop driving. There were about sixty five check points - one every one and a half hours, and the longest stop we had was about forty five minutes! We had to cover every one of the French and Italian

Messrs Richardson and Heathcote look somewhat haggard and worn after a hard night aboard OVC 276. As was usual with Ken Richardson's cars, the top was white (Fred Nicklin).

Alpine routes twice, and the rally was so organised that we always hit the passes at dawn or dusk. I don't ever remember driving so hard for so long, and the only trouble we had was when the dynamo bracket broke during the last night of the rally, luckily not on a narrow pass. I remember having to find a flatish, wedge-shaped stone to jam behind the dynamo to keep the belt tight. The battery had gone flat due to the slack belt, but luckily we came to rest on a slight incline and when I'd finished the necessary repairs Kit pushed the car backwards and I attempted a bump start in reverse. The engine fired up and off we went again. We had about three more mountain passes to cover before to the finish of the rally, which we completed with the stone still in place! We finished first in class, fifth overall, and took the newcomer's award, being only beaten by "tweaked" cars in the specially modified category. Kit was fantastic on that rally, and as I've said before, he never, ever made a navigational mistake. I'm quite sure that the modern rally cars would never stand up to the punishment that ours did in those days" continued Ken, "for unlike now we were not

Kit Heathcote (left) and Ken Richardson lean on a TR2 following the finish of the 1955 Tulip Rally. The car is probably OVC 276, their mount in that event ("Autosport").

allowed any service back up, and if anything went wrong we had to fix it ourselves carrying what spares we could in the cars."

I then asked Ken how he selected his drivers. "Well, we were very fortunate in those days, because everyone wanted to drive a work's TR both because of the known reliability of the cars, and the fact that we could beat many more powerful vehicles on the major rallies, especially the Healeys! We had some superb drivers in the team, many of whom were

characters in their own right. Probably the greatest character of them all was one of my Le Mans drivers, the late Ninian Sanderson, who in fact won Le Mans outright in the late fifties driving a 'D' Type Jaguar for my old pal Wilkie Wilkinson. Ninian was a great practical joker - for instance during the 1955 Le Mans race he was driving a TR2, as indeed was I, both of us part of our three car team. It was teeming down with rain and as we came on to the Mulsanne Straight I noticed Ninian flashing his lights behind me. At first I thought he had spotted something wrong with my car,

Ken Richardson takes SRW 993 through a test on an unknown rally. Note the white top, which Ken always had on his own cars, whether hardtop or soft-top. This car was never part of the official Works team, but Ken used it as his own car for disc brake evaluation (TR Register Archive).

Ken Richardson and his usual co-driver, Kit (JCS) Heathcote look pleased with themselves and SHP 520. The actual event is unknown, but the location looks suspiciously like the South of France (P Clarke)

so I eased up slightly and Ninian came along side. He then shouted "Got a cigarette for me, Ken?" Ninian knew I always carried a packet of cigarettes as indeed he usually did, just in case of a breakdown involving a long walk home! I had a packet in my overall pocket, which I knew was soaked through, so I threw it to him. The next thing I saw in my mirror was Ninian trying to light a wet cigarette in an open cockpit. This attempt failed so he came along side again and shouted "Have you got any dry matches?" This at 115 mph!

Everyone who knew Ninian was extremely fond of him, and even now I often have a laugh to myself at some of the antics he got up to and his quick wit. I recall once at Monza I had hired the circuit for several days to test the twin cams; all the drivers were there including Ninian, but the transporter had not arrived with the car. I received a phone call at the hotel from my foreman Ben Warwick who informed me that all the timing gears had stripped on the transporter's engine, and the cars would be about two days late. By the second day I was getting a little impatient because hiring Monza was an expensive exercise. I was sitting at the bar of the hotel with the drivers, kicking my heels, when Ninian piped up and said "Ken, I've been on many of your secret test sessions over the years, but this is the first one I've been on that's so secret that the car doesn't turn up!" The transporter arrived eventually, Ben and the mechanics having done a superb repair job job on the transporter engine, building up new teeth on the timing gears with their welding equipment.

Another former TR team driver I see regularly is Mike Rothschild. Mike was one of our Le Mans drivers and a great asset to the team, for he was fast and also remarkably consistent. In fact he drove for me for the first time in 1957 at Sebring in Florida where we achieved our first team prize in America in the twelve hour race. I particularly enjoy visiting Mike as he is a superb engineer; his hobby is his considerable collection of antique cars all of which he runs on the road including a 1903 Rambler and a White Steam car. Tinkering with Mike's old cars is a great relaxation for me." Another interesting snippet from Ken during our talk concerned one of the 1955 Le. Mans TRs, these being the cars that were fitted with disc brakes as test beds for the production discs that were to follow in 1956. Following the 1955 race, Ken was using one of these TR2's on the road, and took it to Prescott Hill climb. Upon arrival, he was bet £10 that he couldn't beat a particular Jaguar entered. He accepted the bet and astonished those present by beating all the various Jaguars in the much smaller TR2 and collecting his money!

At this point, I tackled Richardson about Sir John Black, and in particular about the accident that occurred when Ken was driving Sir John in the then new Swallow Doretti. As he had mentioned earlier, Ken himself admired Sir John and always found him both fair and a natural leader, but there were many who found him both difficult and awkward. Sir John Black was ousted in a boardroom coup at the beginning of 1954, and the injuries he had suffered in the accident were publicly mentioned as being the reason for his not being able to continue on the board of Standard-Triumphs. I asked Ken to what extent he thought this to have been the real reason. He confirmed that the accident was indeed serious, but it was not in his opinion of itself sufficient to lead to Black's resignation happening when it did. Rather, it was the straw that broke the camel's back, coming on top of a lot of boardroom friction, personality clashes and politics. Ken recalls that Black was a manic depressive, which is these days believed to be due to a chemical deficiency in the body. "In any event," Ken pointed out, "Sir John was not as badly hurt as I was. In fact it was the worst accident I have ever had, off or on the circuit. I nearly lost the sight of one eye due to my head going through the screen, which necessitated forty nine stitches in my forehead. My ankle was broken and I had a very badly sprained wrist. In fact I remember Sir John himself, by then recovered, coming round to my house after I had got out of hospital to see me with a huge bunch of flowers and fruit. "Even now," continued Ken "in my 82nd year I still occasionally find small pieces of glass from that accident working their way out of my forehead! Sir John's manic depression was a condition that is recognised and treatable today, but which was little understood back in the early 1950's. This illness causes highs and lows and the secret of dealing with Sir John was to know how to handle him when he was in one of his lows. This was one particular factor that contributed in my view to Black's difficulties with the other directors. The main reason for the big bust-up between Sir John and Ted Grinham was, however, a row that I myself witnessed. You see Sir John was always very go-ahead, and he had got himself involved with the Swallow Doretti sports car project. The Doretti used many TR2 mechanical parts, but as the finished car was clearly a possible competitor to the TR2, a potential conflict of interest arose. I was, of course, aware of the Swallow Doretti project as Sir John treated me as his personal consultant and regularly took me to the Swallow Company to ask me what I thought of the progress on the Doretti car. One day Sir John and I had just returned from one of our trips to see Frank Rainbow, the designer of the Doretti, in what must have been in the second half of 1953, when I bumped into Ted Grinham who, as part of our general conversation, asked me where I'd been. I naturally told him, oblivious to the fact that he knew nothing about Sir John's and my trips to discuss the Doretti. Ted went red with rage, and after assuring me that hus anger was in no way due to any fault of mine, he had the

"Mother and Father" of rows with Sir John about having been kept in the dark. This led to a permanent break between them, which I feel played a major part in Sir John's demise. Ted himself left the company shortly after Sir John, I think because of the fact that Alick Dick was made Chairman instead of him, which was a great blow to Ted."

As to the accident itself, it occurred in Sir John's own Doretti, which Ken believes was the first production car, specially finished for Black in Silver Grey. The car was brand new, and Black asked Ken to take him out in it and give his opinion. As the Doretti was still running in, Richardson was driving unaccustomedly slowly when they came back along Coventry's Banner Lane, the road right outside the factory gates. The erratic Black, possibly to impress whosoever was looking, exhorted Ken to put his foot down and faced with an order from the boss, Ken complied. As they sped past the factory, a Works pick up truck turned right across their path to enter the factory gates, and seeing the Doretti, for some reason halted in the middle of the road. There was no hope of stopping, especially with new and unbedded brakes, and the inevitable collision occurred, becoming the talking point of the works for days to come. Ken was off work for six weeks, and his last memory of the accident was of trying to avoid a head on crash with the van by steering the Doretti between the said van and the Works' iron fencing. The rest is a blank in Ken's memory, but luckily the van driver was unhurt. Richardson does not know however what became of that brand new Swallow Doretti!

By this time in my talk with him tea had come and gone, and in our six or so hours we had ranged over virtually all aspects of Ken Richardson's time with Standard's, many hitherto little known pieces of information coming to light. Ken had been able to deal with almost all my questions despite the passage of 40 or so years since the events concerned were current. On only two small points was Ken unable to assist; firstly the reason for the mysterious gap of six commission numbers (TS703-708) in the otherwise complete run of TR2s (were they the six Tourist Trophy cars, Ken wondered, but I thought not, and in fact have subsequently discovered that these were cars assembled in Belgium from parts, part of the pilot scheme for subsequent fairly large scale assembly of TRs in Belgium), and secondly what exactly were the TR2 "speed" models that occasionally crop up in the build records of the early TR2s - Ken had no recollection of these at all, so that is one minor mystery that looks as if it will never be fully solved.

I think that probably the greatest compliment that can be paid to Ken for the many competition successes he and his team had with the sidescreen TRs (which included a world speed record over the measured mile for up to two litre production sports cars, plus eight world endurance records) is

Ken Richardson cutting a celebratory cake in 1988 at the TR Register's International Weekend (TR Register Archive).

in the contents of a letter signed by his foreman Ben Warwick and two of his mechanics. The last paragraph reads -

"We know we can speak for the rest of the old team when we say those far off days were the best days of our lives under your leadership, and you had the deepest of respect from all of us including the drivers, both as our manager and friend, and as Peter Cox, another member of your team says, - "Ken, it was a privilege to have been associated with you."

Ken concluded our talk by telling me that he and son Paul were then shortly off to the USA at the invitation of one of the American TR clubs - how pleasant to know that he retains such an interest in the cars, and that present day TR owners are able to establish direct contact with the man who had overall responsibility for the development of the TR2 out of the doubtful 20TS prototype and the subsequent Competition success of these splendid sports cars!

CHAPTER FOUR:

Contemporary Competition Motoring

I shall try in this chapter to give the reader an insight into what it was like (principally from the amateur driver's point of view) to use a sidescreen TR in competitive events when the cars were in current production. I should say right at the start that this is not a history of all TR involvement in competitions for that would take a whole book in itself - and nor is it a history of the Triumph works team nor the works cars; that subject has been very well covered elsewhere. I do, however, touch on the subject of the Works team in my interview with Peter Clarke, and also in my talk with Ken Richardson set out in Chapter 3.

So far as I know, what has not been attempted previously is a series of interviews with people who owned the cars when new or nearly new, and who used them in the competitive events of the time, in addition in many cases to using the cars as their everyday transport; the TR was that sort of car! I have conducted several such interviews the results of which are incorporated into this chapter, and I have also been lent many unique and previously unpublished photographs, a number of which are reproduced, and which will, I hope give the reader a flavour of those long-departed and seemingly more carefree days.

Competitive motoring (other than on the international scale) was very much more "amateur" then than now, and was taken somewhat less seriously. Fewer people were involved, much less money was at stake and the impression

A very early TR2 seen on the 1954 Morecambe Rally, driver unknown (NMM Beaulieu).

A TR vying with the traditional "enemy", an MG, in the early 1960s, coming out of Woodcote Corner at Silverstone circuit. A bonnet scoop has been added, together with safety straps (NMM Beaulieu).

gained, both from talking today to those who were there and from the contemporary written reports was that it was simply more fun! This is not to say that participants did not try hard, nor that motor competition was not dangerous - rather that there was not quite so much at stake as today, and that the whole thing was treated in a more gentlemanly sporting and lighthearted manner. Cars were usually driven to and from events, and more often than not, maintained by their owners and their friends. Informal clothing was worn, and

The London Motor Club's Little Rally of April 1958 sees a very standard-looking TR3 competing, driver unknown. A badge-less badge bar connects a nifty pair of period 7-inch spotlights. The car behind is a FIAT 1100, a surprisingly popular rally car in the 1950s (NMM Beaulieu).

the only item of compulsory equipment was a crash helmet, and that only for circuit racing. Whether the 1950's period was thereby preferable to the situation today is a matter for debate, and although I hold strong views myself, this is not the place to promulgate them; suffice it to say that I very much enjoyed my days spent talking to 1950's TR drivers about their recollections, and it was clear as they became more animated that the drivers had really enjoyed their TR days, and without exception looked back to the period with fondness and pleasure.

I should make it clear that no particular significance attaches to those TR drivers of the period whom I sought to interview, and those not mentioned should in no way feel that their contribution to TR history is in any way diminished! It was merely a question of who I was able to make contact with at the right time and within a reasonable distance! Sadly also many people are no longer with us, and quite a number proved untraceable despite the placing of "wanted" advertisements in various motoring magazines. I hope however that I have covered what is representative selection of personnel, including several rallyists, a circuit racer and a competition mechanic.

As I said, this is not a history of the factory's involvement in competitions with TRs, although the division between the works and private owners is sometimes blurred when privately owned and entered TRs received works support, as happened with the 1954 Le Mans TR2 entry, OKV 777. As is well known, the Factory did not really expect the success in competitions that quickly followed the acquisition by private owners of those early TR2s, and no competitions department even existed early in 1954. The story of the car's initial success in rallying is therefore very much one of private owner entries and successes, capitalised upon later by the

A very early TR2, with a period windscreen-mounted spotlight, seen on the Redex National Rally dated 10th November 1954 (NMM Beaulieu).

factory once a competitions department had been formed. The great boost to the TR's career and the foundation of its claim to be taken seriously as a sporting car was the outstanding success in the 1954 RAC Rally, which took place in those days in the spring rather November as now. Fourteen TR2s were mentioned on the official entry list, and private entries, although there is some evidence of a 15th TR2 entry in addition. As far as I can trace, no direct Factory support was given to anyone, though the Standard-Triumph publicity department was only too quick to promulgate the results for publicity purposes after the event. I think it is true to say that the participants even paid full list prices for their cars! I will examine this particular rally in some detail shortly, but although by far the most important early TR success, it was not the first occasion in the UK that a TR had obtained an outright win. This appears to have been in the Liverpool Motor Club's New Year Rally, held on 23rd/24th January 1954, where Denis Done won the premier award driving OHP 300. As the photo shows (just), this car had rear wheel spats fitted at this stage, and was Coventry-registered, as were quite a few early TRs. Although Denis Done was himself a motor dealer, it is believed that OHP 300 was a works owned publicity car loaned to him pending delivery of his own TR2, TFM 400 which he later campaigned with much success. Of the 50 or so cars that had reached the home market by the start of 1954, almost all had gone to dealers with some sporting aspirations, or as demonstrators. The paragraph in chapter 8 about Bill Parkes' car shows how long it actually took a private, non trade, individual to obtain a new TR at the time! As far as I can trace, the very first competition appearances in Britain by TRs in any events took place the week before Denis Done's victory, Autosport magazine refers to a TR2 being driven by Ken Bancroft in a sprint meeting which took place on 16th January 1954 at Burtonwood USAF base near Liverpool. In view of the nature of the venue, maybe this was a USA left hand drive TR delivered in the UK to a US serviceman? Unfortunately, no further details are given. Secondly, R.B. James gained a 3rd place in an MG Car Club rally on 18th January, presumably driving his TR2 ORW 600.

Another very early competition TR was registered NHP 49, a left hand drive car, commission number TS 10 (LO). As can be seen from the contemporary colour photograph reproduced in this book, this car was white, though the factory build records state that it was finished in Ice Blue, being completed on 31st August 1953. A note on the record states that it went to Portugal on the 14th September 1953 for the Lisbon Rally and a search through the Coventry local authority's registration records indicates that it was registered new by a Mr Basil d'Almeidea, apparently a private owner, though he must have had some influence to obtain so early a car I presume therefore that the TR2's first competition appear-

ance abroad took place somewhat before its debut in the UK, and that NHP 49 was the car involved, though how this privately owned car came to "change" its colour, and be photographed with Ken Richardson at the wheel as a publicity vehicle remains a mystery. A further very early TR2 success also took place overseas, for on 17th January 1954 E.H. Carvalho won the Gilman Challenge Trophy in Hong Kong in a TR2, possibly the car he later used to win the 1954 Macau Grand Prix? I think that this must have been TS 49, as that was the only 1953 built TR to be dispatched to Hong Kong.

It is interesting to note that no TR2s were entered in the 1954 Monte Carlo Rally which took place in early January, despite the fact that around 300 cars had been built by that time, and that this was the premier rallying event of all in the 1950's - maybe owners were nervous of the car's durability in its early months before the RAC Rally win showed the way. The Liverpool Motor Club promoted another major rally in those days, the Jeans Gold Cup, a tough 340 mile overnight event in the Lake District, held in 1954 on the weekend of 27th/28th February. For the first time that I can trace, a team of TRs was entered in a rally, the three cars being driven by Denis Done, Gillie Tyrer and Lyndon Mills, who was one of the top men in the Standard Triumph Sales Department, though his was ostensibly a private entry. Although they failed to win the team prize, Done and Tyrer finished 5th and 6th respectively.

Thus it can be seen that the TR2's start in rallying up to March 1954 was no more than faltering; what was required was a big win in a major event, and the 1954 RAC Rally provided just that. It is hard to over-emphasise the importance of the results of this rally to the car's credibility, for suddenly and unexpectedly the TR2 became the car that everyone wanted, particularly those with serious competition aspirations who also needed a practical car to carry them around. Supply that was short beforehand became as a result even shorter, and those lucky enough to receive new TR2s found themselves being offered "over the odds" to part with their cars, as a couple of early owners have confirmed to me. It was not just that the TR2 won the rally, it was the fact that it won, came second and fifth, took 8 places in the first 40, won the ladies award and won two out of the three team prizes that really made enthusiasts take notice, and this is why I feel justified in examining the event in some detail.

The RAC Rally of the 1950's was not the rough, special stage event we know today, but it was no less tough in its own way, especially having regard to the technology of the vehicles of the time. It was, as it remains, Britain's premier rally event, and was decided in 1954 by a combination of timed road sections, accurate navigation and special tests of the "driving test" and sprint sort. It commenced at 6.30 p.m. on

On 21st September 1956, during the London Rally, an oil-skinned marshal directs several competitors, our interest being in the TR2 sporting what would today be a most valuable registration number. An early VW "Beetle" and a rare Sunbeam Rapier Mark I add period flavour to the scene (NMM Beaulieu).

Tuesday 9th March, and ran until the morning of Saturday 13th March, with only one night halt for sleep. Roughly 2,000 miles all told were covered, and there were two starting points, Blackpool and Hastings, the majority of the TR2 entries starting from Blackpool. The first part of the route took in the West Country, South Coast, East Anglia, Central and North Wales and the Peak District, the two groups of starters coming together on the Friday morning at Blackpool. Special tests took place both at various motor sporting venues and also at public places such as seaside promenades. From Blackpool on the Friday, the survivors from the 229 starters commenced a non-stop 600 mile all night bash through the Lake District and southern Scotland, which included a night time "round-the-pylons" test at Charterhall. Finally, back at Blackpool on the Saturday, a further driving test took place on the seafront road in front of a large crowd. Fog had been a serious hazard, Johnny Wallwork, the eventual winner, stating that he and his navigator had found it so thick on occasions that they had had to climb signposts to ascertain the way! It was truly an arduous event, and for Wallwork to finish unpenalised on the road section was a major achievement.

Peter Cooper, also TR2 mounted, came second overall, and Bill Bleakley came fifth. Mary Walker took the Ladies Prize, finishing 21st overall, and Triumphs took the 2nd and 3rd team prizes. Some of the TRs were only days old at the start of the event, barely run in, so the owners had not had much time to become accustomed to them. Johnny Wallwork's winning car was registered GJA 205, and it was stated some

Above: Denis Done does a crash stop in TFM 400 as part of the Silverstone Tests in the 1954 RAC Rally. Below: The TR2 of Johnny Wallwork and JH Brooks storm up Park Rash Hill in Yorkshire on their way to winning the 1954 RAC Rally outright (Author's collection).

Bob Dickson's TR2 (ORW 868) alongside Mary Walker's car during the 1954 RAC Rally. Standard-Triumph Sales Manager Lyndon Mills is seen talking to Mary Walker (from the Author's collection).

optional wire wheels. Auxiliary lights and reversing lights were usually added, as were electric windscreen demisters, but bumpers and hubcaps remained in situ, the fashion for stick-on front number plates without bumpers having not then started, other than for the "Jabbeke" car. P G Cooper's second placed TR2 was OEL 505, a black demonstration car borrowed by him from the Bournemouth Standard-Triumph distributor because he was unable to obtain delivery of his own TR2 in time, even though he was himself a Triumph dealer at the time! Here I must correct some previously incorrect information given to and published by me - I now know that OEL 505 was not car no. TS 69, which was exported new to the USA, but I cannot find out what its true commission number was - certainly it was a very early TR, as the registration dates from November 1953. Again, this car seems not to have survived. Mary Walker's car was OWK 888, privately owned by her, and reported by Bill Boddy, editor of "Motor Sport" magazine as "having a disgustingly loud exhaust note". To have occasioned such comment in those

Left: N Jarrett's TR2, OOK 2, tentatively essays a ford in what is possibly the 1954 RAC Rally. Is the brave soul behind really competing in an Austin A40 van? (NMM Beaulieu).

Below: JDN 888 was the TR2 driven on the 1954 RAC Rally by E Elliott and D Wright, finishing in 40th place. Here it poses at a night control, showing off three spotlights sensibly mounted out of the cooling air stream (NMM Beaulieu).

years later by Autosport magazine to have been "the first TR2 to have been released" - this cannot however be true, for recent enquiry of the Stockport licensing authority where it was registered reveals that it was first registered on 11th February 1954. Had it really been the first one released, it would have carried a 1953 registration number, for TR2s did not sit around in showrooms looking for buyers at that period. Wallwork campaigned this same TR2 throughout both that year and 1955, parting with it when he started driving for the works team, but unfortunately no trace has been heard of his winning car for many years, and it seems most unlikely that it has survived. Unfortunately, no record of GJA 205's commission number seems to exist either.

Judging by the photographs, the TRs in the event were in almost standard condition, few even being fitted with the

The peace of a tranquil setting in the Yorkshire Dales is soon to be shattered by the roar of sports car exhausts, as JH King brings his TR2, UJO 440, up to the start of a special test on the 1954 RAC Rally (JH King).

Below, left: At Hastings Control on the 1954 RAC Rally, Barry Leavens and his navigator are seen seated in their TR2, whilst George Hartwell, smoking the cigarette, looks on. Hartwell was a Rootes distributor much involved with motor sport, particularly with Sunbeams. Maybe he was sizing up the new TR as formidable competition to the cars he purveyed! (B Leavens).

Below, right: a group of youthful-looking TR men indulge in a bit of mud-plugging with their TR2. Unfortunately, the photograph reveals neither where nor when (NMM Beaulieu).

days, it really must have produced the famous "TR roar"! I was fortunately able via a TR register member to make contact recently with Mary Walker (now Mrs Frazer), and I deal with her TR career in more detail later in this chapter.

From photographs lent to me and from published information in the motoring press of the time and in the RAC archives, I have been able to assemble a table of details of the 14 TR2s entered in the event, and this is printed below.

Should anyone be able to fill in any of the missing items, I would be most grateful to hear from them. It is possible that a 15th TR2, none other than the Road Test Car OHP 771, was also entered, but it does not appear in the official list. It's driver was said to be W.B. Caldwell, so possibly he substituted the TR for his proposed mount at the last minute, presumably having been lent the TR by the works. A photograph of him driving this car exists, but it is not clear whether it was taken in the 1954 or the 1955 RAC rally. The table of TR entries reads as follows:

No:	Start From:	Driver/Co Driver:	Placed:	Car:
155	Blackpool	JC Wallwork/JH Brooks	1st	GJA205
42	Hastings	PG Cooper/OL Leighton	2nd	OEL505
153	Blackpool	W Bleakley/P Glaister	5th	ONF378
217	Blackpool	B Dickson/G Naugh	14th	ORW868
86	Hastings	J H King/M King	20th	UJO440
215	Blackpool	Mss M Walker/M Dodds	21st	OWK888
213	Blackpool	D Done/Gregory	22nd	TFM400
207	Blackpool	E Elliott/D Wright	40th	JDF888
61	Blackpool	N B Jarrett/ ?	?	OOK2
57	Blackpool	V Cooper/ ?	?	SMB10
131	Blackpool	E Batte/ ?	?	OS9049
208	Hastings	B Leavens/ ?	?	KAK656
184	Hastings	WH Wadham/ ?	?	?
92	Hastings	R Cookson/ ?	Ret'd	UPC700

Of the TR2s that started, only Cookson's failed to finish and that was due to an accident rather than to any mechanical problem. Overall, it was a remarkable demonstration of speed and reliability by the Triumphs, and it occasioned much very favourable press comment at the time.

When I researched this rally for the TR Register magazine some years ago I was able to contact John King, who had finished 20th. He told me that his TR was delivered on 23rd January 1954, and supplied by Messrs Eyles and Eyles in Oxford. He had no choice of colour, and it appeared in

MAX 620 must have been a very early TR2 (sub-TS1000), as it sports the 10½-inch wiper spindle spacing. The driver is unknown, but the event is the Plymouth Presidential Rally in 1954. One of the rubber-sucker-mounted windscreen spotlights is evident (NMM Beaulieu).

Geranium pink, which was not to Mr King's taste, so much so that he had it resprayed black by Eyles and Eyles before it ever went on the road, at a total cost of £12 - 10 shillings! He found the car to be even better than he had expected, ideal for the rallies of the time, and he kept it for four years, eventually part exchanging it in 1958 for a new Peerless. I also heard from Barry Leavens and his anecdote about obtaining delivery of his new TR2 is set out in chapter 8. Both Mr King and Mr Leavens were able to supply photographs, some of which are reproduced here, and which I think give an impression of this most important event in the history of the sidescreen cars.

Later in the month of March, the TR2 scored its first significant international success when a single car was entered into the prestigious Lyons-Charbonnieres rally in the French Alps, a very difficult event covering 800 miles of snowy, tortuous mountain roads at a 38 mph average speed. The TR used was OHP 676, commission no. TS8, which was one of the earliest factory demonstrators and publicity cars, along with OHP 242 and OHP 677 (see front cover). Although not a Works entry, as a Standard-Triumph owned vehicle, the car's entry did receive official sanction, although not apparently any backing or financial assistance. The drivers were Peter Reece, a man of considerable rally experience, and Gregor Grant, the founding editor of "Autosport", and thus an influential fellow with a platform to express his views to those who counted in the motor sporting world. The 1954 event was said to have been the most difficult rally ever then organised in France, and yet these two attempted it without any preliminary reconnaisance, which amazed both the organisers and the other crews! What also amazed them was the result achieved by the lone TR2, until then a car virtually unknown in France. It finished 6th overall, and 2nd in the Sports Car Classification, being one of only 16 unpenalised cars from the 139 starters. Grant wrote up the event in "Autosport" in some detail, and mentioned that they were staggered to realise that the TR had averaged 38 miles per gallon on its trip from England to the French Alps, cruising at 75 mph! He even referred to the TR's performance in the editorial, saying that the French could hardly credit the low price of the TR, and had he been an agent for Standards, he could have taken dozens of orders for this car which set "a new value in money per m.p.h". In the accompanying article, Mr Grant waxed even more lyrical, stating that the TR was tremendous, "mere words being unable to convey just how good this little machine is!" Looking back 40 years, it is difficult to realise how much beneficial effect such praise must have had on the sales and credibility of the TR, but "Autosport" was a weekly magazine that was very much the Bible of anyone interested in competitive motoring of any type. It therefore had a huge influence at a time when motoring magazines could be all but counted on the fingers

The passenger of D Giles' TR, SHW 2, does a "racing sidecar" lean as his driver throws the TR around the pylons during a timed test on the Eastbourne Rally, 26th June 1954 (NMM Beaulieu).

Above: THW 1, a TR2 belonging to CM Seward, is seen blasting up a rough track forming one of the observed sections of the MCC's Exeter Trial in the mid-1950s. The TR2's ground clearance was hardly ideal for such competitions and the three spotlights in the air intake cannot have done much for engine cooling (LAT Photographic).

The driver of this early TR2 looks more like one's bank manager than a sporting motorist, such were the fashions of the day! PBP 2 is seen competing in the Morecambe Rally in 1954 on an alarmingly deserted promenade (NMM Beaulieu)

Below, Bobby Dickson's TR2 is seen during the Circuit of Ireland Rally in 1954. This must be one of the earliest cars fitted from new with wire wheels ("Autosport").

D Giles in SHW 2 competes at London's Crystal Palace Circuit on 19th June 1954. The natty checked shirt was considered pretty racy at the time! (NMM Beaulieu).

of one hand, unlike today when around fifty motoring titles are regularly published.

By the Spring of 1954, the TR was firmly established as the car to have, taking a lead over the more expensive Austin Healey 100, which never did manage to establish itself as a serious rally car, possibly because of its perennial low ground clearance problems. On 3rd April, the TR2 made what was probably its debut in competition in Ireland, when Desmond Titterington, later to become famous as a "D" type Jaguar driver, raced his own TR PZ 6400 at Phoenix Park in Dublin, where "Autosport" reported that the car's appearance occasioned considerable interest. The same issue of "Autosport" also carries a photograph of Bob Dickson competing in an Autocross event in his white TR2 ORW 868 (TS 191), a car which saw considerable hard use during that first year. Autocross - racing on bumpy grass tracks -is not an obviously ideal type of event for a lowish sports car, yet contemporary reports reveal that quite a number of TRs were so used in the 1950's (and much later, for that matter, for the writer recalls several battered TRs being used for Autocross as late as the early 1970's, such was their inbuilt strength). Dickson used this same car later in April for the Circuit of Ireland Rally, where he would have featured in the awards but for a minor error in one test.

Another prestigious event held in those days was the London Motor Club's "Little Rally", which was little in name only, attracting 336 entries in 1954, more than the RAC rally itself! TRs won the team prize, The drivers involved being Messrs King, Isaacs and Toomer. A further opportunity for the TR to be displayed to the Continentals occured between the 12th and 16th April, when the French put on their "Rallye Soleil Cannes", 750 miles of tough road-based event from Paris to the sunny south. Three TRs started, driven by Tracey, Taylor and Gatsonides, who was soon to become very closely associated with the TR Works team then just being formed. Denis Taylor made fastest time in the "round the pylons" driving test, and Gatsonides finished second in his class. Again, the TR2s caused considerable interest, and whilst not winning against the much higher priced continetnal opposition, nevertheless they demonstrated their reliability and value for money. The car used in this event by Gatsonides was OVC 262, an unmodified Geranium pink TR2 loaned by the factory. Following the rally, Gatsonides used this car to rendezvous with Ken Richardosn in OVC 276 in Italy, and they then practised the Mille Miglia route in OVC 262, saving OVC 276 for the actual event, but here I am in danger of straying into "Works car" history! The Dutch organised Tulip Rally took place at the end of April, and Gregor Grant of "Autosport" was again lent OHP 676, this time his co-driver being Stan Asbury. This was a private entry, the embryonic works team being much taken up with the almost simulta-

neous Mille Miglia. By this time, several private entrants in Holland had also acquired TR2s, so Grant and Asbury were not alone. The route covered 2100 miles of tricky navigation, and only 44 crews remained unpenalised, Grant and Asbury being one of these, finishing a creditable 17th overall. TR successes continued and multiplied as more cars became available, so that by the beginning of May, "Autosport" Magazine was able to write "TR2's do it yet again" in their club news section, so prevalent had wins become in all sorts of events by the sidescreen TRs. In view of this, it would be tedious to continue to catalogue them all, but I hope that I have managed to portray something of the rapid build-up during early 1954 in the popularity and credibility of the TR2 as the all-round enthusiast's car.

Evidence of a hard night's driving is apparent on PL Edwards' TR2, as it awaits the final test on the Cambridge University Automobile Club's "Mini Monte" rally at the beginning of 1955. A marshal also appears to be TR2-mounted, further proof of the ubiquity of the TR by this time ("Autosport").

Goodwood Circuit on 7th July 1956 sees two TR2s racing, both fitted with the Works-type aero-screen, mounting on to the bulkhead bolts provided for the purpose. The second car has the later TR2 reveal moulding in place around the air intake (NMM Beaulieu).

Several Standard-Triumph mounted participants in the April 1955 Circuit of Ireland Rally are seen at the event's finish. This 1,000 mile rally took place using some of Ireland's toughest and roughest tracks - and TR2s swept the board, as the cups demonstrate. Crews shown are, left to right: Mr & Mrs R McKinney, Desmond Titterington, Miss PE Davis, Ronnie & Mrs Adams, E McMillen & J Haslett (Dublin Times).

Right: in the "Great American Mountain Rallye", the crew of this TR were Blodgett and Gatsonides, seen here stuck in snow at Lincoln Gap. Eventually, they regained grip by fitting chains and with Blodgett crouching in the boot to provide weight over the rear wheels.

A very standard-looking TR2, belonging to LJ Coe, tries its luck at a muddy trials hill in an unknown location. Waiting to follow it are three Morris Minors and what looks to be a Healey Westland Roadster. Note the ancient roadman's caravan ("Autosport").

Capitalising on these early private owner successes, the Works team, ably led by Ken Richardson began to take over, and the good showings in the Mille Miglia, at Le Mans (a quasi-works effort), and particularly in the Alpine Rally consolidated the TR's reputation as a rugged, all-rounder, a reputation that persisted in the minds of buyers right through to the end of TR3B production. In addition to these events and the RAC Rally win, two further major successes in September 1954 enhanced the car's reputation. One was Johnny Wallwork's outright win in the London Rally, again in his own car GJA 205, by then sporting wire wheels. The other was the showing by the TRs in the Tourist Trophy race run on the difficult "round the houses" circuit at Dundrod in Northern Ireland. Six TRs were entered, in two teams of three; one of the cars was the ex Le Mans car OKV 777, a Works entry driven by Richardson and Dickson, but the remaining five were private entries. All six TRs finished the event, winning both the first and second team prizes. They were probably the lowest priced cars running, and also probably nearer to standard production specification than any other entries. Their showing in this dangerous race was excellent publicity, for as John Bolster wrote, "It must have made many people reach for their cheque books, and serves to underline the Triumph performance at Le Mans."

By good fortune I have been able to trace and interview one of the private entrants in this race, Tom Blackburn, whose car, TTF 1, was one of the three cars forming the winning "team prize" team. I am therefore able to elaborate on the background to the event in some more detail, and to set down Tom's reminiscences of his time with his very successful TR2, for he used it in many different races and rallies in the 1954 and 1955 period.

Tom Blackburn, a Lancastrian, was a keen local car club member in the early 1950's, and knew Ted Lund well, Ted having established a reputation as an engine tuning wizard and someone usually surrounded by interesting vehicles, often MGs. He developed the Lund Special, a supercharged "P" type MG, and Tom Blackburn was able via his friendship with Ted to purchase and to use this car during the 1952 season, the meetings at Charterhall and Bo'ness being amongst Tom's favourites, where he also on occasions competed in a Jowett Jupiter. In mid 1954, Tom was looking to purchase

A period "bobble hat" keeps Tom Blackburn's head warm on 6th March 1955, whilst he conducts a test on Blackpool seafront during the Bolton-le-Moors Car Club Rally. The block on the boot was to enable a second spare wheel to be mounted and a pair of boot handles have been added. An Army surplus breakdown truck and an Austin loudspeaker van enhance this vintage scene (Tom Blackburn).

Below is a delightful view of Tom Blackburn and his fiancee in the paddock at Oulton Park, 30th April 1955. The TR has been stripped for racing. Spare wheels and vintage petrol cans are in evidence. Three TRs are visible in the background, No 30 belonging to Bill Bleakley (Tom Blackburn).

A real impression of speed is conveyed by this action shot of Tom Blackburn driving John Waddington's TR2 in the Six Hour Relay Race at Silverstone, 28th August 1954. Note the small rear brake drums, the early-type rear lights and the pair of tiny reversing lamps (Tom Blackburn).

his first new car, to replace the Jupiter which by then was on its third crankshaft! He needed a vehicle that would acquit itself well both in circuit racing and in rallying, in addition to providing his everyday transport. For reasons we have seen, the TR seemed the obvious choice, Blackburn confirming that his mind was made up by the showing of OKV 777 at the 1954 Le Mans, where he was one of the helpers in the TR pit, being much impressed with the car's speed and reliability.

Although he planned right from the start to enter TTF 1 in the T.T. in September, and although it was modified to Tom's specification in the Works Competition Department prior to delivery, nevertheless the car had to be supplied via a dealer rather than direct from the works. Supply of TRs was still somewhat slow, and there were various delays, causing time before the T.T. to become very short. The car was delivered finally on September 4th 1954 via Hollingdrakes in Manchester, and although no record of the commission number survives, it must have been one of the last of the long-door cars. Tom Blackburn confirms that when it arrived, it had the original type of one-piece rear window hood, soon to be replaced by the later type. (Tom also confirmed that OKV 777 sported what must have been the prototype 3-piece rear window hood, which it had had back in June 1954). Upon delivery, there was exactly one week to go prior to the T.T. race, the car at this stage not even being run in! It was therefore driven virtually day and night for the next four days both to put some miles on it, to loosen the engine, and to enable Tom to gain a modicum of experience with it prior to its being loaded onto the boat for Belfast on the Thursday. Experience was very necessary, for entry into the TT for Tom Blackburn was very much a launch "into the deep end", this being one of the most important sports car races in the whole calender, attracting the cream of international opposition in big engined Ferraris and Jaguars.

I enquired as to the modifications done to the TR by the Works prior to delivery, and these were as follows: competition suspension was fitted, overdrive, an aluminium sump and al-fin brake drums, oversized in that they were 12 inch drums at the front, and 10 inch at the rear. No undershield was fitted in case it should cause overheating, and an oil temperature gauge was installed as a precaution. The engine was fundamentally standard, but was carefully assembled in the way usually referred to as "blueprinting", and it had been equipped with oversized, 2 inch, S.U. carburettors, the only external modification. (Just for the T.T., the standard 1 1/2" carburettors were replaced evidently). The standard cylinder head and manifolds were fitted, though Tom says that they had been well polished! A strengthened, 5 bolt differential was used, but the rear axle was otherwise standard, including the halfshafts, a well-known TR weakness. Uprated wire wheels were fitted, as was a perspex

aeroscreen, and in this form TTF 1 was accurately timed at 128 mph at the end of the straight in the TT. Very surprisingly, the front bumper remained fitted to the car during the race, though Blackburn can't now remember why! It was finished in British Racing Green, but a personal touch was added in that the air intake mouth was picked out in white, predating the yellow mouths seen on Works TR2s later on! Not only did it achieve 128 mph, but it averaged 28 miles per gallon at racing speeds in the TT, truly an amazing performance for the speeds involved. The low-port head TR2 engine was almost freakishly economical in all its forms, as has been demonstrated many times. In view of his participating in the team at the TT, I enquired whether the car was supplied at a favourable price. The answer was yes and no, in that Tom Blackburn paid Hollingdrake's the full list price for the TR2, but the special competition department modifications were incorporated without further charge.

As to the race itself, the team of 6 TRs used as their HQ the Rootes dealership garage in Belfast belonging to Maunsell, one of their number, who drove his TR2 along with

McCaldin. This car was registered B1 6600, and the other three TRs, along with TTF1 and OKV 777 were OKV 72 (Brooke and Scott-Douglas), OON 292 (Merrick and Tew) ans TZ 635 (Titterington and Johnstone). TTF 1, OKV 777 and B1 6600 comprised the "A" team, and the other 3 cars were designated the "B" team, the "A" team winning the team award, the "B" team coming second, TR2's being placed 3rd, 4th, 5th, 6th and 7th in the production car category. Tom Blackburn's co-driver was his old friend Ted Lund, who had worked for some time at the S.U. carburettor factory. He tuned all the TRs the night before the race, and his tuning magic undoubtedly assisted the car's performance and contributed to the excellent fuel consumption. The road surface of the TT circuit was very abrasive, and this led to excessive tyre wear, but otherwise Tom Blackburn cannot recall any specific problems affecting any of the team cars, all of which were almost boring in their consistency and reliability. What he can recall however is that the Standard-Triumph's publicity machine was taken totally by surprise when both the team prizes were won by their products. Nothing had been planned or laid on for such an eventuality, though the advertising lads must have been quick off the mark, for within 6 days a full-page advertisement (reproduced here) proclaming the TR's success in the race was appearing in the motoring press. Overnight following the race all 6 cars were taken to Harry Ferguson's garage in Belfast and securely locked away, and Standard's chartered two Bristol Freighter aircraft to ferry the cars urgently back to Coventry. Hasty arrangements were made for all 6 to go on a nationwide tour of Standard-Triumph dealerships in their "as-raced" condition, and they were thus displayed in various showrooms up and down the land. This meant that Tom Blackburn lost the use of his brand new TR2 for a month, so the Works lent him the factory hack TR, none other than

This side-on view of TTF 1, taken during the Ulster TT Race, clearly shows the over-size Alfin brake drums fitted to Tom Blackburn's car (Tom Blackburn).

OHP 771 (TS 6), the well-used road test car still finished in Geranium, or "embarrassing pink" as Tom calls it. Ken Richardson himself drove the car up to Lancashire for Tom to take over, and so during the next four weeks, Blackburn campaigned OHP 771 both at Prescott Hill Climb and in several rallies, including the Morecambe Illuminations Rally, on which he recalls putting this car through a stone wall whilst negotiating the Trough of Bowland! Mr Blackburn was even able to show me the temporary insurance cover note relating to OHP 771 dated September 1954! Once the tour of dealerships was over, the final showing being at Triumph's London showroom in Piccadilly, TTF 1 was handed back to Tom, and OHP 771 became surplus to requirements. However, Ted Lund decided that he too would like a TR2, and he made an offer for it to the Factory. As by then it was a very well-used demonstrator, and also because the modified, short-door cars were about to be announced, the Factory agreed to let it go to Lund at a favourable price, so he acquired OHP 771. Tom Blackburn recalls that Ted ran it for about a year, competing in all types of events, and sold it in the Autumn of 1955 to be replaced by an MGA, for MG's had always been Lund's first love. It seems likely therefore that the "ex-Works" car advertised for sale by Lund, and referred to in chapter 8 was indeed OHP 771.

I asked Tom whether he had had much experience of driving TR's before he ordered his own, for to go straight into a major race such as the TT with a new car seemed somewhat ambitious! In fact, however, he was friendly with another up-and-coming Lancastrian driver who also made a name for himself driving TRs, John Waddington, and he had co-driven John's TR2 975 BRF on several occasions, In particular Tom drove with John in the 750 Motor Club's 6 hour relay race at Silverstone on 28th August, just two weeks before the TT itself, so he had at least some racing miles in a TR to his credit when embarking on the TT. Tom kept TTF 1 through most of the 1955 season, continuing to use it for all kinds of events, the car having a somewhat hard life! As to further modifications he recalls only the fitting of a Derrington 4 branch exhaust manifold. Reliability was good, though hairline cracks appeared in the pistons which had to be replaced (stronger pistons were soon incorporated in production cars) and he broke a rear spring whilst competing in the 3 day Highland Rally, which was a pity as he had been leading at the time! Surprisingly, no half-shaft breakages occurred, but one continuing problem in circuit racing was boiling of the brake fluid! With the over-sized Alfin drums, the braking was exceptionally good until the fluid boiled, about which little could be done. When finally he sold the TR2, he retained the registration number TTF 1, the car being re-registered 585 BTB, though what became of it subsequently is unknown. I brought up the issue of payment and expenses, and Tom confirmed that he financed his TT race largely out of his own resources, although he was later able to sign up with Castrol and hence receive a smallish amount of money to help defray costs. Not much came his way from Standard-Triumphs however, other than the "gratis" modifications as outlined and certain help with maintenance and spares. As indicated in the interview with Ken Richardson, the Works were on a very tight budget from management even with their own cars, and had no cash to spare to assist non-works entrants, however promising. The company's management did however loosen the purse strings slightly on the 7th December 1954, for they held a dinner at the Park Lane Hotel, London, to celebrate "A Year of Triumph - the outstanding success of the TR2 during the year 1954". Tom attended and still has the menu card, which contains cartoons of TRs by Brockbank, the well known motoring artist. Alick Dick and Ted Grinham attended for the company, along with Marshall of the RAF, Lord Tedder, who took the chair. Virtually all the well known TR drivers were present, and in the foyer of the hotel was a green TR2 mounted on a backcloth lettered "1954, a year of Triumph!" According to the "Autosport report", every guest present received a shooting stick as a souvenir, and Tom confirms that he still has his!

Like so many others that I've talked to over the years, Tom Blackburn retains fond memories of his TR2, and never once regretted his purchase. He has also kept in touch with John Waddington, and so he was kind enough to provide an intro-

duction for me also to meet John, again to spend a pleasant afternoon discussing the great days of the sidescreen TRs.

Like Tom Blackburn, John Waddington is a Lancastrian; one gets the impression both from contemporary magazine reports and from talking to people that that part of Britain produced more than its due share of sidescreen TR competitors. In the 1950's, the motor clubs in the area were particularly strong, and in addition, the county is liberally supplied with interesting "rally" terrain. John started rallying seriously when he was 20 using a Singer Roadster and sometimes a Dellow; by the time he was 25 or so in 1957, he had risen to become one of the country's foremost rally exponents, driving on occasions for the Triumph Works team. Indeed, it was only considerable business commitments in the family textile manufacturing firm that prevented him from continuing his Works team involvement, and which caused him to turn down offers of works drives in 1955 for Sunbeams and for Triumphs in 1958. In November 1957, "Autosport" published a profile of John Waddington, and awarded him the accolade of "perhaps the most successful rally driver in the British Calendar" - this was praise indeed for his competitive driving, most of which was conducted in a series of four sidescreen TRs, his usual co-driver and navigator being Mike Wood. Events which he won outright and/or in which he gained premier awards included the Highland 3-day Rally, Lakeland Rally, Rally of the Dams, Yorkshire Rally, London Rally, Jeans Gold Cup Rally, Morecambe National Rally,

Following the TR teams' excellent results in the 1954 TT, the six actual cars went on a tour of Triumph dealerships, along with their trophies. Tom Blackburn's car, TTF 1, is No 28 (Tom Blackburn).

The six TR2s from the Ulster TT Team Prize-winning teams are seen lined up at the premises of Herts Motors Limited in St Albans, September 1954, where they attract much attention (Tom Blackburn).

Whilst TTF 1 was away on display, following its Ulster TT success, the Works lent Tom Blackburn the original road-test TR2 OHP 771. Here, he is seen pressing this hard-worked car up Prescott Hill Climb on 19th September 1954 (Tom Blackburn).

Concentration is seen on Tom Blackburn's face as he powers round Old Hall at Oulton Park on 16th April 1955 (Tom Blackburn)

Plymouth Rally and the "Birmingham Post" National Rally. As mentioned, he drove for the Triumph works team on several occasions, starting with the 1955 Tulip rally where he co-drove with Jimmy Ray in PDU21. John drove a Works Standard 10 saloon on one occasion, and competed for the team in the 1957 Tulip rally with Willy Cave in TRW 736. During the 1958 Monte Carlo, driving VRW 221, one of the then new works 3A's, he managed to get to the finish despite crashing, albeit too late to count as a finisher. In addition to rallying, Waddington owned a trials car for "mud-plugging" events and also a Fiat 1100 TV for everyday transport, which he also used both for rallying and racing. Although racing was not a primary interest, he managed wins at both Silverstone and Oulton Park, and as has been recounted, competed in the 6 hour relay race in his first TR2, 975 BRF, sharing the car with Tom Blackburn.

I enquired about the acquisition of that first TR; 975 BRF was supplied in March 1954, John being able to obtain reasonably quick delivery via a contact, Jock Jeffs, in the service department at the Canley factory. It was supplied via Byatts of Stoke, hence the Staffordshire registration number. Fortunately, having regard to some of the grim colours then available it came in British Racing Green, and it had wire wheels, although it was otherwise a standard vehicle for which full list price was paid. Unusually, it came fitted with a white soft top. This car was rallied extensively as John's photographs show, and was also raced on several occasions, proving itself reliable and having no major problems. However, after a very busy year, John traded it in for a slight-

ly later TR2, GRN 37, this time a disc-wheeled car in Signal Red. This TR was not new but around 6 months old, and was to standard specification but for the fitment of harder brake linings. John confirmed that the brakes were very much the Achilles heel of the TR2, particularly in any form of competitive motoring. This second TR2 was baptised in April 1955 at an Oulton Park race meeting, and GRN 37 was also used on more than one occasion for some roughish Autocross events. During the 1955 season it had as hard a life as had its predecessor and again it proved reliable, although a comprehensive failure of the lights on the

Above: GRN 37 is seen at Oulton Park in April 1955 overtaking a pre-war 2-Litre Aston Martin and below, during a spin which fortunately caused no damage. This was John Waddington's first event in his second TR2, which looks to be in very standard condition (John Waddington).

The wide-open spaces of Britain's Northern Pennines are seen here as 975 BRF charges up Buttertubs Pass, during the MCC Whitsun Rally in May 1954. A "tweedy" lady spectator on a shooting stick looks on. John Waddington, who won a first-class award on this event, describes this first TR2 as "incredibly and embarrassingly noisy!" (John Waddington).

As an example of the varied forms of competition in which John Waddington used his TR2s, he is seen here thrashing GRN 37 around a bumpy autocross circuit, suffering apparently from terminal understeer. The event was the Liverpool Motor Club's Swan Autocross of 9th October 1955 (John Waddington).

635 KRE was Waddington's very late TR2, bought new with a hardtop and supplied with external door handles, one of which can just be seen in this April 1957 shot, taken on the London Motor Club's "Little Rally" (John Waddington).

TRW 736 is seen here in Austria during the Tulip Rally in May 1957. John Waddington is on one of his Works Team drives, partnered by Willy Cave; they finished first in their class. John confirms that this was the TR3 that he drove in this event, not TRW 735, as has been published previously (John Waddington).

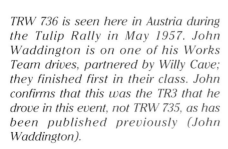

London Rally in September 1955 was not good news - nevertheless Waddington still managed to finish the event! In early 1956, GRN was "getting more than a little worn out", to quote John, so he replaced it with a third TR2, this time a new, black car, 635 KRE. Mindful of winter rallying, a steel hardtop, also black, was supplied with the car, and John confirms, as proved by photographs, that this particular TR2 came from the factory fitted with external door handles without there having been any special order! Although some hardtop equipped TR3s had door handles, even if not ordered as part of the "G.T. Continental Touring kit", 635 KRE is the first TR2 that I have heard of to be so fitted. This merely reinforces what the author has learned over the years in judging "originality" classes at TR events, namely, that it does not pay to be categorical where sidescreen TRs are concerned!~ This third TR2 was however a very late car, being supplied new well after TR3 production had commenced and deliveries of the new model were being made. As mentioned elsewhere in this book, there were considerable

unsold stocks of TR2s at the Works at this time, some of which may have been converted new to TR3 specification, so presumably John's new car was one of the "unsold" TR2s that escaped TR3 conversion. Nevertheless, and despite all his success in TRs over the previous 2 years, Waddington confirms that he still had to pay full list price for the car! 635 KRE saw him through the 1956 season and well into 1957, by which time more business commitments and the various works team events were causing him to curtail his private rallying somewhat. In 1956, however, 635 KRE brought home an impressive series of 'pots' and trophies.

John cannot recall exactly when this last TR2 was sold, but it was not the finish of his involvement with the sidescreen TR's. After a break from rallying for a year or so, he purchased PDB 11, a secondhand, white TR3A bought specifically to compete in the Yorkshire Rally in 1960. This was the first TR he had owned which was fitted with disc brakes, (although of course the works cars he'd driven had been so

John Waddington's days as a Standard-Triumph Works driver are recalled by this photograph, taken at the end of the 1958 Monte Carlo Rally. John is seen second from the right, leaning on VRW 221, the car he drove in the event. Unfortunately, he retired through lateness. Johnny Wallwork is also seen, second from the left, by the tuned Standard 10 that was his mount and in which he finished second in class (John Waddington).

Front wheel tuck-in is much in evidence as GH Breakell flings his hardtop TR around a test in the Highland Rally, year unknown. Although apparently a TR2, this car carries the TR3 wing beading and a reveal moulding that continues all around the air intake mouth: in fact, the TR Register's records reveal that it was TS12773, a late drum-braked TR3 ("Autosport").

equipped) and he recalled how infinitely superior they were for rally work. He did this Yorkshire Rally plus a couple of other events, but soon ever increasing alternative calls on his time caused him permanently to forsake the rallying scene. In addition, John could sense that top level rallying in the 1960's was not going to be as it had been in the previous decade, but would be an altogether more serious affair, harder on the car because of the rough special forest stages then just becoming popular, which in turn would lead to the necessity for specially adapted cars. He felt he had been in at the best time, and was happy to retire, selling the TR3A after only a few months.

On the day we met, I happened to have my own long door TR2 on the road, BRG and with wire wheels, almost a replica of John's first sidescreen car from 40 years previously. Despite his not having been in a TR since the 1960's, John was immediately at home when offered a drive, recalling exactly where all the switches were, and charging off up the road with great confidence and with memories flooding back. He had forgotten how heavy the clutch was compared to a modern car, though!

I asked when we arrived back whether he had ever regretted not being able to take up further works drives in the Triumph team; "Not really," was the reply, "it would all have got too serious, and would have involved driving to orders. In any event," John continued, "we only got £10 a day with no retainer and out of that we had to pay all our living and hotel expenses, so there were hardly fortunes to be made!"

A long-door TR2 with an unusual squared-off aero screen safely negotiates a corner, unlike the Healey Silverstone that was following it. An interesting array of spectators' vehicles add to this scene, taken at Snetterton circuit on 15th April 1956 ("Autosport").

Lady competitor Mrs A Woolley pushes her TR3A through a test on the Morecambe Rally in 1959 ("Autosport").

A wet race produces lots of sports car action, but unfortunately, this photo records no details. Tw TR2s, both with bonnet air scoops, lead and Austin Healey 100 at Snetterton circuit.

A pair of Works TR3As are about to embark on a Bristol Freighter, almost certainly for a Channel crossing. Ken Richardson is in the centre, with John Waddington on the left. VHP 529 carries alarge suitcase on a bootrack, but the identity of the other car is unknown. It was likely to be one of the "VRW" cars (TR Register Archive).

Following my interviews with the two 1950's TR drivers who were on the fringes of the works team, I wanted to talk to an amateur competitor from those days who did not perhaps take things quite so seriously, which is not to say that he was not trying when on events, merely that he had no inside knowledge nor connection with the Works, and competed very much off his own bat. Fortunately I was able via the TR Register to encounter TA "Bill" Parkes, who had a very early TR2 in which he did a lot of amateur rallying in 1954 and 1955. The story of how Bill managed to acquire his car is recounted in detail elsewhere, the car being a Geranium pink TR2 fitted with overdrive, wire wheels, blackberry leather upholstery, competition springs and shock absorbers. Bill's interest lay primarily in rallying, and although he did

compete in several sprints in the car, MUY 334, he never raced it. He had however originally intended to race when he placed the order for the TR, the fact that it just fell into the "under 2-litre" class being a factor which influenced him in ordering the TR rather than an Austin-Healey or a Jaguar. The TF MG he dismissed as being just plain old-fashioned! As to the reason for not racing, Bill recalls that it was doubts about the durability of the crankshaft and bearings under racing conditions, for the word was that fellow competitors in early TR2s were finding out that crankshaft lubrication on the first engines was marginal, and were experiencing problems. These difficulties led the factory hastily to introduce the cross-drilled crankshaft from engine number TS 881 E in March 1954, but unfortunately for Bill, his car had the first type of crankshaft. He tried unsuccessfully to persuade the service department at the Factory to give him the latest cross-drilled part under warranty, but they refused on the grounds that he first had to break the original one, which in fact he never did!

Unlike John Waddington and Tom Blackburn, Bill Parkes had quite a considerable number of problems with MUY 334 early in its life, although he remembers the service department at Coventry as being most helpful and doing all it could to satisfy him and get the TR running again, no charges ever being levied. He always dealt direct with the Factory rather than his local dealer in Worcester, for he felt that with the TR being so new a model - his was the first in Worcestershire - the local firm would know little about it and would not be able to incorporate all the latest modifications as rapidly as could the Factory. Clearly this was a prudent policy, but it did involve Bill in the inconvenience of travelling home to Worcester from Coventry by bus on four occasions whilst the TR was left at the works!

The problems were all mechanical, Bill confirming that the general finish and presentation of the car as delivered was good. Although like most, he did not initially care for the Geranium paintwork, he grew to quite like the colour eventually. Two gearboxes and the clutch were changed under warranty, as was the clutch and the braking system was unsatisfactory, the well known tendency for grabbing and juddering manifesting itself. Again, the service department tried to effect a cure, but were at first only partially successful, leaving Bill with the impression that the braking was the TR's worst feature, and very much its limiting factor in any form of competition. Ultimately his car's braking system was largely cured, however, by the installation of the later TR2 type brakes. A further mechanical derangement concerned the throttle linkage, which fell to pieces on an early rally, and which again was modified by the Works.

As was often stated in contemporary reports, the earliest TR2s were incredibly noisy, Bill's car proving no exception, Mr Parkes Senior being able to hear his son's impending arrival a good five minutes prior to his actually materialising! As Bill says, however, he was still young enough at that stage to enjoy the raucous exhaust note, and declined to have it altered when the works offered fitment of the 24 inch silencer to replace the original 18 inch item. In addition to the legendary noise, another early TR2 characteristic that he confirms from personal experience was the amazing economy, 40 miles per gallon having been normal in everyday motoring. Even on night rallies with lots of flat out low gear work the TR used to average 30 mpg!

Bill had MUY 334 for just over two years, from February 1954 until May 1956, covering in that time around 33,000 miles of mixed motoring. Once the initial problems of the first 6 months as recounted had been dealt with, the car became a very reliable and enjoyable means of transport. During its first few months, it was also an object of considerable public interest and attention, almost embarrassingly so at times, this being compounded by the lurid paintwork and the loud exhaust noise!

Bill remembers his first rally, in March 1954, as being a local Worcester Motor Club affair in which he won a half-bottle of Brandy. His arrival for this event in the TR created something of a stir amongst the enthusiasts, few of whom had seen the new Sports Triumph "in the metal" previously. Over the 1954 and 1955 seasons, about 30 rallies were covered as well as the odd sprint meeting, Prescott and Goodwood in May 1954 being two of the latter. Bill competed in the bigger national events such as the MCC Redex National Rally, the Morecambe Rally and the London Motor Club's London Rally and "Little Rally", as well as in local rallies. He was able to show me several delightful "period" photographs of these events, some of which are reproduced, and although not featuring in the winners lists in any major event, Bill and his TR2 usually managed to finish in the top half of the entry. Probably his best result was taking the second team prize (with a Morgan and an Allard) in the London Motor Club's Little Rally in 1954. Bill Parkes represents a good example of a clubman of the period; able to afford only one car which had to be capable of all types of event, financing his sport privately, dealing with problems as they arose and thoroughly enjoying himself. Although MUY 334 has long gone, when I visited him at his home Bill produced a memento of the period in the form of one of the delightful and accurate 1950's "Victory Industries" plastic model TR2s. Although I had seen these previously, they had always been white, whereas Bill's was finished in the correct Geranium shade, even sporting the registration number of his old car. These "Victory" TRs are well worth seeking out, being around 12 inches long and battery operated. Presumably several different colours were available, and later an updated TR3 version was produced, with the correct cellular front grille. The only example of the TR3 that I know of is finished in BRG, but no doubt there were other colours.

Upon looking through Bill Parkes' photograph albums, I was surprised to see that his TR2 was fitted with the later type of rear lights and reflectors, fitted to post TS 1300 cars. "Surely" I enquired, "it had been fitted with earlier type with the separate, hung-on reflectors?" Bill had no memory of these, and none of the early photographs showed them, and I left thinking that maybe this was another bit of "TR lore" about to be demolished. However, a few days after my visit, Bill rang me to say that he had found another photograph of his TR, this one taken on 10th April 1954 of the car at a control in the London Motor Club's Little Rally, and this picture clearly shows that the original type of rear lights and reflectors **were** fitted. The puzzling thing is that Bill has no recollection of their being changed early on in the car's career (or at all for that matter), and nor did MUY 334 have a rear end accident necessitating new lights. He can only conclude that the service department must have fitted the later type free of charge on one of the car's visits to the Works for warranty work and rectification, and that they failed to mention this. Maybe an enthusiastic apprentice had simply backed the car into something solid and it was mended without the owner's knowledge!

Asked for a recollection of the most amusing incident of his TR rallying career, Bill Parkes recalled driving through a flood at Upton upon Severn, a locality notorious for an excess of water at times. On this particular night rally, Parkes and his co-driver were gingerly fording the river's flood plain when they leaned out to investigate how deep the water actually was. In this process, the doors were opened and the rising river took its course through the car, in one door and out the other! Shutting the driver's door rapidly, Bill caused a tidal wave to flow across the cockpit sideways, drowning everything most comprehensively! Despite this sinking, the engine continued to run and they were able to drive out, continuing their rally in considerable discomfort.

Bill, like others I talked to, still has fond memories of his Geranium TR2, and has often wondered what became;e of it, for he never saw it again following selling it in 1956, and it has never appear on the files of the TR Register - maybe the flood water caused it to rust away earlier than happened to most TR2s!

10th April 1954 sees Bill Parkes' almost new TR2 arriving at a halt on the London Motor Club's "Little Rally". Note the original "hung-on" reflectors that were still on the car at this stage. A rather ungainly Allard passes in the opposite direction (TA Parkes).

Bill Parkes leaves a test start line in MUY 334 at the London Motor Club's "Little Rally" on 21st April 1954 (TA Parkes).

Anxious moments for Bill Parkes and his navigator as they attempt a ford, again on the LMC "Little Rally" in April 1954 (TA Parkes).

A night control provides an atmospheric period shot dating from the 1954 Redex National Rally (TA Parkes).

Typical Pennine weather graces this shot of Bill Parkes in North Yorkshire, again a view from the 1954 Redex National Rally. Altohugh the TR's hood is still down, the Austin Atlantic in the background is caught by the camera in the act of erecting its power-operated hood (TA Parkes).

MUY 334 is thrown hard into a corner at the Prescott Hill Climb in May 1954. Bill Parkes peers around the deep factory aero screen (TA Parkes).

Here, Bill Parkes is seen circuit racing MUY 334, leading a Riley RM Saloon through Goodwood's chicane. The grandstand is hardly packed! (TA Parkes).

Bill Parkes and a jovial bunch of fellow rallyists make a splendid "period" photograph. In the picture are, left to right: Jim Bishop, Bill Parkes, Angela Palfrey, John Pither and, on the extreme right, Michael Smith. The person second from the right is unidentified. TR2 SFD 60 is well-adorned with extra equipment (TA Parkes).

Another driver from the earliest TR days whom I was very gratified to be able to contact was Mary Walker. She won the Ladies Prize in the 1954 RAC Rally driving OWK 888, her own TR2, and also drove for the Standard Triumph Works team, albeit in Standard 10's rather than TRs. TR Register members John and Caroline Edmonds put me in touch with Mary, who following her marriage became Mrs Mary Fraser. She very generously jotted down her memories of rallying her TR in 1954 and 1955, lending me many irreplaceable photographs and mementoes.

Cars were part of Mary Walker's life from an early age, for her father was the proprietor of a garage business at Wooler

in Northumberland, not far from the Scottish border, good rallying country and home to several sporting drivers of repute, notably Jim Clark. Having a fancy to become more competitive in her rallying, Mary opted to purchase one of the new TRs, and with a father in the business, obtaining delivery was less of a problem than it had proved to be for Bill Parkes. Some intervention by Bobby Dickson, who wanted to see a team of TR2s in the RAC Rally, also helped. In fact Dickson had given Mary her first drive in a TR2, following the Scottish Motor Show in late 1953 at the Kelvin Hall, Glasgow. He took her out in a Geranium Pink demonstrator (TS13 probably) along the road to Dumbarton, urging her to go ever faster. She was thrilled with the TR, both with its speed and its sound!

Mary Walker puts OWK 888 through a test on a very damp Hastings seafront during the 1954 RAC Rally. A Sunbeam-Talbot Alpine awaits its turn in the distance (Mary Fraser).

Taken Leeds at the start of the 1954 London Rally, this shot shows Mary Walker in OWK 888 with her co-driver Muriel Dodds, talking to Ian Appleyard. Appleyards were Jaguar dealers in Leeds, Ian Appleyard winning the RAC Rally outright in both 1951 and 1953 driving, not surprisingly, a Jaguar XK120 (Mary Fraser).

OWK 888 was delivered in late February 1954, a white car with wire wheels and overdrive. The car was Coventry registered, but this was because the Home Sales department at the factory first registered it themselves and supplied it direct to Mr Walker's garage, as Mary recalls. However, the factory records state that the car was delivered to Rossleigh Ltd in Newcastle-on-Tyne. From Mary's recollection they did not physically receive it, so this must be a further instance of a Distributor getting a "cut" on a car supplied within their territory, even though they didn't actually sell it or even see it! It was certainly not a works car, as has sometimes been thought. Although she had kept no note of the commission number, my own research at Coventry Record Office revealed that the car was TS 616 "O", with engine number TS 732 E, and that it was first registered on 18th February 1954. Incidentally, the records also revealed that it was last taxed in February 1964, and was then stated to have been broken up, so unfortunately, OWK 888 is not a car we shall see joining the TR Register.

Like other TR2 drivers I talked to, Mary had to pay full list price for her new car, which she nicknamed TRudie! The car was carefully run in locally, the owner gaining experience quickly in what was to her much the most rapid vehicle she had driven to that date. The first big event was, as we have seen, the 1954 RAC Rally, where she finished 21st overall, and won the Ladies Award outright, which was excellent publicity for the company. Mary confirms that in no way were any of the TR entries directly Works supported, but where they were able to assist without spending much cash, the factory certainly did so. An example of this she recalled with some amusement; during the rally, OWK 888 came into contact with a wall somewhere in Wales - as marks were deducted at the finish for any obvious damage to each car's bodywork, Mary was liable to lose a point or two. Bobby Dickson in ORW 868 was having difficulties with his gearbox, and Denis Done in TFM 400 felt his car needed retuning. Dickson suggested therefore much to Miss Walker's horror, that the three of them deviate from the

A hill climb test at Ulpha, in the Lake District, prvides a delightful rural setting for this photograph. Mry Walker's TR2 charges up the hill during the 1954 RAC Rally (Mary Fraser).

The story is related in this Chapter of how OWK 888 received a new wing at the Works during the course of the 1954 RAC Rally. Here, the comparative lack of dirt on the new panel can clearly be seen (Mary Fraser).

Left: a braking test on the 1954 RAC Rally at Bangor sees Mary Walker bring OWK 888 smartly to a halt (Mary Fraser).

Below: Mary (left) and Muriel look pleased as they pose with OWK 888 following the prizegiving at the conclusion of the 1954 RAC Rally. They had won the Ladies' Prize and come 21st overall in the General Classification, out of more than 200 starters. The duffle coats add to the period flavour of the scene (Mary Fraser).

route through the Midlands, and call briefly at the Triumph factory! This took place during a long section that brought the rally not far from Coventry, and the three white TR2s, Dickson leading Mary, with Done bringing up the rear, managed to call at Canley, have repairs effected and regain their correct route without losing time or incurring any penalty! OWK 888 had a new nearside front wing fitted, and one of the photographs of the car taken on the Prescott Hill climb stage clearly shows that this wing is not as dirty as the rest of the car! Dickson's gearbox was changed in record time, as Mary recalls!

Her co-driver for the RAC Rally, and for most of her TR rallying career, was Muriel Dodds, described as "unflappable". Mary opines that Muriel should have had a medal in her own right for sitting alongside throughout that long rally without complaint or any serious navigational error. She also recalls that their way of dealing with any error by one of them, or a difference of opinion, was to be excessively and icily polite to each other for a period; this would eventually culminate in one or other of them being forced to laugh, thus healing the breach. How much more civilised than a shouting match! Looking back from 1994, Mary confesses to "going hot and cold" when she reconsiders and recalls some of her exploits in the TR2. Things undertaken which were not so much dangerous as just plain stupid, some of which she feels lucky to have survived. "Nevertheless," she added, "It was jolly good fun at the time," especially as she was part of one of the very few top flight ladies crews in a world surrounded by chaps in fast cars!

The TR2 was used for everyday transport between rallies, and on more than one occasion, Mary and a companion drove from Northumberland to London for a party, and then back again the same night, around 600 miles in total and on

the old A1, with almost no by-passes and no motorway sections! Duffle coats would be worn over the evening dress that was de rigeur for smart London parties in 1954!

Another major rally tackled that year was the Circuit of Ireland, a team of 4 TR2s being entered. Again, this was not an official Works team, but was to some extent Works sponsored, especially as one of the four cars (OHP 300) was driven by Lyndon Mills and his wife Beryl, Lyndon being head of the Standard-Triumph sales department at the time. Mary and Muriel were in OWK 888, Peter Reece and Barry Davies used TFM 400 and Bob Dickson and Jack Emmerson drove

ORW 868. Mary and Muriel won the Ladies Prize, and the TRs came second in the team prize awards, losing first place only when Dickson incurred penalty points for hitting a gatepost. Mary remembers that this rally included a high proportion of driving tests which she hugely enjoyed, and was particularly good at. In addition to the 4 TRs in the team, there were 2 other TR2s entered, and on one particular hill-climb section, the 6 TRs took the first six places!

The Scottish 24 hour Rally was also tackled, and a Premier award, a class award and the Ladies Prize were all gained. In the Redex National Rally, Mary won the "Silver Garter", a

A night halt on the 1954 Circuit of Ireland Rally sees Beryl Mills snatching a quick drink, whilst Bobby Dickson looks more like an insurance salesman than a TR Rally driver! Beryl and Lyndon Mills drove OHP 300, one of the earliest TRs of all, seen here in the background (Mary Fraser).

Desmond Titterington stands by OWK 888 as Mary Walker and Muriel Dodds are seen at the end of the 1954 Circuit of Ireland Rally. The car has clearly received a wash prior to the final ceremonies (Mary Fraser).

concept that today's feminists might consider somewhat unreconstructed! This was the award for the highest placed lady driver who was not driving a Works car. Sheila Van Damm was the highest placed female finisher, but she was in a Rootes Group Sunbeam, hence the Garter went to Mary Walker. Her photograph album proves that she and Muriel Dodds took part in the London Rally also that year, but Mary has no recollection at all of the event, other than that she thinks that they may have got seriously lost in the Welsh hills - at all events, OWK 888 did not feature in the results. Probably the greatest adventure undertaken by these two intrepid ladies was the Alpine Rally, held between the 8th and 13th July 1954. As we have seen, there was a strong Works team of 3 TR's, but Mary's entry was as usual a private one, though with some support "on the road" from the Works team and its back-up, such as it was. It must be

remembered that in the 1950's even the most major International Rallies did not attract the armies of mechanics, service crews and vehicles which follow even the more minor events today. The drivers largely helped themselves and each other, carrying a few essential spares on the cars, as well as their own personal luggage on most occasions! Standards usually sent a Vanguard Estate car as a sort of mobile office, which doubled as a camera car for Works photographer Frank Callaby and his equipment, and which also carried spares. These items would have been available to private owners competing in TR's, although the works team would naturally have had first call on any particular spare part.

The Alpine included most of the highest passes in both the Alpine and Dolomite mountain ranges, and it was on one of

The start of Mary Walker's attempt on the Alpine Rally of 1954, later to end in near disaster on the Vivione Pass (Mary Fraser).

The Vivione Pass, in northern Italy, was the end of Mary Walker's Alpine Rally in July 1954. The body and steering damage are clearly visible, as are the driver's overalls, quite daring wear for lady in 1954! (Mary Fraser).

the "hairiest" of these, the loose-surfaced Vivione in Northern Italy, that OWK 888 came to grief, as demonstrated in the accompanying photograph. Up to that point, Mary and Muriel had been going really well, but as she now admits, Mary got too enthusiastic on the loose surface and crushed the nearside of the TR2 against the mountain, fracturing the steering linkage with serious consequences for directional mobility! Once all the competing cars had passed through, it was arranged that the Italian army would scour the pass to tow in any disabled vehicles, and they were able to effect a temporary repair to the TR's steering, which enabled Mary and Muriel to drive slowly direct to the finish of the Rally at Cannes. The rally finished with a dinner at the Hotel Martinez, a gastronomic treat that the ladies had no intention of missing, bent steering or not! - Mary still has the menu from the dinner signed by all the Triumph Works team members. OWK 888 was driven sedately back to Coventry

after the event, where it was repaired at her insurance company's expense; repairs which included fitting an entire new chassis.

Following her excellent performances in these several major rallies in 1954, in the Autumn of 1954 the Factory asked Mary if she would drive in the official Works team for the 1955 Monte Carlo and Alpine Rallies. She accepted the Works drive in the 'Monte', an event she had done the previous year in a Sunbeam-Talbot, but for personal reasons, she felt she had to decline the 'Alpine' drive. As events turned out, this did not matter, for the event never took place, a victim of the wholesale cancellations consequent upon the Le Mans disaster in June 1955.

At the end of 1954 Mary not surprisingly was invited to the 'Year of Triumph' dinner given by the company which is referred to in my interview with Tom Blackburn. What was

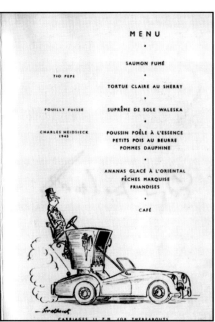

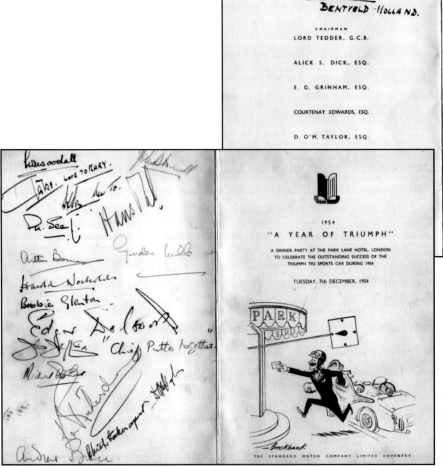

This is the signed menu card from the December 1954 "Year of Triumph" dinner, the inside above and the outside to the left. Several famous names from the TR world are discernible (Mary Fraser).

surprising however was to learn that her co-driver, Muriel Dodds, was not similarly invited, an omission that Mary has always considered somewhat mean. She recalls that the dinner itself was a hugely enjoyable event, uproarious with cabaret entertainment by magician Tommy Cooper. Again, she still has the signed menu from the event, the inscribed shooting stick presented to her and also one of the table centre decorations. This took the form of a plaster-cast model of a newsboy announcing the 'Year of Triumph', holding a chequered flag and a TR2 front medallion!

In the following month, the Monte Carlo Rally took place, but as Standards opted to run a team of the then-new Standard 10 saloons, suitably tuned, rather than the TR2's, Mary's Works drive with co-driver Betty Haig falls outside the scope of this book. In March 1955, it was RAC rally time again, and the Works team continued to field Standard 10's. Mary entered privately in her TR2, in what was to prove its last event. Although Jimmy Ray won the event outright for the factory in his Standard 10, Harold Rumsey's TR2 (LVJ 932) coming second, Mary herself could not repeat the previous year's success. Shortly after the Blackpool seafront tests, OWK 888 was in collision with a heavy lorry whilst Mary's co-driver (not Muriel Dodds this time) was driving. She was later charged with several motoring offences including dangerous driving, but was ultimately completely exonerated. However, it was the end of the Rally for the ladies, and it caused OWK 888 to have to receive its third chassis frame, and this in a car barely 12 months old - what price 'originality' in TRs that are now approaching their 40th year? Although the TR was properly repaired, Mary felt that it had had a sufficiently hard life to justify replacement, and therefore it was sold to someone in the Newcastle area and a

new TR was ordered. This car was a late TR2, with the short doors and chromed reveal moulding around the air intake. It was registered JJR 888, the recurrence of the triple '8' being no coincidence! The original colour was red, but Mary did not care for this, nor for any of the other rather plain colours then being offered on TRs. The colour that had caught her eye was a light metallic steel blue being used by the Rootes Group on Sunbeam-Talbots, and thus she arranged to have the new TR2 resprayed in this colour, called Alpine Mist, shortly after delivery. Other personal touches were added, including chromed rimbellishers, a chromed strip along the sills and front wings, (from a Humber Hawk, Mary recalls) a bonnet mascot and an unusual hardtop. this did not have the works style wrap-around rear window, and was possibly a Universal Laminations top. It came with modified, rigid perspex sliding sidescreens, making the car really weatherproof for the Borders winters.

Although JJR 888 saw limited use in rallies it was not campaigned in the manner of OWK 888, Mary gradually dropping out of the rallying scene. This process was assisted by her marriage to Doctor Fraser, who was not keen on her continuing to take the inevitable personal risks associated with top-flight motoring competition. JJR 888 continued to be her personal transport for some years, Mary still enjoying high speed TR motoring, even if no longer competing. Her notes attached to the photographs she lent me of JJR 888 made it clear that she wondered what today's TR enthusiasts would make of her TR's personal touches and its respray in Alpine Mist, including, dare I say it, the imitation leopard skin seat covers that are just visible in one of the photographs - a real 'period' accessory! In comparison with another TR2 she told me about, however, the Alpine Mist colour sounds quite

Mary Walker's second TR2, JJR 888, was fitted with the luxurious and rare "Universal Laminations" hardtop. Wheel trims and an extra chrome flash add to the distinction (Mary Fraser).

restrained, for in Scotland at that time was a bright yellow TR2, MSP 200, owned by Lord Bruce (now the Earl of Elgin). Evidently this yellow, described by Mary as a 'ghastly yellow' and by the Standard Triumph Review as a "Rich Yellow", was the family colour in which all their vehicles were painted, the TR rallied by Lord Bruce being no exception!

sidescreen TRs, Peter Clarke.

Peter was an apprentice at the Standard-Triumph works in the second half of the 1950's, very much in the heyday of the cars under review, but not only that, he also spent a considerable part both of his apprenticeship and subsequent time

Lord Bruce (now the Earl of Elgin) corners hard in his TR2 on the Highland Rally. This is the car referred to in the interview with Mary (Walker) Fraser which was specially painted in the family colour of "Rich Yellow". Would that this had been a colour shot! ("Autosport").

As to the problems with the TRs, the principal one was of course the brakes, especially with the white car which 'would never pull up in a straight line, especially when cold,' to quote the owner. The usual modifications were tried, but braking always remained marginal, even with wire wheels to aid cooling. Even when fully warmed up, the brakes could still behave oddly, Mary recalls. The second car, which had the larger rear drums was somewhat better, although it was never used as hard as had been OWK 888. Mary did not experience the gearbox and axle problems that visited themselves upon many early TR2's and their owners and mechanically both the cars proved reliable both in competition and in daily transport. She thought the modifications incorporated into the TR2 during its production run made her second car a much better and more practical vehicle than the first one, though one feels that the comfort engendered by the presence of hardtop and heater may have been somewhat influential here!

Mary retains to this day a keen interest in the TR series, and when by chance she encountered a party of TR owners touring the Highlands of Scotland in their cars during the summer of 1993, she managed to have herself photographed in a sidescreen TR, and, as she told me, found it as much as she could do to stop herself charging up the road in the car, such were the memories rekindled!

Following my encounters with several TR drivers from the 1950's, I was fortunate to make contact with someone who was involved with the building rather than the driving of the

with the firm in the Competitions Department, working for the most part under Ken Richardson's direction. Peter's reminiscences are relevant not only to this current chapter, but also have a place in the chapter on car production (Chapter Two) and more of the detail I gleaned from him can be found there. In fact much of his working life has concerned Triumph TRs, for even today he is involved with restoring TRs to a very high standard from his base not far from the old Coventry Plant, which Peter confirms was always known simply as "The Standard" to the workforce!

Clarke joined the factory fresh from school around the end of 1954, at a time when TR2 production was very much into its stride and increasing rapidly. One of his earliest memories is of the amount of hand manufacturing and fitting that went on with TR2 panels (something that will come as no surprise to today's restorers!), including the use of the traditional wheeling machine for fettling panelwork, especially bonnets. Joining as a "lad" he confirms that he had to sit an examination after some months of working to see if he was fit to be taken on for one of the coveted five year apprenticeships. Fortunately he passed and commenced his apprenticeship, initially working for a short period in various sections of the factory to gain diverse experience, including a period in 1956 on the TR3 and Standard 10 production lines. Eventually, he was selected for work in the Competitions Department which not surprisingly was a highly-sought after position, and he spent the whole of the latter part of his 5 years' apprenticeship in that department, right up to its summary closure following the Leyland takeover. In

Top left: an early TR2, with a Works style deep aero screen, driven by Desmond Titterington (who later went on to successfully race "D" Type Jaguars) at Phoenix Park, Dublin, leading an MG TD and a Dellow ("Autosport"). Above: At the Eight-Clubs Silverstone Race meeting in May 1954, PJ Agg's TR2 lost a front wheel. Fortunately, it came to rest without crashing and is captured here by the "Autosport" photographer with the wheel in mid-flight! Left: the dominance of TRs in amateur motor sport is well demonstrated by this September 1955 view of a clubman's race at Oulton Park. There are no fewer than six TRs in the first eight cars, the leading pair here being driven by TH Carnley and TP Taylor. Surprisingly, front bumpers are fitted to these cars! ("Autosport"). Below left: this TR2 failed at Simms Hill on the MCC Exeter Trial and suffered the indignity of being towed up by a tractor! (LAT Photographic). Below: marshals flee from J Gamble's spinning TR2 during the Silverstone "Eight Clubs" meeting ("Autosport").

Left: A really mixed bag of sporting machinery lines up for an unknown event in 1957. The event looks to be a sprint on an airfield and the TR3 stands in front of a vintage 30/98 Vauxhall, a Jaguar XK coupe and a mixed bag of other cars ("Autosport").

Below: SKT 606 acts as an impromptu map table for its crew in early 1955, during the Cambridge University Motor Club's "Miniature Monte" Rally. The driver and navigator were J Pay and A Burgess (LAT Photographic).

Above: Surely a case of: "the pot calling the kettle black"? A TR-mounted marshall carries out a noise check on a (much quieter!) MGA during the Lancashire Auto Club's Lancashire Cup Rally in August 1957 ("Autosport").

Right: Described as "25-year-old schoolteacher turned housewife, this is Yvonne Strawbridge, who was about to campaign her slightly scruffy-looking TR2 in the Swansea Motor Club's "Rally of the Vales". We don't know the year, but can it have been easy to rally drive a TR2 in four-inch heels? ("Autosport").

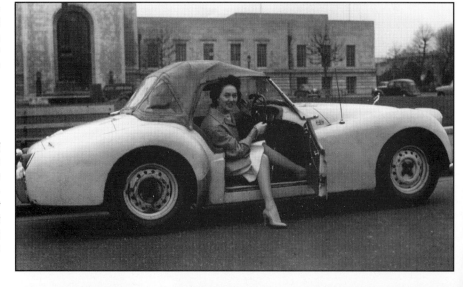

fact, he rejoined Competitions in 1964, helping to build the Works Spitfires amongst others, but that period is outside the scope of this book.

I enquired as to the size of the Competitions Department in the late 1950's, and Peter Clarke recalls that in total around 25 people were involved, comprising perhaps 10 or 12 fitters, 3 body men, 3 or 4 apprentices, a foreman (Ben Warwick followed by Alf Woodyer during his time) a secretary, Ken Richardson and Ken's deputy and assistant. The department was very much linked to the Service Department, and there was some blurring between the functions of the two. Keen TR owners would bring their cars for service and modification to the factory rather than take them to their local dealers, even in cases where they lived a hundred or more miles from Coventry. No doubt they considered (and probably correctly) that they would receive the best attention, and certainly the most up-to-the-minute modifications. Peter recalls working on one particular Geranium TR2 that had a salmon painted on its side, no doubt a tongue-in-cheek reference to its colour. He further recalls that the junior staff in Comps were very much in awe of Ken Richardson, who was seen as "Management" rather than "factory", everyday discipline being left to the foremen, hence only the gravest misdemeanours warranted a "carpeting" before KR himself!

Peter's earliest job in the department involved polishing and gas flowing of cylinder heads, both for Works and customers cars, and such cars would usually be subsequently taken out by the time-served fitters for running in and for road test, Clarke and his fellow apprentices sometimes going along when "second men" were needed to check and record instrument readings. Occasionally cars were taken for test and evaluation to the Motor Industry Research Association test track (MIRA) near Nuneaton, and to be "second man" on such occasions was considered a highly-coveted and fascinating experience. Surprisingly, the Competitions Department had no rolling-road facility, which explains why such "trial and error" testing at MIRA occurred. There were of course more comprehensive testing facilities in the Engineering Department, but surprisingly little direct liaison took place between this department and Competitions. To work in Comps, Service or Engineering was considered very much superior to (and a promotion from) the factory itself, for these departments comprised almost all skilled personnel, the elite of the labour force.

Peter later got involved in the preparation of the TR3A rally cars, both the Works team cars and those of private entrants. Like Ken Richardson, he too confirmed that the privately-owned cars were treated in the same way as the Works cars, and given the same modifications - "which is why they sometimes won" as he wryly observed! It was indeed possible to order an almost exact replica of the latest specification Works TR3As, and Clarke confirms that several such cars were built.

As to the building process undergone by the serious compe-

Peter Clarke lent me an original copy of this well-known photograph, a copy of which was affixed for some years to the Competition Department workshop wall at the factory. The event was the 1960 Tulip Rally, in which David Siegle-Morris, driving his own TR3A, registered D 20, beat all the Works cars! Seen in this picture are, from left to right: Messrs Turner, Ballisat, Siegle-Morris, Elford, Brooks, Crelling and Slotemaker. Note the re-positioned sidelights on WVC 250 (P Clarke).

tition TRs, Peter confirmed that fully finished cars were removed from the production line, taken to the Competitions department, and there largely "unbuilt". The engines were fully stripped for reworking - what is now called "blueprinting", - the gearboxes were stripped and sent for checking and rebuilding to the experimental transmission shop, and the overdrive units were stripped, fettled and tuned by engineers from Laycocks, Peter recalling that during the late 1950's a Laycock man was on site at Coventry virtually full time. The axles were however left alone, which ties in with what TR competition men have found for themselves over the past 35 years, namely that the "Girling" axles on later TR3s and 3As are virtually unbreakable, probably the most reliable part on a very reliable car! After this stripping and checking operation, the cars were then very carefully reassembled incorporating any modifications required by individual drivers, road tested, rectified where necessary and then run in. The Works' own competition TRs were re-stripped and checked after every major event, and in some cases, the engines were dispatched exactly as removed from the cars to the Engineering department for evaluation, accurate measurements of wear being taken. Thus did competition motoring actually help to improve the production car, as it is always to supposed to. As an aside, Peter added that the TR3A rally cars almost always had oil coolers fitted, in addition to the large capacity cast aluminium sumps.

As he was still an apprentice, Peter Clarke was unable to accompany the teams either on Rallies or to Le Mans, time served men only being used for these events. However, he did relate that he visited Le Mans "unofficially" in 1960, having taken some latitude with time off work, in order to see the TR team that he had helped to prepare actually race. He was of course spotted there, and ended up in the pits giving a hand; however, upon return to Coventry he was requested to explain his presence! Peter also mentioned an unofficial way in which the Competitions Department's very limited budget was "stretched", for on occasions parts would be "borrowed" on some pretext from the main production facility, and would fail to find their way back. Having spent time in all the main factory departments, most of the fitting staff working under Ken Richardson were well known around the stores and production line area and their presence would excite little comment - hence trips were made at times of stress for parts - (quite heavy ones at times evidently!) - which did not pass through the official records. As mentioned elsewhere, the Competitions department had to "buy" its cars and spares from the factory out of its meagre budget of around £18,000 per annum (not including salaries)! On a few occasions, ex-Publicity fleet cars were "bought" by the Works team to save money over the cost of a brand new car - SKV 656 being such an example - and this practice also helped to stretch the budget.

Later in his apprenticeship Peter Clarke helped to build the twin-cam Le Mans "Sabrina" engined cars, which were constructed in the Competition Department. He recalls that the machining of parts for these specialised engines was done in the main factory, but assembly of the engines took place the Experimental engineering departments, where the foreman was Ted Silver, and amongst the fitters were Doug West and Lou Webster, engines being tested by Freddie Cooper and the team. Incidentally, I have heard from another source that the castings and some other parts for the twin-cam motors were made by Bean Industries Ltd, but I have not been able to confirm this.

Peter Clarke looks back today on his time in the Competitions Department as a happy one - it was, as he says, "a good gang to be part of" - they could see the direct results of the work they were performing, there was always something of interest going on, and the high degree of autonomy allowed to the Department kept outside interference down to tolerable levels. Budget constraints were always a factor, but there were certain ways round these as we have seen, and it was only in the 1960/61 period when his apprenticeship was expiring that the Company's deteriorating financial position caused a real curtailment of activity. He confirms that the winter of 1960/61 was a really worrying time for the whole of the workforce, and that there was a great sense of relief all round when in the Spring of 1961 the Leyland takeover was announced - even though this meant the demise for a time of the Competitions Department. Peter Clarke himself was transferred to the production lines at at the main plant in Coventry, not a move he relished at the time. By 1964 however, he was back in the re-formed Competitions Department, involved with the rallying Triumph 2000 saloons and the Le Mans and Sebring Spitfires amongst others. Following this interview with Peter Clarke, I propose to deal somewhat more briefly with several other TR drivers from the 1950's and 1960's commencing with Mrs Cherry Osborn.

Through the efforts of John Saunders and Peter Gorrie, long standing TR Register members and owners of several early TRs, I have acquired a copy of a letter written to John Saunders back in 1973 by Cherry Osborn, a lady who, like Mary Walker, was involved with rallying TRs and who drove for the Works team on at least three occasions, co-driving with Lola Grounds. They campaigned TR2 PKV 697 on the 1955 Tulip Rally, a Standard 10 in the 1956 Tulip Rally, and a Standard Vanguard III in the 1956 Monte Carlo Rally.

Mrs Osborn, driving with her husband, who was I understand the Company Doctor at Standard Triumphs during the 1950's, first came to the notice of Ken Richardson whilst

Above left: This TR2 is believed to have been bought new by famous racing driver Earl Howe. Here it is at night on an unknown rally in the 1950s. TPP 2 is not known to have survived, but the TR behind it, OVU 30 is undergoing major restoration. Above right: Outside Broadcast cameras are in action on 25th January 1958, when the Hagley & District CC promoted the Ken Wharton Memorial inter-region driving tests. Here, TR2 RLH 8 is being piloted round the pylons by TD Warren of the South-West team ("Autosport"). Below left: Peter Bolton and Peter Craven, seen here in an early TR2, were a very successful partnership in 1950s rallies. This view shows them about to start the Yorkshire "Mille Miglia" Rally on 13th February 1959 ("Autosport").

Above right: Ron Goldbourn looks somewhat dour as he awaits the re-start at a night halt in the Lancashire Cup Rally on 30th August 1958. 930 DEH was one of several sidescreen TRs he was associated with and, surprisingly for a hard-worked car, it survives. The rally was won by TA Gold, also TR-mounted ("Autosport"). Below left: two TRs are in evidence in this shot of the Bolton Rally on 22nd February 1958. TKA 357 is driven by Ron Goldbourn and navigated by Stuart Turner, who won the event outright. Thier prize was a new Speedwell-tuned Austin A35 which was described as the "most valuable prize ever offered for a motor rally in Britain" ("Autosport"). Below right: the Irish-registered TR2 of Raymond Laird at Blackpool during the 1956 RAC Rally. This car was reputedly borrowed by Standard-Triumph for its "IT" registration to feature in the "Here IT is" series of advertisements for the TR2, though no photographic evidence has been found to support this assertion (David Burrows).

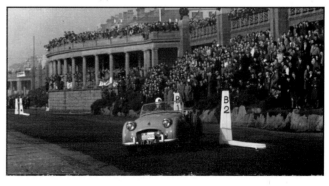

competing with some success in an early TR2, registered OVC 272 (TS 875). Unfortunately I gather that both Dr and Mrs Osborn are no longer with us, so I am only able to quote at secondhand from her letter, written to John whilst he was the owner of OVC 272, a car only four numbers away from OVC 276, the Works Mille Miglia TR2. In this letter Cherry Osborn confirms that she and her husband needed the influence granted to them by virtue of his position within the Company to obtain an early TR2, OVC 272 being supplied to them direct in March 1954 by the Works, hence the Coventry registration, without it ever passing through a dealer's hands. Incidentally, the factory records state that the car was to be supplied to Attwood's Garage in Stafford, which was clearly not the case, and further proves that you cannot necessarily trust all that you read, even in official sources! Maybe a "short-circuit" operated, and Attwoods received a somewhat later car, or possibly it was another case, like Mary Walker's car, of a dealer "supplying" a car that they did not in fact receive, the "supply" being only a paper transaction.

OVC 272 was black, had no extras, not even a heater, yet Mrs Osborn describes it as a "magnificent motor car from the word 'go'." It never did less than 40 mpg, even when pushed hard on rallies, and rallies it did in abundance, 3 London Rallies, 2 RAC Internationals, 2 Daily Express rallies and more, as well as numerous local rallies and club driving tests. It was used also for sprinting, and competed regularly at Prescott and Shelsley Walsh hill climbs, as well as providing everyday transport. She mentions that it was as a result of her efforts in the 1955 RAC Rally that Ken Richardson asked her to join the Works team on an occasional basis. This TR2 was kept I understand for almost three years, and Cherry Osborn makes no mention of any serious mechanical failure. Following its sale to another enthusiast who also

campaigned it with some success, the Osborns replaced OVC 272 with a series of three TR3s and 3As, all bought direct from the factory, and all ex-works rally cars, although unfortunately the letter does not identify them. Each of these was fully stripped, rectified and rebuilt prior to delivery to them, yet Mrs Osborn states categorically that none of the three was the equal of that first TR2 in terms of performance, something that I have heard other drivers who owned both early and later sidescreen cars confirm.

Cherry Osborn describes in her letter what she she called the TR2's "one little idiosyncrasy". This she says taught her to drive better, for it was the car's tendency to plough straight on if one approached a corner a little too fast and then had to brake. "Nothing one did in such circumstances had any effect," she says, adding that she once ended up in a farmyard and did not forget the experience! This car utilised an early set of Michelin 'X' tyres, which she mentioned "really hung on as long as the driver hung on to his or her nerve" - Although we now think of those early radials as marginal, to say the least, on TRs, her description of them shows what an advance they were in the mid 1950's over the primitive crossply tyres in general use. Clearly Cherry Osborn enjoyed her time with her TRs, and looking back some 15 or more years later, had fond memories of the period, although she describes her Works drives as "hair raising as well as interesting!" It was a great pity that I was unable to encounter the lady, but I am sure that she would be pleased to know that OVC 272 is in good hands and is currently undergoing a full rebuild, having survived for 40 years against the odds, for it was certainly for many years a hard worked machine.

Ian Hall, a leading member of the Vintage Sports Car Club these days driving Rileys and a Frazer Nash, was a further

OVC 272 was the black TR2 belonging to Standard-Triumph's company doctor, Dr WH Osborn and his wife, Cherry. It was much rallied by them with no little success, Mrs Osborn eventually being invited to drive for the Works team. The car is seen here on an unknown event in the mid-1950s (John Saunders).

Above left: a TR2, wearing the now-rare TSOA badge, is flung round the bollards of a driving test course in the Fifties ("Autosport"). Above right: spotlamps abound on 897 AEH, driven by J Bullough on the Morecambe CC Illuminations Rally in September 1958. The marshal inspects his watch, sp departure must be imminent ("Autosport"). Below left (upper): a Works drive in WVC 250 was given to Ernest McMillen for the 1959 Circuit of Ireland. Very soon after this picture was taken, a major crash saw his rally ended, the car apparently being recovered by train! ("Autosport"). Below right: Ron Dalglish, winner of the 1959 Scottish Rally, poses with his TR3 after the event. His co-driver was George Brass. Note the heavy-duty winter trads on the rear tyres ("Autosport"). Bottom left: an atmospheric night rally shot sees a TR competitor checked by a well-wrapped marshal who seems to be wearing a lamp on a neck-band! Note the added boot handle on the TR, in place of the original budget lock. The event was the 1956 Lancashire Cup Rally ("Autosport").

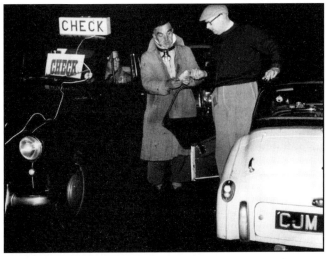

An unknown TR-ist struggles beneath his car in the paddock prior to a race: the car appears to be supported only by a hydraulic jack - not a wise practice! ("Autosport").

1950's TR rally competitor I contacted, and he kindly set down a few of his memories for me. In the main, Ian navigated rather than drove, though then as now, navigators were expected to drive some of the less tricky road sections to give the driver a break. Although he modestly claims little success in the club and national rallies entered, he eventually graduated to the Rootes Group Works team in the 1960's, so clearly Ian was no novice.

His earliest TR2 experiences were as navigator for Ken James in PKF 357 (TS 942), a March 1954 TR2 with wire wheels, finished in the very unusual Olive Yellow paint, and sporting a Geranium pink hood and side screens. As Ian says, "this was a sensation in 1954, but in truth, looking back, it was a quite horrible colour scheme." They did virtually all the North Western rallies during that season, thrashing round the lanes and hills of North Wales in the middle of the night, and generally giving this car a hard time, so much so that it was soon replaced by an ex-works demonstrator, a red TR2 purchased directly from Lyndon Mills, the Director of Sales. Ian considers himself very lucky, for in the first rally that Ken James did in this later car without Ian as navigator, the car turned over and was comprehensively damaged, fortunately without seriously injuring the crew.

On one of the tough Morecambe rallies, Ian Hall found himself navigating for Ralph Whiterley in a further red TR2, and they met a fellow competitor head on while negotiating the ford at Elterwater in the Lake District. This encounter caused the TR's fan to puncture the radiator, a not uncommon malaise. Their rally thus came to an abrupt end, and the rest of the weekend was spent in an alcoholic haze until Ian had come round sufficiently to drive the TR back to Liverpool. He

recalls touching 105 mph along the old A6 on this journey, and adds that upon reflection, he thinks that most of the rally lads of those days were mad! In addition, some of those Northern events were little more than thinly disguised road races - he cites the Bolton Rally as including a lap of the 'B' road surrounding Lake Vyrnwy at an average speed of 56 mph in one of its supplementary sections! Upon reflection, it is hard to see how rally organisers got away with some of their routes and timings, even in the more carefree atmosphere that obtained at that time, and it is little wonder than much more strict regulations later ensued, with rallying becoming more confined to private forestry land, at least for the seriously competitive sections. Still, the thought of a

Ian Hall, the navigator, clings on to the TR2's passenger door, whilst his driver charges around a rally special test (Ian Hall).

Above left: Fred Snaylan waits to be sent off from the Llandrindod Wells control on a major rally in 1958. As can be seen from his TR and the one behind, roof-mounted swivelling spotlights (now illegal!) were de-rigeur at the time. Above right: This TR2 seems to be getting seriously bogged down on a trials hill at an unknown event. The versatility of the sidescreen TR was legendary: anything from muddy hills to international rallies and circuit racing ("Autosport").

Blackpool Tower features prominently in this shot taken on 27th October 1956. WB Holland brings his TR3 up to the timing beam apparatus during the tests that finished the Blackpool Rally. The "free show" seems to have drawn many spectators to the seafront ("Autosport").

TRs are very much to the fore on this starting grid, the eight front runners all being TR2 mounted. Some run with bumpers in place and disc-wheeled cars predominate. The location is Goodwood and the year is believed to be 1956 ("Autosport").

dozen or more TR2s and TR3s blatting through the Welsh Mountain night at 3 am with their raucous exhausts bellowing a concerted war cry does stir the blood more than somewhat!

Also recalled was a "Rally of the Dams" done with Harry Jacoby from St Helens in a brand new red TR3. They drove into a mill pond at high speed at around 3 am and not surprisingly stopped fairly quickly! Ian opened the door and again not surprisingly, the pond came in - Harry opened his door to let it out, but it refused to go, and thus the crew suffered somewhat, as did the new car. They eventually managed to restart the car and drive out of the pond on the other side, only to find that there was no road there. Harry then attempted to drive back through the water to the point of original entry, but in doing so he decided on what to him appeared to be a "better" route through the water, only to find that it wasn't! As Ian now ruefully admits, the TR3 "sank with all hands" and a long, wet walk finally procured a tractor tow at around 5.30 am. This cost a fiver (about £60 in today's terms) and Ian suspects that his driver is still upset about the cost of the affair! The following year the same pair came second overall in this event, this time in a green TR2, 702 FRF, which was one of Ian Hall's best results. He also ral-

lied with Eric Hotley from Haydock, another TR2 campaigner, whose first car was, as Ian describes it, "an early pink one, with tin wheels!". This is recalled as being both very fast and very economical - how often does one hear that in connection with these earliest TRs? - and considerably better than the later, red car that took its place. One night in the "pink" TR with Eric on the "Jeans Cup" rally, they managed to charge up a dried up river bed, having failed to negotiate a left hander following a brow. The car was not too badly damaged, but was unable to extricate itself. It was 1.30 am, but by a handy chance, a group of drunken potholers were abroad in this part of the Dales, and they manhandled the battered TR back onto the highway, whereupon the crew continued. On a later Jeans Cup Rally they stopped to pick up a fellow TR-ist who had stuffed his new TR3 into a wall, and been somewhat hurt. The proximity of the three men in a confined 2-seater caused much blood to soil Ian's maps, but they got to the finish, despite this "merry dash". A further Lakeland Rally saw Eric and Ian put their red TR2 straight through a dry stone wall and into the meadow beyond - no seat belts, no crash hats and no injuries, amazingly. Again, they were able to get the battered TR back to the road, and to continue to the finish, yet another tribute to the strength of the sidescreen TRs.

Interesting machinery is on view in this photograph from 1958, showing a rally checkpoint in Herefordshire. The TR3 is driven by B Smith and M Dando, the Jaguar by Cyril Johnson. Valerie Domleo and Pauline Mayman are Morgan-mounted and Jacoby & Webster bring up the rear in a new TR3A ("Autosport").

August 1958 and a TR2, accompanied by a TR3A, waltz together at Goodwood ("Autosport").

Reminiscing from the 1990's, Ian Hall considers that the best crews from those days, albeit amateur, were really very, very good - indeed, as we have seen, several were invited into Works teams in due course. The events were hairy, and safety precautions non-existent - fun there was in good measure, but accidents were frequent, with bent cars commonplace. Alcohol was not unknown either, both to keep out the cold, and to fire up courage. There were some serious injuries, one has to say, having regard to the nature of the

Above: D Taylor is caught in the act of "having a moment" at Cadwell Park in March 1956. The report does not indicate the outcome, but it must have been during a rally, not a race, as indicated by the loose surface and lack of competition numbers on the car ("Autosport").

events and driving which at times bordered on the reckless, it was remarkable how few really nasty incidents occurred.

Another very early sprint and race competitor in a TR2 was Monty Seal, whose son Roger has provided me with an excellent set of photographs of his father competing during the 1954/5 period. Mr Seal was able to obtain delivery of a TR2 in 1953, his car being TS 122, built on 23rd November 1953. As was usual, no choice of colour was given, the car being a further example finished in the embarrassing Geranium pink colour. It also came with interior trim finished in the unusual metric or wicker pattern, which appeared both on some very early TR2s and again on various early TR3s. The car was supplied and registered in Cardiff, and must have been about the first TR in Wales, the actual registered number being JBO 3.

This TR was competed regularly during its first two years, the photographs showing that it had lost its front bumper very early in life, and had gained one of the rare original factory type aeroscreens. Incidentally one of the meetings in which Monte Seal drove his TR was the Prescott Hill Climb of 9th April 1955. This meeting was notable for the presence of the BBC Television Outside Broadcast vans and cameras - not the sort of event one can imagine national television covering in the 1990's! Many years later, in the mid 1970's, Roger Seal decided to see if he could locate his father's old TR2; after much diligent research, he finally tracked it down to a

Below left: although only a few months old, JBO 3 has already lost its front bumper in the interests of weight saving. Note the extra depth (and extra protection thereby afforded) of the original factory-type aero screen as compared with the modern item (Roger Seal). Below right: the start line at Prescott in May 1954 sees Monty Seal about to commence his climb. A Frazer-Nash, a Jaguar XK120 and a now-classic coach add flavour to the scene (Roger Seal).

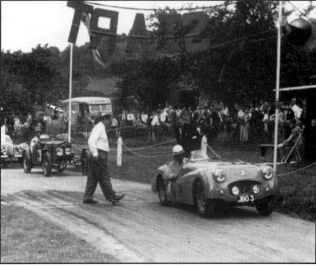

scrapyard in Southern England, only to learn that it had been broken up shortly before his visit!

Another family with long-term TR connections is the West family, Robert West being a keen current TR Register member with a historic TR3A. For many years his grandfather was a director of West's Garage of Lincoln, Standard Triumph agents, and his father, Lawrence West, campaigned a TR2 in the mid 1950's in many rallies with some success, his mother being the navigator/co-driver in several of them! Their mount was a TR2 registered JFE 958, and I have been able to borrow a photograph of the car competing in the 1955 London Rally,

In fact I had a surprisingly large response to my appeals for contacts with people who had owned and driven sidescreen TRs when they were new, more in fact than this book allows space for. I was also fortunate in locating someone who competed in a TR2 when these cars were very much at their low point, in the early 1970's. At this time, when they were worth very little, spares were scarce and when almost anyone with any pretentions to climbing the rally ladder was driving a hot Mini, to find a sidescreen TR in any form of competition motoring was a real rarity, with the exception of Reg Woodcock's highly developed racing TR3.

Ian Griffiths from Somerset purchased his TR2, ODF 538, for £50, in 1969, it having suffered a front end collision. With it came a TR3A-style fibreglass front panel and front wing with which Ian was able to repair the car at minimal cost. By late 1970, the car was again roadworthy and was entered in the Weston Super Mare speed trials. For the next two years, Ian Griffiths entered his battered £50 TR in any sort of Club event he could find, sand racing, club rallying, sprints, as well as using it as his only and everyday transport. Parts were obtained where possible from scrapyards, for sidescreen TRs were commonly found in such places then. As an aside, my researches over the years have led me to conclude that the average lifespan of a TR2/3/3A in Great Britain was 13 - 15 years, the majority being scrapped in the years between 1967 and 1972, for in the latter year, the price trend for sidescreen cars reversed, and values began their slow climb. Quite a high percentage of TRs had been written off as a

Lawrence West's TR2 charges along a loose-surfaced pass during the 1955 London Motor Club's London Rally. The white hood was unusual for the time and the purpose of the two stripes on the rear wing can only be conjectured at (Lawrence West).

Left: Goodwood Circuit was usd for tests in the 1955 RAC Rally. Here, Aubrey Wilds puts his early TR2 through its paces (LAT Photographic). Above: the "Cats Eyes" Rally in early 1955. This TR2 was entered by D Llewellyn-Rees and must have been running cool, judging from the cardboard blanking off the radiator grille (LAT Photographic).

result of accident prior to this period of course, and (as a guess) between 15 and 20% of UK supplied cars survive today.

Ian Griffiths suffered the usual trials of any impecunious novice trying to come to grips with rallying, frequently damaging the car, and spending much of the week putting right the problems occasioned by the previous weekend's competitive motoring. He had to sleep in his broken down TR on more than one occasion, and had constant trouble with wire wheels breaking, so much so that he went back to disc wheels eventually. However, one of his photographs shows ODF 538 competing in a 12 car rally with disc wheels on the front and wires on the back! Finally, after two seasons of hard motoring and hard work, Ian moved on to the inevitable Mini Cooper and the TR2 was sold - does it survive, I wonder? However, even at 17 years old and at the bottom of its depreciation curve, there was enough life left in the car to give a young man a lot of fun and to enable him to start competitive motoring for the proverbial "price of a packet of fags!" His experience was by no means untypical, for although early TRs were rare in competitive events by the early 1970's, in the mid 1960's hundreds of drivers had launched motoring careers of varying success with a cheap, cheerful and reliable old TR! Most sidescreen TR owners these days have had the experience of returning to their parked car to find a gentleman in his late 40's or 50's lurking by the vehicle, only too ready to talk about how he and his friends bought them for pennies in the late 1960's, ran them on hot air, pulled the birds, had lucky escapes and loads of fun, which latter is surely the main point of sports cars!

I hope that in this chapter I have managed to convey something of the flavour of what it was like to use sidescreen TRs competitively in their heyday, as well as providing, via Peter Clarke, a modicum of information on the goings on at the

Left: this TR action shot comes from South Africa. Unfortunately, no details are known, but it would appear to be a gymkhana of some kind (TR Register Archive). Below: in July 1955, a race specially for TR2s took place at Snetterton circuit and from this picture, it would appear some drivers were trying a little too hard! (LAT Photographic).

Ian Griffiths, seen at a night halt on a 12-car rally in the early 1970s, driving his £50 TR2 as described in this Chapter. This car's condition was typical of so many ageing TRs at the time, battered but still giving both transport and pleasure. A fibreglass TR3A front is fitted. The presence of wire wheels at the rear and disc wheels at the front must have raised a few eyebrows! (Ian Griffiths).

Works at the time. What came across to me most clearly in all the interviews was that no-one regretted their time spent with the sidescreen TRs, and without exception all looked back with fond memories to that period of more carefree, informal motoring!

Top left: a driving test on the Rally of the Dams of 16th October 1956 is ideal work for long-door TR2 GCK 670. The crew's names are not noted (NMM Beaulieu).

Above: the unknown driver of this TR2 really presses on up Prescott Hill on 24th July 1955, revealing near to the maximum "lean" available to a TR2 prior to inversion! (NMM Beaulieu).

Left: a splendid Fifties period rally shot, taken on 21st September 1956 during the London Rally. JWH 570 (driver unknown) sports a hardtop, retrospectively fitted as this is an early TR2. The marshals have a snug Sunbeam-Talbot 90 Drophead to shelter in between arrivals (NMM Beaulieu).

Above left: sunglasses adorn the unknown driver of TR2 RXO 881 as he races, probably at Goodwood (wouldn't happen today!) (NMM Beaulieu).

On the right, John Quick races a very unmodified-looking TR3A at Goodwood on 23rd September 1961 (NMM Beaulieu).

Top left: this delightful period photograph appeared on the front cover of "Autosport" on 29th March 1957. It shows racing in Sweden, at the Karslkoga circuit. L Sundin's TR2 sports a home-made aero screen and is seen cornering hard as it leads an MGA ("Autosport"). On the right above, Betty Haig is seen fixing a rally transfer to her TR3 prior to the 1958 Monte Carlo Rally. Hers was a private entry, running alongside the Works team of four TR3As. Whether the box on the boot was a tuning aid or just contained lunch is not recorded! ("Autosport").

Above: this is about the only photograph I've ever seen of a Standard Vanguard racing! The circuit is Oulton Park, the date is November 1960 and the event is the high-speed part of an economy run. The TR3A, which should have had few problems staying ahead of the saloon, was driven by R Grant ("Autosport").

Little can be gleaned of the TR disaster on the right, for the photograph, found in "Autosport" archives, reveals only that the driver was R McArthur. However, BSH 374 must have been rebuilt, for it survives on the TR Register, although its present condition is unknown ("Autosport").

CHAPTER FIVE:
A Sidescreen TR Miscellany

Into this Chapter, and in Chapter Nine, I am placing various items and anecdotes that I hope will be of interest to sidescreen TR enthusiasts, but which do not fall conveniently into any of the main chapter headings. Rather than link each separate section with extraneous words, it seems more efficient of space to utilise numbered paragraphs, albeit at the expense of literary style, and I hope that the reader will forgive this somewhat disjointed approach. The paragraphs are not in any particular order, and are in effect a collection of sundry TR items that have come my way over the years.

1. WVC 251 - this car has been something of a puzzle to TR historians over the years. The four 1959/60 Works team cars were of course registered WVC 247 to WVC 250, but photographic evidence proves that a fifth car, WVC 251, built to the same specification, also existed. Ken Richardson has now confirmed to me that he used this TR as his personal road car for some time, and that it was retained by Standard-Triumphs at the end of 1960 when the other "WVC" cars were sold off. Recent research by Graham Robson has revealed that this car was in fact the last sidescreen TR ever to be used by the Works as an official (or at least, semi-official) entry, for in May 1961 "Tiny" Lewis, partnered by A. Nash, drove it in the Acropolis Rally, finishing tenth overall. The car is not known to have survived and its commission number is unknown, though it would have been in the 39,000's, built in November 1958. A photograph shows Richardson inspecting what must have been the WVC cars though the caption from "Autosport" states that there were six of them, and that they were being prepared for the 1959 Monte Carlo Rally - if Autosport is correct, which was the mystery sixth car, I wonder?

2. At the 1956 Earls Court Motor Show in London, Standard-Triumph exhibited a TR3 with bodywork in "see-through" perspex or plexi-glass, all the mechanical parts thus being rendered visible. The car appears to have been fully operational, though one wonders whether anyone actually drove it! It was in left hand drive form with wire wheels and disc brakes, and was I believe exhibited during 1957 at various others motor exhibitions throughout the world - no-one I have spoken to knows for sure what became of it, although Alec Pringle of the TR Register has heard the following story: evidently it was in store at the Belgian TR importers in the early 1960's, and a Belgian wine merchant tried to purchase it as a display piece for his restaurant! He was told that it was not for sale, for it was only on loan from Standard-Triumphs, so he purchased a new TR4 instead. Rumour is that the 'Plexiglass' car eventually reached the USA.

3. In September 1956, a £50 bet was laid by the Royal Aero Club, and accepted by the British Automobile Racing Club, that an aeroplane would carry two people from Lands End to John O'Groats and on to London using less fuel than a car doing a similar journey! The speed and known economy of the TR led to this being the chosen vehicle, the actual car used being SVC 368. SRW 990 was also supplied as a support car, both cars coming from the Factory's publicity fleet, although SRW 990 did see brief use as a Works competition car. The two drivers were Lord Selsdon and Lord Essendon, who had both been racing drivers pre-war. The TR won the bet by a considerable margin, covering 1573 miles in 43 hours 10 minutes using 36.6 gallons of petrol, which works out at 43 mpg. The aircraft, an Auster J4, was obviously quicker, but used 61 gallons to cover 1347 miles at only 22 mpg, and Standard-Triumphs made much of this exploit in

This is part of the front cover of a Standard-Triumph brochure, put out following the 1956 Earls Court Motor Show in London, showing the "perspex" TR3. One wonders whether it could have been driven? The accompanying model's (how many will recognise her as Rank film starlet Shirley-Anne Field?) profile is typical wasp-waisted 1950s!

Newcastle-on-Tyne police used several sidescreen TRs as rapid patrol cars. In this unusual shot, Constable A Leishman of the Newcastle force demonstrates his black TR3 to a group of Tanganyikan Policemen who were on a fact-finding visit in around 1957 (TR Register Archive).

The advertisement which told the world about the bet, between the Royal Aero Club and the British Automobile Racing Club, that a light aeroplane could fly from Lands End to John O'Groats and back to London using less fuel than a car! As you can see from this illustration, the BARC won the day with a runaway margin.

their promotional advertising for the TR3.

4.   Several TRs were featured in the "Eagle Book of Motor Sport", a book published in 1958 for boys by the proprietors of the "Eagle" boys' comic, hugely popular at the time. A TR2 registered TZ 4747 is shown about to commence a hill-climb, OKV 72 is pictured during the 1954 T.T. race, and the Chapter about rallying depicts RKD 532, 738 BTE, MCG 909 and WBJ 700, confirming the TR's pre-eminence as a rally vehicle at the time.

5.   Various police forces in the UK purchased new TR2/3/3As to use as rapid patrol and traffic cars. These cars were usually supplied finished in black, and often had hard-tops fitted. Uprated suspension was also utilised on occasions. A TR that has recently re-surfaced and which was also believed to have been a Stoke-on-Trent police vehicle, is TS 75653, registered in London as 597 BYX (why it should have been registered in London remains a mystery). The factory build sheet reveals this to be finished in black, with black leather interior, and the record contains the ominous note, "calibrated speedo to be fitted." Stoke police also purchased one of the very last TR3As, TS 82208, registered in 1962 as 455 TVT., as well as some early TR3s, YVT 332 being an example. Among other known police users of TRs were the Newcastle-upon-Tyne force, which had TR2s, including UTN 186 and 187, and TR3A's 491 EVK, 492 EVK, 108 LTN and 109 LTN. A photograph shows Constable A. Leishman of the Newcastle police demonstrating one of their black TRs to a group of Tanganyikan policemen on a visit to this country!

Although I have not seen any other evidence, I am certain that overseas and colonial forces utilised these cars for high speed use. Certainly in the USA at least one Fire Chief had a TR, for I have uncovered a splendid contemporary colour photograph showing Chief Edward Gartland and the firemen of the City of Rochester, New York, posing by a red TR3A in 1959. The car sports white-wall tyres and a giant chromium device that is either a searchlight or a siren!

6.   The British Petroleum Company's experimental department evidently purchased a new TR2 in 1954, allegedly to try to discover how a two-litre engined sports car could be so astonishingly economical! They had had Standard Vanguards previously, so were used to the engine, if not the economy. Once BP had finished with it, this car was sold by them to Roy Johnson, a member of their experimental department staff. He kept it for 6 years, during which time he competed regularly in the TR with some success. The car is believed to have been registered as YPD 273, although I find this to be a 1955 rather than a 1954 registration. Possibly BP either did not register it during their ownership, or used it on "trade" plates?

7.   The December 1955 Edition of the Standard-Triumph Company magazine, "The Standard Car Review" contains a fascinating picture, which shows one of the three TR2s sporting a TR3A style front grille and recessed headlamps, yet this picture was taken a full 2 years prior to the USA announcement of the "restyled TR3" (i.e. TR3A) in October 1957! (the quality of the original precluded its inclusion here). The photograph was taken at the premises of Harris Motors, Triumph dealers in Ventura, California, during a tour

of USA dealers by three TR2's in late 1955. The TR drivers included, from the UK Mr W J Warren, the factory's Export Sales Manager, and Mr H. Pugh, the Spares Manager. One can only conclude therefore that, as this was an official Works promotion, the TR3A style front was fitted experimentally to gauge reaction to it from the USA dealers. If reaction was favourable, why, one wonders, did it take a further two years for this relatively minor modification to reach production? Also, why were neither of the other TRs wearing the then-newly-introduced TR3 front grille? Interestingly, and to deepen the mystery, the article in the "Standard Car Review" that accompanies the photograph makes no reference at all to this strange "TR3A" front - if they did not want readers to become aware of it at the time, then why print the picture?

During this tour by the three TRs, a special luncheon was given in Los Angeles for dealers and distributors from the USA West Coast. One of the guests was a Mr Earle P. Grace, who was said to have sold more TR2s than anyone else in the world, in excess of one hundred in the less than 2 year period that the car had by then been on sale!

8.   The long-door TR2 now in the care of the National Motor Museum at Beaulieu has an interesting history, and is one of the lowest mileage sidescreen TRs surviving. The car (registered RTT417) was purchased new in 1954 by Doug Simes, a garage proprietor from Kingsteignton in Devon, who had been active in motorsport before the war. He campaigned the TR in rallies when new, but unfortunately, the car broke its crankshaft after it had covered about 30,000

miles. Mr Simes for some reason never repaired it, leaving the car (with others) in his garage, where it became progressively more buried under sundry parts. Upon his death in 1987, Mr Simes left five of his cars by his Will to the Motor Museum, but the Museum could only accommodate one of them. The TR2 was chosen, as they had not got an example of an original TR, and the other cars were sold in aid of a Cancer Relief Charity. Although the TR2's instruments and other minor items were missing, it was basically incredibly original, and was beautifully restored in 1988 by Peter Marks in Hampshire, who specialises in sidescreen TRs. The restoration costs were partly funded by the Fund for the Preservation of Technological and Scientific Material.

9.   TRs sometimes turn up in unusual places - a coloured jigsaw puzzle was published in 1954 which included a TR2, the car used being OHP 676. As this was the semi-Works supported car campaigned by Kit Heathcote and Gregor Grant amongst others early in its career, one presumes that the car was lent by the Standard Triumph Publicity Department.. Certainly the car is believed to have been retained in the factory's ownership for some time; it was a very early TR2 indeed, being number TS 8, built 25th August 1953, fitted with engine number TS 10 E, and finished in Ice Blue with Geranium trim! The jigsaw was called "The Hundred Milers", and depicted fourteen cars capable of the magic 100 MPH. It contained 200 pieces and was published by the "Picture Post" magazine - it must be something of a collector's item today.

10.   In 1956, Mr W F Blanchard, described as a Test Pilot

Kit Heathcote has OHP 676 on loan from the factory and is seen undrgoing a special test at Hastings during the MCC Redex Rally in late 1954 (LAT Photographic)

Left: Olympic Gold Medallist for Britain, Chris Brasher, owned at least two TRs, as is related in the text. Here he is seen taking delivery of the first of them, TLT 842, during early 1957 at Bekeley Square House Garage in London. Below left: Jon Laver's ex-Works TRW 735 charges up a trials hill during its latter career. Twin spare wheels helped adhesion, but did nothing for the appearance - and how many men did it take to open the boot? (both pictures from Jon Laver).

around 30,000 miles a year during the first 8 years of its life, it is perhaps not surprising that this car is not known to have survived. This is not however true of an even higher mileage TR, the well known ex-Works TR3 TRW 735, commission number TS 17064-0. For many years in the hands of arch-TR enthusiast Jon Laver, this car is reputed to have covered in excess of 750,000 miles in its 37+ year life to date, averaging more than 20,000 a year since new. Considering its hard life when new, as one of Ken Richardson's 1957 Works team cars and its subsequent competition career in everything from races to classic mud-plugging trials, its survival is remarkable. In recent years it has been rebuilt to excellent condition and refinished in the original Works team Apple Green colour.

When sold by the factory at the end of the 1957 season, the car was acquired by the well-known sporting personality Chris Brasher, an Olympic gold medalist, to replace his previous TR3 TLT 842, which , as he mentioned in a letter to Jon Laver, he felt did not quite have the performance he was looking for. The letter confirmed that the ex-Works TR did indeed perform very much better than TLT 842. As we know that the Works rally TR3s were in substantially standard form, maybe Brasher's original TR3 was somewhat below par, or alternatively possibly the fact that TRW 735 had been what would now be called "blueprinted" by the Competition Department made a substantial difference. The car was used in the 1959 Monte Carlo Rally, a private entry

working for Decca Navigation Ltd., purchased a new TR2, registered NUJ 970. By the beginning of 1964, the car had covered 236,000 miles without any major work being carried out on it, all on its original engine (which was however replaced at that mileage, not surprisingly!) The car was modified with a TR3A front apron and grille, but was otherwise said to be to standard specification. The owner confirmed that he always made full use of the TR's performance, and had enjoyed every mile! Having covered by Mr Brasher, but with some Works support. Following its preparation for this event by Richardson's department, the owner described the car's exhaust note as having "a rich, full-throated burble as if Gigli was gargling down the exhaust pipe!". A further example of high-mileage TRs comes from the USA, where a Mr Ed Sanders of Cincinatti, Ohio, covered around 450,000 miles in his long-door TR2 (TS 3427) between 1956 and 1967.

11.   The fitted suitcase - this factory listed and supplied item of optional equipment was never common, and is now very rare indeed. The case is made "on the slant", to ensure maximum space usage in the TR's sloping boot! It was supplied in various colours to match the interior trim of the car, having three white bakelite handles and brass-bound corners. The one I have seen belongs to John Hopwood, who has been rallying sidescreen TRs for many years and whose TR2 PVU 188 is very original despite the hard usage it gets. The car and owner are shown, pictured in the colour section, with another gentleman who also drove TRs occasionally in his early days, Jackie Stewart, former World motor racing champion. If ever one of these "TR boot-shaped" cases came into the hands of a non-owner or enthusiast, one wonders what they must have thought as to the sanity of the designer/manufacturer of such an eccentrically shaped item of luggage! Incidentally, one reason I imagine that not many of these cases are around is that they cost £9 -18 shillings in 1955, the equivalent of some £125 today! Despite this, the price had risen to £15-10 shillings by 1957!

12.   Was there a TR3C? As I mentioned briefly in my TR2/3/3A Superprofile book, I had heard over the years rumours that a TR variant made especially for the Canadian market existed, namely the TR3C. The specification was reputed to be much as the latest TR3As, or the "TSF" TR3Bs, and the cars were supposed to have been exported to Canada in 1961/2. I have discussed the TR3C with Anders Clausager at the British Motor Industry Heritage Trust, and he has kindly researched his records, and we are now both convinced that no such cars ever existed, the Canadian exports being merely late TR3As or TR3Bs. In 1992 I did receive from an owner in Canada a copy of a Canadian log book/title certificate appertaining to TS 81830, and this clearly includes the suffix "C" could this have been the mysterious TR3C? However, upon consulting BMIHT's build records, the same car was listed as TS 81830 L, and it seems fairly clear that the "L" suffix for left hand steering has, somewhere along the line, been incorrectly transposed as a "C". My knowledge of Standard Triumph's numbering schemes leads me to believe that, even were the TR3C to have existed, it would have been given an "LC" suffix rather than just "C", as any such cars would have had left hand steering. In fact, there **were** some TR3A's with a "C" suffix, but these were the vehicles destined to become Triumph Italias, and exported as rolling chassis to Italy for bodying there. Here, an "LCO" suffix was usual, indicating left hand steering, chassis only, and overdrive fitment.

13.   Tappet noise - over the years many owners, especially those new to TRs, have had cause to wonder at the tappet noise emanating from their engines. In 1958, one purchaser of a new TR3, a Mr N Redford, took the matter up with the factory, and he received from a Mr Brownson of the Service and Repairs Department at the Canley, Coventry factory. It was observed that whilst the Works agreed that the valve mechanism was noisy, they certainly were not going to do anything about it! Nevertheless, their detailed reply was indicative I feel of the level of concern that the Company showed towards the purchasers of its most renowned product. Mr Redford's car was a late TR3 registered LJA999, and I have seen the original supplier's invoice for this car. As a very late TR3, it was one of those cars fitted from new with the TR3A type rear apron panel having separate orange flashing indicators and the appropriate pressings to house them. This TR has only had two owners from new, and now belongs to Ken Rawson in Lancashire. It is a well known car at TR Register events, and is maintained (as it always has been) in exemplary fashion.

14.   Rear wheel covers, or "spats" were available for TR2s and TR3s - and were also still listed for TR3As until around 1960. Original "Stanpart" spats are now rare indeed - I have only seen one such pair in 25 years of being associated with TRs - but Ken Munford in London, a mine of TR enthusiasm, information and parts supply, has had a set made up for his concours-condition TR2. Certainly, spats must have improved airflow at speed, hence their use on MVC 575 at Jabbeke, but ease of wheel changing and rear brake cooling must have suffered, and they do seem to give the car a somewhat "heavy" look, especially with the hood erected. Spats could not be fitted with wire wheels of course, as the knock-off spinner nuts would have hit them! For any TR owner who either obtains an original pair or wishes to have some made up, I am including two factory diagrams that I came across recently showing the fittings and dimensions.

15.   Coventry Registration numbers and "publicity" cars - over the years, many owners of TRs originally registered in Coventry have wondered whether, or even insisted, that their cars were "factory" or ex-works" vehicles. Of course, in some cases this is true; the Works competition cars are now well documented however, and although some "new" factory owned and Coventry registered non-competition TRs do surface from time to time, most are now accounted for. The Company maintained a publicity and loan fleet of TRs for

photographic, advertising and road test purposes throughout the 1954/61 period, and of course these "publicity" cars were Coventry registered. In addition, some of the "Top Brass" at Standards ran TRs as personal transport, these vehicles remaining company owned and again being Coventry registered.

Chapter Ten includes details on all such cases that I have identified to date, but do be aware that a lot of TRs were sold in the Coventry area in the ordinary way, so just because your TR carries one of the Coventry numbers, the odds are against it being anyting special!

The six Coventry registration letter combinations are DU, HP, KV, RW, VC and WK, and in the British system, these combinations are the second and third letter of "three letter" registration number plates. In 1953, when the TR2 prototypes were registered, Coventry licensing authorities had reach letter "M" in their issuing sequence, thus the "Jabbeke" car is MVC 575, and the first TR2 to be registered is MWK 950. By the end of 1959, the three letter combinations with the letters preceding the numbers were exhausted, and the Coventry Authorities started issuing combinations of up to four figures followed by just two letters, hence publicity cars 46 HP and 2242 RW. The system proceeded alphabetically and logically throughout the sidescreen TR build period, with one major exception concerning the "N" series of numbers, which for some reason were issued partially out of sequence. NDU and NHP were issued as expected in 1953, but NRW did not appear until June 1954, **after** the "O" series had been issued. NWK came in April 1955, NVC in December 1955 and NKV

Above left: the letter from Standard-Triumph Service Department to Mr Redford about his noisy tappets. On the immediate left is a photo showing his car, LJA 999. This late TR3 has had only two owners and survives in a very well preserved state in the hands of Ken Rawson. Norman Redford (with pipe) is seen discussing the car's merits with an interested crowd (Ken Rawson).

Above left: Ken James's early TR2 (TS942) is seen in Colwyn Bay in 1954. This is the Olive Yellow car navigated by Ian Hall, as related in Chapter Four (Ian Hall).

Top right: Mrs J Monk corners her TR2 at a race on the Mairehau circuit in New Zealand during 1956, ahead of a Formula III 500cc racing car and a rare Austin Healey 100S (TR Register Archive).

Above: Mary Walker's TR2 climbs rapidly up a Pennine hill track during the 1954 RAC Rally (Mary Fraser).

Left: The Rally of the Midnight Sun of 1955 saw two TR2s entered by AB Nykopings Automobilfabrik. The two cars finished in 9th and 10th places. Here, we see car Number 68 charging up a typical Swedish forest road. The driver's name is not known (Standard Car Review).

Top left: WRA Wyllie sits at the wheel of his TR2, surrounded by trophies. He was the service manager of the Standard Triumph distributor in Singapore during the mid-1950s. The car sports an unusual two-tone finish (Standard Car Review).

Above right: In early 1957, "Miss Ghana" was a guest at the Standard-Triumph factory during her visit to Great Britain. This visit was part of her prize for winning the "Miss Ghana" competition at the time of that country achieving its independence. The lady's name was Monica Amekoafia.

Above: Raymond Laird's TR2 is seen crossing the moors near the army ranges at Otterburn in Northumberland. The event is the 1956 RAC Rally (David Burrows).

Right: British international golfer Harry Weetman is seen posing in the USA at Palm Springs, showing off his newly acquired TR3 (Standard Car Review).

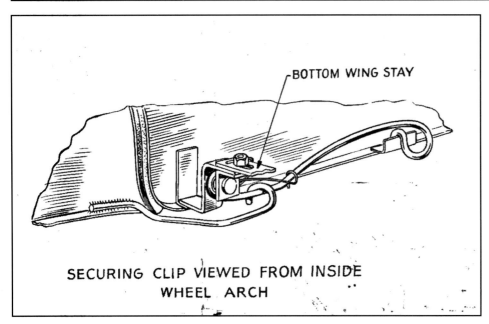

BOTTOM WING STAY

SECURING CLIP VIEWED FROM INSIDE
WHEEL ARCH

Whilst delving among some old TR papers, I uncovered these diagrams relating to the fitment of the rear wheel spats. As can be seen, the fixing arrangement was somewhat complicated.

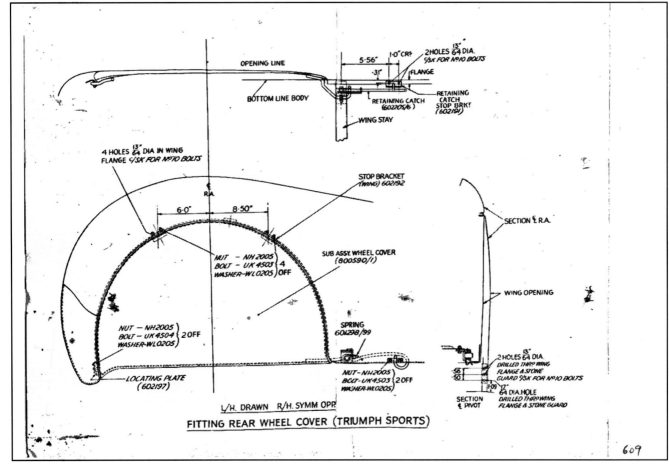

FITTING REAR WHEEL COVER (TRIUMPH SPORTS)

609

not until June 1956, which was by then nearly 3 years out of sequence, and at a time when the "S" series were being issued! This has all caused some confusion to TR historians over the years, and although I have taxed the Coventry Public Records Office on the point, no-one can now recall the reason for the discrepancy. One conclusion that I have come to is that it might have something to do with cars registered temporarily in the City, but ultimately for personal export. Many of the TRs collected personally by USA residents from the factory in the mid to late 1950's and used by them in Europe prior to being taken to the USA had these out of sequence "N" prefix registrations. The author would be most interested if anyone could produce a positive answer!

16.   I relate a story once told to me by a particularly determined TR3 driver - probably true, but possibly "embroidered!" This character was minding his own business, driving his blue TR3 at around 85 mph on a dual carriageway road - the Marlow bypass in Buckinghamshire - when in his mirror he saw an MGB GT approaching very fast behind him. Being a true TR man, he accelerated, for was it not the traditional enemy, an MG? Being in full combat mode with aeroscreens, and as the road was both straight and somewhat downhill, our man had the TR3 round to "Made in England" on the speedo and still the MG pursued him, for this was no ordinary MG but the V8 version! Finally, at what must have been approaching 115 mph, the TR man pulled over and let the MG past only to see the words "Stop - Police" illuminated in the rear window of the MG, which was indeed an unmarked patrol car. (In the early 1970's, as your author can personally verify, Buckinghamshire Police ran at least 3 MG V8's as unmarked patrol cars, **and** they had uprated engines in them!) Fearing a fine of greater value than the worth of the TR, the TR man stopped and trembled as two officers approached. The resulting conversation is said to have proceeded as follows; Policeman "Do you know how fast you were travelling?" TR man - (on the "busted anyway, so what the hell" principle) "Oh, around 120 mph I suppose" - Policeman "Well, I used to have a TR2 and the most I could ever get out of it was around 105, but then I didn't have overdrive, which I see you have, and I imagine that the aeroscreens help!" TR man, "Yes Officer, I suppose that they do." Policeman "Well, as I know from my own knowledge that a car such as yours could not possibly have been doing the speed you were doing, we'd better say no more about it, but remember, not all MG's are driven by idiots, and a few have the legs on TRs!"

17.   "You want a TR2?" - Following the "Jabbeke" runs in May 1953 and the subsequent publicity which began to convince a sceptical, sporting motoring public that the new Triumph Sports might become a force to be reckoned with, quite a large number of orders for the new TR2 began to be received from UK buyers. Production was, however, very slow to build up and only 300 or so cars were built in 1953, of which merely 50 or so stayed in the UK, most going to well

Barry Leavens belts his TR2 up Park Rash Hill in the Yorkshire Dales during the 1954 RAC Rally (Barry Leavens).

known personalities in the motor sporting world, or to main dealers as demonstrators. It was thus next to impossible for a genuine private owner without "connections" to obtain a TR in late 1953 or early 1954, and the convincing RAC rally win by TRs in March 1954 compounded the problem.

Two stories told to me by early TR2 buyers will illustrate what I mean. Barry Leavens wanted a new car with which to compete in the 1954 RAC Rally, and was told when trying to order a TR2 through the usual channels that there was no chance of his obtaining a car in time for this event in early March. He had competed for many years in various rallies, usually using Jowetts. As the Jowett car was going out of production at the beginning of 1954, due to difficulties with the supply of bodies, the Works manager at Jowetts, whom Mr Leavens knew well, used his contacts within the motor industry to pull a string or two at Triumphs. The upshot was that Leavens was told to be outside Banbury railway station at noon one Saturday in January 1954 with a cheque for £1,000, whereupon a TR2 would be delivered to him - no choice of colour, specification or anything! As arranged, the car arrived - a white, wire-wheeled, TR 2 registered KAK656, a Bradford plate, where the Jowett works was based. Presumably the car was initially supplied to Jowetts, and transferred on to Mr Leavens, a clear case of "who you know!" In his letter to me, Barry Leavens recalls the TR2 as being "even better than he had anticipated," although he did not have a particularly happy time on the RAC Rally through no fault of the car.

The second story is that of Bill Parkes, whom I interviewed for Chapter Four. He decided to order the new Triumph Sports immediately after the 1952 Motor Show when the 20 TS was shown. He wanted something new and up to the minute, and placed his order with the main Standard-Triumph agents in Worcester, his local area. By late 1953, almost a year after ordering the car, he had still received no delivery date. However, as he realised from motoring press reports that the car was being redesigned and developed, he accepted the delay on the assumption that what he would eventually get would be a better vehicle, albeit somewhat later than desired. Finally, in January 1954, after constantly pestering the dealers, he was advised that "his" TR was about to be made - no choice of colour was given, nor options!

Bill recalls that the first time he set eyes upon a TR2 was when his own car arrived at the Worcester dealers at the beginning of February. It had wire wheels and overdrive, and was finished in Geranium, which would certainly not have been the owner's choice had he been given one! To cap it all, the dealers insisted on keeping his new car in the showroom for a further 10 days as an exhibit, as it was the first TR2 into the county and was attracting much attention. Finally, Bill Parkes was able to take to the road on 17th February 1954, as proved by the original insurance certificate which he still has (annual cover £17!). He recalls how it was many weeks before he saw another TR2 on the road, and also how his car became a centre of embarrassing attention

Bill Parkes puts MUY 334 through one of the final tests during the 1954 Redex National Rally. The location is Hastings seafront and another TR2, PUE 555, awaits its turn behind (TA Parkes).

whenever he parked it. This car was registered MUY 334 and although Bill has not kept a note of its commission number, my own records indicate that by a process of elimination having regard to colour and the fitment of wire wheels and overdrive, it must have been TS 428 "O", built on 21st January 1954. Thus can it be seen that a private owner with no special contacts had to wait the best part of 18 months from placing his order to driving away in his TR!

The difficulty in obtaining TRs in those early days explains why the earliest (non-Company) advertisement I can find for one in the motor sporting press is in the issue of "Autosport" dated 12th March 1954, when London dealers Basil Roy Ltd describe the new Triumph as being "on view" in their showrooms and that "orders are now being taken." In the following week's issue, the Northern dealer, Gillie Tyrer (who himself rallied TRs with some success) was offering "One only, TR2 - ex-Works on 25th March 1954, with wire wheels, list price" - as the advert did not appear again, one imagines that this stray car without an owner was quickly snapped up!

18.   Jim Clark's TR3 - double World Champion racing driver Jim Clark had a new TR3 early in his career, both using it as a road car in 1957/58, and also campaigning it in races, rallies and sprints whilst he was making a name for himself. The car was a white, disc-braked TR3, and although its com-

World Champ's Car

Purchased by Local Man

A local young man, Mr Archie Brown, Sauchie House, Burrell Street, Crieff, had quite a surprise this week when he examined the Registration Book of his newly-bought sports car — the vehicle was first owned by "Messrs James Clark and Son, Edington Mains, Chirnside, Berwickshire."

Mr Brown mentioned this to a "Herald" representative who decided to check on the name and address.

PHONED CLARK

A phone call on Wednesday morning to Chirnside confirmed that the car did indeed once belong to World Champion motor racing driver, Jim Clark. "R.S.C. 190?" said Clark over the 'phone, "Yes, quite a nippy little job (good for 6000 r.p.m.— 130 m.p.h!) I used it in competitions—mostly hill-climbs at Bo'ness and Rest-and-be-Thankful. The car belonged to me for just over a year."

The vehicle, a red 1,991c.c. Triumph T.R. III, was first registered in November 1957. It was white when Jim Clark bought it and has changed colour twice in six years.

"It feels great to own a car which once belonged to Jim Clark, but I won't be trying to emulate him!" added Mr Brown, who is employed by Messrs. D. McBirnie & Son Motor Engineers, Crieff as a mechanic.

A former pupil of Morrison Academy, he learned his apprenticeship with Albion Motors Ltd Glasgow.

mission number is unknown, it must have been a very late TR3 as it was first registered in November 1957, when the TR3A production was commencing. The registration number was RSC190, and the car was said to have been a Motor Show car, though whether this meant the London or the Scottish Motor Show I cannot ascertain. It was fitted from new with wire wheels and overdrive, and is believed to have had a white hood and sidescreens. Clark used the TR3 for just over a year, and when questioned about it some years later described it as "a nippy little job, good for 130MPH, 6,000 r.p.m. in top!" This seems to have been something of an exaggeration, though it is of course possible that the engine was well modified. The car has not been heard of in recent years, and one suspects it may not have survived. However, I have a newspaper cutting from 1964 that shows a Mr Archie Brown with his "newly acquired TR3", which he was surprised to learn, after he bought it, had formerly belonged to one James Clark!

19.   The TR3 "Junior" - the Standard-Triumph factory supported the production of a half-scale TR3A, and I have seen a copy of the advertising leaflet incorporating official Standard-Triumph badges and insignia. The car was indeed roughly half full size, although I understand the prototype was built at one third size. Through the good offices of TR Register member John Saunders, who has one of these cars, I have received a copy of a letter from Peter Hunt, the son of the designer David Hunt, who was I understand the proprietor of Coventry Laminates Ltd, the firm which produced the cars for sale by Standard-Triumphs. The cars were produced in fibreglass, and as detailed in the sales leaflet, had many working features, being altogether a "cut above" the average child's pedal car. Roughly one hundred were sold, which at a price of £48 in 1960 (equivalent to around £550 today) was good going. The car was evidently exhibited on the Standard-Triumph stand at the London Motor Show (probably in 1960), and the factory even provided a miniature transporter to carry these diminutive TRs! It is not known how many survive today in addition to John Saunders' car, but in view of their solid construction and non-rusting bodywork, there must be quite a few of these highly collectable devices around. Evidently some copies were made later by a different firm, but I have no further details of these.

20.   TRs have been around for longer than the average owner may think, for there are evidently two (at least) references to them in the Bible - namely "and Jesus also rode into Jerusalem in Triumph" together with "and the sound of Moses' Triumph could be heard throughout all the land" - he must have been driving an early TR2 with the single 18 inch silencer box!

21.   "Wicker" or "Metric" trim - this mysterious TR trim

variant has caused much correspondence over the years in the columns of the TR Register magazine TRaction, although as yet no official reference to its existence has been found in any Factory sales, development or specification literature, and it is not even mentioned on the build records of those cars to which it was fitted. That it exists is beyond doubt, for I have personally owned a TR3 fitted with a full set of original trim made of this strange basket-weave style fabric. The trim is a vynide material and came, it is thought, in several colours roughly approximating to normal TR trim colours - the trim in my TR3 is a sort of off-cream colour, but has probably faded. When fitted in a vynide-trimmed car, it appears to have been used on all surfaces, including door panels and dashboard, but where fitted to a leather-seated car, the seat facings were of course in leather whereas the seat backs and the sides of the cushions were believed to be in the basket-weave material.

As to during which build periods it was used, there is some conjecture. In some photographs of OHP 771, the original Road Test TR2 (TS 6) it looks as if this car had the basketweave trim, but one cannot be certain. What is certain is that it was fitted to the car bought new by Monte Seal, which was TS 122 (registered JBO 3), and also to several other early TR2s. Monte Seal's son Roger now owns TS 1997, and this car also has this trim, as does TS 1021 L, a very original TR2 recently reimported from the USA by Jim Lowry. I have not seen any reports of later TR2's being so fitted, but a "glut" of basketweave trimmed cars reoccurs shortly after the introduction of the TR3, at least 5 such being known to me, the lowest numbered being TS 8713 and the highest numbered being TS 10195. In all the factory build records for these TR3s, this trim is referred to as "Grey", either leather or vynide. In his thoroughly researched article on TR trim materials which appeared in the TR Register magazine No. 35, Alan Robinson refers to this trim material as "metric", but does not explain where this term comes from, or why it is pertinent. One feels that there is more yet to come to light on this subject!

22.   Thanks to Ian Gibson, one of the original TR Register members and the possessor of a vast fund of Sidescreen TR knowledge, I have acquired several copies of original Standard-Triumph service information sheets. These were circulated from the factory to dealers and repairers, and were in effect commentaries on modifications and an updating of the workshop manuals in the light of practical experience. As examples of how the system worked, I examined three separate bulletins, the first dated September 1958 and dealing with rationalisation of tyre sizes; the second dates from October 1958 and concerns a possible problem with excessive brake pedal travel, this being an item issued by Girling Ltd and presumably relevant only to disc brakes. The

SERVICE   INFORMATION

STANDARD AND TRIUMPH VEHICLES

ep No. 3/8	RATIONALISATION OF TYRE SIZES	Date SEPTEMBER, 1958.
	T.R.3. Models	

The Dunlop Rubber Company have amalgamated certain tyre sizes in order to reduce their current range.

This policy will affect T.R.2. and T.R.3. vehicles fitted with 5.90 - 15 tyres which now become obsolete. The revised tyre, now quoted as 5.90 - 15 (5.50/5.90 - 15), is a compromise between the original 5.50 and 5.90 tyres and is therefore suitable for rims within this range.

The alteration in rolling radius of the new size is such, that no speedo correction is necessary.

NOTE :   The instructions are for information only and do not constitute an authority to carry out modifications at the expense of The Standard Motor Company Limited.

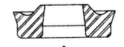

GIRLING *Service* BULLETIN
THE BEST BRAKES IN THE WORLD

KINGS ROAD · TYSELEY · BIRMINGHAM 11. TELEPHONE ACO 3371

OCTOBER 1958	TECHNICAL	BULLETIN NO.491,T.103.

EXCESSIVE BRAKE PEDAL TRAVEL

TRIUMPH TR.3

Instances have been reported of excessive brake pedal movement developing due to the entry of air into the system across the master cylinder seal, which cannot be permanently eliminated by normal bleeding.

Investigation has revealed that the complaint has arisen since the introduction of an alternative seal from approximately Commission No.TS.28000 to TS.34311. The difference between this seal and the original type Part No. 504807 can be clearly seen from the illustrations.

Experience has shown that this alternative seal is more sensitive to the extreme limits of normal production variation, and it has now been withdrawn from both production and spares stocks.

Should cases of excessive brake travel be experienced which cannot be rectified by normal bleeding procedure, the seal should be examined, and if conforming to design 'A' should be replaced by the type 'B' Part No. 362453 Standard Part No.504843 and the system refilled and re-bled.

Each master cylinder is coded with a letter and a serial number for example:-

'B' 1428 = 14/2/58
'B' 478 = 4/7/58

The figures represent the day, month and year of manufacture, and the alternative seal was introduced between 14th February (1428) and the 4th July (478), and all master cylinders with code number representing the time between these dates are suspect. As a further identification of the reintroduction of the original seal a letter G. has been added to the code reference e.g.B.478.G.

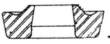

A   B

STANDARD 🦅 **TRIUMPH**

SERVICE DIVISION: BIRMINGHAM ROAD
ALLESLEY COVENTRY
Telephone: Coventry 22118

T.R. PISTONS.

T.R. Models.

Alterations to piston assemblies have been made subsequent to the introduction of Triumph T.R. models.

The following information is therefore, issued to enable Distributors and Dealers to provide the correct pistons when replacements are necessary.

The original piston assembly Part No. 107581 was replaced at Engine No. TS.4882E by piston assembly Part No. 110516 which had a strengthened crown, and the rib on the skirt at the split position was extended to run into the bottom skirt rib.

A revised piston ring layout fitted to piston assembly Part No. 113560 was introduced at Engine No. TS.9731E and incorporated a taper faced second compression ring and a modified scraper ring. This assembly was later replaced at Engine No. TS.26698E by piston assembly Part No. 506691, which had further stiffening of the crown.

Distributors or Dealers holding stocks of the early piston assemblies are advised to fit them as applicable. If no stocks are held, however, piston assembly Part No. 506691 may be used for all replacements, but because of the differences in weight between pistons of different Part Nos. care should be exercised to ensure that they are fitted as a set of four.

Left, above and below: the three bulletins, mentioned in the text, which deal with rationalisation of tyre sizes, brake pedal travel and piston specification changes (via Ian Gibson).

Group 1/36.   - 2 -

	Piston Assy.	Bare Piston.
Up to and including TS.4882E.	107581	201592.
TS.4883E. - TS.9730E.	110516	202436.
TS.9731E. - TS.26697E.	113560	202436.
TS.26698E. - Date.	506691	205005.

PISTON RINGS.

Up to TS.9730E.		
Compression rings	8 off	107582.
Scraper rings	4 off	107583.
TS.8731E and Subsequent.		
Compression rings		107582.
Compression rings (Taper)		113550.
Scraper rings		113549.

NOTE.- These instructions are for information only and do not constitute an authority to carry out modifications at the expense of The Standard-Triumph Sales Limited.

third item is undated, but Ian Gibson reckons it to have been issued in late 1960 or early 1961. It is most interesting, and deals with the various piston specification changes that took place during the production run.

Also provided by Ian is some positive evidence that the Works intended to fit an overdrive switch mounted on the gear lever, as was in fact done on later Triumphs. The extract taken from a page listing high speed equipment in a TR2/3/3A parts book shows part number 109048 listed, described as "Knob and switch assembly, change speed lever." Interestingly, the "TS" number at which it was said to be introduced was left blank! As we now know, this item never reached production for TRs, although hollow gear levers were fitted which would have allowed the necessary wiring to reach the switch in the knob. Later events showed that such an item could work reliably, so one wonders why the gear lever switch was not used on TR3As?

23.   The Triumph Sports Owners Association was the original club for TR owners, and was in effect founded by and (initially at least) run from the Public Relations Department of the Standard Motor Co at Canley, Coventry, the P.R.

Below: the document which refers to the "knob and switch gear assembly" confirming the factory's intention to fit an overdrive switch to the gear lever (via Ian Gibson).

HIGH SPEED EQUIPMENT

Part No.	Description	Plate No.	No. per Unit	Remarks
501803	**ELECTRICAL OVERDRIVE UNIT KIT— R.H.S. ONLY**		1	Fitted up to Commission Number TS only
502104	**ELECTRICAL OVERDRIVE UNIT KIT— L.H.S. ONLY**		1	
502375	**ELECTRICAL OVERDRIVE UNIT KIT— R.H.S. ONLY**		1	Fitted from Commission Number TS and future
502376	**ELECTRICAL OVERDRIVE UNIT KIT— L.H.S. ONLY**		1	
301339	Overdrive unit	AT1	1	
108788	Solenoid, overdrive unit	AT2	1	
109521	Cover, rubber, solenoid		1	Fitted from Commission Number TS2673 and future
102332	Bolt, overdrive unit attachment		6	
WP0107	Washer, plain, on bolt		6	
30047	Wire, locking bolt		3	
SS778	Washer, joint, between gearbox and overdrive unit		1	
110736	Mainshaft, gearbox	AT3	1	
110735	Plug, in ends of shaft		2	
400096	Cable, assembly, speedometer		1	
400097/0	Cable, outer, speedometer	AT4	1	
400097/1	Cable, inner, speedometer	AT5	1	
602037	Grommet, fitted on outer cable		1	
42781	Switch, isolating, fitted in gearbox cover	AT6	1	
108253	Relay	AT7	1	
TK4504	Screw, relay attachment		2	
WP0005	Washer, plain, on screw		2	
NH2005	Nut, locking screw		2	
WL0205	Washer, spring, under nut		2	
107285	Switch, operating overdrive	AT8	1	Fitted up to Commission Number TS only
108437	Knob, operating switch	AT9	1	
59445	Washer, rubber, in knob		1	
110729	Bracket, sleeve		1	
110730	Sleeve, rubber, fitted in sleeve bracket		1	
110731	Bracket, clamp		1	
TF2202	Screw, set, clamp bracket to change speed lever		1	
NH2002	Nut, locking screw		1	
WL0202	Washer, spring, under nut		1	Fitted from Commission Number TS and future
110728	Clip, cable, fitted on bolt securing change speed lever to top cover		1	
109048	Knob and switch assembly, change speed lever		1	
502282	Block, terminal		1	
YA0105	Screw, terminal block attachment		2	
502283	Clip, cable		1	

In early 1956, more than 50 members of the Triumph Sports Owners' Association took their cars to the factory for a guided tour. These two pictures were taken during that visit. Among the cars visible in the top picture is Leslie Brooke's former Ulster TT car, OKV 72. In the lower view, Mr Hain's TR3 which was registered "TR3" is prominent (TR Register Archive).

Manager Mr. Prentice being in overall control. The idea seems to have gelled into action in late 1954, and new TR buyers were encouraged upon buying their cars to register as members of this group. Benefits of membership included a TSOA handbook, which was loose leaved and had information for the more competition-minded owner. The idea was that as improvements were made to the cars in the light of experience, the TSOA office circulated information sheets detailing these to the members who incorporated them in the loose-leaved book. The book in my possession includes such sheets numbered up to 18. The book also included space for the owner to insert details of his or her individual TR, together with a log in which to enter up "competition results". A car badge was supplied, this being cast in "Mazak" and enamelled in red and black, as per the front apron badge. In the late 1950's, the TSOA regalia was changed to blue and white to match the later TR3A badge colours, but the red and black ones seem much more common now, although all surviving TSOA items are hard to come by. A lapel pin carrying the Triumph shield was also said to have been issued, though I have never seen one.

Members received a newsletter giving details of improvements to the cars (this was in addition to the bulletin sheets) and their various competition successes, and a "sales and wants" column was also available. This magazine was roughly bi-monthly, but its publication seems to have been somewhat erratic over the years that the TSOA existed. The first copy I have is dated November 1955, being volume 1, number 7. The final one that I have seen is dated July 1960, said to be volume 5 number 8. By this time the magazine was quite a professionally produced 24 page affair, whereas the early ones are no more than four pages, and at times seem little more than factory advertising handouts! By 1960, the TSOA was being run from 54 Regent Street, London W1 by the Standard-Triumph Automobile Association, which I believe to have been an "umbrella" club for owners of all Standard-Triumph vehicles. The factory's Sales and Publicity Department were still however clearly supporting the club, which by then had several local and regional groups, some of which issued their own duplicated monthly newsletters.

I have not been able to locate any precise details as to when the TSOA was wound up, if indeed it was - maybe it just faded away in the early 1960's as times moved on? Possibly the various local groups continued on an informal basis, but I do not think that the TSOA survived long once the TR3A was out of production and the TR4 was well established. The TR4 and its successors were aimed at a wider, less competition-minded market, and with the shortage of funds and the Leyland takeover of the early 1960's, it seems most likely that Standard Triumph's support of this club would have ceased, leaving TR owners in the UK with no club at all devoted specifically to them until the formation of the TR Register at the start of 1970. The last mention I can find of the TS0A is in late 1962, when it's headquarters seem to have been at the premises of Triumph Dealers L.F. Dove and Co. in Wimbledon - maybe this company financed it once Factory support ceased?

The foregoing details apply to the UK TS0A, but I should add that there was a USA branch of the same organisation, formed in 1956 by Standard's North American Company. It seems that this was run on similar lines to the UK Club, with newsletters and information sheets being issued, the USA club growing to become very large and successful. Indeed, by the early 1960's it boasted 14000 members and was the USA's second largest sports car club! It was this USA TS0A that promoted the various European tours by North American TR buyers that are dealt with in Chapter Nine. Eventualy, the Norh American arm of the TSOA became incorporated into the Vintage Triumph Register, so in that format at least, it still survives today.

24.   The "split" two-piece steering column - As I mentioned in my "Original TRs" book, uncertainty surrounds the introduction point of this item in that no direct reference to any specific commission number change point can be found. We can surmise from the published parts books that its introduction occurred, or rather was phased-in, from around the middle of 1958, somewhere between commission numbers TS 26000 and TS 34000. The lack of written evidence as to the point of introduction is all the more surprising given that it was such a major change, the two piece column requiring extra supports and bracketry. Two piece columns exist in both "adjustable" and "non-adjustable" steering types, the latter type being by far the more common. As anyone who has had to remove a steering column will confirm, the two-piece type is far easier to deal with, so I assume that ease of original fitment and subsequent replacement was behind this specification change. Recently I came across factory build records for TS 40161 and TS 60152 and on the records it clearly says "fit old type steering", which can only refer to the one-piece column. This is clear evidence that the change-over point was not precise but was phased over a period, and a long one at that, for TS 40161 was a November 1958 built car, and TS 60152 was

built as late as September 1959!

The implication behind the notes in the build records is that by then the later-type steering was normal, but that the earlier type of one-piece column **could** still be fitted - by request, one wonders? And if so, why should anyone request it? Maybe a stock of the earlier items had come to light, and the parts controllers were anxious to use them up, or maybe the new type had gone temporarily out of stock. It is clear therefore that over a range of many thousands of cars, either type could be fitted - maybe this is why the official literature "ducks" out of stating when a change occurred, i.e. because they knew that the fitment was ad hoc and random, and didn't wish to admit this!

25.   Unusual colours: it was possible to order a new TR finished in a special colour at extra cost and there is clear evidence from the surviving build records that such one-off colours did exist. For instance, TS 5478 "0", a UK supplied car built on 11th February 1955 was finished to special order in "Athens Yellow" with a red leather interior and black hood. Athens Yellow was presumably a standard colour of one of the major paint manufacturers, but was certainly not used on other Standard-Triumph models - it sounds rather devastating in combination with a red leather interior! I have never seen any evidence as to the extra cost involved in ordering a unique colour finish, but I would guess that it was quite expensive having regard to the disruption of production that must have occurred. A further yellow TR2 was MSP 200, the long door car purchased in mid 1954 by Lord Bruce and used by him for rallying. Lord Bruce, now the Earl of Elgin, has himself confirmed to me that the car was specially ordered from new finished in the family's "ancestral" colour of rich yellow, as indeed were all the family's vehicles! Another "one-off" TR2 was TS7875, delivered to a lady by the name of Lorna Doone Snow! This was supplied finished in Midnight Blue, with white trim piped in dark blue, a navy-purple hood (sic), a white plastic steering wheel, white painted brake drums and white wall tyres! Presumably this car was the height of fashion in 1955, but imagine how sceptical concours judges would be now as to its originality - yet it was original!

What I did not know until recently was that it was possible to order a car finished in primer. For instance TS 24692 LO was supplied to the USA in primer in late 1957, and was presumably finished locally in a one-off colour, as otherwise there would have been no point in so ordering it! Completely Knocked Down (CKD) cars supplied in kit form for local assembly (in Belgium or South Africa for instance) could of course appear in all manner of different paint finishes, although it does seem that in the main, factory colours were used more than non-factory ones. The more one researches the factory build records, the more oddities and inconsistencies one turns up. I mentioned several "rare" colours in the table of colours and finishes set out in my "Original TR" book, but since compiling that, several more have come to light. For instance a colour called Wedgwood Blue was used on TS 17047 L, TS 22580 L and TS 24223 LO, and probably on several other cars around this time. This was I imagine a pale blue, and its use predates the TR3A Powder Blue by some months. Is it one wonders the same Wedgwood Blue as occurred later on TR4s? TS 20888 L is described as finished in "Sebring Red". As "Sebring White" did not arrive until a year or more later, I assume that a this is not a misprint for Sebring White and that there really was such a colour as Sebring Red. TS 13624 is described in the records as finished in "Ivory-trial colour", the word 'trial' clearly appearing in the records.

The grey shades provide a rich vein of confusion, for in addition to the "official" shades of Pearl Grey used from late 1957 until the beginning of 1959 and Silverstone Grey used thereafter, I have found also Phantom Grey (TS 39267 LO), Slate Grey (TS 65107) and Silver Grey (with silver grey hardtop), this latter being on TS 51164 LO whereas TS 52664 L was Silver Grey with silver grey vynide trim. Platinum Grey also I recall seeing on a build record in the past, together with Plover Grey and South-Sea Grey! Whether these were really all different shades of grey or whether some were different names for the same colour is not certain. I can recall seeing a TR 3A finished in a metallic grey finish said to be original - which grey was this one wonders - any of the foregoing, or maybe yet another shade and name!

TR3B's tend to be much more conservative in colour, the choice of shade being restricted normally to Spa White, Powder Blue, Black and Signal Red. Even here however there was obviously some leeway, as two cars at least were supplied in a colour called Prussian Blue, these being TCF 624 L and TCF 2009 L. I have no doubt that as I and others have time to research more of the 83,000 or so sidescreen TR build records, further interesting variants will materialise! Just as an aside on the question of paint finishes, British Racing Green as a colour seems to have become steadily less popular as the production run progressed. A large number of TR2s and TR3s were supplied in this shade, and it was still relatively popular during the first half of the TR3A production run. After 1958 however, when the primrose yellows, greys and powder blues became available, its use declines quite sharply until very few TR3As in the 70,000's and 80,000's are being finished in BRG, and indeed, it was not available at all on TR3B's. In view of its popularity today, this is I find somewhat surprising. Signal Red was ever popular, along with the various whites, and was I would guess the individual colour most frequently specified on

sidescreen TRs - maybe one day someone will go through all the factory build records and prove me right (or wrong!).

26.   I have been able to obtain from old Standard Triumph factory records a detailed breakdown for the year 1954 of export numbers and destinations of TR2s built and delivered in that year. Unfortunately it appears that records for the following years have not survived, so we must be content with this one year as representative of TR export sales. In 1954, 2831 TR2s were exported, mainly left hand drive cars, but quite a few RHD cars to the colonial markets. 575 went to Northern Europe (not including the UK), 118 to countries surrounding the Mediterranean, 27 to the Near East, 15 to the Middle East, 57 to the Far East, 49 to Africa;, 149 to Central America, 182 to Australasia, 1391 to the USA, 251 to Canada and 17 described mysteriously in the table as exported to "miscellaneous!"

Some surprising facts emerge; for instance, only 4 TR2s reached South Africa that year, despite the fact that the TR later became sufficiently popular in that country to justify the setting up of a CKD assembly plant. A large total of 176 went to Belgium (some as C.K.D. kits and some to be turned into TR2 Francorchamps Coupes no doubt), but only 8 to Holland! Sweden took 91 whereas Norway took only 8. Only 9 went to Italy, presumably because the Italians produced sports cars of their own, but the Libyans took 24! Spain had only 3, Morocco had 39 and not one reached Turkey at all! Why only one TR2 reached India in 1954, yet 13 reached Ceylon (Sri Lanka) can only be conjectured at, and 2 cars even found their way to Borneo. Considering its size, it is amazing that 50 went to Venezuela, yet none reached either Chile or Brazil. As might be expected, Australia accounted for the comparatively high total of 121, whereas 59 made it to New Zealand, a remarkable figure having regard to its relatively tiny population. The figure of 1,391 to the USA is much as one would expect, showing that even in 1954 that country accounted for almost half of all the TR's exported. What became, one wonders, of the two cars exported to Madagascar, largely without roads in 1954 I believe, the one car sent to the Canary Islands or the 11 to Gibraltar - low mileage examples, one presumes?

27.   Appropriate registration numbers - unlike the situation that obtains in the USA, where one has, I believe, long been able to obtain a registration number appropriate to one's car, in the UK it was and is a matter of luck, and possibly "pulling some strings." The two British numbers TR2 and TR3 have over the years graced appropriate TRs, these two numbers both being originally issued by the Borough of Southampton in February 1925. In the November 1955 issue of the TSOA newsletter, it is mentioned that a Mr L. T. Cornish "has been able to obtain the number TR2 to go on

Right: A fascinating picture from the Spring of 1956 displays the new TR3 of Mr Hain, alongside the TR2 of Mr Cornish. Both cars carry the most appropriate registration numbers and even the Standard Vanguard's number is somewhat special. The TR2 wears what looks like Ace wheel discs and a nice pair of 7-inch spotlamps. The photo was taken at Triumph dealers Lankester Engineering. Below: at first sight, the registration number of this TR3A appears of no particular note, until one converts the "3" into "tri", when it begins to make more sense!

his car, a TR2 of course." Then in the May 1956 issue of the same publication, it was reported that a Mr E Hain of London SW3 had obtained TR3 to go on his brand new car of that marque. Both these gentlemen were said to be members of the Surrey and Hampshire branch of the TSOA and the cars appeared together for a photograph, reproduced here, taken at Surrey dealers Lankaster Engineering Ltd. "TR2" certainly remained on a TR2 for many years, as I myself saw it in the mid 1960's on a very smart British Racing Green TR2 parked in North London. The number is believed still to be in issue and circulating but is thought now to be on a modern vehicle. Similarly with the number "TR3" - I do not know for how long this survived on an appropriate vehicle, but in "Autosport" magazine for 14th August 1959, the number "TR3" was offered for sale complete with a TR3A upon which it was then mounted for a total price of £875, the sellers being Lankaster Engineering Ltd again. In recent years this number has been noted several times by TR Register members on a succession of modern cars; a pity, but I suppose inevitable in a world where the value of such a number now exceeds the value of a TR upon which to put it!

28.   I relay the following exactly as it appeared in the TSOA magazine for March 1956, "Iran to Germany and back - we have just received an interesting account of his exploits from Djamil Mehdinia of Teheran, providing yet another proof of the car's toughness and speed. No sooner had his new car arrived in Teheran than the Mr Mehdinia took it on a journey through Turkey, Greece, Italy and Switzerland to Germany covering 6702 kilometres of the world's worst road surfaces in 11 days without the slightest trouble. During his stay in Germany, he drove from Dusseldorf to Hamburg, a distance of 456 kilometres, at an average speed of almost 80 mph. Imagine his astonishment when he discovered at a local service station that one carburettor had been disconnected for some of the way! Germany back to Iran was even tougher, as the TR2 carried three persons, two trunks and four bags behind the seats, loose luggage in the boot and four trunks on the luggage grid. Not a single mishap, so Mr Mehdinia sends his grateful thanks to our engineers for what he calls "my little monster TR2!" How, one wonders, does one get a passenger, two trunks and four bags behind the seats in a TR2? Also, one presumably has to be fairly unconversant with one's car not to realise that one carburettor is disconnected! Still, it shows what some people expected of their TRs and presumably rightly so, for there were no problems!

29.   Further items of note from the Triumph Sports Owners Association Magazines - A trawl through the TSOA "Newsreel" reveals some interesting items alongside the usual notifications of pub meetings and visits for owners to Canley. In the July 1957 issue, when the rally successes for TRs were probably reaching their zenith, the magazine reported that TR3s had taken the first 6 places in the production sports car category at the Grand Prix des Frontieres at Chimay in Belgium. It is also reported that the Alpine Rally

was cancelled that year as many of the Alpine passes were in a dangerous state due to storm damage and Ken Richardson expressed his disappointment, for the team cars would surely have done as well as in the previous year. By this time, it is clear from the classified adverts appearing in the TSOA magazine that many TR2 owners were busy updating their TR2s into "TR3s", both cosmetically by adding the new grille, and also mechanically by substituting the larger carburettors and high-port cylinder heads. The September 1957 issue reported the Works team's best ever result in the Liege-Rome-Liege rallyand also reported in that month was the formal opening of a new pub in Coventry by Alick Dick, the Company's managing director. It was called "The Standard" and incorporated the "Vanguard Lounge" and the "TR Snug.".

Another TSOA magazine I have been able to obtain (they're very scarce these days, not surprisingly) is March 1958. This issue confirms that the TR3A (referred to as "New Style TR3") was introduced to the UK market on 1st January 1958, at a basic price of £699, plus the £350.17 shillings purchase tax. In July 1958 it was announced proudly that TR production was being stepped up from 340 to 450 a week, to try to keep up with the demand from the USA. The USA marketing organisation comprised by then six distributors and no fewer than 600 dealers.

A Canadian owner of a TR2 wrote in to tell of his holiday trip to Mexico and back from Ottawa, a total of 9,924 miles covered in 26 days. The fuel consumption was said to be 39.9 mpg, all the more remarkable as the "competition type" rich "GC" needles were left in the carburettors by mistake for half this mileage, the owner having forgotten to substitute the

Mike Hawthorn, Britain's first World Champion racing driver, squashes himself into the back of a TR3A, in the front of which are seen TV personality Eamonn Andrews and "Miss Triumph 1958", Sheila Lunnon, October 1958 ("Autosport").

normal "touring" needles following the car's last competitive event! The classified adverts reveal that by this date Derringtons were marketing 64 spoked wire wheels with wider rims for TRs. Clearly the desirability of something stronger than the 48 spoked variety had been identified, especially for competition purposes, notwithstanding which the Works continued to produce cars standing on the 48 spoked wheels right into the TR4 era! On this subject of TR4s, the August 1958 issue predicted the coming of the TR4, but was at pains to assure owners that demand for the TR3A was at such levels that it wouldn't be replaced for a very long time, and thus they need not worry about having an "out of date" car. The possibility of the Twin-Cam engine was also mentioned, but again it was said to be a long time thence and also that it was going to be expensive! Clearly the Works were worried that rumours of these new cars might affect sales of the TR3A, notwithstanding that the same paragraph also mentioned that there were substantial waiting lists for the car in every market except the USA, where of course most of the was production going.

In October 1958 the "Miss Triumph" contest was held, an event which today would no doubt be viewed with suspicion as "deeply unreconstructed!" The winner was a Miss Sheila Lunnon, described as "blonde, beautiful and from Watford!" Her "vital statistics" (remember them?) were said to be 37-23-36, and she was selected from 80 applicants by a panel of "experts" including Eamonn Andrews and Mike Hawthorn. The TSOA News actually came out with the exhortation that TR enthusiasts should come to the Motor Show to see this "Honey" on the Triumph Stand! At that Autumn's Earls Court Motor Show, five TRs plus one exhibition chassis were shown; the chassis, a hardtop car and a softtop car on Triumph's own stand, plus two cars on the stand of Mulliners Ltd, who built the TR bodies. In addition, a rally specification TR3A was shown, though it is not clear on whose stand this was. Its specification was given in detail, and it sported the following items;   heater, overdrive, 4.1 axle, 48 spoke wheels (surely nothing to crow about?) Dunlop "Alpine" tyres, foglamp, long-range spot lamp, two Smith's clocks, Halda Speed Pilot, fire extinguisher, map reading lamp, map reading torch, stone-guards (presumably on the headlamps) cigarette lighter (vital in those days!), two-pin plug, screen washers, two continental horns, and "heavy-duty electrical equipment" (unspecified). These days one quite frequently hears of cars said to be "the Motor Show car" - maybe one should not be so sceptical in view of the fact that five TRs appeared in 1958 alone, and that sidescreen TRs appeared at 10 London shows, including the prototype car in 1952!

Further correspondence was coming in relating to the amazing economy of the TRs , especially the early TR2s. Vic Derrington himself told of a journey of 275 miles in his TR2 (converted to TR3 specification) where no more than 5 1/2 gallons of fuel was used, giving exactly 50 mpg. He claimed to have been cruising at 80 mph whenever possible, and admitted that this performance was "so fantastic as to be unbelievable." Indeed it is, but similar claims of up to 50 mpg from TR2s appear so frequently over the years that one simply has to give them credence. Indeed, the Mobil Economy Run in 1955 was won by a TR2 certified to have covered 71 mpg! On the question of running costs, an article setting these out for a 1955 TR2 run for 21,000 miles over 2 1/2 years made it clear that depreciation at £354 over the period exceeded all the other running costs put together, and that on a car usually considered to have relatively low depreciation!

Below: the bulletin issued about Michelin "X" tyres, giving owners details of the reduced rolling circumference and effects on speedometer readings.

MICHELIN 'X' TYRES

Two months ago we mentioned the speedometer inaccuracies caused by fitting Michelin 'X' tyres, and this has given rise to so much correspondence that we have decided to ask our engineers for a full explanation of the extent of the error. Here it is.

The Dunlop tyres as normally fitted to the TR are of the woven type and these increase their diameter with speed. All TR's are fitted with speedometers which are corrected to take account of this phenomenon which commences at 50 m.p.h. Michelin 'X' tyres have a steel tread support which prevents this, and to find true speed after 50 m.p.h., the following formula must be used.

$$Vc = V \left(1 + \frac{V^2 - 900}{210,000}\right)$$

where V = Speed as indicated

Vc = True Speed

There is one further calculation to be made however, because Michelin 'X' tyres have a slightly smaller rolling radius, and for this reason the figure arrived at by allowing for tyre growth has to be reduced even further in the ratio 826 : 807 tyre revolutions per mile. This gives the following comparative data.

Car Speedo corrected for Dunlop Tyres	Car Speedo uncorrected for Tyre growth	Car Speedo uncorrected for tyre growth Plus Allowance for smaller Tyre Radius
50	50	49
60	59	57½
70	68½	67
80	77¼	76
90	87	85
100	96	94
110	105	102½
120	113½	110½

In other words, the last column shows your true speed if you have Michelin 'X' tyres. As mentioned in September's Newsreel, it is possible to obtain special speedometers for cars with Michelin 'X' tyres from the Competitions Department, Smiths Motor Accessories Ltd., Oxgate Lane, London. N.W.2.

The February 1959 issue revealed that no fewer than 12 TRs were entered for the Monte Carlo rally, said to be Triumph's "jinx event." Certainly no TR ever came near to an outright win. Production continued to rise in 1959, and by June a record number of 110 TR3As were stated to be produced each working day, of which 90% were going to the USA, where in March 1959 alone, 2,000 new TR3As were registered! This figure of 110 cars daily conflicts considerably with my figures given in Chapter Two - I think that the 110 figure must have been the very best, possibly freakish day, and that a more normal average daily production was around 60/70 cars at that time.

The final copy that I have is dated July 1960, and is much concerned with the visit of the three "TRS" cars to Le Mans, where, as the magazine modestly states, "no prizes were won!" The members' small adverts continue to make fascinating reading, many people wanting to purchase hard tops for their cars, and also desiring items to enable them to upgrade TR2s into 3s and 3As. Alfin brake drums were another common "want," as were sliding sidescreens to replace the early fixed-pane type. The prices paid inevitably cause some amusement now - for instance, £5 for a brand new tyre, £2 for a new sidescreen and "fifty shillings" (£2-50) for a complete door!

30.   The November 1957 TSOA magazine contained an interesting item on speedometer inaccuracies caused by fitting radial ply tyres, and as this is of moment still today, I am reprinting it below exactly as originally set out. As can be seen, a car correctly registering 100 mph on the speedometer when fitted with the original Dunlop cross-ply tyres would in fact only be doing a true 94 mph when fitted with Michelin "X" tyres, a difference of 6%. As indicated, Smiths Industries produced specially converted speedometers for TRs fitted with "X" tyres, these being reference numbers SN/6307/11 for the 3.7 axle and SN/6307/10 for the 4.1 axle. I hope that the publishing of this information will enable the more mathematically-minded to avoid unwarranted boasting about their TRs' top speed in future!

31.   The following anecdote from 1958 is said to have been a true story - if so, I wonder how long the TR in question lasted as a plaything, and I hope that I never meet the boy now that he has presumably grown up! An "Eastern Potentate" was inspecting new American cars for sale in a motor showroom when his 9 year old son noticed a new TR3 parked in a corner. "I want it," he said firmly, repeating the demand when the salesman attending to his father patted his head soothingly. The salesman eventually fetched a model TR from his office to placate the child, which the awful boy promptly threw violently into a corner. "I want

that one!" he demanded, pointing to the real thing. The father agreed to this request, but unfortunately this particular TR had already been sold. After some frantic telephoning (and presumably bribery), the purchaser of the TR agreed to relinquish it in the boy's favour, for the boy would have no other than the one in the showroom, and the salesman was anxious to conclude a big deal with the father. The boy duly acquired the TR3 there and then, and was last seen driving (at 9 years old) the luckless TR round and round a hotel car park! Such is the power of money!

32.   In the Spring 1974 issue of the TR Register's magazine TRaction a brand new TR3A was offered for sale, at least 13 years after it must have been made - the price in 1974, £1,250! One wonders what the story behind the storage and non-use of this car was, and what became of it. At the time, good used TR3As were fetching £3/400, so laughable as it may seem in the 1990's, £1,250 was not perhaps such a bargain in 1974.

33.   Unfortunately, over the years many people have lost their lives in sidescreen TRs, particularly in the car's early days when crossply tyres or the early radials offered less grip than we are accustomed to today. One well-known person to suffer thus was Denis Brain, the virtuoso French horn player whose records are still sought after today. Denis Brain was always interested in sports cars as well as music, and he had a British Racing Green TR2, registration number SXX3. He was playing at the Edinburgh Festival in 1957, and at the time was living in London. After a concert one evening in Edinburgh, he elected to drive his TR back to London through the night, but unfortunately he left the road and hit a tree in Hatfield, Hertfordshire early in the morning, having almost made it to his destination. It is believed tiredness overcame him; no other vehicle was involved and he was killed outright. Terry Simpson, the founder and former President of the TR Register happened to live in Hatfield at the time, and vividly recalls inspecting Denis's TR shortly after the accident when it had been taken to the premises of a local garage. It was of course badly damaged, but I cannot find out whether it was written off or was eventually repaired. Either way, it was a sad fate to befall a lovely car and a fine musician who was much missed.

The story is told that Denis Brain used to take his motoring enthusiasm into the concert hall, being seen on more than one occasion with motoring magazines propped up on his music stand whilst playing under various famous conductors!

34.   When looking through back numbers of motoring magazines from the 1950's and 1960's whilst doing research for books such as this, I occasionally find intriguing adver-

tisements for TRs for sale at temptingly low prices! For instance, in the January 1969 issue of "Motorsport" a TR2 described as an "ex-Works" car (which one, I wonder?) was advertised for sale for £85 - the owner thought it necessary to add that no offers would be entertained on this price! This period in the late 1960's to early 1970's was when sidescreen TR prices were at their lowest, and the cars generally at their most run-down and uncared-for stage, many being run into the ground by impoverished students and the like eager for something rapid and noisy to impress the girls! On the very same page in that edition of "Motorsport" is the advertisement from DCM Auto Services, a company with a reputation in the late 1960's for selling some of the best sidescreen TRs available. Among their TRs for sale is a "Le Mans" TR3A, said to have been placed 19th at the 1960 Le Mans race. No price is quoted, but the advert states that the previous owner said that the car was so fast that it could only be driven in brown trousers! One can only presume that this car was one of the twin-cam TRS cars, possibly 926 HP which was known to be around in the UK in the early 1970's - and yet it is described as a TR3A, which it certainly wasn't!

In an issue of "Autosport" magazine published in September 1955, I came across an advertisement for a "two-tone red" TR2, said again to be an ex-Works car. Two-tone colours were rare on TRs at the best of times, and two-tone red would I suggest probably be unique, at least in the UK. It had overdrive, competition suspension and 10 inch brakes all round with racing linings, and the advertiser was Ted Lund, a well known competitor at the time both in TRs and MGs, and a man with something of a reputation as a tuning wizard. As mentioned in my interview with Tom Blackburn in Chapter Four, Ted Lund acquired OHP 771 in late 1954, and I am sure therefore that the car he was advertising a year later was none other than that same car, the original Road-Test TR2. It was painted Geranium, and possibly the "two-tone" effect was caused by the fitting of a hardtop in a contrasting red? Tom Blackburn confirms that the car was still finished in Geranium whilst Ted had it. Although it had belonged to the factory for its first year, it could not really be called an "Ex-Works" car in the Competition sense, for it was never part of the factory team. Tom cannot recall who purchased it, and as Ted Lund is no longer with us, the fate of this historic TR remains a mystery, for it has never resurfaced.

One of the ex-Works Alpine Rally TR2s, PDU 20 appeared several times in adverts in the late 1970's at various prices, and was even offered to your author at that time. It seemed too expensive at around £500, so to my great regret, I did not buy it. Even the "Jabbeke" car MVC 575 appeared for sale on the open market in the late 1970's, and the other development prototype TR2, MWK 950 was sold several times for very little money around then. Motoring magazines of the period make fascinating reading now, and nothing more so than the advertisements. Unfortunately, it is a most time-consuming task, and one I have not had the time to complete, so there is more TR history to be found if anyone has the opportunity!

35.   The "Grand Touring Conversion Kit" - this unusual item was developed largely to enable the Works Rally TRs to run in the closed car categories in continental rallies in addition to the open sports car categories, and this was something of an early "homologation special" item. It was conjured up in the 1956 period to be used in conjunction with the then already available hard top, and consisted principally of special sidescreens and a locking external door handle kit, because of course production TR3s did not have external door handles. The part number applicable to the whole kit was 554313, and Ian Gibson, who has seen one installed on a car, assures me that the whole thing was more complicated than might appear at first. The door handles and their mechanisms were **not** the same as were later used on the production TR3As, but are much sturdier and more elaborate, incorporating some 25 different parts.

The sidescreens differed as well from the normal item, and had a beading rather than lift-a-dot fasteners along their lower edge. Works competition TR3 SHP520 was evidently the vehicle that the factory used upon which to develop this kit. The conversion first appeared in the factory parts catalogues as late as August 1957 according to Ian, but a bulletin issued by the Works as early as March 1956 refers to the kit and it was used on the 1956 Alpine Rally cars. Taking into account the cost of the hardtop itself, the whole thing was

an expensive items that must have been rarely specified other than by competition minded people who wished to take advantage of "closed" or "GT" competition categories."

SHP 520 was an interesting car being, it is believed, initially an Engineering Department development vehicle, hence its use to perfect the GT kit. It became one of the 1956 and 1957 factory team cars, being used in May 1957 by Nancy Mitchell in the Mille Miglia. (it was fitted with wire wheels by then). Ken Richardson himself drove it in the 1956 Alpine Rally, and it was used again in the 1957 Liege-Rome-Liege event. It was probably the only one of the four mainstream 1956 Works team cars not to go to the USA, as it seesm that the other three, SRW 410, SRW 991 and SRW 992 went there in March 1957 for the Sebring race. They were replaced in the team by the "TRW" series cars, alongside which SHP 520 continued to run. It also had a pre-production set of front disc brakes for proving purposes, although it was initially built with drums. Another unique feature was the fitment of a long-range, 25 gallon fuel tank for the Mille Miglia.

36.   SRW 993 - both SRW 991 and SRW 992 were well documented Works team cars, and SRW 990 (which did one event as a Works car) has been referred to in paragraph 3 of this chapter. However, another "SRW" TR was SRW 993. This car was mentioned in an early issue of TRaction magazine, and was believed to have been a factory development car. It was not used in official competitions by the Works, but it is thought that Ken Richardson ran it as his own car for a period to try out disc brakes on the road, though Ken himself couldn't recall this when I interviewed him. Certainly the car was fitted early on with four-wheel Dunlop disc brakes, presumably for evaluation and comparison with the

French woman driver Anny Bousquet poses with one of the Works TR3s at the start of the Alpine Rally in 1956. This car was in fact driven in the event by Messrs Richardson and Heathcote who, unfortunately, did not finish (BMIHT Archive).

Girling two-wheel disc brakes that eventually reached production. It also had the GT conversion kit and hardtop and was fitted with a 2138 cc 86 mm bore engine, although presumably not from new. Maybe it was the car that Richardson used for his clandestine experiments with this larger engine, as described in the interview with him in Chapter Three. SRW 993 survived into the late 1960's, but has not been heard of in recent times.

37. Aluminium-bodied TR3As - for many years I have heard persistent rumours of the existence of such cars and as these have come from at least six separate sources, I do not think that they can be discounted. As is well known, the very earliest TR2s had certain aluminium body panels, notably the bonnet and spare wheel door, but in the case of the alleged aluminium TR3As, the whole outer body was said to be aluminium. Whether this material extended to the inner body and sills I do not know, but one can only presume that the reason was purely one of weight saving for competition purposes. The ancillary advantage of corrosion-resistance ought to have meant that any such cars built survived well, but I know of no existing example and would be pleased to learn of one such.

I discussed the possibility of the existence of such cars with Ken Richardson and although he could recall three such cars being built, he could not throw any light on the surrounding circumstances. They would be unlikely to have been Works rally cars as these are too well documented and well remembered, so possibly they were prototypes or private entrants' cars specially ordered. That one at least was a prototype is lent credence by the recollection of a TR Register member whose friend purchased an all-aluminium TR3A fitted with a twin-cam "Sabrina" engine in the mid 1960's. This was a road-going vehicle (not a Le Mans car) with an outward appearance exactly as a normal TR3A. Indeed, the friend, who had no previous TR experience, purchased the car ignorant of the fact that it should not have a twin cam engine or aluminium body! It was, needless to say, a very rapid machine, but its eventual fate is unknown. TR Register stalwart Alec Pringle clearly recalls a car answering to this description being in the Brighton area in the late 1960's and early 1970's, so just possibly this is the same car.

What is doubly strange is that although it is almost certain that Standard-Triumphs **did** fit twin-cam engines to some road-going cars for evaluation and development purposes, they normally removed these and substituted standard engines prior to selling off the cars. The owner of this twin-cam TR3A, upon realising that his vehicle was far from standard, telephoned the factory which confirmed that the car was indeed a development vehicle that "escaped". The other stories I have heard about aluminium bodied TR3A's

do not include twin-cam engines, so maybe in these cases the normal procedure of substituting an ordinary motor prior to sale was followed. I should add that we are not here talking about any of the three 1959 Le Mans race TR3S cars, for these had fibreglass rather than aluminium bodies, as well as extended wheel-bases and I think that we can rely on TR enthusiasts to be able to tell the difference! Although not made in aluminium, one lightweight steel panelled TR at least did exist, for a factory record card for TS 32618 states "special lightweight body in 22 gauge steel, for the attention of Mr. A.E. Ballard in the Engineering Department" - another mystery car!

38.   The "speed" models - I have written before concerning the mysterious "speed" model TR2s, three at least of which were built but a little more information has now come to light. The first such car was numbered TS 19 (SP) LO, and was built on 22nd September 1953, finished in white with Geranium trim and left hand steering. The build record clearly indicates that the "SP" letters were part of the car's commission number, but we do not know whether they were actually included on the bulkhead plate. I feel certain that this particular car was constructed as a "Jabbeke" replica for the 1953 London Motor Show, for it was fitted with the same streamlined body equipment as the Jabbeke car. The November 1953 issue of the "Standard Car Review" magazine, when reporting on the Motor Show, refers to one exhibit as being "an identical car to the Jabbeke car, but in white." TS 19 is the only TR built to that specification in time to have been shown at that event, so this must have been our first "speed" model, and the conclusion must be that "speed" model TR2s were meant to be full Jabbeke replicas. Maybe the Works hoped to sell quite a few, but if they did, they must have been disappointed, for an exhaustive search through the first 2,000 TR2 build records has only revealed two more such cars, both of which, amazingly, were supplied to New Zealand!

These cars were TS 612 (SP) and TS 767 (SP), and strangely, neither appears to have been fitted with overdrive. TS 612 was built on 12th February 1954, right hand drive, finished in Ice Blue with Blackberry trim, and a note in the build record says, "fit all high-speed equipment." The delivery destination is listed as Invercargill, New Zealand. TS 767 was an identical car as regards colour and specification and was built on 3rd March 1954. The delivery destination is listed as Christchurch, New Zealand. One wonders why two of these three Jabbeke replicas should have gone halfway round the world? Perhaps a New Zealand TR enthusiast can do some digging and enlighten us! As to the fate of the first car, TS 19, I would surmise that being left hand drive, it was sent to North America; I have recently received a letter from a Mr Wogan in Canada which might possibly shed some light on it. Around 20 or so years ago a friend of his, the owner of a long door TR2, so presumably a man who knew his TRs, was shown in the Toronto area a TR2 fitted with a metal ton-neau cover, undershield and rear wheel spats. This car was also said to have had an extremely low commission number, though the exact number is not recalled. Could this have been the speed model TS 19? It certainly seems possible! TS 612 (SP) is listed as still in existence by the New Zealand TR Regisgter, but of TS 767 (SP), nothing is known. As to the letters 'SP', one would assume that they were an abbreviation of "speed", but it has also been suggested that they stood for "special project". - I can believe this in relation to TS 19, but TS 617 and 767 were production cars, so the designation "special project" would seem inappropriate.

French ladies crew, Lise Renaud (left) and Annie Soisbeault are pictured during the 1958 Lyon-Charbonnieres Rally. Their Paris-registered TR3A received some Works assistance, but was a private entry ("Autosport").

TR2 STO 555 leads an unidentified sports car at Mallory Park on 14th September 1957. Maybe the secons car is one of the fibreglass Jowett Jupiter R4 prototypes? (NMM Beaulieu).

Above: this looks as though it could be the marshalling area at Silverstone and what a superb example of a typical Fifties race day, with Austin-Healeys (a rare 100S front left), Healey Silverstone, Jaguar XKs, early Lotus and a whole panorama of typical 1950s traffic in the car park behind. Below is a very tidy and standard-looking TR3 being propelled round Brands Hatch by an unknown driver at Brabds Hatch on 18th August 1957 (NMM Beaulieu).

Fifties Silverstone! No courtesy suites to block the view of Wooscote from the parking area and a chance to get close to the action. Here a TR2 is doing what it should be doing - and pretty close to the limit, too, by the attitude of the driver (NMM Beaulieu).

Goodwood this time. A TR3A (UYM 8) presses on, having suffered some frontal derangement! (NMM Beaulieu).

Above is an outwardly standard-looking TR3A with a hardtop, racing at Brands Hatch. The event and driver(s) are unknown, but the date is 22nd March 1959. From the dual competitor numbers on the side, it is clearly a shared car, though (NMM Beaulieu). Below: what a perfect way to spend a Sunday. The location is Firel Hill Climb in Sussex and the date is Sunday 31st May 1959. JR Henley gets away from the start in his TR3 ("Autosport").

A TR CAMEO WITH COLOUR

This rare colour photograph shows the launch of the TR2 and Swallow Doretti in California in January 1954. Full details of this event are in Chapter 9 (Standard Car Review).

Film star Eva Bartok poses with producer Michael Carreras on the set of the feature film "Break in the Circle", filmed in 1954. A rare and delightful period colour shot, showing the correct shade of British Racing Green for TR2s. PDU 730 was a Publicity Department car, which is believed still to exist (TR Register Archive).

An unusual colour shot, taken in 1955, which proves that the existence of two-tone colour schemes on sidescreen TRs dates right back to the mid-1950s. As far as is known, these were not offered by the Factory, but were frequently dealer-applied later. Here, the driver is Duane Rice, waiting at the start of a race at Stockton, California (TR Register Archive).

A contemporary colour shot from the Summer of 1955 sees the TR2 of JW Reid-Jones parked by Llyn Llydon in North Wales, with the summit of Mount Snowdon in the background (J Woolverton).

A general view of the car park at a TR Register national meeting in 1974. Sidescreen TRs were still then in everyday use and, as can be seen, their condition was frequently fairly disreputable!

A marvellous colour transparency used for advertising purposes by Cal-Sales Incorporated in early 1956. The shot was taken at the Lido Yacht Anchorage at Newport Beach, California, and shows a TR3 in the rare Beige colour, with a contrasting Sunset Red hardtop. This picture manages to convey the wealthy life style into which so many USA-bound were delivered at the time, so different from the cut-and-thrust of Winter rallying in northern England, yet just as much a part of the TR scene (Cal-Sales Inc).

A 1980s photograph of ex-Works TR3 TRW 735 in its restored state, showing the correct Apple Green shade, in which the 1957 and 1958 Team cars were finished (Jon Laver).

A transparency taken by the Works official photographer, Frank Callaby, shows a TR3 in an idyllic seaside setting in Summer 1956. The perfect calendar shot! (TR Register Archive)

Ladies quite frequently raced TRs and here we see Gillian Spooner pressing her TR2 round Copse Corner at Silverstone Circuit. The year is believed to be 1957 ("Autosport").

Above: a varied selection of new TR3s are seen in full colour in Austria on the 1957 "Tour of Europe" TSOA Rally. Note that all the cars visible carry "NKV" Coventry personal-export registration plates (TR Register Archive).

Right: Pictured from another car on the route is Mr Dundas' TR3; it is believed the event is the Highland Rally, probably in 1958 ("Autosport").

This extraordinary colour scheme was seen on the Cal-Sales Incorporated stand at the Los Angeles Motor Show at Christmas 1956. Presumably, the paint finish was dealer applied in the USA - maybe the car was one of the very few which left Coventry in primer? Chrome wire wheels (48 spokes) are in evidence, along with white-wall tyres (Cal-Sales Inc).

Two Works TR3As are seen at a control on what is thought to be the Circuit of Ireland Rally in 1959 ("Autosport").

This car (owner unknown) is included as a representative example of a modern restoration to a good standard, both of condition and originality. It also makes a very agreeable picture! (TR Register Archive).

On the Terrace at Monte Carlo Casino, one of the "VRW" Works TR3As is seen, following the finish of the 1958 Monte Carlo Rally. The Apple Green colour shows to advantage, but note the garish un-Rover-like colour scheme on the car behind! This car (VRW 219) was the Ladies Team car, driven by Ms Annie Soisbault and Ms P Ozanne, who retired due to cumulative lateness (TR Register Archive).

Above: A TR3A is used as a fashion accessory - "Vogue" fashion models are seen posing with the TR at the American Pavilion, which was part of the 1958 Brussels Exhibition. Note the heavy-weight television camera! (TR Register Archive).

Left: A West London street scene from 1972 sees the author's TR3A alongside one of London Transport's classic and long-lived "RT" Series AEC-built double-decker buses. A parked Sunbeam Rapier provides further interest.

The pit crew of Hyde Motors Incorporated of San Francisco, pose by their equipe at Palm Springs, California in 1958. This company sponsored a successful TR3 racing car, just visible on the trailer (BMIHT).

A TR3A in Spain; whilst on holiday in 1959, Mr GG Evans took this impressive colour view of car, mountains and girl in appropriate dress, on the road from Leon to Oviedo (GG Evans).

Above: The Fire Chief in the City of Rochester, New York, chose a TR3A as a rapid-response vehicle in 1959, appropriately painted in red. Here he poses with the TR, which seems to be equipped with either a mighty siren or possibly a search light (TR Register Archive).

Right: this TR3 belongs to Martin Lodawer, of California. USA style "wind-wings" are in evidence, as are wheel trims, but Martin tells me that the British registration plates are only for photographic purposes. The car would appear to be finished in the unusual Winchester Blue, obtainable only on 1956/57 model year TR3s (Martin Lodawer).

Above: a USA TR3A speeds along in the hills of California, showing off its Powder Blue paintwork. The car is being driven by its owner, Steve Bergath (Martin Lodawer).

On the left is Bob Woodley's Coventry registered, drum-braked, TR3, which was believed to have been originally a press demonstrator. It has been beautifully restored to its original colour of Salvador Blue, a rare and attactive paint finish used only on 1955/56 model year TR3s (Bob Woodley).

Above: This is one of the extremely rare 1953 colour shots of a production TR. NHP 49 is seen here with Ken Richardson at the wheel: this car was TS10-LO and it makes a splendid picture finished in Pearl White, with what was probably Geranium trim (Julian Stephens).

On the right is a photograph to show the state into which some sidscreen cars had declined by the 1970s. Leaving them outside for years was not conducive to survival, but even disasters such as this can be rebuilt with the vast array of spares now available (TR Register Archive).

John Hopwood poses with former World Grand Prix Champion, Jackie Stewart, by John's very original TR2, which is used today in historic rallying. John also rallied TRs many years ago and it is said that Stewart was seen in sidescreen TRs in his early days (John Hopwood).

Left: Ron Gouldbourn and Stuart Turner (right) look pleased with themselves as they lean on Ron's TR3. They have clearly collected a prize or two in their most recent event; the date is November 1958 ("Autosport").

Above: the reader may recognise these two images of the 20TS Triumph Sports from the black-and-white brochure picture in Chapter 7. This is the artwork for the early colour publicity material distributed at the 1952 London Motor Show (TR Register Archive).

The German-owned TR3A on the left carried a well-painted Union Jack under its bonnet when presented at a TR Register concours in the late 1970s. The car's condition was superb, but unfortunately, it met with an accident going to the event. The judges, however, decided to ignore the dent and the car duly won top prize (TR Register Archive).

CHAPTER SIX:

Contemporary Tuning Items & Accessories

I shall examine in this chapter those items available to the private owner during the production currency of the TR2/3/3A series, in an attempt to show what could be done at the time both to give the car extra performance and to make it more individual and better suited to the owner's requirements. A great deal of such extra equipment was (and in some cases still is) available for the sidescreen TR; the large numbers in which the car was produced created a big enough potential market to justify production of many accessories and performance aids, and the fact that many cars were used in competitions also encouraged suppliers and designers. Of course, in the 1980's and 90's, following the considerable resurgence of interest in tuning four-cylinder TR's consequent principally upon the introduction of the TR Register Race Championship, many more sophisticated aids to TR speed and safety have become available, and the cars can now be made to perform in all respects better than in their heyday. Admirable as they are, however, these modern items have no place in a book written from a historical perspective, and in any event, information on 1990's TR tuning items is readily available from the specialists.

As was mentioned in the chapter dealing with Ken Richardson, the Standard-Triumph factory carried out surprisingly little tuning development work on the TR engine, or on other aspects of the car for that matter, and the Works cars were genuinely little different from the production machines. Most of the equipment fitted to them was available to the public either as optional original equipment or for "after-market" installation, and the factory-produced accessory and options leaflets to set out what was available, one of them being reproduced in this Chapter.

In the absence of much "factory" development therefore, the field was wide open to individual entrepreneurs to devise and sell performance items to the TR owner who wanted to go just that bit faster then his neighbour in an ostensibly similar car. Principal among the tuning firms supplying performance equipment for TRs in the 1950's and 60's were S.A.H. Ltd, V. W. Derrington and Co, Wilen Engineering and Lawrencetune. These firms, with others, plugged the gap left by the factory's comparative lack of interest. Unlike MG's Abingdon works, which supplied a well proven series of engine modifications for their cars in progressive stages, and backed them with supporting literature and even guarantees in some cases, Standard-Triumph did not even list so much as a Stage One cylinder head! It is true that it was possible to have one's TR worked upon by the Competitions Department in Coventry, but this was an informal arrangement, and in any event, with even the Works TRs so standard in specification, concentrating on strength and reliability rather than outright performance, the Factory had little to sell. It was not surprising therefore that private enterprise stepped in with tuning equipment; what I find the more surprising is that, having built and developed the clubman's sports-car par excellence, the factory should have neglected so obvious a market. It is small wonder that by 1960, Austin Healeys and MGs began to eclipse the TR as the rally car for the keen amateur to have, and that the TR4 never had anything like the competition success at any level as its sidescreen ancestors.

For the sake of completeness, I list below that Factory-supplied equipment which could be called performance related (as opposed to comfort, safety or appearance related):-

1.   Overdrive: usually ordered from new, but could, at considerable expense, be retro-fitted. Initially this operated

on top gear only, but from car no. TS 6266 in May 1955, overdrive operated on 2nd, 3rd and top gear, endowing the TR with what was in effect a seven-speed gearbox, for there was no useless overlapping of the overdrive gearing with the direct ratios, all seven speeds being distinctly different.

2.   Cast aluminium engine sump;- at 12 pints, this had a greater oil capacity than the normal item, and its aluminium finned construction gave better oil cooling at speed, particularly as it projected downwards into the airflow under the car by about 1 1/2" more than the steel sump. However, for rough rallying purposes this was far from ideal as it was very vulnerable, and the fitment of a sump shield was not practical for lack of ground clearance.

3. Wire wheels; these provided better brake cooling, and also much more rapid wheel-changing possibilities, useful for racing work. They were, however, heavier than steel wheels, more vulnerable to damage, needed regular maintenance and cleaning of the spokes and did not allow the fitment of tubeless tyres. Perhaps for these reasons (and cost?) they were rarely specified on new TRs, possibly only around 10 to 15% of new cars being thus fitted. It has however become much more fashionable to fit them in recent years, the conversion being a very easy matter due to the use of bolt-on splines utilising the same hubs as the standard steel wheels. I should add that TR2's and Lockhead drum braked TR3's built new with wire wheels had a different arrangement whereby the hubs and halfshafts were particular to the the wire wheel fitment. The wire wheels themselves were of the 48 spoked variety on almost all sidescreen TRs fitted with them as new, but it was possible later in the TR3A's production run to specify 60 spoked wheels, these being considerably stronger for competition purposes. Chromed wire wheels were also available, although these seem principally to have been supplied for the USA market.

4.   4.1 to 1 rear axle ratio:- this could be supplied (only in conjunction with overdrive) for TR3 and 3A owners who felt that the standard gearing was too high for competition work. It gave marginally improved acceleration at the cost of slightly increased fuel consumption and a certain loss of the TR's legendary high speed cruising ability. In my experience, it was very rarely specified.

5.   Competition (i.e. uprated) front shock absorbers and larger, stiffer rear shock absorbers.

6.   Uprated (stiffer) front and rear springs.

7.   Aero-windscreens; these can be called a performance item as their fitment considerably reduced the TR's frontal area (by almost 20%) thereby increasing maximum

speed by around 5 mph. The original factory supplied type (very rare today) were deeper than the modern "Brooklands" type, and they bolted direct to pre-drilled mountings in the scuttle top. For some reason, these mounting points were deleted in April 1958, at car no. TS 32833.

8.   Undershield

9.   Rear wing spats (more detailed information on these in Chapter 5)

10.   Metal tonneau cockpit cover.

The above items were catalogued in the early days of the sidescreen cars, and all were useful in streamlining the car for maximum speed racing work. However, accessibility, brake and engine cooling were all impaired, and few such items were sold or fitted.

11.   Skid plate - this was a rally-developed sump shield which bolted under the steel sump. It could not be fitted with the aluminium sump due to its extra depth. The skid plate had holes drilled in it to facilitate cooling.

12.   Anti-roll bar - this item had a Standard-Triumph part number (508397) but does not appear in the accessory list I have seen. It appears only to have been available for the TR3A. The example I have picks up on the TR3A type front bumper supports, and for this reason cannot fit the TR2/3 cars without modification. I do not think that the Factory ever catalogued an anti-roll bar specifically for the TR2/3.

13.   Dunlop "Road Speed" and "High Speed" tyres, together with Michelin "X" radials, were listed at various times as options.

14.   Aluminium brake drums - these were manufactured by the firm of Wellworthy and Co, and marketed as "Al-fin" drums. They were cast aluminium, fitted with steel liners, and gave much better heat dissipation and thereby brake cooling. Available in either 9 inch or 10 inch sizes, they usually had lateral cooling fins, though some I have seen had circumferential fins. Although not a product of Standard Triumph, they had the company's blessing, were marketed along with the various official factory extras, and could be ordered on a new car.

15.   Lucas Magneto: this mystery item definitely existed for the TR (I have seen one installed), but I can find no Lucas part number and only an implied reference to it in official Works literature. Presumably fitted primarily for racing purposes, it replaced the coil and distributor, the Magneto being more efficient in providing reliable sparks at high engine

A sprint meeting at Staverton airfield on 30th September 1956 included this hardtop-equipped TR2. Observe how the "go-faster" stripes that heralded the "boy-racer" era have materialised on this unfortunate TR in embryonic form (NMM Beaulieu).

An unusual "accessory" is seen fitted to Works TR3A VRW 223. An adjustable "hood" is positioned above the two additional spotlights - presumably to prevent glare and to direct the beam to some extent? This device was used in the 1958 Monte Carlo Rally.

speed as compared with the early types of coil ignition. However, by the 1950's coil ignition systems were fully capable of providing all the sparks even a racing TR would need, so I am somewhat surprised that a Magneto was made for the TR. It did have an ancillary advantage in that no battery was needed for racing (thus saving quite a lot of weight), but this would not have applied to a road car with other electrical equipment to power.

16:      2138cc engine option available from early 1959, using 86mm bore pistons.

As mentioned earlier, Standards left it to private enterprise to provide and develop engine tuning items, and I now propose to look at the more important of these firms in detail. The firm of S.A.H. Accessories Ltd, founded by Sid Hurrell, is probably the most well known of the Triumph equipment suppliers, for they concentrated heavily on the TR series, although taking in Spitfire and other Triumph models during the 1960's and 70's. They always maintained a supply of performance items for even the earliest TR2s right through the lean years of the early 70's, when the cars were worth very little and being driven into the ground by the impecunious. With the one honourable exception of Reg Woodcock's highly developed TR3, almost no four cylinder TRs were being raced in the UK at this period, and very few were being road tuned, so in retrospect it is surprising that S.A.H. were able to continue to supply such parts in the face of declining interest. Presumably the business was buoyed-up by demand for later TR equipment, and also items for the Herald/Vitesse and Spitfire series. Gradually, the firm moved away from Triumph items into SAAB equipment, supplying accessories for the Swedish make, having commenced as a sideline around 1959. Sid Hurrell retired some years ago, but his son, Terry, continues to this day manufacturing and supplying many of the items developed for TRs by his father, Terry's firm trading as Triumphtune Ltd, a firm under the umbrella of the Moss Motors Group. New items are also still being developed.

A full grid of cars lines up at Goodwood for a "TRs-only" race, such was the popularity of the sidescreen TR at the time (August 1958). Interestingly, on the front row can be seen Sid Hurrell's later TR, SAH 137, plus his TR2 PYU 430, which had presumably been passed on by this date ("Autosport").

Sid Hurrell began his association with TRs with an early TR2, registered PYU 430, which car he raced and tuned himself in the mid 1950's. It was developed progressively by Hurrell until it was one of the fastest TRs on the circuits, and inevitably a demand grew up from fellow competitors for Sid's modified parts, leading to the formation of S.A.H. in 1956. By 1957, the company was operating a fully equipped TR tuning and maintenance workshop from premises at Leighton Buzzard in Bedfordshire, Sid soon moving on to a TR3A specially registered SAH 137, which, like its predecessor, was one of the very fastest of TRs. This car was both a test bed for modifications and also a mobile advertisement for SAH, whose business increased in proportion. A comprehensive catalogue was produced, which went through several editions and which contained virtually everything that a TR racer, rallyist or road tuner could need, from an S.U. carburettor needle right up to an "off the shelf" 135 or 140 BHP engine. This "full S.A.H. engine" was fitted to a surprisingly large number of road going TR's, and consisted of a modified high-compression cylinder head, a matched and polished inlet manifold and competition valve springs. A high lift "SAH 26" camshaft was fitted, together with the later specification, cross-drilled crankshaft and 86 mm pistons and liners, though the 83 mm items could be supplied to keep the car under the 2 litre limit for competition if required. Special "Glacier" bearings were installed, the flywheel was lightened and the whole engine assembly and clutch was carefully balanced. A four-branch, extractor-type exhaust manifold was fitted, along with a Lucas sports-type coil. The conversion utilised the original 1 3/4" S.U. carburettors, only the needles being changed, and in this form the modified engine produced 135/140 B.H.P. gross, as compared with a standard output in TR3/3A form of 100 BHP gross.

"Low port" cars with 1 1/2" carburettors could be converted,

but the final power produced was down by around 10 BHP. The cost of the full conversion, which also included what was in effect an engine rebuild, was £172 exchange in 1966, an outright purchase being possible for £227. Fitting to a customer's car, including setting up (SAH had its own rolling-road facility) and final testing cost a further £25. Although these figures look risible today, it must be borne in mind that the full conversion cost probably half the then current value of an early TR in the mid 1960's, so it was a major investment, albeit one that could be fully justified if the existing engine was well worn. Buyers in search of even more horse power could purchase a further 8-10 BHP by having a pair of 45 DCOE Weber carburettors fitted in place of the SU's. Substituting these demanded a special inlet manifold which SAH could supply, together with a different throttle linkage system. These 45 DCOE carburettors then needed to be "set-up" as regards jets and chokes to give of their best for each individual engine, so it is small wonder that the whole twin Weber carburettor system cost £72, or getting on for £900 in today's terms! SAH's catalogue carries a warning note to the effect that Weber carburettors should not be fitted to an otherwise unmodified engine, as not only will their full potential not be released, but fuel consumption will be adversely affected!

For those not wanting the full engine conversion, SAH supplied cylinder heads of types A, B and C specification and these were recommended as a first item of performance tuning, the type A head claiming to produce an extra 10 BHP when used with the SAH "free-flow" silencer. Type B was similar, but with all new valves and springs, whereas type C had ovesized inlet valves. All heads had a raised compression ratio, balanced combustion chambers and enlarged and polished inlet and exhaust porting. An extractor type 4 branch exhaust manifold was suggested as the next stage, this item being said to be worth between 5 and 8 BHP, and it

Sid Hurrell of SAH Limited, in PYU 430, keeps just ahead of RF North during a race at Goodwood in June 1956 ("Autosport").

Below: Sid Hurrell's TR3 is shown at Silverstone in 1958, demonstrating its front as modified for aerodynamic efficiency.

was also claimed to give cooler running.

Among other performance items supplied by this enterprising firm were oil cooler kits, reground camshafts, carburettor ram pipes, high pressure fuel pumps, "Kenlowe" electric radiator fans, sports coils, uprated springs and shock absorbers, lowering kits for racing, anti-roll bars, wire wheel conversion kits magnesium "Minilite" wheels, "Powr-lok" limited slip differentials, Girling "Powerstop" brake servo kits, lightweight, glass-fibre body parts and much else besides. Incidentally, I was most surprised to see from their 1966 catalogue that a transistorised ignition system was available for TRs at that early date, at a cost of 14 guineas complete!

With the copy of the company's catalogue that I have came a reprint of a road test by "Sports Car" magazine in July 1962 of an SAH modified car. Admittedly this test was of a TR4, but there is no reason to believe that a TR3A similarly modified would perform any more slowly. The 135 BHP engine conversion was fitted, using the original SU carburettors and the car had overdrive with the standard 3·7 to 1 rear axle

ratio. A "Kenlowe" electric fan was used, and in this form the car proved capable, in this presumably independent test, of a genuine 130 mph, 0-60 in 8.6 seconds and 0-100 in 22.8 seconds, quite impressive figures. In addition, it was tractable enough to idle at a regular 800 RPM and was also able to be driven smoothly at and to pull away clearly from that engine speed. Clearly therefore this was a well developed vehicle, capable of racing at weekends with a good chance of success in its class, yet docile enough to be used as everyday transport. Incidentally the TR4 involved was registered SAH 137, as successor to Hurrell's TR3A.

I have devoted quite some space to SAH, but I feel that this is fully justified, for they were **the** name in TR tuning from the late 1950's onwards, and were the only firm who, ath the time, specialised solely in Triumphs and their conversion. SAH claimed to carry the largest stock of TR2/3/3A spares in the country, and they liaised closely with several former Works-trained mechanics who had been involved in Ken Richardson's Competitions Department. As the company was also officially sanctioned by Standard-Triumph as TR conversion specialists, SAH could be said to have been the true heirs to the 1950's Works Competitions Department. They carried on the tuning and development of the four cylinder TR in a way that one presumes Ken Richardson and his men would have done had the company's management authorised it and had funds been available. Truly the words "SAH Converted" were a virtual guarantee of a well-sorted, rapid TR when the cars were at their zenith. Although SAH were the largest specialist TR tuning equipment producers during the period under review, they were not the earliest on the scene; this honour goes I think to the Surrey firm of V W Derrington Ltd.

Vic Derrington had considerable experience of tuning and of manufacturing "go faster" items for various types of performance vehicles, and his shop in London Road, Kingston,

Reprinted from **AUTOSPORT**, September 16, 1955

JOHN BOLSTER TRIES

A TR2 – *PLUS*

Derrington modifications add even more performance to an already outstanding car

ABOUT the beginning of 1954, I road-tested a new Triumph sports car. At that time, incredible to relate, the cognomen "TR2" meant nothing to the man in the street, and all the many competition successes were still hidden in the future. How time flies!

It's fun to say, "I told you so", and, therefore, it is pleasant to turn back to that old report. The very first sentence reads—"The Triumph TR2 is the most important new sports car which has been introduced for some time". For once, Bolster was right. All of which introduces the subject of the current test, which is a "tuned" version of the same model.

The Triumph TR2, in standard form, gives a genuine 100 m.p.h. performance, coupled with remarkable reliability and fuel economy. That, one might think, is enough to be going on with from a relatively cheap and well-equipped sports car. The answer, of course, is that it's only enough until you want to beat another TR2! These cars appear in club events every week-end, and so a demand has grown up for special equipment that will extract a few more b.h.p. from the willing engine.

V. W. Derrington, of 159-161 London Road, Kingston-on-Thames, has long been known as a purveyor of bits and pieces for the man in search of extra speed. He has now turned his attention to the TR2, and, in fact, races one of these cars himself. I recently borrowed this machine for a week, and these notes are the result.

Bigger Carburetters

The most important modification is a new induction system, with larger carburetters. These are SU instruments, as are the standard ones, but they have a bore of 1¾ ins. instead of the normal 1½ ins. The new inlet manifold has a balance pipe, and blends the larger carburetters with the existing ports, so that only the minimum of "marrying up" is necessary.

In addition, Derrington's car has a new exhaust manifold. The swept pipes pair off cylinders 1 and 4, 2 and 3, entering the standard silencer via a junction box. An extra straight-through silencer has been fitted in the tail pipe that well-known raucous note.

The induction side of the job, including the two big carburetters, costs £40. The exhaust manifold comes to £20, with an extra £1 5s. for the tail pipe silencer. Incidentally, the test car also has a Scintilla Vertex magneto, and a few other detail modifications of which more anon.

On the road, the first impression is that the "tuned" car is quieter than the standard model. I like fast cars to be silent, and so I applaud this exhaust manifold. No loss of flexibility is occasioned by having larger carburetters, and the traffic manners are impeccable. Cold starting is instantaneous.

Standing ¼ mile—17.6 secs.

The acceleration is identical to standard up to 30 m.p.h., wheelspin being the deciding factor in this range. Further up the scale, a steady improvement is recorded. Naturally, a very large power increase would be required to make spectacular gains, but those few useful fifths of a second may make just the difference to beating the other chap into the next corner. I did 0-60 m.p.h. on a re-calibrated speedometer in 10.8 secs., and the standing quarter-mile occupied 17.6 secs.

As regards speed, I got a timed maximum of 107.1 m.p.h. In case you are a Triumph owner, this means 116/118 m.p.h. on the speedometer, if yours is a similar instrument to the one on the test car. These runs were made with the hood and sidescreens in position.

It is needless to remark that one cannot get something for nothing. The improved power output is obtained by passing more air through the engine at maximum revs., mixed with an appropriate quantity of petrol. In the hands of a fast driver, the modified car uses up to 20 per cent. more fuel than a standard one, which is about what one

would expect. Apart from this greater thirst, however, there are no other disadvantages.

Modified Bucket Seat

Another useful modification had been made to the driver's bucket seat. Its side had been extended to hold one from slipping towards the passenger's seat, and a padded buffer was also fitted inside the offside door. There are many other makes of cars that would benefit from such treatment, some of them actually being dangerous through the lack of lateral support provided. I am repeatedly telling puzzled drivers that their mysterious steering maladies and cornering difficulties may all be traced to the seat of their pants. I enjoyed flinging Derrington's Triumph through the corners with my posterior firmly anchored in the seat. Would-be competition drivers should certainly check this point.

A common fault among sports cars is loose spokes in their wire wheels. Modern wheels seem particularly prone to this, and the test car has rebuilt rear wheels. These have 64 spokes each, and the 4.50 ins. rims give extra support to the tyres. The battery has also been taken from the bonnet to the boot, which supplies a little more weight to hold down the rear axle at the expense of luggage room.

Very beautiful is the wood rimmed steering wheel. Of laminated and riveted construction, this adds greatly to the appearance of the driving compartment, and is pleasant to the touch. It is the kind of thing that makes a popular model stand out from the crowd, if one has £12 to spare.

The Triumph TR2 is an excellent sports car, and in standard form it will satisfy the majority of owners. For those who want a TR2 with a difference, however, a visit to V. W. Derrington is more than worth while.

WAY IN is through a pair of 1¾ ins. SU carburetters (instead of 1½ ins.) plus a new manifold with balance pipe.

WAY OUT is via this new exhaust system which pairs off cylinders 1 and 4, and 2 and 3. An extra tail-pipe silencer is available.

Modified Cylinder Head	6 B.H.P.
Extractor Exhaust Manifold	7 B.H.P.
High Speed Inlet Manifold	3 B.H.P.
Ram Pipes for S.U.	2-3 B.H.P.
Modified Camshaft	6 B.H.P.
Twin Choke Weber	10 B.H.P.

This recommended equipment has been tested by the Works Experimental Department on an otherwise standard engine unit producing 90 B.H.P. gross at 4,400 R.P.M. with the following increases of B.H.P. at the same revolutions.

As these increases generally improve as a direct percentage of the gross power developed, the actual power given upon a tuned engine for any one may therefore be considerably higher. Thus the extractor manifold giving 7 B.H.P. more at 90 B.H.P. would be over 8 H.P. better on an engine delivering 100 B.H.P.

COMPARATIVE ROAD PERFORMANCE FIGURES

for the various modifications to TR2 and TR3 models. First column of figures are those obtained from tests of the particular car as delivered, and second or third columns modified as described. Maximum speeds were attained over approximately 1½ miles and not true speeds attainable.

	1955 TR2 fitted inlet and exhaust manifolds and H6 carburetters		1954 TR2—mileage 30,060			1957 TR3—mileage 2,500 Modified cylinder head, inlet and exhaust manifold	
				Modified cylinder head only	Plus exhaust manifold only		
0–30 m.p.h.	2.8 secs.	2.2 secs.	2.8 secs.	2.4 secs.	2.0 secs.	3.2 secs.	2.8 secs.
0–50 "	5.4 "	4.8 "	6.2 "	5.8 "	5.3 "	8.6 "	6.2 "
0–70 "	11.3 "	9.3 "	13.2 "	12.6 "	11.8 "	14.4 "	12.6 "
50–80 " 3rd gear	6.5 "	5.8 "	Not taken	—	—	8.4 "	7.2 "
20–60 " top gear	Not taken	—	15.8 secs.	12.1 secs.	11.5 secs.	14.8 secs.	13 secs.
Maximum 3rd gear	82 m.p.h.	86 m.p.h.	80 m.p.h.	85 m.p.h.	88 m.p.h.	79 m.p.h.	88 m.p.h.
Maximum top gear	103 "	110 "	101 "	106 "	110 "	103 "	113 "

On the left, a reprint from an "Autosport" article by John Bolster, reviewing Derrington's TR2 tuning kit and on the right, a copy of the TR page of Derrington's catalogue.

V.W. DERRINGTON LTD
KINGSTON 5621-2

**159 & 161 LONDON ROAD
KINGSTON - ON - THAMES
ENGLAND**

Open 9a.m.-6p.m. Sunday 9a.m.-1p.m.

RACING AND HIGH SPEED TUNING EQUIPMENT

As the original specialists on tuning equipment for the TR2, introducing these first in early 1955, our modifications and equipment have been eminently successful and extensively copied. Successes include winning the Belgian Sports Car Championship held on the Spa Circuit for successive years 1956 and 1957, with fully Derrington equipped TR2 & 3 models, using steering and road wheels, modified cylinder heads, inlet and exhaust manifolds, oil radiators and fume screens.

TUNING FOR RACING

The cylinder head is the greatest source of power, so this should be the first modification. Better "breathing" and exhausting are largely contributory, so these should be next. Higher maximum speeds can be obtained from the use of a high lift camshaft, at the expense of low speed torque and irregular low speed running, whereas the other modifications improve both. Continuous high speed motoring causes the oil and bearings to overheat, so these should be cooled by the use of the large capacity aluminium sump and the oil radiator, the latter reducing the oil temperature by 15° to 20° Centigrade.

Improved road holding and braking are necessary for high speed safety, and thus competition springs, shock absorbers, front anti-roll bars, broadbase road wheels, special brake linings and Alfin brake drums for non-disc brake models, provide these vital improvements. Control of the car at high speed is greatly assisted by our conversion to the bucket seats, which also gives greater comfort.

Our Tuning Department, staffed by fully experienced engineers, is at your service for Tuning, Modifications, Overhauls and repairs, and our Mobile Workshop is present at the more important Race Meetings for Racing Driver Service.

MODIFIED CYLINDER HEADS

These have the compression raised to 9 or 9.5-1, inlet ports and seatings "gas flowed" for high velocity filling and improved flow from the exhaust ports. The combustion chambers are reshaped for better filling, exhausting and thermal efficiency, and with the ports are ground and highly polished, which also slows down the rate of carbon deposit. The valves are specially seated and tested for gas tightness. These improvements develop considerably more power with no greater tendency to pink, but "harder" or cooler sparking plugs are necessary for racing. The engine is equally tractable with the extra performance, and also has slightly better fuel consumption.

Cost upon exchange or to own cylinder head ... £25 $70.00
„ „ of modified head c/w valves and springs, outright sale ... £50 $140.00
„ of head only, less valves, TR3 high lift ... £16 17s. 6d. $47.25

TR 3 HIGH SPEED INDUCTION MANIFOLD

High Speed Intake Pipe for H.2. or H.6. S.U. Carburetters, de-siameses the inlet and feeds the mixture evenly to each port with higher gas speed. Polished internally, plated finish ... £11 10s. 0d. $32.60
or complete with H.6. carburetters, control linkages, flexibly mounted float chambers and fuel pipe line ... £36 0s. 0d. £100.80

Ram Pipes for S.U. intakes, as developed for maximum power, patented design for equalising depression between intake and S.U. suction chamber, retuning unnecessary. In light alloy, 1½" and 3½" ... per pair £1 17s. 6d. ($5.25)

CAMSHAFTS, HIGH LIFT, OVERLAP
Specially developed, producing good torque from 1,000 R.P.M., and more power at maximum revolutions, with similar fuel consumption ... £19 10s. 0d. $54.60
Allowance for unworn standard camshaft ... £4 10s. 0d. $12.60

EXTRACTOR EXHAUST MANIFOLD (illustration on front page)
Develops 7-8 B.H.P. more than standard, and is under half the weight, connecting on to the standard straight through exhaust system for both T.R.2. and T.R.3. high port models. Essential for use with special camshafts and Weber carburetters, to enable full power to b developed. ... £19 0s. 0d. $53.20

OIL THERMOMETERS, with bulb, 5 ft. capillary tube and adaptor for fitting into crankcase, reading 40°C to 140°C ... £3 3s. 0d. $8.85
LIGHT ALLOY SUMPS, double capacity, ribbed for extra cooling ... £11 15s. 0d. $33.00
LIGHT ALLOY ROCKER COVERS. Highly polished, cast L/A ... £6 5s. 0d. $17.50
CHROMIUM PLATED ROCKER COVERS ... £2 15s. 0d. $7.70
"VARIFLO" adjustable rear DAMPERS, most effective ... £6 5s. 0d. $17.50
WOODHEAD MONROE front DAMPERS, most effective ... £4 15s. 0d. $13.20
COMPETITION front coil SPRINGS, per pair ... £4 4s. 0d. $11.80
COMPETITION rear leaf SPRINGS, per pair ... £14 14s. 0d. $41.30
ANTI-ROLL BAR kits, fitted without drilling ... £6 5s. 0d. $17.50
BRADEX FIRE EXTINGUISHERS, R.A.C. approved, the lightest and most compact, chromium plated, re-fillable ... £1 19s. 0d. $5.53
„ do. „ Double capacity ... £2 15s. 0d. $7.70
BONNET STRAPS, tan or black, chromium fittings, pair ... £1 2s. 0d. $3.15

Double Twin Choke Weber carburetter assembly fitted to Triumph T.R.3 £52. Can be fitted with standard cast iron exhaust manifold, but when used with our Extractor Exhaust manifold, develops 7-8 B.H.P. more at 4,400 R.P.M. as tested by Triumph Experimental Dept.

V. W. DERRINGTON LTD.
AUTOMOBILE DESIGNERS
ENGINEERS ● MANUFACTURERS
159 - 161 LONDON ROAD,
KINGSTON - ON - THAMES, ENGLAND

"FEATHERWEIGHT" STEERING WHEELS
(Pat. No. 791052)

As used by most racing drivers for reduction of weight, complete safety in case of accident, perfect grip in hot or cold climes, and beauty of appearance. Laminated wood rims in contrasting colours of white obeechi and rich red mahogany, with finger grips formed on underside.
Frames cut from Birmabright of stout gauge for strength, lightness and finish, and fitted with alloy boss to fit TR2 and TR3 column and controls. Handmade throughout by craftsmen.
Flat. 16" dia. £12 0s. 0d. 17" dia. £12 15s. 0d. Dished 15s. extra. Postage, inland, 4s. 6d. U.S.A. and Canada, $3.50.

LIGHT ALLOY OIL RADIATORS
Reducing running temperatures by 20° to 25° C. Easily fitted to obtain correct circulation. Kit includes L/W high pressure hoses, adaptor and connections for full flow oiling system and necessary bolts.
TR3 and 4 Oil Radiator Kits ... £15 10s. 0d. $43.40
TR2 Oil Radiator Kits with full flow filter ... £17 10s. 0d. $48.00
OIL Filter Elements (new one must be fitted every 3,000 miles and cleaned every 1,000 miles) ... 9s. 6d. $1.02

WELLWORTHY ALFIN BRAKE DRUMS
The definite answer to brake fade, and when used with HINTEX M.20 or other "Non-Fade" brake linings give superlative retardation, without grab. Can quite safely be used at speeds of 100 m.p.h. and over with maximum pressure. Transverse finned, for maximum cooling and can be fitted without any alteration.
Per pair £17 12s. $49.60
BRAKE LININGS, MINTEX M.20 "non-fade". Per set 8 linings and rivets. £8 17s. $22.00
Per set 8 linings and rivets, exchange shoes. £9 13s. $27.20

ROAD WHEELS. Steadiness on high speed cornering can be greatly improved with considerably less tendency to "break away" by rebuilding the wheels with broad base rims and respoking with 64 instead of 48 spokes. Cost inclusive of trueing, balancing and stove enamelling silver ... £6 per wheel $16.90
New wheels complete: £3 18s. per wheel $33.95

SEAT CONVERSIONS
Driver's seat can be fitted with a high side, with foam rubber padding and upholstered to match, and a similar finished buffer pad for attaching to the door, giving a firm seating position. Cushion comfort can be improved by a layer of foam rubber fitted under the trimming, which prevents seat fatigue and cramp.
Cost of converting each seat, as above ... £7 $19.70
„ to high side only ... £4 $11.25
„ door buffer pad ... £1 5s. $ 3.50
„ lining seat cushion foam rubber ... £2 5s. $ 6.30

LUGGAGE CARRIERS
Made of stout gauge steel tubing for strength with light weight and durably finished, heavily chromium plated upon copper and nickel undercoatings. With our design, the weight is taken by the internal ribs and spread over the panel, to prevent distortion. Supplied with rustproofed bolts and chrome acorn nuts and strap staples. 30" × 17" £7 15s. 0d. $21.70
De luxe model, fitted by strainers and rubber suction cups, avoiding drilling ... 370 × 18" £9 15s. 0d. $27.30
Both types allow of lid being opened when fitted with grid. Extra heavy webbing straps ... 7 ft.; 7s. 8 ft.; 8s. each

Polished light alloy frame, shaped to fit the scuttle, with rubber draught strip, rain and wind proof. Glazed with moulded curved perspex for maximum protection and minimum wind resistance. Will fit existing attachments where supplied on the scuttle. L.H. and R.H.
Triumph T.R.2 £3 15s. 0d. each ($10.50), £7 5s. 0d. ($20.30) pair; Triumph T.R.3, M.G.A, Austin-Healey £4 0s. 0d. each ($11.55), £7 15s. 0d. ($21.70) pair, other makes to order.

Racing Screen

An efficiently designed induction system, when fitted with two or more carburetters, depending upon inlet port design, in conjunction with an effective exhaust manifold, can give a considerable increase of power and torque, resulting in greatly improved acceleration, hill climbing and maximum speed. Due to better distribution, improved breathing and better scavenging, fuel consumption is invariably improved under similar driving conditions, compared with the original design, but when full advantage of the extra performance is taken, fuel consumption may be slightly more, for "speed costs money." Under similar conditions of hard driving the multi carburetter units give not only better performance but lower fuel costs.

For thirty years, Mr. V. W. Derrington has led with designs for improved carburation and exhaust manifolds, having been closely associated with the development of many successful racing cars, racing motor boats and aircraft, therefore our experience is unrivalled. The knowledge thus gained, has been used for the production of these high efficiency units for use on touring and sports cars.

Surrey had been a mecca for sports car enthusiasts for many years, well prior to the introduction of the TR2. During the mid 1950's, Derrington developed and raced a TR2, and like Sid Hurrell at SAH, he thereby built up both considerable expertise in the cars and also developed a stock of proven TR tuning items. The car Derrington raced was a red TR2, registered VPJ 770, and by a considerable coincidence, this same car, after being previously unknown to the TR Register, resurfaced as the author was writing this chapter in March 1993. The owner contacted me via the club, and I was able to inspect the car, which was in surprisingly original condition, still carrying most of the Derrington modifications made to it in around 1955! This same TR2 was tested by John Bolster for "Autosport" magazine in September 1955, and I have included a reprint of this test in this chapter. In addition, I have come across a leaflet detailing the various Derrington products for the TR range, and again this is reprinted here. As can be seen, a comprehensive range of items was available, from a leather bonnet strap to a full Weber carburettor conversion. At £52, this is noticeably cheaper than the SAH price, but I imagine that SAH may have included the fitting, tuning and rejetting that would have been necessary. One item of particular note and, I think, exclusive to Derringtons was the 64 spoke wire wheel, fitted with a "broad based" rim. The standard 48 spoked wire wheel was found to be marginal for racing purposes very early on, and these 64 spoked replacements seem to predate the 60 spoked rally-proved wheels as used on some of the Works cars. Even the first TR4's had 48 spoked wire wheels unless either 60 spoked ones were specially ordered or steel wheels were fitted. The high sided driver's seat conversion is also worthy of note.

Derrington's also had a mobile workshop which attended the more important race meetings, and which was on hand to provide support for TR drivers (and others) using their products. Although this firm did deal with other marques as well, they were in the mid 1950's very much concerned with TRs and they did much of the pioneer development work on TR tuning and modification. However, they did not stay in the TR market for as long as SAH and seem to have wound their TR operation down once the heyday of the four cylinder TR was over, although I believe that some items remained available to order and the Kingston shop continued in business beyond the death of Vic Derrington himself in 1972. Certainly original Derrington tuning items are now quite sought after as "period accessories," and I know of one of their four branch extractor exhaust manifolds that is still giving good service after 32 years continuous use!

Another firm which specialised in sidescreen TR engine conversions was Wilen Engineering, based in North London and later at Esher, in Surrey. Although I had seen their advertisements in the contemporary motoring magazines, I had not been able to find out much about them until a TR Register member in Guernsey, Mr T J de Putron, sent me a photocopy of their catalogue dated January 1959. Their development car seems to have been a long-door TR2 registered PYT 2, which was campaigned in the mid 1950's by a Mr D A Wilcocks. I cannot ascertain whether he had a direct connection with the firm, but this TR certainly appears in their advertisements; PYT 2 was fitted with an extraordinary aerodynamic nose cone/front apron panel which did nothing for its looks, but presumably was found beneficial in increasing top speed, and in fact one or two other racing sidescreen TRs also utilised a similar item. Included in the Wilen catalogue is a road test of a converted TR2, stated to be fitted with a modified nose cowl (possibly this was PYT 2). The car

Vic Derrington's TR2 is seen here being hurled round Goodwood circuit by Peter Gammon in August 1958. This car, VPJ 770, came to light after years of storage as this book was being written, still carrying its Derrington-modified engine: it is now being fully restored ("Autosport").

had a high port cylinder head, H6 1 3/4" carburettors, Wilen inlet manifold and ram pipes with a bonnet top air feed, but was stated to have the standard cast iron exhaust manifold . I reproduce the road test results here, for the acceleration figures, if accurate, are remarkable for such a relatively unmodified car. Indeed, the 0-60 time quoted of 8.1 seconds comfortably beats that of the 2.2 litre SAH fully modified TR4 in the test cited above, yet the "Wilen" car appears to have been to almost standard 1957 TR3 specification plus the special induction system and an aerodynamic front (which would not have counted for much in the 0-60 dash). The mean maximum speed quoted of 118 mph is credible, having regard both to the 124 mph achieved at Jabbeke by MVC 575 with an unmodified engine, and also to the fact that the Wilen car had the aerodynamic nose and (presumably) one of their similarly aerodynamic, wrap-round aeroscreens. I must however express some scepticism as to the acceleration figures claimed based on my own personal experience with modified TRs, and also on the fact that this car had the standard exhaust manifold and, as the report does not state otherwise, the 83 mm bore 1991 cc engine. From all I have read and experienced, to obtain 8 second 0-60 mph times with a sidescreen TR requires not only a "full house" road conversion like the SAH one, but also the larger bore engine.

Wilen's range of items was nothing like as large as those of the two firms dealt with previously, and consisted mainly of these induction and carburation modifications, airflow improvements and a very smart looking polished light alloy valve rocker cover. This item was priced at £7 15 shillings in 1959, whereas the polished, light alloy manifold cost £12-10 shillings and the rampipes £2 15 shillings a pair.

Another company that became prominent in TR engine tuning was Chris Lawrence's Lawrencetune firm. Although not around in the early 'sidescreen' days, Lawrencetune became in the 1960's an important source of TR tuning equipment. TR engines were of course fitted to Morgan Plus Four cars from 1954 onwards, and as these weighed considerably less than the TR models, they tended to be somewhat faster, even if less practical in every day motoring. A demand grew up from the Morgan racing fraternity for performance parts in the same way as it had done from the TR boys, and Lawrence was one of those catering for this market, he himself racing a very successful, highly modified Morgan Plus Four. Obviously most of the engine modification parts developed for the TR2 and 3 were equally suitable for the Morgan. When fitted with a "full house" TR engine and a lightweight aluminium panelled body as was the Plus Four Super Sports, the Morgan became a very rapid machine indeed. Although I have not been able to obtain any specific literature relating to Lawrencetune TR items, these evidently consisted of a full range of TR cylinder head and

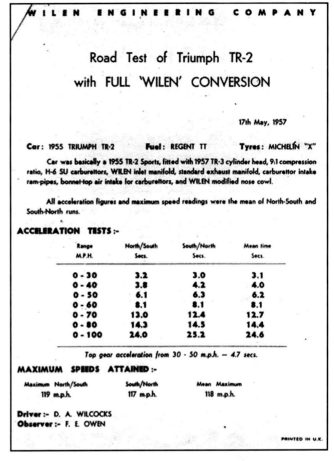

induction/exhaust modifications, together with oil coolers and suspension modifications. A Tecalamit/Jackson fuel injection system was also offered, though I've never heard of one being fitted to a sidescreen TR as opposed to a TR4. Another item of particular note was the Lawrencetune light alloy crossflow cylinder head. This achieved a desirable combustion chamber shape without the usual resort to twin overhead camshafts, by means of a clever arrangement of push rods and rockers driven from the standard camshaft. Its crossflow design also considerably facilitated the engine's breathing, but unfortunately, the cost penalty was heavy, the alloy head being priced at £195 in the early 1960's. As this equates to more than £1500 now, not surprisingly, demand was limited.

For people who really wanted ultimate TR performance , Laurencetune offered special pistons and liners which gave engine sizes of 2480 cc and 2598 cc, and a steel crankshaft capable of sustained high revolutions. Similar items have again become available from other sources in recent times, but Chris Lawrence was very much a pioneer in the art of

making TR-engined vehicles, especially racing ones, as rapid as possible.

In addition to the specialist firms already mentioned, several of the other well-known tuning shops from the 1950's and 60's offered TR conversions, again principally cylinder head and carburation modifications. Among those that did so were Mangoletsi, Alexander Engineering, Downton, Speedwell and Barwell.

Of the Standard-Triumph dealerships and distributors, some were very much keener than others to stress the competitive and performance potential of the TR series, certain dealers going so far as to supply and fit some of the proprietary conversions already referred to. None, however, appeared keener than the Wimbledon firm of L F Dove & Co, who set up a specialist TR maintenance, repair and conversion cen-

tre, and advertised it as such.

As far as I can ascertain Doves did not actually produce tuning items themselves, but they would supply both new and used TRs ready converted, and provided the support and spares back up necessary. How the manufacturer's warranty (6 months only in those days) was affected when a new TR received a performance conversion I am not sure, but I would guess that it may well have invalidated it. Doves remained active on the TR scene for many years, and of course they marketed their own "2 + 2" fixed head TR4s and 4As in later years. Indeed, in the early 1960's their Wimbledon premises was being quoted as the correspondence address for the London headquarters of the Triumph Sports Owners Association, so clearly they had some very keen TR men on the staff.

Although carburettor and cylinder head modifications are the usual and most obvious route towards extracting more power from engines, there is a different, very efficient but not as frequently utilised way to a similar end, and that is by means of forced induction, which in the 1950's meant supercharging. No review of TR performance aids would be complete without a reference to this, for two different supercharging systems were available for sidescreen TRs. The supercharger had been a common means of increasing performance in pre-war days, but gradually it had declined in popularity as engines became more efficient, and possibly also because insurance companies imposed considerable premium loadings on "blown" cars, often out of all proportion to the performance increase.

A supercharger will generally release around 30 to 40% more power from a given engine, at a penalty of increased fuel

A contemporary advertisement for Wilen Engineering, whose TR products are described in this Chapter.

consumption if the extra available performance is actually used. Torque is also proportionately increased, and the blower (unlike the modern turbocharger) will do its beneficial work at low engine speeds. A properly fitted supercharging system is akin to increasing the cylinder capacity of the engine by around 40%, so a supercharged 2 litre TR should behave as if it had nearly 3 litres under its bonnet. Having regard to this, and to the fact that there is plenty of room for the installation in the engine compartment of the TR (a limiting factor with many vehicles), it is in retrospect surprising that the fitment of forced induction did not prove more popular. Cost must, however, have been a factor, the price of the full kit being around £100.

Two firms which developed blowers for the sidescreen TRs were Judson in the USA and Arnott in Great Britain. Both were low pressure items, blowing at around 5 psi, but this was evidently enough with the Arnott installation to reduce the 0-50 acceleration time of an otherwise standard TR3 from 8.8 seconds to 6.4 seconds. The USA manufactured

Two supercharged TRS: on the left is the Judson blower installed on Ian Gibson's TR3A, showing the Holley carburetter and in the right top corner, the oil tank for lubrication. On the right is the Arnott supercharger installed in a TR2. As can be seen, it is mounted on the opposite side of the engine from the Judson and uses a single large SU carburetter (both photos: Ian Gibson).

Judson supercharger was fitted on the induction/exhaust side of the engine, sitting where the carburettors would normally be and on top of the dynamo. The light alloy casing was bolted via a special manifold direct to the cylinder head, and the fuel was fed through a Holley carburettor mounted to the rear of the installation, near the bulkhead. Both superchargers were belt driven, a longer than standard fan belt being required to drive the Arnott, whereas the Judson was driven by an auxiliary belt.

To take advantage of the larger volume of spare space available, the Arnott was mounted on the other side of the engine, on the outside of the distributor, this necessitating repositioning the ignition coil on the front inner wing. In order for the compressed fuel mixture to reach the inlet ports on the opposite side of the engine, a long pipe crossing over above the valve cover was necessary, this splitting into two, one pipe feeding each pair of cylinders. Such a long delivery pipe was not ideal, and in situ, the Judson certainly looks to be the neater arrangement. A single large (2 inch)

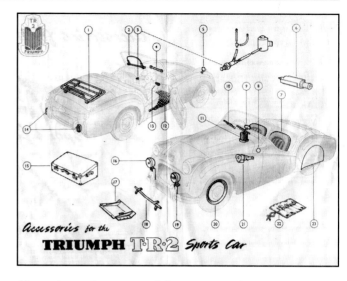

Accessories for the
TRIUMPH T.R.2 Sports Car

These three pictures, and the one opposite, show the 1955 Triumph accessories catalogue for the TR2.

Accessories for the
TRIUMPH T.R.2 Sports Car

ISSUED BY
TRIUMPH MOTOR CO. (1945) LIMITED
(A Subsidiary of The Standard Motor Co. Ltd.)

ACCESSORY BROCHURE TR2

Description.	Part No.	Price. £ s. d.	Remarks.
1 Luggage Grid	552398	10 0 0	
Special Carburettor Jet	108809	3 9	each. Two off.
Needles (G.C.)			See Owners' Handbook.
2 Aero Windscreen	700896	4 0 0	each
3 Windscreen Washer	500898	5 5 0	
(Hand Operated)			
4 Defroster (Windscreen)	59844	1 10 0	
5 Wing Mirror	70326	15 6	each
6 Cigarette Lighter	502041	1 8 6	Subject to Purchase Tax
7 Seat Covers			See Note
8 Licence Holder	602226	2 9	For use when Aero Windscreens are fitted
9 Driving Mirror	70400	2 0 0	
(Anti-dazzle)			
10 Dual Speed Windscreen	501843	13 5 0	
Wiper Kit			
11 Heater Kit	551877	15 0 0	
12 Tailored Link Floor Mats	552164	1 18 6	per set. Subject to Purchase Tax. See Note
13 Ashtray—Swivel type	701019	8 5	Subject to Purchase Tax
14 Reversing Light c/w Switch	502251	2 7 6	
and Cable			
15 Fitted Suit Case	800608	9 18 0	Colour to match trim
16 Spot Lamp	501703	4 2 6	
17 Skid Plate	301644	1 8 6	May be fitted for Rally and Trials events
18 Badge Bar	552399	3 5 0	
19 Fog Lamp	501702	4 2 6	
Fog Lamp	70377	5 8 0	
20 Wheel Rim Finisher	502160	1 0 0	each. Fitted to Disc Type Wheel only
21 Overdrive Unit Kit	501803	47 10 0	
(Right Hand Steering)			
Overdrive Unit Kit	502104	47 10 0	
(Left Hand Steering)			
22 Tool Kit Complete	301413	2 2 6	See Note
23 Rear Wheel Cover Kit	552083	7 15 6	When ordering please state colour required

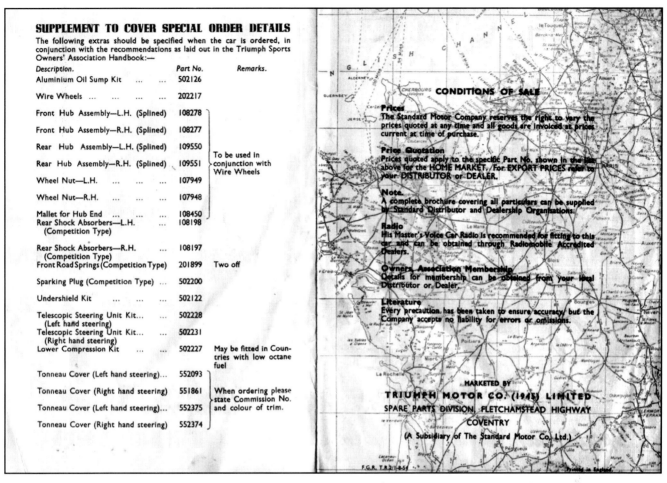

SUPPLEMENT TO COVER SPECIAL ORDER DETAILS

The following extras should be specified when the car is ordered, in conjunction with the recommendations as laid out in the Triumph Sports Owners' Association Handbook:—

Description.	Part No.	Remarks.
Aluminium Oil Sump Kit	502126	
Wire Wheels	202217	
Front Hub Assembly—L.H. (Splined)	108278	
Front Hub Assembly—R.H. (Splined)	108277	
Rear Hub Assembly—L.H. (Splined)	109550	
Rear Hub Assembly—R.H. (Splined)	109551	To be used in conjunction with Wire Wheels
Wheel Nut—L.H.	107949	
Wheel Nut—R.H.	107948	
Mallet for Hub End	108450	
Rear Shock Absorbers—L.H. ... (Competition Type)	108198	
Rear Shock Absorbers—R.H. ... (Competition Type)	108197	
Front Road Springs (Competition Type)	201899	Two off
Sparking Plug (Competition Type) ...	502200	
Undershield Kit	502122	
Telescopic Steering Unit Kit... ... (Left hand steering)	502228	
Telescopic Steering Unit Kit... ... (Right hand steering)	502231	
Lower Compression Kit	502227	May be fitted in Countries with low octane fuel
Tonneau Cover (Left hand steering)...	552093	
Tonneau Cover (Right hand steering)	551861	When ordering please state Commission No. and colour of trim.
Tonneau Cover (Left hand steering)...	552375	
Tonneau Cover (Right hand steering)	552374	

CONDITIONS OF SALE

Prices
The Standard Motor Company reserves the right to vary the prices quoted at any time and all goods are invoiced at prices current at time of purchase.

Price Quotation
Prices quoted apply to the specific Part No. shown in the list above for the HOME MARKET. For EXPORT PRICES refer to your DISTRIBUTOR or DEALER.

Note
A complete brochure covering all particulars can be supplied by Standard Distributor and Dealership Organisations.

Radio
His Master's Voice Car Radio is recommended for fitting to this car and can be obtained through Radiomobile Accredited Dealers.

Owners Association Membership
Details for membership can be obtained from your local Distributor or Dealer.

Literature
Every precaution has been taken to ensure accuracy but the Company accepts no liability for errors or omissions.

MARKETED BY
TRIUMPH MOTOR CO. (1945) LIMITED
SPARE PARTS DIVISION, FLETCHAMSTEAD HIGHWAY
COVENTRY
(A Subsidiary of The Standard Motor Co. Ltd.)

F.G.R. T.R2/1.4.5/ Printed in England.

SU carburettor fed the Arnott blower, room being found for this right up near the battery,

Examples of both systems can still be found in use today on cars belonging to TR Register members, one long door TR2 known to me having had the Arnott system fitted for most of its life with very few problems reported by its owner.

I shall now turn to those contemporary items available to the sidescreen TR owner that were not performance related, but were rather aimed at increasing the comfort and practicality of the car, or making it look "that bit different." I believe that another American firm, Paxton, also marketed a blower for the TR Series in the USA.

It seems logical to commence with those items actually available from Standard-Triumph's themselves, of which there were a great many. More than with with most cars of the period, there was a huge difference between a basic, as delivered, TR with no options (which could be very basic

indeed), and a fully equipped car with all the available factory equipment. In these more affluent days, the great majority of sidescreen TRs still running are fitted with some, if not most, of the optional equipment available, to the extent that to find a basic TR is a rarity. Nevertheless, the factory build records prove that many basic specification cars were built, particularly those not built for specific customers and thus destined for the "Home Reserve", which in reality meant the car parks where unsold new TRs languished awaiting owners during periods of slack economic activity. Very many fewer basic TRs were supplied to the North American markets; presumably the greater affluence there caused buyers to opt for "extras" even if they did not particularly need them, although a heater was rarely fitted to cars going to the southern USA states, even when the car was otherwise "fully loaded".

A publicity leaflet detailed the various options and their prices, and although not fully comprehensive, it certainly listed most items. As with "performance" equipment, most options could be specified on a new car, though there appears to have been nothing that could not be retro-fitted, albeit at higher cost. Certain items were "dealer fitted" and in such cases, the Works usually produced a service leaflet detailing the fitting procedures.

The full list of factory equipment is as follows:

1)   Hardtop - on a new car it could be ordered in various standard factory colours, but if ordered subsequently for dealer-fitment, it came in primer at a cost of £44-10 shillings. Both steel and fibreglass Works hardtops were made, the steel type being much the more common.

2)   Luggage grid - this could be the bolt-to-the-bootlid type (early) or the later, hinged type that avoided drilling the boot lid, being mounted on the hingepins at the front, and clamped at the rear to the trailing lip of the lid. It seems dear at £10!

3)   Interior heater - a 'retro-fit' kit available for £15, the heater itself being a Smiths Industries 9-row unit variously described as 2, 2,5 or 3 kilowatts rating. Some early heaters were only of 7-row type, and these were rated at 2 kilowatts.

4)   Leather upholstery - this was one item that could not really be retro-fitted - it is something of a misnomer, for the whole of the upholstery was not leather, many pieces still being made in Vynide. A common error made by Concours contenders these days is to have every item of trim finished in leather, whereas only the seat facings, dash, cockpit cappings and occasional seat facings (if fitted) were actually leather.

5)   Radio - several different types were available over

the years, both with push-button or conventional tuning, and also incorporating single, dual and "all" wavebands. The usual make was the Radiomobile, sometimes marketed under their 'HMV' label. Push button sets were available almost from the start of TR2 production, and a photograph reproduced here shows one fitted to a 1955 TR2 as original equipment. Placing the radio in the glove box cover was the usual and the Works-recommended practice, the 6 1/2 inch speaker being normally fitted in the passenger's footwell on the outer side, where a cut-out was incorporated in manufacture. These valve radios had a separate power pack containing the valves, and again this was fitted in the glovebox or footwell, space or sometimes under the centre of the dashboard if no heater was fitted. The recommended place for the aerial was in front of the windscreen, on the outside of the front scuttle, on the opposite side to the steering. However, many cars had the aerial placed on one or other side of the rear bulkhead saddle, and I have seen a factory build record (for car no. TS 31211 "0") which clearly states "Electric automatic aerial to be mounted on the rear of the car," so although never listed, an electric aerial **was** available, and as early as 1958!

6).   Tool roll and tools - basic wheel changing items only were supplied with most TR2s and 3s, but 42 shillings and sixpence bought you a supplementary and comprehensive tool kit. According to the parts book this tool kit was supplied as standard with TR3As, but I do not believe myself that this was the case, as confirmed to me by two original owners of TR3As, neither of whom received a supplementary tool kit with their cars.

7)   Telescopic steering column. This is quite a rare item, and it was only practicable to incorporate it upon original manufacture. The adjustment was operated by turning a

This photograph shows an original radio installation, fitted from new in this TR2. The set is a Radiomobile and the valve pack was mounted separately in the passenger's foot well. The glovebox lid was the factory's recommended location. Also seen on this car, by the steering wheel is the chain that pulled up a radiator blind, another period accessory (Peter Rix).

large knurled ring on the column below the steering wheel, which gave around 2 1/2 to 3 inches of movement, though this meant that the wheel was brought nearer to the driver, whereas most drivers would have preferred it further away! When the adjustable column was fitted, an alternative steering wheel was supplied having its spokes arranged in a different manner to the normal wheel.

8) Tonneau and hood stick covers. Strictly speaking, these were optional items, though it seems that they were what are now called "delete options." Thus, each car was supplied with them unless specific instructions not to supply were given at the time of ordering, or unless the car was built new with the factory hardtop. The hood stick cover, as it name implies, neatened up the rear of the cockpit when the car was open and the full tonneau cover was not in use. Colours of these items could be supplied to match the interior trim, or else be black, fawn or white.

9. Two-speed wipers - these were available right from the start of production (Lucas Type DR1), although at least two different types of control knobs were in use. Unlike the standard, single speed wipers, the two speed ones had a self-parking arrangement. In the author's experience, there was not much difference between the two speeds! In today's terms, they could perhaps best be described as "slow" and "very slow" - an accessory of doubtful efficacy!

10. Fitted suitcase - a wedge-shaped case designed to make maximum use of the boot space in the sidescreen TR. It had brass bound corners, 3 white "Bakelite" handles and came in colours to match the interior trim. It seems extraordinarily expensive at £15 10 shillings in the TR3 accessory list, yet it was priced at only £9 18 shillings in the TR2 list - raging inflation even then!

11. Screen washers - unlike the suitcase, the manually operated screenwasher seems a bargain at £1/3s/6d! It was manufactured initially by Trafalgar, although Tudor screen-washers were later fitted, particularly to TR3As. These had a large, squarish glass reservoir, and could be either manual, vacuum operated or electric.

12. Windscreen defroster - these items were available from the factory, and were manufactured (I think) by Lucas. Other proprietary brands of much the same design were also available such as Desmo. For those who have not seen one (few now seem to survive), the defroster was a brown, "Bakelite" device about fifteen inches long and an inch and a half wide, with rubber suckers at each end. It was attached by these to the inside of the windscreen, and had small 12 volt heating elements built in. These provided reasonably effective de-icing and demisting in winter condi-

tions, keen rally-types often fitting two to enable the navigator also to enjoy the benefits of vision!

13. Radiator Blind - this winter accessory was operated by either a cable or a fine chain from the driving seat, and consisted of a roll up, spring loaded blind that could be pulled up to occlude the radiator, either fully or partly, in order to raise engine (and hence heater) temperature in severe weather. The cost of the complete kit seems modest at three pounds! Most TR3As of my experience needed the opposite, even in mid winter, tending usually to run too hot. An aside to current owners of overheating TR3As - make sure that the fibreboard air deflector is in place between the grille and the radiator. If it is not, airflow will bypass the radiator, taking the line of least resistance, and overheating will result. The more functional front cowl of the TR2 and 3 did not of course allow this to happen!

14. Occasional rear seat. This was never listed for the TR2, although the TR3 type will in fact fit (access will be difficult as the TR2 does not have a hinged passenger seat back). First introduced in October 1955, the TR3 seat dropped in to the rear cockpit space, and had two steel legs that were bolted to the floor. For extra security, there were two top brackets that fixed to the top of the rear of the cockpit. This first type of one-piece occasional seat had a bow-shaped leading edge to the cushion, which, like the backrest, was pleated to match the main seats. TR3As prior to TS 60001 had a roughly similar arrangement, but the backrest was formed as part of the cockpit trim with the seat cushion separate, unlike the earlier, one-piece seat. Post TS 60001 TR3As had to have the occasional seat altered slightly to reflect the different "flat floor" arrangement that came as part of the retooled bodyshell. All TR3A occasional seat cushions were of oblong, rather than bowed shape.

15. Wing mirrors - no wing mirror was included in the standard specification, rear view being granted solely by the tiny interior mirror. Most owners therefore fitted wing mirrors, and the "official" type was a round glass, non-handed item, with a flexible ball joint fitting to prevent accidental damage. Many other types of mirror were available, the "bullet" shaped "high speed" mirrors being particularly favoured by the keen types. An anti-dazzle driving mirror was also available for interior fitment, being suspended from the windscreen top rail. This was usually fitted in addition to the original rear view mirror.

16. Cigarette lighter - this was an "official" extra, available for dashboard mounting.

17. An external, weatherproof road fund licence holder was available, this being usually bolted to the outside of the

front scuttle and used in conjunction with aeroscreens.

18.　　Ashtray - two distinct types of ashtray were fitted; the earlier type was a swivelling bowl-shaped device that could be swung out from its mounting under the bottom edge of the dashboard, whereas the later one slid in and out on guide rails; again this was mounted along the bottom of the dashboard, and it had a fluted front in brownish bakelite.

19.　　Tailored, link floor mats - these came as a set of two, and were specially shaped to comply with the footwell contours. Finished in basic black, they cost £2 /11s/0d a pair, but if one rashly wished them to be coloured to match the car, then the cost rose alarmingly to 4 guineas, getting on for twice the price!

20.　　Reversing light - again more than one officially supplied light existed, a round type and an oblong type. The usual mounting point was on the rear overrider bracket, and a special, white plastic pull-out switch with an illuminated central "tell-tale" was supplied, total cost £2/7s/6d.

21.　　Badge bar - the standard item mounted onto the brackets inside the front overriders. In addition to carrying the badges so beloved of the 1950's sporting motorist, it was strong enough to be used to mount some types of fog and spotlight, though these were more usually mounted as detailed below..

22.　　Fog and spot lamps - in fact there were too many different types of these to allow accurate listing, but those sold with official sanction appear only to have been of Lucas manufacture. The usual method of mounting, shown in the accessory catalogue, was by way of angle brackets picking up on the overridder to bumper bolts.

23.　　Low compression kit - strictly speaking ,this is an engine modification, and hence should have been in the first part of this chapter. However, it can hardly be called a "performance" item, having exactly the opposite effect! Aimed at owners who were compelled to run their TRs on low-octane fuel, presumably for geographical (or political?) reasons, it consisted of a compression plate for interposing between the cylinder head and the block, longer pushrods to allow for this extra spacing, plus a new set of gaskets. Once fitted, the compression ratio of the standard TR2 was reduced from 8.5 to 1 to 7.5 to 1, and maximum brake horse power fell from 90 to 87. Presumably also fuel consumption was slightly increased, due to the engine's resulting reduced efficiency.

24.　　Polished wheel rim finisher. Obviously these were only for fitting to disc wheels, being manufactured in either polished aluminium or chromed steel. Some were merely a "push" fit onto the rim, whereas the superior types had proper mounting clips (but see the section on "Ace" rimbellishers later in this chapter). I have been unable to discover which manufacturer made the "officially" supplied rim finishers - it may be that they emanated from more than one source; certainly there were several styles during the whole sidescreen car production run.

25.　　Chromed exhaust tailpipe finisher - it appears that this came as standard with most of the first TR2's, but quite early on it seems to have become a 12s/6d option!

26.　　Seat covers - both the TR2 and TR3 accessory catalogues list these, though no details are given except the price, which is somewhat arcanely quoted as "from £7 10 shillings a pair, according to quality" - clearly therefore they were not always of the **best** quality!

27.　　Continental touring kit - these kits were very popular with the adventurous owner in the 1950's when he was determined to drive his vehicle beyond the reach of the factory's spares and dealer organisation. They could usually be hired for a nominal sum, and then only those items actually used were paid for upon safe return. Alternatively, the kit could be purchased outright by those who reached foreign parts more frequently. I have not seen such a kit, nor a list of its contents, but a line drawing in one of the catalogues reveals it to have included fanbelt, coil, valves, valve springs, bulbs, set of hoses, condenser, rotor arm, contact set and probably more besides.

28.　　Sliding window sidescreens - these were available as an optional, after-market "extra" to owners of earlier cars fitted with the non-sliding, zipped sidescreens. Fitment of the Works-style hardtop to an early car with the fixed-window sidescreens also made employment of the sliding window sidescreens a good idea, for ease of entry and ventilation purposes.

29.　　Grand Touring Conversion Kit - this was something of a competition "homologation special" item, fitment of which (in conjunction with the hardtop) made the car eligible for the "Grand Touring" or closed car categories in certain events. It principally consisted of "uprated" sidescreens plus external door handles and locks, and thus was irrelevant to the TR3A which came with these as standard.

30.　　Reveal Moulding Kit - this refers to the chromed strip that surrounds the "mouth" of the TR3. A very similar item was fitted as standard to very late TR2s, this differing from the TR3 type in that it did not continue along the top of the "mouth." The reveal moulding listed as an optional extra

A good view of the special sidescreens, with beading at their base, that came as part of the factory "GT Touring" kit with the hardtop. As the observant will notice, the door handles are not the same as the later TR3A type, there being no keyhole. The photograph is dated April 1956 (TR Register Archive).

in the official accessories catalogue was of the TR3 type, and the note states "Finished in chrome, this accentuates the outline of the intake cowl and should be fitted with grille part no. 801255".

31.   Grille - this is the item referred to above, and is the TR3 cellular radiator grille. Clearly therefore Standard-Triumph recognised the desire of TR2 owners to upgrade, at least in looks, their car to TR3 status, for the grille and reveal moulding were sold to them for this sole purpose with "official" sanction. The catalogues states that "the grille is continentally styled, and undoubtedly adds to the elegance of the motor car" - Hmmm!

As far as I can ascertain, the above is a full list of Works supplied or sanctioned accessories for the TR2/3/3As, but it may well be that other items were added which failed to get into the accessories catalogues, or that there were items details of which have not survived for other reasons. A small example concerns the list of options set out in the "Motor" magazine road test of the TR2 in 1954. This states that a "dished steering wheel" was available as an option, but I have never seen any other reference to such an item, and can only conclude that it may simply be an error.

A drawing, taken from the Triumph Sports Owners' Association handbook, showing what purports to be the TR's toolkit. Much controversy surrounds which tools were supplied and when. At one time, the toolkit was actually listed as an "extra", apart, of course, from the basic wheel changing tools.

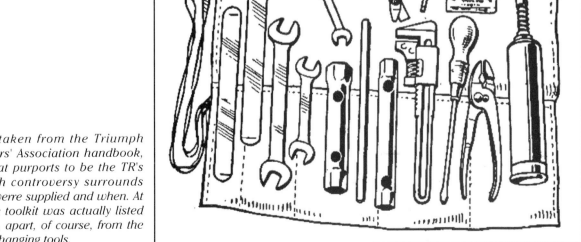

A TR interior, showing how the jacking post actually passes through the floor of the car to raise and lower it for wheel changing.

Left hand drive TRs awaiting delivery (they have clearly apready been shipped, as they are fully fitted and the wooden shipping "buffers" have been replaced with the cars' own bumpers.

By courtesy of Roger Ferris of the TR Register, I have obtained a document dated 26th April 1962 produced by the Standard-Triumph Motor Company Inc. of the USA (South-Eastern Zone). This was sent to dealers selling the TR3B, and set out the price structure (including profit margins) for these cars. Also set out were the options available, a restricted list as compared with the catalogue above for the 2/3/3As. I reproduce the price list here, and would also add that the covering letter to dealers indicated that the first 500 TR3Bs to be supplied (the "TSF" cars) would all have leather trim, as a sort of "non-optional" option!

In addition to the Works supplied or sanctioned accessories, a good number of small private firms found it worth their while to tool up to fill perceived gaps in the range of equipment available for such a popular enthusiast's car as the TR series. The 1950's and 1960's were the peak of the "bolt on goodie" era and the motoring magazines of the period were filled with ingenious ideas and products to part the enthusiast from his money, some genuinely useful and some downright daft. In retrospect, for instance, it is hard to believe the drivers could have paid money for headlamp hoods, which served no useful purpose but must have cut top speed and increased fuel consumption, yet such things were indeed fit-

Here and opposite: the TR3B and East Coast USA price lists which were circulated by the Standard-Triumph Motor Company Inc (South-Eastern Zone) (via Peter Ferris).

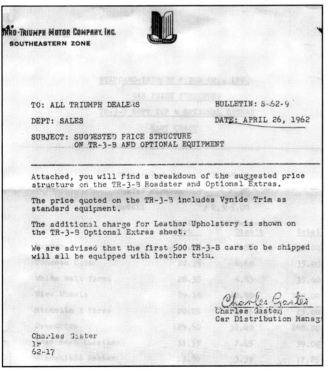

STANDARD-TRIUMPH MOTOR CO., INC.
CAR PRICE STRUCTURE
TR-3-B SOFT TOP & OPTIONAL EXTRAS
EAST COAST

	Dealer Net		
Dealer Net	1,965.00		
Dealer Mark-up	400.00		
Retail	2,365.00		

	Dealer Net	Dealer Disc't	Retail
Heater	36.45	8.55	45.00
Tonneau Cover	28.35	6.65	35.00
White Wall Tires	28.35	6.65	35.00
Wire Wheels	89.10	20.90	110.00
Michelin X Tires	20.25	4.75	25.00
Overdrive	129.60	30.40	160.00
Rear Seat (Leather)	31.55	7.45	39.00
Windshield Washer	13.86	3.39	17.25
Leather Upholstery	40.00	10.00	50.00

S-62-9
4-26-62

ted to TRs, as well as to more mundane saloons, as contemporary photographs prove.

A trawl through the magazines of the period has enabled me to put together a review of some proprietary items available for the sidescreen TR, although I do not claim the following review to be exhaustive.

To return to the subject of "updating" TR2s into TR3s, very prophetically the firm of Cosmic Car Accessories launched their "TR2" grille, looking suspiciously like a TR3 one, as early as March 1955, many months before the official showing of the TR3. It was of the same cellular, "egg-box" construction and differed from the later production item only in that it had a slight "bow" towards the front, and in that it had somewhat more "cells." One can but wonder whether this was happy coincidence on the manufacturer's part, or did someone, somewhere, get wind of Triumph's plans? A photograph of TR2 OFD 876 modelling the Cosmic grille for TR2s is reproduced here, this first appearing in "Autosport" dated 25th March 1955. Note also that the car is fitted with headlamp hoods, wing mirrors, and extra lights. The surround of this TR2 grille was said to be die-cast, with the "cells" of light alloy, and the manufacturers ambitiously stated that it could be fitted to the TR2 "without the drilling of holes" - per-

This TR wears one of the proprietary bootracks that were widely available in the 1950s and 1960s. They involved drilling the boot lid, unlike the factory item, which was more cleverly arranged to clip on at the rear and attach to the hinge pins at the front. A good shot of a vintage DC3 aeroplane, too! ("Autosport").

haps it was fixed with sticky tape! Retail price was 10 guineas, something like £130 in today's terms, so it could not be said to be cheap.

The firm of Key-Leather Co Ltd marketed several items, as can be seen from the reproduced advertisement opposite. How about a "handsome and dashing shield against sun-glare?" This can be seen fitted to an unfortunate TR3, SLX 9, and it must have knocked hooded headlamps into a cocked hat as regards increasing both wind resistance and fuel consumption! Still, as the advert says, it was rapidly becoming a "must" for sports car owners! It was also claimed to replace

Above: in March 1955, many months before the public first saw the TR3, Cosmic Accessories Limited marketed this grille for the TR2. It bore an uncanny resemblance to what was to come and was not cheap at 10 guineas. OFD 876 also wears headlamp hoods and wheel rim embellishers ("Autosport"). Right: Key Leather's advertisement for its TR sun visor - not the prettiest of accessories. The advertisement also mentions the K-L "thermo-gauge" for cars not fitted with water temperature gauges, K-L "Kerb- finders", those funny little "cats whiskers" for drivers unable to avoid doing damage to their wheels and tyres as they parked and finally, the "Sit-rite" back support designed more for bench-seated saloons than such cars as TRs.

the radio-aerial - presumably the metal strips surrounding the perspex fulfilled this purpose! Perhaps not surprisingly, I have never seen an example of this accessory - few surely can have survived. Another TR item was the "Venta" extractor, stated to be the "definite answer to the problem of body ventilation." These were made of moulded "Vybak" (the material used for hood rear windows), and were attached to the forward ends of the sidescreens by six self-tapping screws. They were claimed to allow circulation of air without draughts, although it is not clear exactly how. Priced at £1-9s-6d a pair, however, they looked good value! Into the same genre fall the "wind wings", much beloved of USA TR enthusiasts, and these really do seem quite a sensible idea. Unlike the "Venta" extractors, wind wings were for use with open TRs where no sidescreens were in place. They clipped to each side of the windscreen, and being made of rigid perspex and adjustable, they deflected much of the buffeting air away from the cockpit. I cannot see that they were ever marketed in the UK, but photographs (and reimported cars from sunny USA states) show that very many TRs utilised them in North America. A USA advertisement I have extols the virtues of the "Centurion combination five-position window and wind-wing". This bizarre device seems to have replaced the sidescreen altogether.

The fact that TR 2/3/3As never had proper rear bumpers was seen as a manufacturing opportunity, and the Shelford Engineering Co Ltd produced some rather odd quarter bumpers to protect the rear corners of the TR from knocks and dents. There were two distinct types; in 1956/57, they were tubular, made of 3/4 inch twin 16 gauge tube, bolted from the bracket of the rear overrider onto a special bracket on the chassis rail projecting out under the side of the rear wing from which they were spaced by a rubber buffer. The manufacturers claimed them to be stronger than a normal rear bumper, and to be capable of fitment in 5 minutes, which seems optimistic. The retail price was £2 -12 shillings

Below: the "Venta" air extractor, maded of moulded "Vybak" plastic - do any survive, I wonder?

a pair, and the photograph showed them fitted to a TR2 registration number NCE 152. By 1959, the tubular construction had changed to flat chromed steel, and the price had risen to £3 - 9s - 6d a pair. The company now claimed to have USA agents; in view of the "parking by feel" habits of some North Americans, maybe there was indeed a greater sale for these bumpers than in the UK. The later type were shown in the advertisements fitted to TR3 registered RER 400. The author once purchased a TR3A fitted with a pair of this type of bumper, and he is happy to confess that removing them was the first thing he did upon getting the car home!

Additional rear end protection would have been obtained by the fitting of a towbar, despite this not being its primary purpose. The position of the spare wheel door and the lowness of the chassis at the rear, below ideal towing ball height,have always made fitment of towbars to sidescreen TRs somewhat difficult. It was not until 1958 that the firm of C.P. Witter and Co Ltd, in conjunction with Standard Triumphs, introduced a towbar specially for the TR, modestly priced at £4. Presumably towbars fitted prior to that date had been "one-off" affairs. Witter's bar is shown in a photograph fitted to a TR2 (HJA 750), and it seems clear that spare wheel access would have been very difficult with the towball in position, although this could be removed in the event of a puncture requiring access to the spare. The towbar kit included uprights to enable the height of the ball to be raised if desired, and the bar itself looks to have been bolted both to the main chassis rails and also to the rear chassis cross tubes. In later years, several other types of towbar became available, some of these clamping directly to the cross tubes alone, thus requiring no drilling of the chassis rails. As to the suitability of the sidescreen TR for towing in general, Standard Triumph's were somewhat coy, stating that "in many respects, the TR is not an ideal towing vehicle, being essentially a high-speed model." The Standard-Triumph Review however, the official "house" magazine, carried several reports over the years of owners using TRs as tow-cars perfectly satisfactorily, although loads appear to have been limited to around 12 cwt. This seems somewhat conservative, for with plenty of power, low down torque and a strong, separate chassis, the TR ought to be a good towing vehicle, despite the handicap of this less-than-ideal towball position. Certainly the author has towed a ton of loaded caravan with both a TR2 and a tuned TR3A without problems, although the chassis mounting points need regular checking and the cooling system needs to be in excellent condition to prevent embarrassment!

A popular fitment for disc-wheeled TRs in the 1950's were chromed or polished alloy wheel rim embellishers, and several proprietary suppliers of these existed. Probably the best known and most widely used were the "Ace Rimbellishers"

Left: RER 400 shows off its "Shelford Engineering" rear quarter bumpers - "A boon for parking at only 69/6d a pair!" Below left: TR2 NCE 152 models the Shelford quarter bumpers for a contemporary advertisement. The boot of this car also sports a pair of external handles, another accessory of unknown make. Below: The first officially endorsed tow bar for the sidescreen TR was made by CP Witter & Company available from 1958. One is seen here on HJA 750, a long-door TR2. Spare wheel access involved removing the tow-ball! This is also a good view of the single-window hood.

Sports Owners Association newsletter carries a warning to owners of disc-braked TRs who had the Ace items fitted. The four worm-drive clips that held each rimbellisher to the wheel passed very close on the inside of the wheel to the hydraulic brake bridge pipe on the caliper housing, and in some cases had been known to foul it with obvious results. Clearly this was a potentially dangerous fault, and the manufacturers therefore issued a revised type of clip free of charge upon request, and also ensured that all new Rimbellishers had the redesigned clip. All owners of TRs fitted with disc brakes and Rimbellishers were strongly urged to check the clearances on their cars without delay. I doubt if there are many such adornments in circulation today, but if the reader should have a TR fitted with any kind of disc-wheel trim, it might be as well just to check!

Although not of course specifically aimed at TR owners, for the sake of completeness I must mention the "Halda" speed pilot in a review of available accessories. These boxes of

manufactured by Cornercroft Ltd in Coventry. This firm had a long history of automotive wheel adornment, and had I believe manufactured the "Ace" wheel discs fitted to many superior makes of car before the war. The Ace Rimbellisher fitted drum-braked TRs without problems, but unfortunately, once the disc-braked cars were introduced in 1956, a difficulty came to light. The March 1958 issue of the Triumph

Right: all that is known about this photograph is that it was taken in Fowey in Cornwall during 1957. Clearly much love and money had been lavished on this TR2, for many different accessories are evident, not including the rather oversized bonnet mascot! Julian Stephens).

Immediately below: a hardtop-equipped TR3A is used by its first owner to tow his racing hydroplane round the country. This car, XOK 754, still survives, despite such hard usage (TR Register Archive).

Bottom: a TR interior is seen with the Halda Speed Pilot installed. This was an essential tool for any serious rally competitor in the 1950s and working examples are much prized by the historic rally fraternity today ("Autosport").

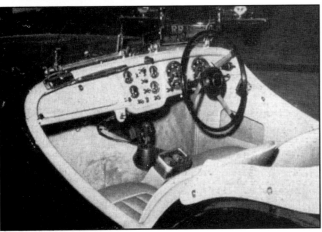

tricks were an essential tool to the serious rally driver of the 1950's, and are much sought after today by the historic rallying fraternity. They were able accurately to measure average speed, elapsed time and distance travelled, all essential information to the co-driver in the navigation-based rallies that preceded today's special stage affairs. The Halda box could be fitted to a TR in the glovebox space, under the dash, or between the seats on a special console.

I have dealt with the Works manufactured steel and fibreglass hardtops, but there were at least three, possibly more, other suppliers of hardtops for the TR2/3/3A cars. The firm of Universal Laminations Ltd from West London produced a fibreglass top which had very similar lines to the Standard Triumph one, and priced at £48 in 1955 it was no cheaper than the "official" item. It was available in any colour, had a fully washable headlining and was fitted with an interior light, which was "one up" on the Works top. This firm also offered its own sliding sidescreens to match for £15, or could convert your own non-sliding sidescreens for £8 the pair.

Microplas Ltd, based in Mitcham, Surrey, were a company with considerable experience in fibreglass mouldings of many types, and they moved somewhat later into the sports car hardtop market. Through the courtesy of Tony Wemyss, the man who used to run Microplas Ltd, I have acquired an original leaflet detailing the "Microbond" tops for TRs, these remaining in production throughout the 1960's. As fibreglass manufacture became more common, so prices fell, and in 1966 the TR2/3/3A hardtop was priced at only £26 - 15 shillings, plus £6- for spraying in a special colour, and a further £4 to fit it to the car. This latter figure was a bargain ,for

TR 2, 3, 3A

The **MICROBOND** hardtop for the TR 2, 3 and 3A has been designed to be adaptable to accommodate the variations which are experienced in the bodywork of individual cars. Initial fitting at our factory takes about four hours, but subsequent fitting or removal can be accomplished in about 20 minutes. The hardtop is secured to the car making use of existing provisions and consequently no drilling of the car is required. The front of the hardtop is held by studs which replace the hood buttons along the top of the windscreen frame, while the main fixing points pick up on the soft top frame-brackets. The rear window which has to be individually trimmed to suit a particular car on initial fitting is secured round its lower edge by fittings at the rear soft top button positions. This method of window construction gives the maximum vision to the rear of the car and in fact both rear light assemblies can be seen from the front seat positions.

Above: the Microbond advertisement for its hardtops on TRs. Top right: The interior of a rally TR3A, showing the Halda Speed Pilot, plus perspex deflectors to direct hot air to the most efficacious places (BMIHT Archive).

the leaflet explains that initial fitting took around 5 hours at their works, as it was found (as TR rebuilders also know!) that variations existed in the fit and dimensions of individual TR bodywork which the Microbond top was designed to accommodate. Unlike the Works top, the Microbond one was held by studs along the front screen rail, these studs replacing the standard hood "Tenax" posts which thus meant that no drilling was required. At the back, the hardtop fixed to the set screws that otherwise held the soft top frame, which was removed. The rear window, which had to be trimmed to suit each particular car and hardtop on initial fitting, was held at its base by further fittings picking up on the rear soft top fixing buttons. This hardtop also had similar lines to the Works hardtop, but the rear window "wrapped around" slightly more, enabling the manufacturers to claim that one could see both rear lights from the driving seat with it in position! The car featured in the leaflet showing the hardtop was a disc-braked TR3, TYY 535, which Mr Wemyss told me belonged to one of his staff, he himself running another TR3, UHP 289. Lenham's also offered a TR2/3/3A hardtop during the 1960s and 1970s, I believe.

The TR accessory business extended further than just items for the cars themselves, for artefacts such as key fobs and cigarette lighters bearing the TR shield emblem were available, and no doubt made useful presents for purchase by the wives and girlfriends of the sporting TR driver.

The Triumph Sports Owners Association, in July 1957, was offering "strictly to members only" a "Rolstar" cigarette lighter with the red and black TSOA shield motif embossed thereon, priced at one pound. This must be a rarity today for serious collectors of TR ephemera to seek out! Similarly, a TSOA silk tie could be obtained, priced at 14 shillings; it was in silver and light blue stripes on a dark blue background, and carried the TSOA motif, again in silver and light blue. A very neat leather key fob with TR shield emblem was issued, in both the red and black colours of the TR2/3 and early 3A

Right: yet another maker of hardtops for TRs was Universal Laminations, who displayed in this advertisement their sliding sidescreen installation.

DETACHABLE FIBREGLASS HARDTOPS

FOR THE TRIUMPH **TR2** SLIDING WINDOW SIDESCREENS

Price **£48.** This top really is quickly detachable in a few minutes. In any colour, full washable headlining, beautifully finished, with interior light. Soft hood remains always on the car. Draughtproof sliding window sidescreens to match (**£15**) or your own converted (**£8**)—available separately.

Also for :—
**AUSTIN-HEALEY 100
SUNBEAM ALPINE
XK 120 AND ALL
SPORTS CARS**

Scottish Distributors :
EASTERN MOTOR CO. LTD.
52, GEORGE STREET,
EDINBURGH, 2.

UNIVERSAL LAMINATIONS LTD.

58, HOLLAND PARK MEWS, LONDON,   W.11.   Telephone : PARK 4310

Below: ties and other accessories available from the Triumph Sports Owners' Association at the time.

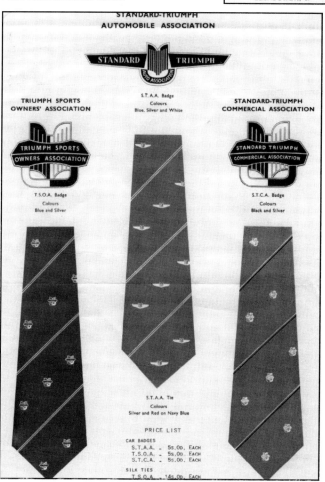

STANDARD-TRIUMPH AUTOMOBILE ASSOCIATION

S.T.A.A. Badge
Colours
Blue, Silver and White

TRIUMPH SPORTS OWNERS' ASSOCIATION

T.S.O.A. Badge
Colours
Blue and Silver

STANDARD-TRIUMPH COMMERCIAL ASSOCIATION

S.T.C.A. Badge
Colours
Black and Silver

S.T.A.A. Tie
Colours
Silver and Red on Navy Blue

PRICE LIST
CAR BADGES
S.T.A.A. . 5s.00. EACH
T.S.O.A. . 5s.00. EACH
S.T.C.A. . 5s.00. EACH
SILK TIES
T.S.O.A. . 14s.00. EACH

series, and also the blue and white of the later TR3As. I have seen this with the 'TR3' motif, and have been told that it also existed in 'TR2' form, but have not encountered one. I believe that the Factory had them produced for distributors to hand to new owners upon their taking delivery of a new TR, but it seems that they may also have been available for separate purchase, though they do not appear in any accessories list, nor do they seem to have been a TSOA item.

The TR2 was also used by at least one manufacturer to advertise clothing, an advert for the "Silverstone Twelve" motoring coat appearing in contemporary magazines, the coated driver standing proudly by his TR2. It cost 12 guineas, and had 'tailoring which lifts it out of the class of a "duffle", a duffle-coat being of course the standard TR winter outer wear for the period.

In addition to the many different accessories of all types that I have described, some owners had individual requirements that necessitated "one-off" items being manufactured, a good example being the TR shown in the photograph fitted with a canoe-carrying rack! There was apparently no limit to the lengths of "personalisation" to which some owners would go, and in Chapter 9 will be found details of a TR2 registration number NFH 33 that sported at least fifteen additional personal touches!

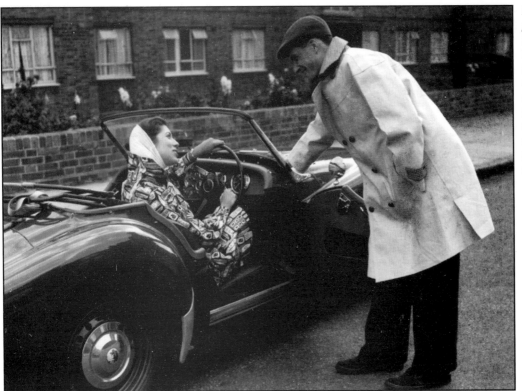

Motoring dress of the period is well illustrated in this posed shot of a late TR2 or early TR3. Headscarves were essential for ladies, but skirts must have been somewhat draughty - few women resorted to wearing trousers ("slacks" as they were then called) in the 1950s ("Autosport").

One of the more bizarre accessories made for a sidscreen TR was this rowing skiff carrier, made for Mr Roger King of Grimsby. It carried a 28-foot long boat and speeds of up to 80mph, loaded, were said to have been achieved.!

Above: Germany-based American serviceman Daniel Fowler beat all the Porsches with his TR2 at an amateur drivers' race at the Nurburgring in Summer 1955 (BMIHT).

Top left: a somewhat eccentric accessory, a foot-operated spray gun, is seen in action wit TR2 WPL 259. Centre left: the

original caption for this picture implies all this luggage would go into the boot of a TR2. In fact, I suspect the space behind the seats was also used. This publicity shot was released around the time of the 1954 Earls Court Motor Show ("Autosport").

Left:an enormous reversing light graces the rear of AC Taylor's TR3A as it leaves a control on the Jeans Gold Cup Rally on 3rd September 1960 ("Autosport").

Above: with roof spotlight blazing, Mick Green takes TR3A NDP 50 off on a rally section. Detailed study of the photograph reveals the front tyres to be of the original type of Michelin "X" pattern (TR Register Archive).

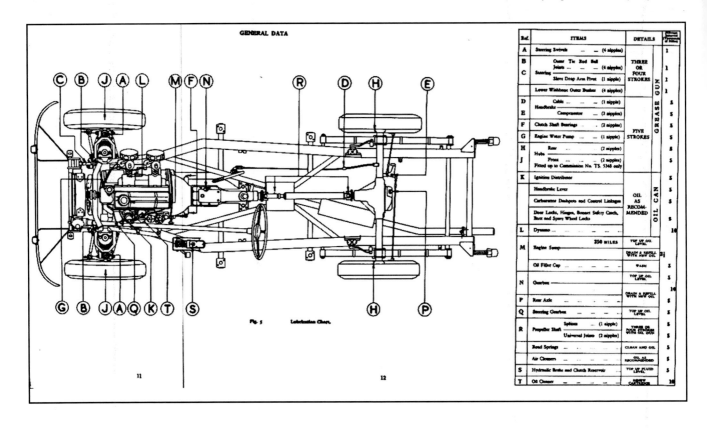

Fig. 5   Lubrication Chart.

CHAPTER SEVEN:

TR Literature,

Advertising & Publicity Material

In this chapter I propose to take a closer look than any that has been published previously at the literature (in its broadest sense) and advertising material that supported and sold the sidescreen TRs. I do not of course mean the books published from the 1970's onwards dealing with the cars historically, nor do I mean the various TR Register club magazines and publications; rather I refer to the printed word relating to the cars both as disseminated by Standard-Triumphs themselves, and by other companies whose products were used in the TR. In addition I shall deal with contemporary dealers' advertisements and other peripheral items that may be of interest. Road tests and other related matters are dealt with in Chapter Seven, but for light relief I have included at the end of this section some cartoons which involve TRs, even if their inclusion stretches the definition of "literature" to its furthest extent! I have been greatly assisted by Ian Gibson, who must have one the the largest collections extant of Standard-Triumph publications, and whose knowledge of these publications is, I submit, unrivalled Even so, neither Ian nor I claim that what follows is either exhaustive, comprehensive or fully accurate. for "new" items continue to come to light, causing old theories to be revised!

In the first part I shall cover the factory publications that actually instructed owners and repairers how to deal with the cars, namely owner's handbooks, workshop manuals and parts catalogues. The first edition driver's handbook naturally covers only TR2s, and was part number 501528/1, the final "1" referring to the edition number. This item is undated, but must presumably have been ready to go out with the very first TR2s supplied to private owners at the end of 1953. The same handbook was current throughout 1954 and presumably into 1955, for the second edition, again undated, as

well as dealing with the TR2 (part no 501528/2) refers also to the TR3, which of course only arrived in the Autumn of 1955. The photograph at the front is of a TR3, and both Lockheed and Girling braking systems are referred to, although the change from Lockheed to Girling is quoted as occurring at car TS 13001. This is incorrect, and leads Ian Gibson to conclude that this 2nd edition handbook must have been printed and ready sometime in advance of the actual braking system change taking place.

I would add here that each handbook, workshop manual and parts catalogue not only went through successive editions as I shall reveal, but within those individual editions, several actual printings took place, and at times the opportunity to change some minor items was taken at a reprinting rather than waiting until a full edition change occurred. However, as the subject is complicated enough just dealing with the editions themselves, I propose to ignore reprintings within each actual edition. Similarly, I shall not deal with any foreign language editions, principally as I have very little information on these.

The 3rd edition handbook which one must conclude was issued in 1956 does not include the TR2, but does cover both Lockheed and Girling brake fitted TR3s, whereas the 4th edition (1957?) includes only the post TS 13045 Girling disc brake fitted cars. The 5th edition covers the TR3A (referred to only as the TR3, in accordance with the factory's practice at that time) and was issued at the start of 1958. This edition appears to have run through many printings for a number of years, as by 1958 the sidescreen TR specification was largely settled, and few modifications of note took place thereafter, the principal one being the post TS 60,000 body changes, which were not really relevant in a driver's handbook. The

6th edition (part number just 501528 with no suffix) did not appear until November 1966, assuming that the printer's code mark is correct, several years after production ceased. Thus it was supplied not with cars, but only to owners who had lost theirs or who had not had the original passed on upon a change of ownership. This edition appears to have been a combined USA and UK book, for it shows a photograph of a right hand drive car but appends a note regarding left hand drive vehicles. The photograph of the engine compartment depicts a left-hand drive car, but the word "bonnet" is used, which is of course UK usage. To avoid any problems with the word "hood", the publicity department cunningly referred to "soft top" whereas previously in earlier editions "hood" had been used for soft top, which must have puzzled many Americans to whom "hood" meant bonnet! This 6th edition refers to the all synchomesh gearbox, which only appears on TR3B's. It assumes that 2138 cc is the standard engine capacity, and it depicts TR4 type rear brakes, which were only fitted to TR3Bs and some very late TR3As. As regards the TR3B, Ian Gibson contacted the works in the late 1960's to enquire whether any literature specific to this model had been produced, and they confirmed that there was none, the TR3A items being supplied. It is possible that an insert detailing the mechanical changes was put into those TR3A handbooks supplied to TR3B purchasers, but no evidence of this has come to light.

As to parts catalogues, these were loose-leaved, ring-bound items, the idea being that dealers could substitute amended pages sent out to them by the Works as parts were improved or otherwise changed. For this reason, it does not pay to be categorical about parts catalogues, for surviving original ones may well have been updated and changed by their previous custodians. The first edition that either Ian Gibson or I have seen bears the printer's code date of December 1954. However, as the car had been on sale by that time for more than a year, during which time numerous specification changes had been made, this cannot have been the very first parts catalogue, for otherwise dealers and repairers would have been "working in the dark" throughout 1954! One must presume therefore that although dated December 1954, this was but a later printing of an item originally issued around the start of 1954. Ian Gibson is doubtful that the system whereby the Works sent parts catalogues amendment sheets to individual garages had commenced as early as 1954/5, for he has not seen any that date from earlier than the late 1950's. Rather than issue actual amendment sheets, (which were obviously amendment sheets because they referred to themselves as such!) in the mid 1950's the factory appears merely to have sent reprinted loose-leaved pages to the dealers for incorporation in the parts books, these not being referred to as amendment sheets! Thus, once these had been incorporated in an individual parts book, it

became impossible to know whether they were additions and/or substitutions, or whether they had been there all the time! This as can be imagined leads to great difficulty in trying to date parts catalogues. In addition to amended parts catalogue sheets, the factory also circulated service bulletins to keep dealers abreast of developments. These were "service" rather than "spare part" items however, and were not incorporated into parts catalogues, although of course any actual revision of parts numbers and specifications consequent upon a service bulletin item **would** be so incorporated! - complicated I'm afraid!

The highest commission number referred to in the December 1954 parts catalogue is TS 4229 for the introduction of the "Dzus" fastened bonnet. This thinks Ian could have been ahead of actual car production, having regard to a copy deadline to allow for a printing in December 1954, a theory that is lent weight by the absence of any printed commission number for the associated deletion of the cable release type of bonnet. Clearly the works planned most specification changes some way ahead, and although they usually got things correct, i.e. correctly predicting at exactly what commission number a planned specification change would occur, there are instances of them getting things wrong! The second edition parts catalogue appears to be undated, but as it concerns itself only with the TR2, it must have been issued prior to September 1955. To this edition were later added two separate supplements, the first in August 1957 which dealt with the disc braking system, and the second (undated but presumably early 1958) which dealt with the "TR3, 1958 model," which was factory-speak for the TR3A. The true third edition materialised later in 1958, and went through at least 6 printings during its currency. No printer's code is found on it, and the highest commission number referred to is TS 34404. It does, for the first time, include the "split" steering column. The final parts catalogue was the fourth edition, part number 501653 and the frontispiece of my copy describes it as applicable to "TR2 commission number TS1 to TS 8636, TR3 commission number TS 8637 to TS 22013 and TR3 (1958 model) commission number TS 22014 and future". Ian Gibson's copy (presumably printed later) adds "TR3A (sic) TSF1 to TSF 500 and TR3A TCF1 and future," these being of course TR3B serial numbers. This last edition incorporates specification changes right into the TR3B production, although some of the earlier TR2 and 3 specification changes have by then been deleted, this meaning that no one edition of the parts catalogue is fully comprehensive!

Concerning workshop manuals, none of these appear to bear any date codes. The earliest edition owned by Ian Gibson covers modifications up to commission number TS 5251, though Ian suspects, and I agree, that there must have been an earlier printing of this edition as otherwise dealers would have been without any "book of words" for the whole of 1954. If you find a TR2 workshop manual that does not, for instance, refer to the addition of the battery box drain tube, then you can be reasonably sure that you have acquired one from the very first printing. Only the 3rd edition of the workshop manual actually declared itself as such, the others do not identify their edition number. However, there was clearly both a first edition, TR2 only, workshop manual, and a second edition which incorporated a TR3 supplement. The third edition went through at least six printings, lasting well beyond the production currency of the cars. My own second edition manual (part number 502602) incorporates a TR3 supplement at the end, but this was clearly produced prior to September 1956, as there is no reference to disc brakes. I have however seen an expanded "TR3 supplement" to a 3rd edition manual, and this **does** deal with the disc brakes and the associated, later rear axle. No specific TR3A or TR3B manual appears to have been issued, and that the manual is not infallible is shown by the TR3 supplement to the 3rd edition stating that engines from TS 9350E onwards were fitted with the "high-port" cylinder head, whereas this only arrived in fact from TS 12606E onwards, and even then not on all engines! The parts books I have seen were printed by the firm of H A Smith and Sons Ltd of Coventry, but the drivers handbooks and workshop manuals were printed by W W Curtis Ltd, again, not surprisingly, from Coventry.

Various other "official" explanatory publications were published by Standard-Triumphs from time to time, these usually being to do with the retrospective incorporation on earlier cars of later modifications. For instance, I have a publication (part number 554279) which is the Works leaflet detailing (and very detailed it is) how to retro-fit a hardtop to a TR2 or 3 that was built without one. Similarly, there existed a Works leaflet on the incorporation of overdrive second and third gears into a gearbox built with the early TR2 type top-gear only overdrive, although by the second edition of the workshop manual these instructions were incorporated into the manual itself. Another fascinating document is the "Schedule of Repair Operation Times," which sets out the time allowed for mechanics at Authorised Dealers to carry out various repair operations. My copy describes itself as the "First Edition", but it refers only to the TR3. I have seen another copy of this item that purports to cover TR2s as well, and this had no edition number. The time allowed to remove and refit the engine and gearbox as a unit, including detaching and refitting the gearbox from the engine once the unit was on the bench is quoted as 16 hours. This time limit must assume that the front apron nuts and bolts will easily undo; however, those who have worked on elderly TRs will confirm that they will not! Some times seem surprisingly

lengthy, yet others are painfully short, such as the four hours allowed to dismantle a gearbox completely, fit any necessary new bearings and to fully reassemble! However a full 20 hours, or 2 1/2 days work, was allowed for the fitting of a hardtop to a car that was built without one, which seems absurdly generous. Having regard to the cost of the hardtop itself and then this 20 hours of labour, the item looks to have been a very expensive luxury!

To remove and refit the front apron panel one was granted a bare two and a quarter hours - optimistic to say the least, yet to renew and adjust the fan belt one was given three hours! Upon investigation, they included in this time the 2 1/4 hours allocated to remove and refit the front apron, a quite unnecessary operation in this case, as well as a further half hour to remove, drain and refit the radiator! As any long term TR owner will confirm it is perfectly possible to change the fan-

---

Repairs Time Schedule

TRIUMPH SPORTS CAR (Model TR3)

ENGINE AND CLUTCH

Note : With the exception of S.E.2, road test times are not included.

Operation No.	Unit Description	Time Hrs.	Mins.
S.E.1	**Engine and gearbox,** to remove and refit as a unit only, detaching and refitting gearbox (includes Op. S.E.38 and 38a) ..	16	00
	(a) Extra to change over all ancillary equipment	2	00
	(b) Extra to reset or renew crankshaft rear oil seal only	2	00
	(c) Extra to partially dismantle engine, fit new crankshaft and bearings, leaving cylinder head, etc., in position ..	7	00
	(d) Extra to dismantle engine and refit all parts to new cylinder block. (Does not include decarbonizing and grinding in valves).	11	30
S.E.2	**Engine tune up :** includes cleaning and adjusting sparking plugs, distributor points, carburettors and petrol pump, adjusting tappets, checking ignition timing and road testing	2	15
S.E.3	**Distributor points.** To clean and adjust only		15
S.E.4	**Ignition timing.** To check and reset only ..		20
S.E.5	**Valve timing.** To check only		45
	(a) Extra to reset if necessary. (Consists of Ops. S.E.28 and 28b)	5	30
S.E.6	**Rocker cover joint.** To renew		20
S.E.7	**Tappets.** To remove rocker cover and adjust tappets		20
S.E.8	**Rocker shaft.** To renew assembly complete and/or push rods. (Includes Op. S.E.7).		45
	(a) Extra to dismantle assembly and fit new shaft and/or rockers		30
S.E.9	**Cylinder head.** To tighten down nuts only. (Includes Op. S.E.8)		55
S.E.10	**Cylinder head.** To remove and fit new gasket and adjust tappets	2	00
S.E.11	**Valves.** To decarbonize and grind in valves. (Includes Op. S.E.2)	7	00

1

belt at the side of the road in half an hour; however, the vital piece of information you need to know and which the workshop manual neglects to tell you, is that the car needs to have its steering on full lock, for this causes the centre tie rod to drop away from the fan extension piece just far enough for you to be able to squeeze a new belt through the resultant gap, which you can't do with the front wheels set straight ahead! (I am assuming that your engine mountings are in reasonable condition, for if they are soft, the engine sits lower and there may still not be enough room). Perhaps the company kept quiet about this dodge in the 1950's as a way of giving its dealers a "nice little earner" each time an unfortunate owner broke his fan belt! I should also add that one has to "wangle" the belt between the fan and the radiator core sideways and from underneath, at great risk to one's knuckles, but as for having to remove the front apron, never!

Moving on from instructive to promotional literature, the company issued several price lists during the production period of the sidescreen cars, though price movement was a much less frequent phenomenon than it became in the 1970's and 80's. As a representative example I am reproducing a price list for the 1959 models, issued in October 1958. The prices of many of the major accessories are included, and again, one is surprised at how relatively expensive some items were. To ascertain a comparative price in 1994, one needs to multiply by a factor of approximately 12; in doing

this the overdrive option works out at around £750, so it is hardly surprising that so relatively few TRs were thus originally equipped. At a basic equivalent price of around £12,500 today, a TR3A with no extras equates roughly with a 2 litre fuel-injected sports saloon - but bear in mind that the TR carried tax at the horrific rate of 50%, whereas in the UK today only 17.5% VAT is levied. A TR3A ordered "fully loaded" as the Americans say, with hardtop, radio, heater, overdrive, wire wheels, leather upholstery and a few other items could however cost the best part of £1,350, equivalent today to around £16,000, at which price it begins to have looked a little expensive, especially as in the late 1950's, one tended to have to pay the list price rather than shop around for the large discounts of today. The real "killer" however was the radio at £45 for a simple receiver - imagine paying £550 or more today for such a product! An additional small item of promotional material that I have seen recently is a factory-produced card for placing on the windscreen of TRs standing unsold in showrooms - this had the price on one side, and the word "Sold" on the reverse, as confirmation that the vehicle had found a buyer. These cards must be rare indeed today.

The company issued a series of special leaflets listing and describing the many different factory accessories that were available, both for original fitment and for later addition. At least four editions of this publication were produced, but I

TRIUMPH T.R.3 SPORTS CAR

	List Price £ s. d.	Purchase Tax £ s. d.	Total Price £ s. d.
Basic Model	699 0 0	350 17 0	1049 17 0
Hard Top with Sliding Windows	734 0 0	368 7 0	1102 7 0

Optional Extras fitted on production to special order

	£ s. d.	£ s. d.	£ s. d.
Heater	10 0 0	5 0 0	15 0 0
Radio	30 0 0	15 0 0	45 0 0
Leather upholstery	12 0 0	6 0 0	18 0 0
Adjustable Steering Unit & wheel	5 0 0	2 10 0	7 10 0
Aluminium Engine Sump	5 0 0	2 10 0	7 10 0
Road Springs— front (competition)	1 0 0	10 0	1 10 0
Shock Absorbers— rear (competition)	1 0 0	10 0	1 10 0
Tyres (Set of 5) Dunlop 'Road speed'	6 0 0	3 0 0	9 0 0
Michelin 'X' Tyres	5 0 0	2 10 0	7 10 0
Wire wheels & hubs (centre lock type)	25 0 0	12 10 0	37 10 0
Overdrive	42 10 0	21 5 0	63 15 0
Tonneau cover	9 0 0	4 10 0	13 10 0
Occasional Seat Vynide	9 5 0	4 12 6	13 17 6
Leather	10 0 0	5 0 0	15 0 0

Conditions of Sale. Prices: The Company reserves the right to vary the list prices at any time and all goods are invoiced at the prices current on day of delivery ex works.

Serial No. 126/10/58

THE STANDARD MOTOR Co. Ltd.

Registered Office and Tractor Division	THE STANDARD MOTOR CO. LTD. BANNER LANE COVENTRY 'Grams : Stack, Coventry 'Phone : Tile Hill 65211
Standard and Triumph Car Division	THE STANDARD MOTOR CO. LTD. CANLEY COVENTRY 'Grams : Flywheel, Coventry 'Phone : Coventry 3181
Service Division	THE STANDARD MOTOR CO. LTD. BIRMINGHAM ROAD, ALLESLEY COVENTRY 'Grams : Stanser, Coventry 'Phone : Coventry 2115
London Service Depot	THE STANDARD MOTOR CO. LTD. STANDARD ROAD, CHASE ESTATE PARK ROYAL, LONDON, N.W.10 'Grams : Stantri, Norphane, London 'Phone : Elgar 6511-7
London Office	15/17 BERKELEY SQUARE LONDON, W.1 'Grams : Flywheel, Wesdo, London 'Phone : Grosvenor 8181
Spares Division	THE STANDARD MOTOR CO. LTD. FLETCHAMSTEAD HIGHWAY COVENTRY 'Grams : Flywheel, Coventry 'Phone : Coventry 62471

REG. TRADE MARK

In addition to country-wide service The Standard Motor Company offers a generous guarantee with all its products, and all Stanpart replacement units.

PRICE LIST OF 1959 MODELS

TRIUMPH STANDARD

HOME SALES DIVISION

OCTOBER, 1958

deal with these in Chapter 6 where I cover the subject of accessories more widely.

The principal item of sales literature was of course the colour sales catalogue, nearly always of a fold-out type and containing either artists' impressions of the cars or actual photographs (frequently retouched) or sometimes a combination of both. I will deal with these chronologically, but do not claim that this survey is exhaustive, for "new" original material keeps turning up! Again, for reasons of simplicity, space and lack of availability, I am concentrating on English language editions, although catalogues were known to have been produced in several other languages, notably French, German, Italian, Spanish and, dare I say it, American!

As might be expected, there was a colour brochure printed for the 20 TS sports car, despite its lack of readiness for production, presumably so that this could be distributed at the 1952 Motor Show. The car is very much an "artist's impression," and it looks distinctly elongated. The brochure is undated, but must have been produced in around October 1952. It is possible that a second or different 20 TS brochure was also produced, but I have not seen it. By July 1953 a black and white 4 page TR2 brochure was available, this

actually referring to the car as the "TR2." Again, no photographs were included, only artist's drawings, but at least the front cover TR2 drawing is reasonably faithful to the real thing. The car is shown still wearing the "20 TS" type front badge, and the sidelights differ from the production items, but the front overriders have been changed to the TR2 type. The car is drawn left hand drive, and the brochure includes full details of the speeds achieved by the prototype at Jabbeke, then of course the big news! I cannot be certain that this item was the first TR2 brochure, carrying as it does the printer's date of 7/53, for I wonder what publicity was handed out at the Geneva show in March 1953 when the first TR2 was first shown to the public. Presumably the Triumph people would not be giving out 20TS brochures, so maybe there was a French/German TR2 brochure that predates this July 1953 item? The first widely available TR2 brochure was an 8 page fold-out colour one, of which at least two editions were printed. Again, it was all drawings rather than photographs with the exception of a photograph of Ken Richardson standing alongside MVC 575 following the Jabbeke record runs. The car is shown in left hand drive form, finished in Ice Blue with blue upholstery and darker blue wheels, a non standard colour scheme - presumably artistic licence! The first edition of this brochure shows the

The Triumph Sports

TR2 still carrying the 20 TS type front badge, whereas the second edition shows it carrying the production "shield" type badge. The surprising thing is that the car is on the front referred to as "The Triumph Sports Car" rather than the TR2, despite the fact that the earlier brochure referred to above did call it the TR2! The first edition appears to have been created for the October 1953 Earls Court Motor Show, the second edition appearing in early 1954, my copy being dated February 1954. However, it refers to the win by the TR in the 1954 RAC Rally, and this did not actually take place until March 1954, so one wonders how much one can actually rely on the dates in these items of official literature!

By later in 1954 the company were giving away cardboard "TR2" blotters, an example of which is reproduced below. It carries a genuine photograph of a red, long-door TR2 in right hand drive form being driven through what is apparently a park, and the reverse side is a blotting pad. The principal 1955 TR2 brochure was a more ambitious 12 side fold out, containing both colour and black and white photographs, some clearly retouched. It also contained a list of the car's principal competition successes during 1954 and 1955. The hardtop version was also featured, and the TR appeared in both left and right hand drive form, though the registration numbers on the colour pictures of the UK cars

THE TRIUMPH T.R.2 SPORTS

The Triumph T.R.2 Sports, with its 2 litre engine (1991 c.c.) and four speed gearbox opens up exciting new possibilities for the sporting motorist. In its standard touring trim without Overdrive it is capable of at least 100 m.p.h. On the Belgian Jabbeke Highway, in speed trim, the T.R.2 reached a speed of 124 m.p.h., while subsequent successes in international competition have amply proved its capabilities.

R.A.C. 2,000 miles International Rally: 1st, 2nd and 5th. Le Mans 1954: Finished 15th — 1,793 miles at 74 miles per hour. Alpine Rally: Coupe des Alpes—2 Team Prizes and Cup for best aggregate performance on tests. A privately owned T.R.2 in touring trim was recently driven 1003 miles round Britain in 24 hrs. averaging 37.286 m.p.g. and 41.6 m.p.h.

THE TRIUMPH MOTOR COMPANY (1945) LTD.

COVENTRY   ·   ENGLAND

Above is the blotter referred to in the text, the original of which is in colour, showing a red TR2.

To the right is the front panel of the brochure for the TR2 "Francorchamps". This is not reproduced in colour here, but the original shows a "Steel Blue Metallic" coloured car and it is worthy of note that this brochure seems even rarer than the car!

TRIUMPH *"Coupé Francorchamps,,*

THE *Triumph* T.R.2 SPORTS

Details from the first TR2 catalogue of July 1953; left is the front cover page and below are two artist's impressions from the inside. Drawings were utilised for the simple reason that production cars were not yet available to photograph - and in any event if they had been, they wouldn't have stood still long enough for the cameraman to focus on them!

On the right is a detail from the interior of the same brochure.

Above is the front panel of the first disc-braked TR3 brochure. Note the embargo date on the top right hand corner of 17th October 1956, the start date of the Motor Show at which the disc brakes were first revealed.

On the right is a detail from the interior of the same brochure.

Available with occasional passenger seat

THE Triumph Sports T.R.3 is the latest version of the famous T.R.2 which, during the last two seasons, has made such a name for itself in leading motoring events throughout the world. The T.R.3 has more power, developing 95 B.H.P., and includes many modifications which make it even better than its predecessors. There is also greater space behind the seats—sufficient to install, as an extra, a seat for occasional passengers. The back of the front passenger seat tips to give access to the rear.

For real versatility there's nothing to beat the Triumph Sports. Take it out on to the open road and feel the swift, surging power of the 2 litre engine—then you'll know what inspired motoring really is. Yet, how easy it is to manœuvre in city traffic; how quickly off the mark; how reassuring the smooth, instant response of the Lockheed hydraulic brakes; and then in the gruelling, back-breaking competition courses, what verve and staying power. Yes, the Triumph Sports T.R.3 has all that motoring enthusiasts need.

The Triumph T.R.3 has been designed for comfort as well as really outstanding performance. Instruments, for instance, are neatly grouped in front of the driver; the screen is easily detachable and provides first-class protection without promoting dazzle. Facing the passenger is a glove locker and each door has a pocket. The seats, of the adjustable bucket type, are roomy and comfortable, while the floor is carpeted and the remote gear-lever is conveniently placed, enabling rapid gear changes to be made. There is a luggage boot in addition to the space behind the seats, while beneath, the spare wheel is located in a compartment of its own. Hood and side screens will keep driver and passenger snug and dry. A Hard Top model is available for those who wish to combine the above attractions with the snug comfort of a smart modern coupé. The all round visibility of this model makes it an ideal sports car for all weather motoring. The hard top is easily removed if the car is required for open-air motoring. The detachable side screens have sliding windows and with the scuttle ventilator air-conditioning can be adjusted to a nicety. Thus, for the motorist who wants a car for touring or sport the Triumph T.R.3 is the ideal choice.

A page from the 1956 TR3 sales brochure, showing the newly-available occasional rear seat. The front seats are pushed fully forward!

appear to have been tampered with! The front cover shows what looks like a Geranium TR2 with wire wheels in a beach setting, with a white TR2 in the background. The Geranium car is a short door model, which is an inconsistency as Geranium was no longer a listed colour in 1955 for short-door cars! Maybe it was a Signal Red car and poor colour reproduction! This brochure was issued in the summer of 1955, and I feel sure that there must have been an intermediate one produced for the 1954 London Motor Show, but I have not seen a copy. My own copy of the 1955 brochure bears the date of October 1955, by which time the TR3 had been announced! However, it is well established that there were quite a number of unsold TR2s around when the TR3 came out, and it was listed side by side with the TR3

(at a lower price) for some months, hence the reprinting of the TR2 brochure as late as October 1955.

For some reason, the October 1955 TR3 brochure was only a 4 page affair and in black and white at that! Maybe there was a more comprehensive colour one? This black and white item used real, retouched photographs, the car featured on the front being RHP 560, a wire-wheeled publicity car that I believe was converted from a TR2, for I have seen a photograph of both this car and its sister car RHP 557 wearing TR2 fronts! The Belgian-built TR2 "Francorchamps" had its own colour brochure, in the French language; the front cover of one of the few surviving copies is reproduced in this Chapter.

and the safety of disc brakes

Speed and safety. These are the merits which distinguish the Triumph T.R.3. Engineered for fast, safe driving yet convenient for travel in rush hour traffic. Proven by its outstanding success in competitive events throughout the world. Rapid acceleration; a top speed of over 100 m.p.h., and disc brakes to ensure a firm even stop. Form hugging seating, and firm but comfortable suspension allow for relaxed driving no matter what the road conditions. Drive with speed. Drive with safety. Drive the Triumph T.R.3.

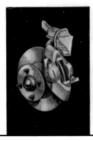

DISC BRAKES

Girling disc brakes are standard equipment on the front wheels of the Triumph T.R.3. They grip firmly and evenly under all weather conditions. Other advantages are

1. No brake fade
2. Unaffected by water.
3. Self-cleaning.
4. Self-adjusting.
5. Longer life friction pads.
6. Friction pads renewed in matter of minutes.

Above is an inside page of the 1958 UK edition of the TR3A brochure, showing the heart of the City of London, with an excess of Standard Vanguards in the background.

The panel to the right is the front cover of the German-language edition of the same brochure. This is referred to later in the text and is merely a reversal of the cover of the UK edition.

From time to time, as with the TR2 blotter, the Publicity Department produced smaller items for dealers to give away, one such being an elongated four page TR3 brochure that I have. The format is about 8 1/3 x 3 inches, but as the typeface is very small, there is a surprising amount of information therein. This hand-out is dated September 1956, and it refers to the fitment of Girling disc brakes, although not in the triumphant tones that one might have expected, given that it was the world's first true production car to be so fitted! A month later the full, new, disc braked TR3 brochure arrived, the year (1957) being mentioned on the front for the first time. My copy is actually stamped 17th October 1956 - maybe this was an embargo date which concurred with the revealing of the disc brakes at the Earls Court Motor Show that month. This particular brochure is about the most comprehensive and nicest of all the items of sidescreen TR publicity, being a full twelve pages in length and in book, rather than fold-out, form. It relies entirely on drawings rather than photographs, and is a mixture of colour and half-tones. On the cover is a beige TR3, whilst inside is a Winchester Blue open car and a Signal Red car with a Red hardtop. Much is made of the occasional rear seat, and of course the disc brakes. The existence of the "GT" hardtop conversion is referred to, stated as being available "for the competition minded enthusiast," and the 4.1 rear axle ratio is also listed as a no-cost option (although only when an overdrive was specified). The list of optional extras still includes the rear wing spats and short front undershield, incidentally - maybe the factory had unsold stock of these items! By this time, the engine power was quoted as "100 BHP," indicating the fitment of the "high-port" cylinder head. This brochure continues to show, as do most others, a combination of left and right hand drive cars, presumably so that the same artwork could be used for export brochures, even though the wording (for the USA) and the language (for Europe) would have been changed.

By 1958 and the introduction of the TR3A one gets the distinct impression that the Works Publicity Department was resting on its laurels, content that their product was so good and so successful that it would sell itself! The 1958 TR3A brochure was used right through 1959 and well into 1960, and, as far as the UK and Europe were concerned, it may well have lasted right until the end of production. I have no doubt that there were several different North American TR3A brochures and probably a TR3B one, but unfortunately these are not around on this side of the Atlantic. This principal 3A leaflet was not, in all honesty, anything like as nice as the 1957 TR3 one just described. As usual, it relies on the artist rather than the photographer, and one feels that the proportions of the TR3As on the front cover are not quite right, the bonnet being somewhat elongated, maybe to convey the impression of power! This leaflet was an 8 page fold-out

type, claiming for the car "110 mph and the safety of disc brakes" - however, on that very page is shown a picture of the car stationary near the Bank of England in the heart of the City of London, hardly 100 mph stuff! The car is shown finished in a strange blue/green colour that was never available, and the background is suffering from a surfeit of Standard Vanguards! On another page a white 3A is shown in "competition trim" which appears just to mean with aero-screens, and on the front, the elongated 3As referred to are shown with a stylised motor race going on in the background. As I write I have in front of me two copies of this brochure, one 1958 edition for the home market, and one dated May 1960 printed in German. The "cheap-skatery" at the Publicity Department by 1960, when money was tight, is all too evident.

The German brochure has the same cover as the UK one, but the drawing is reversed to make the cars appear left hand drive! In the background the racing circuit scene is also reversed, but the artist remembered that almost all racing circuits are run in a clockwise direction, and he therefore redrew two of the racing cars to continue to revolve in the usual direction! However, he seems to have forgotten the stationary racing car being worked on in the background, for this is still facing the "wrong" way, and as soon as it rejoins the race, a collision will ensue! What happened to the City of London one may ask? Well, the same girl still has the same car (albeit reversed left to right), but the background has changed to what looks like New York, and the Vanguards have turned into Chevrolets! Not very German, but maybe the same drawing was used in North American publicity material? I have also seen a second UK edition of this brochure, and it carried the date of August 1960, even later than the German one, proving that the same leaflet was being distributed for at least two years. Of course, this is defensible on the ground that the TR's specification was very largely settled by 1958 and thus there was little need to update the publicity - in addition, throughout late 1958 and all of 1959 sales were going so well on the strength of the vehicle's proven record that publicity hardly mattered, and it is noticeable that the number of magazine advertisements being placed by the company dropped considerably after the initial publicity that had surrounded the launch of the TR3A.

The only significant difference between the 1958 and 1960 brochures is that in the latter, paint and trim combinations are listed in a separate tabular form appendix, whereas in the earlier copy they appear within the general specification. This incorporation of colours into the general sales brochure is a further example of money saving, for no mention of either body or trim colours appears in the pre-1958 catalogues, these items being dealt with by separately issued colour and trim charts which I shall refer to later. Amazingly,

THE STANDARD CAR REVIEW   *May,*

Another Triumph for DOCKERS' FINISHES!

A car with a splendid "presence" — enhanced, we are proud to say, by its gleaming finish — the Triumph Sports Two Seater is the latest Standard product for which Dockers' Specialised finishes have been chosen.

Maintain that superb finish by regular
★ use of Dockers' CELLUSOL LIQUID ★
POLISH or CELLUSOL WAX POLISH

DOCKER BROTHERS

Makers of Paints, Lacquers and Varnishes for every purpose

LADYWOOD BIRMINGHAM · 16

230

Above: Docker Brothers were proud to be associated with the TR2, as their advertisement makes clear. Top right: A TR3 shown (almost) by Cal-Sales Incorporated at the Los Angeles Motor Show in December 1956 had an extraordinary paint job, as can be glimpsed. Attractive young ladies have long been used to sell cars, but as to relevance of the rocking horse, one can only speculate - maybe it was present in case it produced something really rare? (BMIHT). On the right is a TR2 being tried out in Australia by actor Ron Randall, seen with his wife Hildegarde Christian in April 1955 (BMIHT).

One of odder uses for a TR is shown here - the tractor unit of a miniature articulated truck! Mr and Mrs Brammer set out from California in 1959 in this device on a 7,000-mile trip around the USA, to publicise the Smyth Van Lines trucking company, calling at Triumph dealers en route (Standard Car Review).

the rear wing spats were still listed as an extra as late as 1960, though I have seen no evidence of a 3A having being supplied with them. Also listed were "fixed side screens" as part of the GT conversion kit. I imagine this means "fixed" to the car in some semi-permanent way, rather than with "fixed" as opposed to "s;iding" side windows.

As regards official colour charts, these are now very hard to come by, and I have never seen a 1956/57 colour chart specific to the TR3s, though one must have existed as the brochure reveals nothing about colour. The most comprehensive colour catalogue I have seen (part number 502378) is one held in the TR Register's archives, and this deals with all Standard and Triumph models. It is undated but must emanate from around late 1954 or early 1955, for the Signal Red and British Racing Green colours are listed as being available for the TR2, but there is no mention of either the TR3 or the Phase III Standard Vanguard, both of which came out in October 1955. The chart includes the infamous Olive Yellow colour, the intriguing Ice Blue (really an eau-de-nil green) and the somewhat garish Geranium Pink. Salvador Blue, which later became a TR3 colour, is shown, but only as applicable to Standard models at that time. This is a twelve page catalogue, but the company also produced concurrently single page cards showing colours on one side and trim choices and specifications on the reverse. An August 1954 one that I have lists only four colours for the TR2, Black, Pearl White, Signal Red and British Racing Green. One presumes that these were handed out to potential buyers who seemed serious in showrooms along with the brochures, and that the colour charts were produced separately to obvi-

ate having to reprint the brochures each time a colour specification change was made.

That other promotional handouts were on occasions produced by the company is shown by a 1956 8 page leaflet describing itself as a "Motor Show Retrospect." It covers in detail and photographically the Standard and Triumph stands at the Earls Court Show of that year, having a picture of the Perspex-bodied TR3 on the front. Obviously it could not have been available during the Motor Show, so I conclude that it was produced for dealers to hand out subsequently. I do not know whether this item was repeated in other years, or whether 1956 was in some way special. Although not specific to the TR series, a survey of TR literature needs to make mention of the company's in-house magazine, the Standard Car Review, which appeared monthly, priced ninepence! It expressed itself to "incorporate Triumph News," and covered all the latest happenings at Coventry. Most months it carried several items of TR interest, as well as many excellent photographs some of which are used in this book, and it appears to have been on sale to the general public rather than just to employees and owners. There were also of course the various publications concerned with the Triumph Sports Owners Association, but I deal with these elsewhere in this book. The 1954 "Autosport" magazine road-test of the TR2 was reprinted as a four page leaflet for showrooms to hand out, and other road tests may have been similarly treated.

At least two oil companies produced lubrication charts for the TR2 and TR3, Castrol co-operating with the company itself to produce a detailed wall chart about 24 inches by 18. Shell also produced a wall chart, not quite as large or detailed, and although it states that it had been checked by the company, it does not look quite as "official" as the Castrol one, which even bears the company's shield badge. Finally, reprinted from the December 1954 issue of the Standard Car Review, was an eight page leaflet entitled "The TR2 Story",detailing the car's design and development process, incorporating power curve graphs, and listing the various competition successes between January and September 1954. This item was given out by dealers, the example that I have seen being stamped by L.F. Dove Ltd, the well known South London firm.

I shall now attempt to review the advertising of the sidescreen TR throughout its nearly 10 year production run, although in fact very little advertising was done during 1953. In addition, advertisements tailed off dramatically during 1959 and 1960, at least as far as UK publications were concerned. Clearly as an enthusiasts car the TR tended to be promoted more in the sporting magazines, Autosport, Motorsport and the like, but some more general advertising

The Triumph Sports Owners' Association.

INFORMATION SHEET No. 4

AERO SCREENS

Provision has been made for the fixing of aero screens by the inclusion of four chrome headed setscrews and nuts placed

in the cowling just behind the windscreen. To fix the aero screens, remove the windscreen and loosen the nuts of the set-screws, thus allowing the slotted arms of the aero screens to slide under the setscrew heads.

REAR WING SPATS

Spats are intended for appearance and to reduce wind resistance for maximum high speed work, they can only be fitted with the pressed steel wheels.   To fix the spats into position insert the protruding bar at the forward end of each spat into the locating plate which is

fixed on to the bottom inside forward edge of each rear wing, lift the spat into position with the upper two tongues placed inside the wing rim and secure by swinging the spring steel hooked rod (secured to the rear wing) to the rear and hooking it on to a bracket fixed on to the inside of the wing.   This hooked rod engages in the loop of the bar fixed on the rear end of each spat.   When the spats are not in use the securing rod should be hooked on to its bracket, where it will be held in position by a light spring load.

An interesting page extracted from the Triumph Sports Oowners' Association handbook, referred to in the text.

was done in Autocar and Motor, and also on occasions in non-motoring magazines, for instance "Country Life!" I have myself a vague recollection as a child of TRs being adver-tised on billboards or hoardings, but cannot find any evi-dence of this. As a specialist product, I think it most unlikely that the TR ever received any direct television advertising, especially as this form of promotion was in the UK at least, very much in its infancy during the TR period. It is possible

that there were cinema advertisements, particularly ones placed by local dealers in their local cinemas, but again, I cannot prove this.

The 20 TS appeared as a last minute addition to the 1952 Motor Show, and it was not specifically included in the com-pany's publicity campaign - there were however one or two advertisements for it at around the time of this 1952 show, but presumably as there were no actual production vehicles to sell, the firm decided to save the main advertising budget until the car was actually available. The reception given to the 20 TS could not have inspired confidence in any event. It was therefore not until the successful conclusion of the Jabbeke record runs in May 1953 that the Publicity Department felt sufficiently confident in the product to spend cash on promoting it (and presumably in the factory's eventual ability actually to build and deliver some cars!). In the June and July 1953 issues of the Motoring publications several advertisements for the "New Triumph Sports Car" appeared, the price of £555 plus tax being quoted. The 124 mph speed record was emblazoned across all of these adverts, as well it might be, for it really was a very significant velocity for a 2 litre production car in 1953. The car was not referred to as a TR2 however, and photographs were not used in the Company's own advertisements, merely a line drawing of the car during its record run. The artist, however, failed to get it right, for the car is given a front bumper, which it in fact ran without. The opportunity to advertise this suc-cess was also taken by several other companies whose products were used in the car and/or the running of the Jabbeke runs, so highly comprehensive publicity coverage was achieved, which was, of course, the point of the run.

Once the euphoria surrounding the Jabbeke event had died down, the Publicity Department temporarily ceased promot-ing the TR, again presumably because of the delays caused by the development process and the lack of any actual cars to sell. As it was, I gather that the record run elicited quite a number of orders which were unable to be fulfilled for some time. Certainly a search through the motor sporting maga-zines for the second half of 1953 reveals virtually no adver-tisements for the TR2 at all, neither company ones nor any by individual dealers; the Standard Triumph publicity prior to the 1953 London Motor Show concentrating very much on the new Standard 8 family saloon, with hardly a mention of the TR. Having regard to the numbers of Standard 8's expected to be sold compared to TRs, this is understand-able, but one would have thought that the Company would have made more of the "prestige" effect of the TR in its advertising - again, maybe they were frightened of eliciting orders that could not be fulfilled, at least in the short term, and nor must we lose sight of the fact that the USA was seen as the principal market for the TR. The one major exception to this lack of promotion was a coloured TR advertisement that appeared on the front cover of "Autosport" magazine for 30th October 1953, and also I believe in other publications. The car shown was a drawing rather than a photograph, the same drawing of an Ice Blue car that had appeared in the October 1953 catalogue. Again the car was only called the "Triumph 2 litre Sports Car", and the price was quoted at £555 plus tax.

Advertising in Britain only really began in earnest following

the 1954 RAC Rally successes, where of course the TR swept the board and suddenly became a desirable commodity. This coincided roughly with better availability of production vehicles, so adverts were duly placed making sure that the RAC Rally success was well promoted. In fact, in early 1954 one Triumph dealer in Essex was advertising the TR2 as a "124 mph car" - stretching the truth more than somewhat as regards production cars! Again, other companies were anxious to be associated with this success and placed their own adverts maintaining that their products had been used on

An early North American advertisement for the TR2 in its original form at the initial price of $2,499.

the successful TR2 cars. The "official" advert was a very bland affair solemnly listing the RAC Rally successes; no price was mentioned and it did not even picture the winning car! In May 1954, Docker Brothers, the paint manufacturers who supplied Standard-Triumphs, placed a large advert in the Standard Car Review stating how proud they were to supply the paint for the "Triumph Sports two-seater." A photograph was used, showing a left hand drive TR2 carrying the 20 TS badge and the original wiremesh grille. This was a commonly used early publicity photograph, one of a series taken of the same car, and I cannot be categorical as to which TR its was. As a left hand drive car, it cannot have been ORW 666, the 3rd prototype, for not only was this right hand drive, but it also had the 20 TS type front overriders as is clear from other shots of it. It must therefore have been either MVC 575 or MWK 950; it cannot have been a production car as these photographs were in circulation prior to even TS1 and TS2 having been built.

The Cal-Sales advertisement which proclaims 45 mpg for the TR2 (wonder if this was a case of "advertiser's licence", referring to an Imperial gallon for the sake of boasting something approximating to the truth - remembering that the US gallon is 20% less than the Imperial gallon?

The early USA advertising for the TR2 (priced at $2,499 plus taxes and delivery) stressed the economy aspect, claiming up to 45 mpg (US gallon?), but also mentioning the car's 100 mph capability. "Give yourself real 'Grand Prix' performance at a down to earth price" was another US slogan, presumably relying on USA buyers not knowing too much about what Grand Prix performance really was! By the end of June 1954 the company were placing adverts headed "Triumph at Le Mans" - well, no, they did not actually win, but at least the sole TR entry did creditably, especially as it was probably the most standard production car in the race. It was not a Works entry, but it did receive a measure of Works support, and the Publicity Department were certainly eager to claim it as theirs, the advert mentioning in bold letters the excellent fuel consumption. The price was quoted, now £625 plus tax, and a line drawing of a production TR2 was included. Following Le Mans, the next two Company advertisements also had competition successes to proclaim: "Triumph in the Alps," which appeared in August 1954, referred to the gaining of the team prize in the Alpine Rally, and then there was "Triumph at Ulster," which appeared in the October. This should surely have read "Triumph in Ulster", and it referred to the gaining by the six TR2s entered in the Tourist Trophy race of both first and second team prizes. It was certainly a feat worth shouting about, and a photograph of a racing TR2 actually appeared in the advert for the first time. The wording chose to stress the "reliability" of the TR, which had led to "such consistent success internationally." Thus it can be gleaned that the company's 1954 advertising campaign was very much competition orientated.

By early 1955, a different type of advert appeared, the first of the "IT" series, which took in the Standard 8 and 10's as well. "Here IT is!" was the new slogan - what is "it"? Well, the TR2 of course. As to what "IT" meant, other than the obvious, several later company advertisements stated that it stood for "Internationally Tested," but this is certainly not made obvious in the February 1955 TR2 publicity. A photograph is used, the car shown being registered as OHP 242. Now this car was TS 14 '0'; one of the very first publicity cars. It was a long door car, but in the 1955 advert, it appears to have short doors and outer sills! It also has the late TR2 type chrome reveal strip around the air intake, although this was not introduced on production TR2s until later that year. One wonders, therefore, whether this photograph was of the real OHP 242 which had been updated, (it appears to retain the early 10 1/2 inch wiper spindle spacing) or was it of a later car to which OHP 242's identity had been affixed? Maybe also the photograph had been retouched, but if so, it was very expertly done. Identity swapping was quite common in the motor industry, (I believe it still goes on) and I cannot believe that Triumph's were immune from this. There is a driver in the car who could be Ken Richardson, but the photograph is not clear enough to be certain.

In June 1955 the "IT" campaign continued, but by then a line-drawn TR2 had replaced the photograph described above. In this drawing, a young lady is in the driving seat, and a fellow alongside her wears a loud, checked sports jacket. Another sporty looking couple stand alongside, clearly mighty envious of the TR2! The TR is described as "having brought a new inspiration to motoring!" Competition successes continued throughout 1955, and the 3 car team at Le Mans in 1955, all of which finished strongly, occasioned a company advertisement. However, not as much was made of this Le Mans effort as one might have expected, but probably the terrible publicity surrounding this 1955 race, with its horrific accident and more than 80 deaths, made it something that advertisers and copywriters fought shy of being associated with. One must remember that following the accident, there were many calls for motor racing to be banned entirely, and competitive motoring almost came to a halt on the Continent that summer. Consequently the Works publicity people chose to stress the "summer touring" aspect

of the TR, and to play down its competition use, unlike in 1954. The "IT" adverts continued through 1955 by showing a wire-wheeled, hardtop equipped TR2, again a line drawing. It was described as having won more International honours than any other post-war model in its class: Britain's most exciting sports car! Price, with hardtop, was quoted at £670 plus tax.

Late 1955 brought the TR3, which was at once heavily promoted, although as I said earlier, the TR2 remained listed for a few months. The TR3 campaign emphasised "bringing you more power, speed and comfort," which one has to say was only partly true, and they certainly did not mention the increase in fuel consumption! The availability of a hard top was stressed (even though this had been around since late 1954), as also was the occasional rear seat, which really was new, albeit of limited practical value. In the initial TR3 adverts, a large photograph was used of a car by a harbour with a yachting background, a couple seated in the car talking to a "keen type". The car used is white with wire wheels, and it bears the registration number PYY 166, although there seems to have been an attempt to make this illegible! Certainly it was not a Coventry mark, being a London issue from April 1955, so maybe this is a further example of jiggery-pokery with Publicity Department vehicles! A subsidiary photograph shows to advantage the new, optional rear seat, though the front seats have (not surprisingly) been pushed forward to their fullest extent. Another version of the same advert has the car with registration number OYR 905.

Around March 1956 a full page advertisement appeared exhorting owners to take advantage of the "Standard and Triumph Maintenance Voucher Scheme" - this provided for regular servicing of the cars "to a special formula and at modest cost." The car featured was a line drawn TR3, the line drawing clearly being taken from the actual photograph of the TR3 in the harbour setting mentioned above. By April 1956 the TR3 was being described as "The car that gives you more," and the "IT" slogan had reappeared, albeit in less prominent form. A photograph of an (unregistered) car was shown alongside a glider, again to emphasise the sporting aspect, and a petrol consumption of 32 mpg was mentioned in the text, along with 100 mph capability. "For sheer value for money, there is nothing to beat the TR3" the advert modestly proclaimed. At the same time, the Company's United States advertising was putting all the emphasis on speed, (flat out 100 mph and 0-50 in only 8 seconds) and exhorting potential owners to "Zest-drive a Triumph soon" - ugh! The possession of 100 bhp was mentioned, and the adverts claimed that the TR3 "was new from the word Go," which of course was far from the truth, for in reality it differed very little from the TR2. The USA price in 1956 was set at $2,599, plus taxes and delivery, which could be a considerable extra

cost with the distances involved.

In the September 1956 issue of "Motor Sport" magazine one finds one of the few advertisements specifically for the hardtop version of the TR, priced at £715 plus tax. Billed as having "race track performance and saloon car comfort," a white TR3 with a black hardtop was featured, its sports-jacketted driver standing alongside and gazing into the sky at a TR3 shield badge which appears to be hovering in mid-air - a portent, perhaps? Saloon car comfort seems to be stretching the imagination a little far, even when comparing the hardtop TR to the relatively-primitive saloons of the day. My own memories of hardtop fitted TRs are of exceeding noise caused by the drumming of the steel top, and draughts from the lack of good sidescreen to hardtop fitting. Later in 1956 the advertisement relating to the "TR3 versus light aircraft" duel referred to in Chapter 5 appeared, but in general the publicity people appear to have continued their 1955 policy of not specifically mentioning competition results in their

The Standard & Triumph Voucher Maintenance Scheme provides for the regular servicing of your car by your local Standard & Triumph dealer to a special formula prepared by Standard factory engineers. It enables you to obtain, at a modest cost, smooth, trouble-free running under all conditions. Another example of Standard & Triumph Service.

★ For further details apply to Service Division, The Standard Motor Co. Ltd., Allesley, Coventry.

STANDARD CARS   TRIUMPH CARS   STANDARD COMMERCIAL VEHICLES   STANDARD DIESEL ENGINES   FERGUSON TRACTORS

promotional material. This was not for lack of good results to promote, one hastens to add, for this period was the start of the TR's most successful time as one of the world's greatest rally cars. As an instance of the lack of competition information, if there was a TR3 advert featuring the 1956 Alpine Rally, in which 5 TR3's took Coupes des Alpes for unpenalized runs, then I cannot find it. In late 1956, the Bakelite Company took advertising space to promote their "Vybak" plastic used for sports car hood windows, and they chose a TR3 to use as a model. Similarly, I.C.I. Ltd also used TRs to promote its "Vynide" upholstery material on occasions. By October 1956 disc brakes had arrived, and this did indeed give the Company something to shout about, for their fitment as standard equipment to a production vehicle was genuinely big news, and was well featured in the contemporary advertisements. In the USA the price had risen slightly to $2,675 plus taxes, and the disc brakes were being highlighted, though not as much as speed and acceleration.

TR drivers were said to "have a tiger in their power" (makes a change from in their tank!), and prospective owners were told that they'd be wise to arrange for delivery now! Many of them did of course, the real USA sales boom commencing around this 1957 period, so one assumes that the USA advertising was doing its job, naive as much of it may seem to us now. North Americans were assured that "no other car at its price can match it - or catch it!" Disc brakes and their associated safety benefits were being stressed, but as before, the real accent was on the performance available in relation to the purchase price. By the Autumn of 1957 TR3 adverts were appearing with "100 mph" plus" emblazoned across them in huge black letters, this velocity being somewhat counteracted by the statement, in smaller letters, at the foot of the page "In city traffic - so docile, no fuss!" Wisely the Company were bringing out the fact that in the TR they built a car just as at home in town as on the race track or in rallies, for in the same way that the huge majority of modern buyers of offroad vehicles never use them as such, so the large majori-

An impressive line-up of TR2s is arrayed outside the premises of London sports car dealers Performance Cars Limited. This shot was taken in 1956, while that company was in its prime and was Britain's largest dedicated sports car dealer.

Above: Its a TR, but is it art? An unknown artis takes the opportunity to sketch a TR3A on the Standard-Triumph stand at the 1959 Earls Court Motor Show.

ty of TR buyers by 1957 were purchasing the car as everyday transport rather than as a competition vehicle. That its versatility allowed it to be all things to all people was of course one of the major factors behind its phenomenal success, and the advertising copy reflected this, emphasising its docility (sports cars were then still usually looked upon as fierce and temperamental) and manoeuvrability, plus the size (!) of

its luggage boot. Well - I suppose it is big compared with a "T" series MG, and at least it was not full of battery and spare wheel as was the contemporary 100/6 Austin Healey.

As late as October 1957 advertisements were still appearing in the UK for the TR3, even though the 3A was by then being built and shipped to the USA. "Time goes further with a

Throughout the

American Triumph Rally of Europe

every car was driven on

BP Energol motor oil SAE 30

and BP Super

DRIVE IN WHERE YOU SEE THE BP SIGN BP

THE BRITISH PETROLEUM COMPANY LIMITED

Top left: 1950s glamour in the form of model Margaret Bramaghim of Hawaii. She poses with the new TR3A for the local dealership in 1959. Left: SKV 655, the "Autosport" road test TR3, has a slower duty at the end of 1957: it transports Santa Claus through Coventry on his way to switch on the Christmas lights. Above: BP associated itself with the TR3, claiming that all cars in the USA "Tour of Europe" rally in 1957 were fuelled and oiled by that company.

Triumph" was a new slogan - apparently meaning that you could cover more miles in a given time in your TR - which presumably left you more time for other pursuits! One of these must have been the playing of golf, for in the photograph a golfer with period "flat 'at" lounges against a white TR. Incidentally whenever photographs were used in advertisements the cars were almost always white - one imagines that experiment must have proved that these reproduced better in the half tone printing processes used at the time.

The TR3A arrived in Britain during January 1958, billed as "A new look for the New Year." The TR was stated to be "still way ahead," and the first TR3A adverts not surprisingly listed the salient new features where genuine improvement had

occurred. One very questionable statement was made, however, in that the new style front with recessed headlamps was said to give smoother air-flow. This is manifest nonsense, the air penetration of the old TR2/3 front air intake being greatly superior, even allowing for the headlamps being more prominent. Looking back from now it seems most strange that the TR3A (or TR3 1958 model as the Company continued to call it) was not in fact called the TR4. After all, the differences between the late TR2 and early TR3 were considerably fewer (and less noticeable) than the differences between the late TR3 and early TR3A, and yet that earlier changeover had occasioned a change of number, whereas the later one did not. By February 1958, TR3A buyers were being ordered to "thrill to inspired motoring" in a

TR that "sets the pace for economy, speed and safety" - this is the first time that I can find that the word "safety" was used as a selling feature - maybe times were changing, for Ralph Nader was only a year or two away! The price quoted had now risen to £699 plus taxes, a rise of around 25% on the original late 1953 price of £555. This was a significant jump over a 4 year period in those days of very low inflation, and even taking into account the improvements in the quality of the product, it seems to indicate that the Company were taking the opportunity of the TR's worldwide success to increase their profit margins on each car sold - well, they would, wouldn't they?

By mid 1958, the slogan had changed to "Ask the man with a Triumph", because if you did, he would tell you that there was nothing to equal his Triumph TR for sheer value for money! We were now back to artists' impressions following the photographic period during the TR3's currency, a TR3A in "competition" trim being shown, which was a half-tone version of the coloured picture appearing in the 1958/60 TR3A catalogue previously described. Similarly, in October

1958 one of the TR3A's from the front cover of that brochure had been sequestered for appearance in various magazine advertisements, the driver still wearing his cravat! A small line drawing of a rally TR3A (it looks like VRW 221) also appeared in some advertisements, but this was the only concession to promoting the TR3A's illustrious rallying career as a selling point. No results were given and in fact rallying success does not appear to be even mentioned in the TR advertising of the time, which I find very surprising. The headline on one particular advert was "still unchallenged!" An admission of the TR's declining fuel economy was made, for the formerly quoted figure of 32 mpg had now been revised to 26/32 mpg - so much for the "smoother airflow" over the new style front!

As we have seen was the case with the contemporary sales brochures, in 1959 very little effort was being put into new publicity material for the TR3A. As well as the fact that it was selling very well anyway, another reason for this was probably that the Triumph Herald had been announced in April 1959, and most of the publicity budget was clearly being spent on that car, the TR3A being left to look after itself. The same advertisement for the 3A using drawings from the brochure continued to appear, with some variations, during 1959, but with apparently much less frequency than in the year before. However, in the Summer of 1959 a TR3A (XHP 259) was taken by a team of Cambridge University students to Monza in Italy, and a number of international records were broken, including the 10,000 kilometre record at an average of 102.6 mph, quite an achievement for an almost-standard production car. This feat was utilised in advertising the TR3A, both by the company and by Joseph Lucas and Co, a photograph of the car being used in each case. One of these "Monza" advertisements made use of a photograph of the car showing all the drivers, with the car stationary, whereas the other advert showed the car travelling at speed. This latter advertisement was appearing as late as September 1960, the TR3A being described as "The world's fastest selling sports car," and the slogan used was "for safety, power and economy" - notice how the word "safety" had now moved to the front of the slogan rather than the rear! Sales of the TR3A were in decline by the middle of 1960, and production was tailing off. An economic recession in the UK

did not help, and nor did the ever more persistent rumours of the impending arrival of a TR4, with or without a twin-cam engine! At all events, the Company appears, at least in Great Britain, to have virtually abandoned promoting the sidescreen TR by the end of 1960, the financial crisis that enveloped Standard-Triumph at this time (just prior to the Leyland takeover) presumably having something to do with the lack of money for promotion and advertising generally. As a last gasp, the advertisement used to promote the TR3A at the time of the October 1960 London Motor Show called the car "the World's most popular sports car", but in truth, the copywriters found nothing new to say! Incidentally, the TR3B seems scarcely to have been promoted at all in North America. I have not so far seen a single advertisement relating to the model!

Finally, to conclude this section on "TR literature" on a humourous note, I am reproducing several cartoons, both contemporary and more recent, in which sidescreen TRs have appeared. The "Autosport" cartoon by Raymond Groves gives some indication of how popular TRs were in rallies, the cartoonist having chosen a TR as the "archetype"

*Above: Independent Television produced a magazine pro-
gramme in 1958 called: "Motoring Club". One of its transmis-
sions included racing drivers Mike Hawthorn and Duncan
Hamilton, discussing the merits of the TR. Here they, and the
car, are seen in a studio setting (BMIHT).*

*On the right is one of the most unusual uses yet discovered
for a TR. Trapeze artiste Maritella swings from a twenty-five
foot pole, anchored through the floor to the TR's chassis.
Evidently, her husband drove the car rapidly around pylons
as part of their act, while she hovered up the pole!*

*Below left: "Miss Triumph" in 1959, Sheila Lunnon, poses by a TR3A in the time-honoured manner and outfit! Below right:
Works rally TR3A VHP 529 lurks behind team driver Annie Soisbault in January 1959. She shows off the Standard-Triumph
Photographic Department's 16mm Paillard-Bolex used for making publicity films (TR Register Archive).*

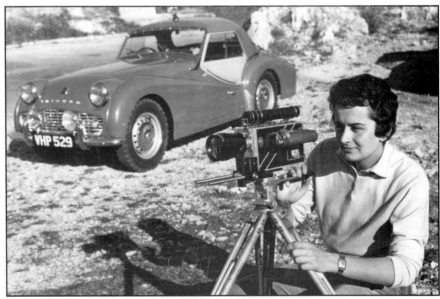

The world's fastest-selling sports car

The T.R.3 is the greatest name in sports motoring . . . safer, more powerful, more economical. On the track or on the road, the T.R.3 surges ahead of its world-wide reputation for reliability and performance.

For safety, power and economy . . .

TRIUMPH T.R.3

£9 9 1.7.6 (inc. P.T.)

STANDARD TRIUMPH

STANDARD·TRIUMPH GROUP · COVENTRY   LONDON SHOWROOMS: BERKELEY SQUARE

This advertisement appeared in September 1960, a very late TR3A advert, and was one of the rare occasions when the Company's Publicity Department used a photograph of a competition car to sell the product. The car was XHP 259, the "Monza" record breaker, and as can be seen , it was fitted with a radio for communication to the pits. A perspex fly deflector was mounted on the bonnet and a quick-lift jack socket projects below the rear of the car (TR Register Archive).

The cartoons below come from Jan May (the upper one) and "Autosport" (drawn by Raymond Groves).

rally car - note the obligatory duffle-coat on the Marshal! Mr Giles, the famous "Daily Express" cartoonist, produced a very workmanlike drawing of a TR2 for his 1955 cartoon showing a snow scene, and the Dutch TR club provided an instance of what the power of a TR3A could do in a cartoon headed "De Avonturen van Truusje Trippel". This was reproduced in an early TR Register magazine, but regrettably, my negligible knowledge of Dutch does not allow me to translate. However, I can see that the young lady certainly appears to suffer somewhat as a result of her encounter with a TR! Also appearing at intervals in the TR Register's magazine were a series of most amusing "TR Man" cartoons, drawn by Dave King, and I have chosen for inclusion a representative example of "TR Man's" exploits. "TR Man" became something of a cult hero in the late 1970's, several prominent club members modelling both their dress and driving style on him! Finally, another Dave King cartoon appears alluding to the amount of filler in the average TR, (in the 1970's) and Jan May puts the female point of view on the doubtful benefits of aeroscreens in winter!

Love is ___

___ letting him drive with aeroscreens

"Holidays here every year at this time— chairman of a rubber company, I believe. . . ."

An extract from a "TR-Man" cartoon, a series of which appeared in the TR Register's magazine some years ago. The printed quality of the second half of the cartoon is not shown here as the original was damaged and unsuitable for reproduction. Suffice it to say, however, that "TR-Man" prevailed as usual and "Noddy" got nicked! Drawn by Dave King.

"And *I* say there *is* a pedestrian crossing here."

The cartoons above and below need no embellishment, save to acknowledge the one above to Express Newspapers (the artist Giles needs no introduction to most). The caption to the one on the right bears repeating. It says: "No, it's not for his house - it's the filler arriving for his TR restoration (drawn by Dave King).

RIGHT-HAND SIDE OR OFF SIDE

RIGHT-HAND STEERING

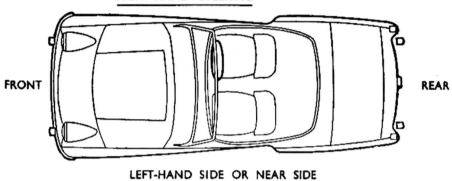

FRONT   REAR

LEFT-HAND SIDE OR NEAR SIDE

COMMISSION NUMBERS AND SUFFIX

Right-Hand Steering	...	...	...	...	TS	...
Left-Hand Steering	...	...	...	...	TS	... L
Right-Hand Steering (with Overdrive)			...	TS	...	O
Left-Hand Steering (with Overdrive)			...	TS	...	LO

RIGHT-HAND SIDE OR NEAR SIDE

FRONT   REAR

LEFT-HAND STEERING

LEFT-HAND SIDE OR OFF SIDE

CHAPTER EIGHT: *Some Contemporary Views of the Sidescreen TRs*

This chapter aims to review some of the technical and road-test material published, and the opinions expressed about the sidescreen TRs when they were current models. To do this, I have drawn on magazine articles and surveys, factory hand-outs, published road tests and letters written to the motoring press at the time. Unfortunately, there is not the space for an exhaustive review of everything published concerning these cars, even presuming it could be located, so I have concentrated on drawing from sources that, as far as I can tell, have not been utilised in recent years. I do not therefore propose to deal in over-much detail with those road tests that have been reprinted elsewhere since their original publication, for these are now both too well-known and are also available to the reader in recent publications elsewhere. Rather I have been able to unearth some "new" items which will I hope shed some further light on how the TR was viewed in its day, both by professional motoring writers and also by those who bought and drove them on an everyday basis.

Much was written about the 20TS prototype upon its introduction, not all of it complimentary, but there were of course no published road tests, which in view of what we now know about this car was probably just as well! The 20TS was described in some splendid exhibitions of the sport of "damning with faint praise" as "an interesting newcomer", a "last minute surprise" and "Sir John Black's hope for the future!" The press could be little other than vague about driving the new Triumph, for it was only revealed at a very late stage in the build-up to the 1952 Motor Show. Reasonably comprehensive technical details were released, plus just two or three photographs, and even these appear somewhat "doctored". Although the motoring press was invited to a test session shortly after the Motor Show, no more than a few anodyne sentences regarding driving impressions appeared in any publication, and the car was said to be still "under development" and "not expected to be available in the showrooms for some time to come". When what became the definitive sidescreen TR did finally appear at the March 1953 Geneva Motor Show, press interest was strangely muted considering that here was what was arguably the World's cheapest 100 mph car. Maybe the "relaunch" of the TR taking place on foreign soil had something to do with this, for British journalists were notedly parochial in those days. The lack of any actual TR2s to drive clearly did not help! Following the successful "Jabbeke" run in May 1953, further comment was occasioned, articles appearing in both the "Motor" and the "Autocar". The "Autocar" journalist was even afforded a short run in the record-breaking car, but his impressions were vague and inconclusive. In fact, it was not until the very end of 1953 that the Autocar managed actually to procure a TR2 for a proper test, this first detailed analysis of a production TR appearing in the January 8th, 1954 issue. "The Motor" had to wait until April 1954 to test the same car, OHP 771; by this time quite a number of TRs had reached private buyers, and the RAC rally victory had already been won, so the journalists were hardly in "scoop" territory!

"Motor Sport" magazine, perhaps the most influential publication with the sporting fraternity who would make or break the TR's reputation, had to wait until February 1955 to publish their impressions of the TR, almost two and a half years after the Triumph's Earls Court debut! I suspect that Editor Bill Boddy's reputation for fearless reporting had something to do with this delay; maybe the Standard-Triumph press office wanted to be sure that their car was absolutely right before submitting it for what actually turned out to be a pleasantly complimentary test by Mr Boddy. Incidentally, the

TR's principal rival, the Austin Healey 100, was never tested by "Motorsport" at all, because at that period the British Motor Corporation had imposed an absolute ban on the testing of any of its products by this magazine, presumably because of "Motor Sport's" objective reporting and its refusal to toady to the bigwigs of the British Motor Industry by being kind to products that merited criticism!

Very surprisingly, the car "Motor Sport" was given to test was a "long-door" TR2, PHP 727, this despite the fact that the "short" doors had been introduced some four months earlier for production vehicles. One would have though that a vehicle to the latest specification would have been produced for so important a test! The manufacturers asked "Motor Sport" not to submit the TR to "the full road test ritual", so no performance figures were published. However, unlike its weekly contemporaries, "Motor Sport" was much more in the business of providing its readers with detailed driving impressions rather than accurate stopwatch figures, so this was no particular hardship - nevertheless, one wonders why this request was made when the TR2 performed so well!

John Bolster, writing for "Autosport", got his hands on the hard-worked OHP 771 in March 1954 and he, like others, was generally highly complimentary. The exhaust note came in for stern criticism, and there was, as from most testers, a certain measure of "modified rapture" concerning the handling, but in terms of performance, value for money and economy, the car was said to be "virtually without equal".

Although a descriptive article about the TR2 had appeared in the USA (Road and Track Magazine) in September 1953, North Americans had to wait until April 1954 before a full road test appeared in this same magazine. Again, I find this a surprising delay having regard to the importance placed upon this particular export market by the Company.

By late 1954 the TR was well known, and in October that year the magazines carried descriptions of the smart new hardtop and the door modifications. Somewhat surprisingly, the modifications to the TR2 were considered enough to justify "Autocar" carrying out a further full road test in early 1955, this time of the hardtop-equipped demonstrator registered PRW 137: the data page of this test is reproduced here. The car tested, although the revised model, still had overdrive on top gear only, and interestingly, a photograph shows the full tool kit. However, it appears that this was not a standard item at this time, TR buyers having to purchase the tools (other than wheel changing tools) as an extra. Another surprising detail is that photographs show PRW 137 to carry the chrome reveal moulding around the air-intake, despite this not appearing on production TR2s until quite some months later. (The actual date of introduction of this

item has never been ascertained).

Also reproduced in this Chspter is a short test of what was described as "The bread and butter sports car" - a TR2 tested by Robert Walling, who was presumably a major newspaper motoring correspondent. Although someone has dated the cutting 1st June 1955, it is not apparent from which paper the test comes, but the advertisements that appear on the reverse side of the original cutting lead me to suspect that it must be from one of the London evening newspapers. Despite the poor quality of the cutting, its rarity I feel justifies its inclusion. I like the precision in the statement that the hood "takes 50 seconds to erect", and the debate as to whether a woman could drive it! 88 marks out of 100 seems a good score, although without other tests with which to compare it, one does not know whether this gentleman was a generous marker or not!

One of the very few published tests of a modified TR was published by "Autosport" in September 1955, when John Bolster put Vic Derrington's tuned car VPJ 770 through its paces and that test is reproduced in Chapter 6. Although it does not say so, the implication in the test is that the performance was somewhat disappointing, being barely better than the standard vehicle and at a cost of fuel consumption having been increased by some 20%! It is apparent that almost any modification to the TR2's original engine specification spoils the phenomenal economy of these early cars - Triumph's themselves found this when the TR3 was introduced, test TR3's never being able to approach the wonderful economy of the TR2 with its 1 1/2 inch S.U. carburettors.

In addition to specific road tests, the success of the TR gave rise to several excellent, more general, articles, in particular a marathon two part description of the development of the TR, written by technical writer John Rabson and published in the "Autocar" on the 8th and 22nd of April 1955. As a chronicle of how the 20 TS was refined into a serious production sports car, this treatise could hardly be improved upon and is well worth seeking out. (It is reprinted in full in the excellent "Brooklands" TR2/3/3A volume). OHP 771 again found itself the subject of comment in an article entitled "A taste of Triumph", published in September 1954 in the "Autocar", for Douglas Clease borrowed this TR2 to take on a 2400 mile Continental tour. He was delighted with its performance, even commenting upon how snug and dry the interior remained in torrential rain on Alpine passes!

The TR3 was road tested shortly after its introduction by several periodicals, about the first being the USA edition of Sports Cars Illustrated in March 1956. Their car was a hardtop version, but they had to admit that a TR with a hardtop was not the equal of a proper fixed-head coupe when it

TRIUMPH TR2 HARD TOP

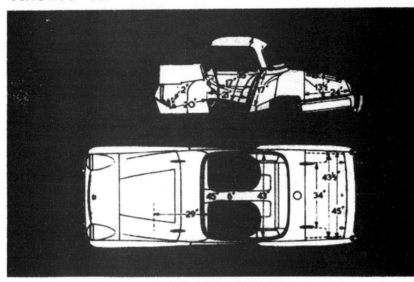

Measurements in these ½in to 1ft scale body diagrams are taken with the driving seat in the central position of fore and aft adjustment and with the seat cushions uncompressed

DATA

PRICE (basic), with hard top two seater body, £670.
British purchase tax, £280 5s 10d.
Total (in Great Britain), £950 5s 10d.
Extras: Radio, £42 10s 0d.
    Heater, £14 3s 4d.
    Overdrive £40.
    Windscreen washer, £5 5s 0d.
    Wire wheels, £25.

ENGINE: Capacity, 1,991 c.c. (121.5 cu in).
Number of cylinders: 4.
Bore and stroke: 83 × 92 mm (3.26 × 3.62in).
Valve gear: overhead, pushrods and rockers.
Compression ratio: 8.5 to 1.
B.H.P.: 90 at 4,800 r.p.m. (B.H.P. per ton laden 78).
Torque: 117 lb ft at 3,000 r.p.m.
M.P.H. per 1,000 r.p.m. in top gear, 20. In overdrive 24.4.

WEIGHT (with 5 gals fuel): 19½ cwt (2,184lb).
Weight distribution (per cent): F, 53; R, 47.
Laden as tested: 23 cwt (2,570 lb).
Lb per c.c. (laden): 1.29.

BRAKES: Type: F, Two leading shoe; R, leading and trailing.
Method of operation: F, Hydraulic; R, Hydraulic.
Drum dimensions: F, 10in diameter; 2⅛in wide. R, 10in diameter; 2⅛in wide.
Lining area: F, 87.5 sq in. R, 87.5 sq in (152 sq in per ton laden).

TYRES: 5.50—15in.
Pressures (lb per sq in): F, 22; R, 24 (normal). F, 28; R, 30 (for fast driving).

TANK CAPACITY: 12¼ Imperial gallons.
Oil sump, 11 pints.
Cooling system, 13 pints (plus 1 pint if heater is fitted).

TURNING CIRCLE: 30ft 0in (L and R).
Steering wheel turns (lock to lock): 2¼.

DIMENSIONS: Wheelbase: 7ft 4in.
Track: F, 3ft 9in; R, 3ft 9½in.
Length (overall): 12ft 7in.
Height: 4ft 2in.
Width: 4ft 7½in.
Ground clearance: 6in.
Frontal area: 15.5 sq ft (approximately).

ELECTRICAL SYSTEM: 12-volt; 51 ampere-hour battery.
Head lights: Double dip; 60-36 watt bulbs.

SUSPENSION: Front, Independent, wishbones and coil springs. Rear, half elliptic leaf springs.

PERFORMANCE

ACCELERATION: from constant speeds.
Speed Range, Gear Ratios and Time in sec.

M.P.H.	(3.03) to 1	3.7 to 1	4.9 to 1	7.4 to 1	12.5 to 1
10—30	—	—	10.6	7.8	4.8
20—40	13.4	10.3	7.2	4.6	—
30—50	13.9	10.2	7.0	—	—
40—60	14.8	10.5	7.4	—	—
50—70	15.8	10.9	8.4	—	—
60—80	19.9	12.8	—	—	—
70—90	24.6	19.3	—	—	—

From rest through gears to:

M.P.H.	sec.
30	3.8
50	8.8
60	12.6
70	17.1
80	25.6
90	37.4

Standing quarter mile, 18.8 sec.

SPEEDS ON GEARS:

Gear		M.P.H. (normal and max.)	K.P.H. (normal and max.)
Top (normal) (mean)		103	165.76
(best)		107	172.2
3rd		64—76	103—122
2nd		40—50	64—80
1st		22—28	35—45

SPEEDOMETER CORRECTION: M.P.H.

Car speedometer	10	20	30	40	50	60	70	80	90	100	110	113
True speed	13	20	28	36	45.5	54.5	64	74	84	94	103.5	107

TRACTIVE RESISTANCE: 25 lb per ton at 10 M.P.H.

TRACTIVE EFFORT:

	Pull (lb per ton)	Equivalent Gradient
Overdrive	180	1 in 12.4
Top	250	1 in 8.9
Third	350	1 in 6.1
Second	550	1 in 3.9

BRAKES:

Efficiency	Pedal Pressure (lb)
94 per cent	75
80 per cent	50
52 per cent	25

FUEL CONSUMPTION:
31 m.p.g. overall for 875 miles (9.21 litres per 100 km.).
Approximate normal range 28-38 m.p.g. (10.1—7.6 litres per 100 km.).
Fuel, first grade.

WEATHER: Damp surface, slight wind. Air temperature 36 deg. F.
Acceleration figures are the means of several runs in opposite directions.
Tractive effort and resistance obtained by Tapley meter.
Model described in *The Autocar* of October 15, 1954.

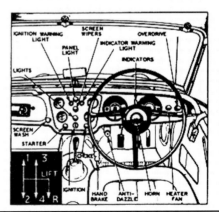

The data page from the "Autocar" road test of the hardtop TR2, published in early 1955.

MOTORING by ROBERT WALLING

1. 6.55.

They call it the bread-and-butter sports car

The Triumph TR2 Sports.

This road-test by Robert Walling appeared in an unknown newspaper around June 1955. His comments make interesting reading.

HERE comes the Triumph TR2, the bread-and-butter sports car that leaps into the front line. They call it that because some of its parts, like the engine, were originally designed for the normal saloon models its Coventry factory makes.

The price, at £886, purchase tax paid, is certainly low, but I can also report that the butter is lushly spread. For the TR2's gait up to 102 m.p.h. is richly sparkling. There are not many cars under double its price with which you can change gear from third to top at—yes—90 m.p.h.

This is really a new sports model for the not-so-rich motorist. It gives him the edge the wealthy man has—but for half the price.

Low weight

Costly on petrol? You would think so. Yet in ordinary fairly-fast driving it worked out at about 30 miles to the gallon. This was without snapping into operation too much the over-drive button on the dashboard which saves petrol by slowing down the engine without slowing down the car. This economy even surprised the designers. They put it down to an efficiently-streamlined body and low weight.

If the road is clear I find the car cruises at 80 m.p.h. in the way others drift along at 50—that is to say, with little noise or fuss. You use the gears to slow down for cross-roads, then change up again to resume the top-gear rate. If you need the brakes in a hurry you find they are so powerful that safety belts would improve comfort for such quick pull-ups.

Now for the criticisms. The car CAN be driven quietly in congested traffic, but you have to get to know it well if you want a smooth result. There is no harshness, the controls are easy, but the throttle foot

must be made to gentle the engine. Over bumpy cobbles in the City the ride is not so soft as it might be.

On the open road the front coil-springing is lively when you take a roundabout a shade quickly on a rough road surface. Again, at high speed, you have to watch your steering

unless the road surface is top grade.

Could a woman drive it happily? My companion did. Although she did not exceed 60 m.p.h. she said later: "The car seems a handful at first, but the acceleration soon gives you confidence and you drive better for it in the end."

MY TEST CARD

	Marks Possible	Marks Gained	COMMENTS
COMFORT	10	7	Tall drivers would like the foot pedals fixed farther from the seat to give more knee freedom under the steering wheel. The top of the short gear-lever is too near the under-edge of the dashboard, causing the left hand to jam when changing into and out of third gear. But the passenger can sit with legs fully outstretched, and elbow room is ample.
ENGINE	10	9	This is a well-tested version of the Standard Vanguard unit "hotted-up" to give 22 more brake horse-power. One mark off for a noisy exhaust at high revolutions.
PERFORMANCE	10	9	As good above 50 as below it. For that quick get-away: 60 m.p.h. in second gear. Watch for bad road surfaces at speed.
GEAR-CHANGE	10	9	Quick, and gear-lever is handy. Clutch movement is extra long.
BRAKING	10	10	Don't be too enthusiastic or you can lock your wheels and skid.
VISIBILITY	10	9	Needed—slightly more view of the nearside front wing.
STEERING	10	8	Could be lighter in action, and is affected by bumps at speed.
LUGGAGE	10	10	For a two-seater sports car—excellent. See the deep boot at the back, and the space behind the seats.
PETROL	10	10	Unusual, especially since two carburettors are working.
SOUND IDEAS	10	7	Press-buttoning of the hood into position takes 50 seconds. An over-drive for those long Continental roads. Marks off for direction-indicator lights which could be bigger and brighter. *Note: The over-drive is an optional extra.
TOTAL	**100**	**88**	

came to draught sealing and general comfort, though it did of course have the advantage of being easily convertible back into a roadster. They did concede, however, that the hardtop greatly stiffened the car and made it less prone to scuttle-shake, an opinion that many hardtop TR owners

would share. What was not mentioned though was the considerable increase in interior noise occasioned by the fitting of the steel hardtop as compared with the normal hood. "Motor" magazine tested TR3 RKV 335 in April 1956, again with a hardtop in place - in fact, almost all published TR3

A charming contemporary shot of what the well-dressed female TR driver was wearing in 1955. The ladt concerned is Mrs M Baddiley, winner of the Ladies Sports Car Section of that year's Scottish Rally .

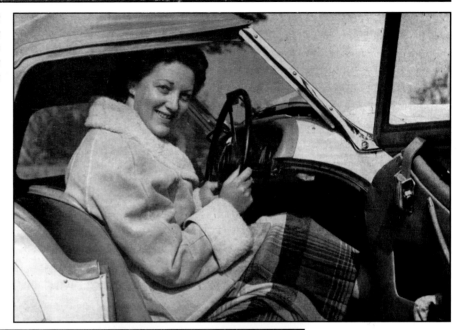

TR3s are seen on the Cal-Sales Incorporated stand at the Los Angeles Motor Show in the Winter of 1955/56. Not surprisingly, whitewall tyres are in evidence (TR Register Archive).

tests seem to have been of the heavier, hardtop equipped cars for some reason. As these generally had the optional rear seat fitted as well, they were for the most part slower as regards acceleration than the TR2s had been, although as mentioned they consistently used more fuel! Top speed was usually improved by the smoother lines of the metal top.

Despite the introduction of the TR3 in the previous Autumn, the Australian Magazine "Cars Today" produced a full test of a TR2 in their January 1956 issue, and thanks to TR Register member Nigel Wiggins, I have been able to examine a copy. The car tested was a privately owned example, but it produced performance figures that were very similar to the various tests of factory provided TR2s, proof positive that the Works road-test demonstrators were not "doctored" in any way, unlike the notorious Austin Healey 100 NOJ 392 provided for early road tests! Reverting to the TR3 in early 1956, a further press cutting I have been able to acquire is a test of RKV 335 by none other than Mike Hawthorn, probably Britain's most charismatic racing driver.

Mike asserts that all the gossip about the tendency of the rear wheels to break away is nonsense, which is interesting not only for his opinion, but for the fact that it demonstrates

such gossip was indeed abroad at the time. Hawthorn was generally enthusiastic about the car, but does have a point in criticising the extra 8s / 5d charged for an ashtray, at a time when smoking was almost a universal habit. A point at which neither I nor the run of the professional TR testers agree with him was concerning the car's trim and finish. He marks this aspect down, but the general opinion seems to have run counter to this, most feeling that the trim and finish were perfectly adequate for the type and price of the car. Maybe as an over-worked demonstrator, RKV 335 was showing signs of hard use? My favourite sentence is his reference to "Fleet Street to Silverstone in 1 hour 23 minutes" - as the distance is quoted at 67 miles, and as it includes at least a dozen miles of built up area, Mike must really have pedalled, having regard to the lack of Motorway in those days! Possibly he went at midnight, or maybe (dare I suggest?) he didn't go at all, and the time was purely theoretical!

An unlikely place for a TR3 test to appear was in the "Tatler" magazine dated the 7th March 1956, this being a magazine much read by the English upper classes of the time. The car involved was RKV 352, described in the article as "one of the smartest looking medium priced sports cars" - this was unusual in itself, for good looks were not something for which any sidescreen TR was usually praised - rather they were normally described as "functional", "purposeful" or "rugged". Few I feel can dispute (either then or now) that the TR's obvious rivals, the Austin Healey 100 and the MGA, were more stylishly elegant. The magazine seemed somewhat miffed that the heater and overdrive were not included in the basic price (as they were on the Austin Healey), but nevertheless conceded that "however you look at the price, it buys a great deal of performance and motoring pleasure". The acceleration was stated to be "electric", the wheels

Above: a young TR mechanic is seen in the person of 10-year old Adrian Kaye, grandson of John Kaye, Triumph dealer of Leeds. He was said to be the envy of his schoolmates (Standard Car Review). Right: what the Standard Car Review described as "sports car therapy" in action. Members of the San Antonio Sports Car Club brought their TRs to show the patients at a US military hospital in Texas in 1956, some fortunate patients being treated to fast rides in the cars, all in the cause of getting well (Standard Car Review).

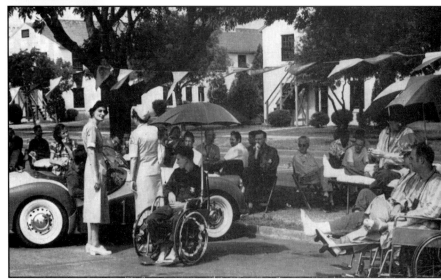

The TATLER and Bystander,
MARCH 7, 1956   400

THE TRIUMPH TR-3 handles lightly on the bumpy tracks of the countryside, as well as on main road macadam. Top speed is over 100 m.p.h. and under pressure the engine never feels unduly extended

Motoring

by

Oliver Stewart

THE LIGHTWEIGHT FURIES

SPORTS cars are the British motor industry's present to the world. At this time of year parcels of sports cars are being made up in England for dispatch to many countries. May I preface the paean of praise I propose to sing in this article by suggesting to all young recipients of new sports cars that they should preserve—mentally if not physically—the label "*Handle with care. This way up.*"

Because it is one of the smartest looking of the medium priced sports cars on the market today, I elected to try the Triumph TR-3 and to report upon it here as an overture to springtime motoring. I took over the TR-3 hard-top, which costs in standard form with sliding windows £1,043 17s., inclusive of purchase tax. The car had a number of extras, among them an overdrive and a heater, items which, with tax, put on £75. However you look at the price it must be conceded that it buys a great deal of performance and of motoring pleasure.

The roads were icy during the period of my test and, being of a cautious disposition, I was forced to make a reconnaissance of my private "straight" before I dared to make an all-out run. But the weather did not spoil the entertainment which this car gives. When it is considered that the weight, inclusive of fuel, oil, water and equipment, is well below one metric ton and that the engine is of 2 litres capacity, it can be understood that the acceleration is electric.

The first time I went away through the gears a speedometer 60 was reached in 12.5 seconds and later on I succeeded in getting this down to 12 seconds. The top speed is well over 100 m.p.h. and the wheels can be spun on the accelerator on a dry road under many conditions. In short, there is ample power available and one gains the impression of working always well within the car's capacity—which is one of the joys of the sports car in ordinary use. The engine, however, in spite of a compression ratio of 8.5 to 1, is not harsh and takes the car quite smoothly from 20 to 50 (in third gear) in 7.5 seconds.

The hard top gives good protection, although I found that, however the sliding windows were arranged, there was a good deal of draught inside the car. But the heater kept the feet and legs warm and consequently there was a reasonably high degree of over-all comfort. The TR-3 is exceedingly low, the roof top being only 127 cm. from the ground. The model I tried had occasional rear seats in which one grown-up person could be accommodated in moderate comfort, or two children. The slideable bucket seats for the driver and front passenger are well arranged and there is a small boot.

A road test taken from an unusual source, namely "The Tatler" magazine. This gives a somewhat different view of the TR from that normally found in motoring magazines.

being able to be spun on dry roads "in many conditions". "Even under pressure," stated the tester, Oliver Stewart, "the engine never feels unduly extended and is not harsh, taking the car smoothly from 20 to 50 mph in 3rd gear in 7.5 seconds". As usual, the test car was hardtop equipped, but the driver found that "however the sliding windows were arranged, there was a good deal of draught inside the car. Despite this, the heater kept the feet and legs warm and consequently there was a reasonably high degree of overall comfort" - again a case of modified rapture? Possibly the addition of the expensive hardtop was causing testers to be less forgiving than they had been only two years earlier when they judged the TR2 with its ordinary hood, which was frequently described as "comfortable and cosy".

Upon the introduction of disc brakes for the TR3 in September 1956, press coverage was very wide, not only in the specialist motoring magazines, but also in the daily papers, for this was the first true series production car to carry these new aids to safety. Today, when disc brakes are standard equipment even on the humblest vehicles, it is difficult to realise how exotic they seemed in 1956; at that time, even some Formula One racing cars were still using drum brakes, so their use on a cheapish production sports car was worthy of much comment. The general opinion was that they were well worthwhile, unaffected by water or fade, although one or two testers did note that they appeared to get very hot, the discs even glowing in the dark at times! The only minor criticism was that of increased pedal pressure as compared with the drum brakes, for no servo system was ever fitted as standard. This occasioned more than one writer to question whether the car was any longer suitable for female drivers! Having regard to their undoubted benefits, however, and particularly as the basic price of the TR3 remained unchanged at £680 before tax, the disc brakes were unequivocally welcomed.

This revolutionary innovation allowed Triumph to "relaunch" the TR3 with some considerable success, many new advertisements trumpeting the arrival of the disc brakes. Their arrival had coincided with the political Suez Crisis and its consequent period of petrol rationing, so the introduction was most timely in enabling Standard-Triumph's to promote the vehicle at a time when sales of all cars were poor, competition motoring was under threat, and new car purchase was far from most people's minds. Nevertheless, by early 1957 new TR3s were being discounted by dealerships, as much as £100 being offered off list price, a 10% reduction at a time when the discounting of cars (or any new product for that matter) was rare in the UK.

The "Autocar" was, as usual, the first to get it's hands on the revised hardtop TR3 for testing, SKV 656 being assessed by

them in January 1957. The performance figures were somewhat slower than formerly, possibly due to weight increases, and they seemed a little circumspect regarding the handling, rear end stability being criticised, particularly on less good road surfaces. At about the same time as this test, Richard Bensted-Smith, a journalist with the "Motor" magazine, published an interesting article about his two TR2s, used as both everyday cars and competition vehicles. He was effusive in his praise, an opinion to be respected as he had lived with and used the cars hard over a 3 year period rather than having just tried them over the usual 1000 miles or so of a formal road test. He stated that "provided the TR suited your pocket and your normal burden of luggage, so useful an all-rounder seems too good to be without".

Bensted-Smith's first car, SYA 176, triumphed both in the Mobilgas economy run, returning 71 miles per gallon overall, and also in the Vintage Sports Car Club's prestigious Pomeroy Trophy, winning it outright! This was a considerable achievement, for this unique event used a formula designed to equalise the performance of all competing cars, irrespective of age and power. It was only open to cars of over 1950 cc, so the Triumph was one of the smallest vehicles competing, yet its overall performance, coupled with it's lapping of the Silverstone racetrack flat out at better than 30 miles per gallon, gained it the top honours. When the article was written at the end of 1956, Bensted-Smith was using PXL 640, a short-door TR2 with wire wheels and Michelin "X" tyres, which he considered to be a great improvement, albeit at the expense of heavier steering. In conclusion, this experienced sports car driver described his TRs as "not perfect, but coming as near perfection as you can expect from a mechanical maid-of-all-work".

Following the "Autocar" test in January 1957, the earliest of the remaining batch of TR3 tests seem to have been the April 1957 one in Sports Cars Illustrated, followed by the May 1957 article published in the American magazine "Road and Track". The car tested by the latter journal had overdrive, and interestingly it was equipped with the 4.1 to 1 ratio rear axle. This latter fitment probably enabled it to record a standing-start quarter mile in under 18 seconds, quite a lot faster than the time for this sprint recorded for TRs by most contemporary sources. The top speed, however, remained as normal at around 105/107 mph. The test seemed to imply that all new, overdrive-equipped TR3s were by then being fitted with the 4.1 ratio as standard, a fact that I have seen reported elsewhere, but one which time has proved not to have been true. Even most USA bound TR3/3As fitted with overdrive still had the normal 3.7 to 1 axle ratio (although only a low percentage of USA delivered cars had overdrive at all), and as to UK cars, the 4.1 axle was (and is) extremely rare - in 25 years of sidescreen TR involvement, I have only come across two cars originally so fitted! Concerning the disc brakes, "Road and Track" called them "tremendous", producing hard, fast stops from 100 mph with neither fade nor smells, and nor did they find the pedal pressures high. The concluding paragraph of the report stated that in its price class, the TR3 had "no competition", and in terms of performance per dollar, it had "no equal as a competition and fun machine!".

The "Motor" magazine got hold of SKV 656 in July 1957, which still sported a hardtop despite the Summer. They managed to obtain better performance figures from the same car than had the "Autocar", but ominously stated that the wet weather handling on the Dunlop "Road Speed" tyres "left a lot to be desired!". The smallest touch of the throttle was said to put the rear of the car out of line, although when the ordinary, non- "Road Speed" Dunlops were substituted, the wet weather handling was noticeably improved. The "Autosport" test followed in September, John Bolster predictably preferring an open TR, and hence he was allocated SKV 655. He was most pleased that the exhaust note had been considerably tamed, liked the disc brakes and thought that the TR was still excellent value for money and a soundly engineered vehicle. However, reading between the lines, the rear end handling clearly concerned him, for he said that for some reason not easy to define, the car does not encourage the man at the wheel to take risks! He conceded that the cornering power was in fact better than it had first appeared, but clearly the "SKV" TR3 demonstrators had not inspired their testers in this department. The top speed was also a little disappointing, 102 mph being all that could be obtained in top gear, with a bare 100 available in overdrive.

A Scottish magazine, "Top Gear", published a test of a dealer-supplied TR3 in 1957, registration number RGB 3. This particular car was still producing an exhaust "blare" that required toning down, and adverse comment was made on mechanical noise, principally tappets, a sound that will be familiar to all sidescreen TR owners! Door catches, bonnet and boot locks also came in for criticism, but the heater was said to be "effective" and the hood "excellent". As to the revolutionary brakes, these were said to offer "no great improvement" at low speeds, but to be of "real benefit" whilst driving hard. The car supplied had no overdrive, and proved capable of 104 mph flat out, with a 0 - 60 mph time of 11 seconds dead, which was slightly faster than the average. Yet again, this tester was impressed by the overall functionality of the TR, its outstanding value for money and its economy, for uncharacteristically, this TR3 produced around 35 mpg except when performance tested, when it dropped to around 28 mpg. Of the wayward rear-end behaviour highlighted by others, nothing was said; in fact the handling characteristics were said to be "safe"!

My own view, having driven sidescreen TRs for 25 years, is that the car **is** fundamentally safe on modern radial tyres; in fact it holds the road very well in dry weather and is not bad in the wet. However, upon recalling those examples I have driven fitted with crossply tyres, and particularly those with the early Michelin "X" radials, these could be truly alarming in the wet. It was perfectly possible to "lose" the back end at 15 mph on a roundabout, and the car would sometimes turn right round with no warning when accelerating hard in 2nd gear (mine did it one wet Sunday night at Hyde Park Corner, which was somewhat embarrassing!). I feel in consequence that those early TR testers did indeed have a point, especially as "their" cars usually had cross-ply tyres. In fact, one wonders whether discretion alone prevented them from being much more forceful in their criticism of the car's wet-weather roadholding? Modern day owners need however have no fears, for a sidescreen TR fitted with 165 section radial tyres, a front anti-roll bar and with its shock absorbers and suspension in good condition is perfectly safe, and cannot be made to produce the antics described above, even when provoked on wet corners!

The North American magazine "Motor Trend" also got its hands on a TR3 in July 1957, and managed to produce the best performance figures I've seen of a standard TR3 (assuming it **was** standard of course!) - these included a 0-60 mph time of 9.2 seconds, and a standing start quarter mile in a remarkable 16.9 seconds. These figures are so much better than average that one speculates as to their accuracy, especially as the car was stated to have the normal 3.7 to 1 axle ratio. As was becoming quite usual, they named it as about the best sports car "buy" on the market in value terms, and they gave the new brakes wholehearted endorsement, although commenting that a series of panic stops from 60 mph produced "smoke in amazing quantities!".

The influential "Motor Sport" magazine procured a TR3 for test in July 1957, the car used being SKV 656 yet again. Amazingly, despite what must have been a hard early life, this car has survived, and has now been fully rebuilt by a long-standing TR Register member. As this particular test seems not have been reproduced before, I am taking the opportunity of including it in full without comment, for as an objective assessment of the TR3, it is hard to fault. As usual, "Motor Sport's" editor Bill Boddy gives driving impressions rather than stopwatch figures, and it would appear that he was impressed. Interestingly, he calls for the car to be restyled for the USA market, and this is of course exactly what was happening at that time, with the revised frontal treatment of the TR3A. Maybe Mr Boddy had seen a prototype on his visit to the factory that Summer? At the end of each year, it was his custom to write a long article reviewing all the cars he had driven during that year, such an article

JULY, 1957   347   MOTOR SPORT

TRIUMPH TR3 ROAD-TEST

Latest Version of a Popular British two-litre Sports Model has Commendably High Performance and Excellent Brakes.

FAST HARD - TOP. — The Triumph TR3 has more power and space than the TR2 and possesses the truly excellent Girling disc front-wheel brakes. As tested the total price is £1,219 19s.

AS regular readers of MOTOR SPORT may remember, we published a full road-test report on the Triumph TR2 sports two-seater in the issue dated February, 1955. Since that time the TR3 has made its appearance, with an engine giving ten more b.h.p., with a well behind the seats and Girling disc brakes on the front wheels. We recently put a TR3 hard-top through its paces and were impressed by this well-known sports car's twin abilities, to go and to stop !

In specification and arrangement the TR3 differs little from the TR2. There is the same short, rigid remote central gear-lever for changing gear as rapidly as the driver wishes and the sensibly-placed fly-off hand brake with big grip set between propeller-shaft tunnel and his left leg. The facia has a 120 m.p.h. speedometer and 6,000 r.p.m. tachometer, both by Jaeger (the former embodying trip and total mileage recorders and headlamps full-beam warning light), before the driver, supplemented by a neat central panel containing—refreshing, this—clear dials indicating fuel amounts, dynamo charge, oil pressure (80 lb./sq. in. at 3,000 r.p.m.) and water temperature (normally 140 deg. F.). Left of this panel is a large lined cubby-hole, irritating because its lid can be opened and closed only with a key. Lettered refined knobs spaced about the facia control lamps, panel lighting, choke and wipers (self-parking), and there is a separate ignition key and push-in starter knob. Before the driver further knobs look after the screen-washers, Lucas fog lamp, Lucas long-range spot lamp and heater, while the flip-switch controlling the Laycock de Normanville electrically-selected overdrive (an optional extra) is very conveniently located for operation by the right hand. The T-spoke-sprung steering wheel calls for 2¼ turns, lock to lock. A recessed button in its centre operates blatant twin-tone horns. Too bright indicator lights on the facia warn of direction indicators in use or ignition on. The indicators are self-cancelling, actuated by a control on the steering-wheel boss.

The bucket seats are not particularly comfortable; both slide easily and the squab of the passenger's seat folds forward to induce into the well behind the seats any person or animal sufficiently misguided to occupy it for more than a very brief distance. As the floor of this space slopes downwards it does not readily accommodate luggage and it is difficult to see why provision was made for it, although a proper seat, of restricted dimensions, can be obtained to special order. The trailing doors have catches released by pulling interior leather-cords, sliding Perspex windows in the side-screens enabling this to be done when all is " buttoned-up." The lined hard-top is securely bolted in place and the aforesaid side pieces peg into sockets on the doors, rendering the car weatherproof when the signalling flaps have been done up. There is a big grab-handle before the passenger. After 10,000 miles rust was forming on the fittings and the driver had to be careful not to hurt his right elbow on the rear metal strut of the off-side side-screen. The doors were not particularly easy either to open or shut; each has a deep rigid pocket, in which small objects can enjoy a distinct elusiveness. They are wide doors, providing an easy exit.

There is a reasonable-sized, quick-action fuel filler on the centre line of the tail and the unobstructed boot is of commendable capacity, its heavy lid needing to be propped open and calling for a carriage-key as well as an ordinary key to unlock it. The spare wheel is properly accommodated in a separate compartment, but jack and starting handle remain to savage my lady's suitcases.

Visibility is good, the hard-top possessing a large back window, the screen pillars being thin and both headlamps and front wings visible to a driver of average height. The pendant pedals are rather far from the floor and easy heel-and-toe gear changes are not possible. However, there is decent accommodation for the clutch foot and the

foot-operated lamps-dipper is well placed. The body is free from rattles, nor do the side-screens contribute any.

When parking the driver finds the steering exceedingly heavy but it becomes almost too light at speed. It transmits little road shock or vibration, while there is mild castor-action. It is, however, rather " dead " steering, lacking in immediate response. The TR3 rides well for a sports car, although on rough roads there is a good deal of up-and-down movement (but no pitching), for the rigid back axle calls for stiff springs to locate and damp it. In enterprising cornering roll is virtually absent. Front suspension is by wishbones and coil-springs. Corners can be taken fast, but a tendency to dart about spoils absolute precision, which vagueness of the steering does nothing to mitigate. If provoked the back wheels will break away in a conventional tail slide.

In normal driving this Triumph goes round corners safely at high speeds and it is only when trying hard that a certain uncertainty and untidiness intrude. Even then, the TR3 is an exceptionally quick A to B motor car, because the performance is of no mean order for a value-for-money 2-litre. The rev.-counter has a red mark at 5,000 r.p.m., equal to maxima of approximately 15 m.p.h. in first, 45 m.p.h. in second, 55 m.p.h. in overdrive-second, 75 m.p.h. in third, 90 m.p.h. in overdrive-third and 105 m.p.h. in top. Translated into through-the-gears acceleration, we did a s.s. ¼-mile, two-up, in 18.6 sec., finishing at 75 m.p.h. in normal-third gear. The speedometer needle keeps steady at set readings but surged too much for us to record acceleration figures at intermediate speeds, and there is an optimism of 1.8 m.p.h. at 30 m.p.h. and 3.7 m.p.h. at 60 m.p.h. to be taken into account. The mileage recorder was 3½ per cent. too optimistic. The needles of speedometer and rev.-counter move in the same plane.

RUGGED POWER.—The 2-litre engine of the TR3, developed from the Standard Vanguard power unit, has " wet " liners and, as can be seen, twin S.U. carburetters, etc.

FAMILIAR FRONTAL ASPECT of the Triumph TR3 hardtop, showing the re-located grille, Lucas head and spot-lamps, the flat screen and sliding side windows which also have signalling flaps.

ANOTHER VIEW of the Triumph TR3, familiar to drivers of less potent cars, showing the large boot, spare-wheel compartment and wrap-round back window.

From the foregoing it will be appreciated that the latest Triumph sports car will attain a maximum of about 110 m.p.h. given a reasonable run and in this country the speedometer goes quickly to over 100 m.p.h. along normal straight roads.

In normal-third over 70 m.p.h. is available, and a flick into o/d third allows the speed to creep up to 80 or more m.p.h. The possession of overdrive on all three of the higher gear ratios is thoroughly worthwhile to a driver willing to make full use of the indirect ratios because he is thus able to fit seven forward speeds to the requirements of the moment. Bottom gear is for emergency use only, which puts normal-second on the low side. Not only is acceleration from a standstill most impressive but it is exceptionally well maintained, even from 80 to 100 m.p.h. in top gear, for instance.

To match the performance of this 110 m.p.h. car there are superlative brakes, Girling disc on the front wheels. These stop the Triumph without anxiety with a mere caress of the pedal and the only indication of the hard work they undertake so uncomplainingly is a smell of hot-pad after frequent or heavy applications. These disc brakes are foolproof and fade-free and constitute a major attraction of the TR3. The wheels can easily be locked, causing tyre protest, but in fast cornering the Dunlops do not make undue noise. The steering lock is good (turning circle approx. 32 ft.).

The action of the clutch is reasonably light and smooth but the pedal travel is too long; the excellent placing of the little remote gear-lever has been commented on, but it earns a black mark because the knob feels unpleasant to handle. The gear change is apt to be harsh as the synchromesh is beaten; considerable vibration is transmitted by the lever. Over rough roads the scuttle vibrates very mildly but this is scarcely conveyed to the steering column. There is less wind noise than would be expected, although the wind past the side-screens is reminiscent of an aeroplane, and no objectionable exhaust noise, but a good deal of mechanical noise intrudes and the test car had an unpleasant tap in the engine, the breather of which could be heard breathing at idling speed. The Triumph commenced promptly with a minimum of choke and did not exhibit any tendency to " pink " or to run-on after spells of hard motoring. The choke control can now be locked in various positions.

Apart from providing notable speed and acceleration the well-tried wet-liner four-cylinder engine of the TR3 works commendably within itself, 3,000 r.p.m. in top gear sufficing for a cruising speed of over a mile-a-minute, while the same engine speed in overdrive-top equals nearly 74 m.p.h. Driven thus, baby-car petrol economy is obtained and at the more probable habitual cruising speed of 80 m.p.h. the engine is called upon to run at only 3,250 r.p.m. in overdrive-top gear. In fast main-road driving we recorded a fuel consumption of 25.4 m.p.g. of Shell and B.P. Super, or 24.6 m.p.g.

after milometer correction. After 625 miles scarcely any oil had been consumed. The brake stop-lights were inoperative on the test car.

The bonnet top is unusual in that it is secured by Dzus fasteners that require a carriage-key to release them. It is heavy, has to be propped up, and didn't shut absolutely flush. Engine accessibility is excellent, as is that of the Lucas battery and the electrical fuses, etc., and it is pleasing to find rod-linkage between accelerator and the twin S.U. carburetters with their A.C. air cleaners. The dip-stick is particularly well located, on the near side. The valve cover is polished on the TR3 engine. There are air vents at the back of the bonnet top to direct hot air on to the windscreen, apart from demisting vents on the scuttle behind the screen. The screen washer has a glass, not plastic, John Sydney water container. A knob on the facia sill opens a ventilator flap in the scuttle to provide the TR3's occupants with cool air, and no fumes reach the interior.

To sum up, the Triumph offers good performance and possesses superb brakes for a car which, although its basic price has risen from £886 to £1,021 since we tested it in TR2 form (the price of the TR3 hard-top being £1,073 7s. inclusive of p.t. in standard form and £1,219 19s. with the extras. including wire wheels, as tested) is still definitely in the value-for-money class. It is selling splendidly in dollar-markets and should continue to do so for a long time to come, especially if it could be re-styled, because proven reliability and economy allied to potency are qualities sought after in all parts of the world.—W. B.

THE TRIUMPH TR3 HARD-TOP

Engine : Four cylinders, 83 by 92 mm. (1,991 c.c.). Push-rod-operated o.h. valves. 8.5 to 1 compression-ratio. 100 b.h.p. at 4,800 r.p.m.

Gear ratios : First, 12.5 to 1; second, 7.4 to 1; overdrive second, 6.07 to 1; third, 4.9 to 1; overdrive third, 4.02 to 1; top, 3.7 to 1; overdrive top, 3.03 to 1.

Tyres : 5.50 by 15 Dunlop on centre-lock wire wheels.

Weight : 19 cwt. 2 qr. 0 lb. (without occupants but ready for the road, with approximately one gallon of petrol).

Fuel capacity : 12½ gallons. Range approximately 307½ miles.

Wheelbase : 7 ft. 4 in.

Track : Front, 3 ft. 9 in.; rear, 3 ft. 9½ in.

Dimensions : 12 ft. 5 in. by 4 ft. 7½ in. by 4 ft. 2 in. (high).

Price (with extras as tested : £1,219 19s. (inclusive of p.t.).

Makers : Triumph Motor Co. (1945) Ltd., Coventry, England.

appearing in the January 1958 issue. He stated unequivocally that he regarded the TR3 as **the** finest value for money sports car, and went on to say that in view of this, he was prepared to forgive it "certain minor failings and crudities!" The gearchange he thought to be "about the best there is" and the engine was "seemingly indestructible". Overall, Bill Boddy called it "a car that commands respect", and he finished by saying that, "were a sports car not unsuitable for his particular circumstances, he would like to own a TR3!"

Thus it can be seen that Standard Triumph's publicity men obtained wide press coverage for their disc-braked sports car, almost all of it favourable and some of it positively glowing. The 1958 model was on its way, however, this of course being what we now know as the TR3A. Production of the 3A had started in September 1957, but as the initial batch all went overseas, the first that British enthusiasts knew of it was when the motoring periodicals carried descriptions in early January 1958, concurrently with these revised TRs becoming available in the showrooms. Probably because there were no significant mechanical changes, coupled with the fact that the TR had now been around for some years in much the same form, there were very few road tests of this car, despite its nearly 5 year production run.

Neither of the principal UK weekly magazines tested the car, nor did "Autosport " and nor, it seems, did the main USA periodical "Road and Track". However, the USA version of "Sports Cars Illustrated" ran a full test of the TR3A in its March 1958 issue, despite its having carried a full test of a TR3 only a very short time previously. They fully approved of the new styling, which was after all designed to appeal to the vital dollar market, and were pleased to see the more substantial front bumpers. Quality control at Coventry was praised, and they said that one could run a Triumph TR for 100 years, yet it felt as if nothing would fall off! Draughts in the cockpit (it was snowing during part of the test) were criticised, but acceleration was said to be "neck snapping" and braking "left nothing to be desired". Performance seemed slightly down on former cars, 0-60 mph occupying 12.6 seconds. Despite a moderate price increase, the magazine felt that the new improvements were well worthwhile.

The only British test published of the TR3A seems to have been that in February 1958 by the British edition of Sports Cars Illustrated. They obtained a demonstrator registered VDU 565, although the photographs accompanying the test show the vehicle running on trade plates for some reason. The car had the optional hardtop and overdrive, and they recorded the startling 0-60 acceleration figure of 9.4 seconds. As they also criticised the speedometer for a considerable amount of over-reading, one suspects that the acceleration times may have been taken without using accurate equip-

ment. Fuel usage had climbed to around 26 mpg overall, which seems typical of a TR3A in daily use, and they considered that at £1100 including the hardtop and tax, the TR could no longer be called the "poor man's sports car", although it was pointed out that it was still the cheapest 2 litre sporting vehicle available.

The new seats were described as "most comfortable", and the interior was praised as "warm and snug", the car providing "ample touring comfort for two persons". That the speedometer in this car was indeed wildly optimistic was shown by the maximum speed runs, when it registered in excess of 120 mph - i.e. off the scale, or round to "Made in England" as keen owners have been heard to claim! It was admitted that the test car came with Dunlop racing tyres, and as their rolling radius was different to that of the normal boots, presumably this explains the excessive speedometer error. Roadholding was said to be excellent, with an acceptable standard of comfort. A particular point of praise was the accessibility of things mechanical under the bonnet, a great bonus in a car likely to be owner-maintained. In fact, the under bonnet layout was said to "command respect", which seems a strange choice of phrase!

The Motor" magazine produced an article in April 1959 which chronicled the development of the TR series, and this not only referred to the "20 TS" prototype as the "TR1", but also used the TR3A nomenclature for the first time. Therefore, despite the Company's refusal to rename the TR3, pressure from the press and public was ensuring that the 1958 model had a different description to its predecessors.

"The Autocar" magazine ran an informative series at this time entitled "Used cars on the road," when a secondhand example of a popular car was borrowed from a dealer and put through its paces. In March 1958, the subject was a 1955 TR2 with a hardtop, registered VUG 6. This car had covered but 23,000 miles, yet it was said to be full of "squeaks, rattles and booms" and the hardtop and sidescreens were, predictably, described as "letting in draughts from all directions". In fact, the tester could see no advantage in having a hardtop, particularly as the standard hood was good "of its type". Fuel consumption was up to scratch at between 29 and 37 mpg, but at 13.4 seconds for the 0-60 mph test, performance was slightly dulled. The green paintwork and the chromium were said to have withstood three years excellently, but bad scuttle-shake was evident on this car, surprising in a hardtop-equipped version. In fact, over 60 mph it was said to be such that the instruments were difficult to read!

The speedometer was called "so erratic as to be almost useless," but in general they were pleased with the car,

VDU 565, one of the very few TR3As ever road-tested by a contemporary magazine, is seen displaying its spare wheel and wheel-changing tools. Despite being a Factory-owned car, it sports the additional tubular quarter bumpers described in Chapter 6 (TR Register Archive).

although the exhaust roar was described as "embarrassing". The price asked was £695; as the original price of a hardtop TR2 with tax was around £950, this represents a 3 year depreciation of only just over 25%, which was surprisingly good. In fact, it is obvious from looking at advertisements in late 1950's and early 1960's periodicals that TR2s and TR3s were in such demand that prices held up amazingly well, and that even by 1960 the cheapest price for which the earliest of TR2s could be bought was around £500, more than half the original price, and that for a 6 year old car that might

have been heavily raced or rallied! This £500 is equivalent to around £5750 at 1994 prices, so joining the ranks of the TR owning classes was not at all cheap, despite the vehicle's "poor man's sportscar" epithet.

In October 1959, this same "Autocar" series focused on a one-year old TR3A, registered 12 EAR. This powder blue car was offered, with hardtop but without overdrive, for £865, the mileage being only 15,000. The article affirmed that as compared with TR2s tested earlier, the whole car felt much more rigid, with the sealing of doors and sidescreens vastly improved. In addition, it was said that the excessive scuttle shake of the earlier cars had been eliminated (but see later). As the car was so relatively young, there had been virtually no deterioration in any department, although the clutch was giving problems with clean disengagement. As usual, the exhaust noise came in for comment, despite this car being fitted with the later, two box, silencer system. An interesting sequel to this piece was that the car tested was purchased after the report by Stuart Bladon, a staff journalist with the "Autocar", and he wrote up his experiences with the car after he had owned it for 3 years. Although not fitted with overdrive, he soon found the need for it, and £15 purchased a reconditioned unit. However, the factory fitted it for him and charged an "exorbitant fee" for this service. Fuel consumption, driven hard and in daily business use averaged around 25 mpg, and on the whole, the car was a most reliable purchase.

I recently contacted Stuart Bladon, who is still a motoring journalist, and he has fond memories of this TR3A. Indeed, he still runs a TR today (a 1982 TR7). He did not care for the powder blue colour of the 3A and soon had it changed to dark blue. Scuttle shake was however a problem, particularly when fitted with the Dunlop RS5 tyres and with the car in open form. Although it diminished in winter with the hardtop

Stuart Bladon's TR3A, 12 EAR, which was the subject of an "Autocar" used car test, as described in the text ("Autosport").

re-fitted, it was never absent, despite what was written in the original article! Incidentally, when he sold 12 EAR in 1962, he retained the hardtop, later selling it separately - as he recalls, the telephone never stopped ringing, such was the demand! In his 3 years of ownership, Stuart took the mileage from 15,000 to 55,000, and he only parted with the TR in 1962 because the Autocar's bosses insisted he had one of the then-new Morris 1100's, which he describes as "the worst car I ever ran"! Overdrive solenoids on the TR3A proved to be consistently unreliable, about 6 months of daily use being the maximum that they would tolerate without attention or replacement. Upon receipt of the Morris 1100, he managed to sell the TR3A for £480, it having cost him £850 three years earlier. As can be calculated, this is a greater percentage depreciation than was occurring in the 1950's, reflecting the fact that by 1962 the TR3A was no longer a current model, and also that there were many more TRs available by then on the second-hand market.

One of the final contemporary magazine articles to feature the TR3A was carried in the October 1960 issue of "Motor Sport", when Editor Bill Boddy was lent a press demonstrator 3A registered 46 HP. This car and 2242 RW appear to have been about the last sidescreen TRs on the press fleet, being supplanted by the TR4's in 1961. Although the resultant article is much more about the trip to Italy that he made in the TR than about the TR itself, Boddy was still impressed with the car as a long distance express, providing relaxed and economical cruising in overdrive. No performance figures were taken, which may have been just as well, for by 1960 the TR's rivals were beginning to outpace it. As is well known, the performance of the TR remained virtually constant between 1954 and 1961 (and right up to the TR4A's demise in 1967, for that matter!), so clearly this was not any longer an aspect of their product that the company would have wanted highlighted. Incidentally, 46 HP was found in the 1980's in very original condition, having been stored in a shed for many years. Fortunately, it has now been rebuilt, and is seen on occasions at TR Register events. For the sake of completeness, I must add that no test of a TR3B seems ever to have taken place, not even in the USA press. This is however hardly surprising, as the factory clearly did not wish to promote the sidescreen TR at a time (1962) when the TR4 was all the rage and when it was only supplying the TR3B reluctantly following dealer pressure.

A further aspect of sidescreen TR press coverage that I need to deal with is that of published letters written by owners, both of the TR and of its principal rivals. The great majority of these seem to have appeared in "Motorsport", which was always noted for a lively and controversial letters page. Indeed, it was this page that indirectly led to the formation of the TR Register in 1970, as we shall see.

The first letter, published in August 1954, was from a Mr J R Brown, who was one of the pit crew working on the privately-entered TR2 OKV 777 at Le Mans that year. He considered, I think correctly, that the magazine's report on the race did an injustice to what was certainly the most standard car in the race, and I reproduce the letter here as I feel it makes some valid points. A year later, a letter in the April 1955 issue sparked off a long-running correspondence on the relative

Richard Attwood belts his TR3A around Silverstone on 12th August 1961. The rear track seems to be wider than standard on this car, as the wheel fillls the arch more than normal - maybe the axle has just moved sideways under hard cornering! (NMM Beaulieu).

merits of the TR2 and its "deadly" rival, the Austin Healey 100. It suggested that standard TR2s outperformed Austin Healey 100s (and also XK120s!) to the extent of beating them in scratch races, and further suggested that the TR's road-holding was better! Whilst the former statement was true to some extent, the latter statement was very much open to question. In May, a Mr Trimble leapt to the Healey's defence, stating why he had chosen the 100 in preference to the TR for competition purposes. His main points were that while the TR was a little quicker off the mark, the Healey would catch it up in the higher speed ranges, both cars having virtu-ally the same top speed. As to handling, he asserted that the Healey was considerably better than the TR2, which "appears to hop round bends and then weave its way down the straights, whereas the Healey normally corners neatly".

Having myself owned many examples of both models, I feel that there is no doubt that the standard Healey 100 **does** have better roadholding than the standard TR2, and that this difference would have been more marked on the tyres avail-able at the time. The correspondent mentions that at least four TR2s had overturned whilst racing in the previous 6 months, whereas no Austin Healey was known to have com-mitted a similar indiscretion. This may well have been true, but takes no account of the fact that there were vastly more TRs racing than Healeys! The final reason Mr Trimble gives for having preferred to purchase the Austin Healey was the capability of its engine to accept further tuning; indeed, he claims that "very little tuning can be carried out on the TR2 without impairing its reliability" - time and S.A.H. Accessories Ltd subsequently proved this statement to be

---

THE TRIUMPH AT LE MANS

Sir,

As one of the pit staff for the Triumph TR2 entry at Le Mans, it is felt that your comments in the report of the event do injustice to one of the few private entries, and certainly the most standard car, in the race.

As this was our first run in the event, and we could entertain no hopes of a class win against the Maseratis and the works Bristols, all costing several times the price of our car, we set ourselves the target of finishing at all costs, and if possible of achieving the qualifi-cation speed of approximately 76 m.p.h.

This speed was maintained with a satisfactory margin throughout the night, and without stressing the car in any way. With better light, if everything appeared favourable, it was our intention to increase speed. At this time, however, the driver reported that clutch slip was becoming evident, thus having the effect of limiting revs on all gears, but particularly on overdrive, thus reducing the indicated maximum from in the region of 118 m.p.h. to little over 100 m.p.h., and bringing the lap speed below that required for qualification. It was decided, however, to keep the car running rather than have a lengthy pit stop to permit our purely amateur crew to investigate the trouble.

The result is now well known. Our car averaged over 75 m.p.h., and it is felt that this is by no means discreditable. A careful watch was maintained by both drivers, and no grounds for complaints of baulking were given.

In view of the foregoing, it will be seen that the car was at all times run well under its potential performance, and your remarks suggesting that the organisers reject entries of this type, which surely present an accurate indication of a production car's capabilities, can only serve to give an unfortunate impression. It is not cars like the Triumph which should be refused, but rather the thinly-disguised centre-seating racing cars with whom your grossly unfair comparison is made.

Incidentally, the car finished in first-class order, and on examina-tion after its return the clutch slip was found to be due merely to excess grease from the thrust-race having fouled the clutch plate.

I am, Yours, etc.,

Burnley.   J. R. BROWN.

Mr Brown's leter referred to in the text, from "Motor Sport".

absolute nonsense, though the easy availability "off the shelf" at that time of the "Le Mans" tuning kit for the Austin Healey, with no comparable offering for the TR, might have made the Healey appear more tuneable. In modern times, the TR engine, of smaller capacity that the Healey's, has been developed to produce considerably more power more reliably than even the most highly developed 100's, the long stroke of their engines being a severe limiting factor.

Mr Trimble's final statement was, however, partially correct, namely that the TR was "essentially a rally car, while the Austin Healey was essentially a circuit-type car". Yes, the TR won countless rallies at all levels whereas the Healey won virtually none, at least until the 3000 came along many years later. However, the TR **also** won races, did better at Le Mans than any standard Healey, and was very much more of an "all rounder", as well as being significantly cheaper to buy and a lot cheaper to run! Trimble's letter really set the correspondence pages alight, and for the next few months the "TR2 versus Austin Healey 100" controversy was the main topic, both cars having their fervent detractors and admirers. One or two lucky correspondents had already owned both cars, even at that early date, and these gentlemen conceded that both vehicles had their good points, but on balance, the correspondence came out overall in favour of the TR2 by a factor of two to one. Rather than tediously repeating all these letters, I will attempt to summarise the general points made. Incidentally, as to other rivals of the TR, little mention was made; the Morgan had a TR engine in any event, but was clearly less of a practical, everyday car, the Jaguar XK 120/140 was in a different price bracket altogether, the Jowett Jupiter had ceased production, the MGA had not yet been announced, and the premium prices of foreign sports cars put them out of reach for most enthusiasts. In mid-1955 therefore, it really was a TR2 or a Healey 100 if one wanted an affordable, usable sports car.

Principally, the TR2 had price in its favour; the basic TR with tax cost £886, the Healey cost £1,063, a difference of £177, or roughly £2,000 in today's money. However, the Healey came with overdrive, a heater and wire wheels as standard, whereas these were options on the TR. This did at least allow the purchaser of a TR the choice of whether he wanted these items, and even if all of these were added, the TR was still significantly the less expensive car. One correspondent went so far as to say that the Healey, with an extra engine capacity of 700 cc, doing about 10 miles per gallon less and costing a lot more, jolly well ought to be more comfortable (which it was) and perform better (which was arguable), as otherwise there was little point in it! Another correspondent recalled Mike Hawthorn's published opinion, "that for the money, there cannot be a sports car in the world to touch the TR2!". As to performance, it is now well

known and was indeed known to some at the time, that the "Motor"/"Autocar" magazine road test Austin-Healey 100, NOJ 392, was fitted for the test with most of the "Le Mans" performance modifications, thus being a far from standard car. These helped it to achieve a 119 mph top speed and a 0-60 mph time of 10.3 seconds, both significantly better than the TR2. No standard Austin Healey could however achieve these figures, for the test car produced around 103 BHP as compared to the 90 BHP of the showroom car.

As far as I have ascertained, no sidescreen TR submitted for testing was ever other than to standard catalogue specification, and this is borne out by those owners I have talked to, whose cars would replicate the road test TR's figures. Those correspondents who averred that the Austin Healey had better performance were, I submit, mistaken. Yes, it may have handled better, but then its fuel consumption was nowhere near as good as that of the TR.

Looks are obviously entirely subjective, but few can doubt that the Healey was a prettier car than the more starkly functional TR2 - in fact there are those (and I am one of them) who believe that the Austin Healey 100, particularly in two-tone colours and with the louvered bonnet, is the most beautiful car ever built bar none! In terms of practicality, the TR wins; - the Healey's disastrously low ground clearance does it no favours, its engine accessibility is poor compared to the TR, and nor can it carry a third adult or two children behind the seats. You also need to remove luggage from the Healey's boot to gain the spare wheel, whereas the TR's spare has its own little, extremely accessible, box to live in. The TR hood may be a "kit of parts", but it is swift to erect, and takes up a lot less space on the car than does the Healey's permanently-attached item. To erect the hood on a 100 is not a one-man job; one no sooner erects the frame on one side than it collapses again when one scoots around to the other side! Anyone who has tried this sport in pouring rain will know what I mean! The TR also has a full set of clear instrumentation, unlike the Healey, plus spare parts prices that have always been significantly cheaper than those of the B.M.C. product.

Time and again the various correspondents mentioned the Austin-Healey's gearbox as being its Achilles Heel, as indeed it was. Whereas the TR had a proper four speed box with a neat, remote control lever, (and as one writer emphasised "did not need overdrive to make it a sportscar") the 100 had to make do with three speeds, which made overdrive essential. Presumably this was why it was a standard fitment? The gear lever was of the "long wand" variety, and was thus not at all sporting, though to be fair, the great torque of the engine did mean that gearchanging was required less frequently. However, I cannot imagine anyone changing gear for fun in an Austin Healey 100, whereas in a TR2.......! Not only was the Healey's gearbox far from sporting, it was also not adequate to do the job in hand, and breakages were frequent. In "Motor Sport" for September 1955, a Mr Roberts wrote to say that although he owned an Austin Healey with which he was basically happy, he had just broken the gearbox and been told that no spare boxes nor parts were available, and that he would be without his car for three months! His letter concluded - "My advice - stick to your TR2s". The TR had faults in service of course, but it had no one specific problem anything like as serious as the Austin Healey gearbox debacle.

One letter concerning the TR which did not refer to the rival product was published in June 1956, and as I have heard of this problem occurring elsewhere, it bears repeating. Flight-Lieutenant Sims wrote to say that he had had to brake very hard in his TR2 whilst carrying out an "accelerating manoeuvre". He avoided an accident, but the engine moved forward under braking so far that the fan punctured the radiator. Soft, worn-out engine mountings can exacerbate this problem, which was cured by this owner by attaching a cable between the bell housing and the chassis cruciform.

By September 1956, when the disc braked TR3 arrived, the British Motor Corporation had produced their Austin-Healey 100/6, which incorporated major changes from the previous four-cylinder model. That the Standard-Triumph management perceived this car as a serious threat is evidenced by a Product Comparison memorandum that I have been fortunate enough to obtain. Prepared for internal circulation only, this document (dated 28th September 1956) is here reproduced in full, and the results of the analysis must have satisfied the Triumph managers, having regard to the final paragraph. The 100/6 Healey did at last have a proper four speed gearbox, although the gear change lever was still somewhat eccentric. However, the previously standard overdrive was now deleted, as were the wire wheels, so taken all in all, the Healey was still more than £100 dearer - and it had to make do with drum brakes for another 3 years! In fact, the performance comparison was even more in favour of the Triumph, for no acceleration figures are quoted, and those of the early 100/6 were not good, 0-60 mph taking more than 13 seconds once the road test results were revealed. Even when the Healey received a revised cylinder head a year later, it's performance could only just match the TR's. Space precludes further reference to the comparison of the TR with its principal rival, but the final word and the acid test is what did the customers buy? In the 1953 to 1961 production period of the TR2/3/3A, around 80,000 TRs were sold, whereas in the same period fewer than half that number of Austin Healeys found buyers, for world sales totalled only around 39,000. I should add that it is true that during the 1955 to 1961 period nearly

---

Product Information Service

New Model Comparison
The new Austin-Healey 100 Six compared with the Triumph T.R.3

1. Introduction
        The only major differences in the specification of the Austin-Healey 100 Six compared with the previous model lie in the installation of a six-cylinder engine instead of the previous four-cylinder unit, provision of occasional seats for children at the rear and a slightly re-styled front end appearance. Such items as overdrive, knock-off wire wheels and adjustable windscreen, which were previously standard equipment, are now optional extras at additional cost. Previously the provision of the over-drive and knock-off wheels as standard equipment gave the old Austin Healey a better all-round specification than the Triumph T.R.3. With the new model this is no longer so and, in spite of a reduction of £66 in the basic price, the Austin Healey continues to be substantially dearer than the T.R.3.

2. Engine

	T.R.3	Austin Healey
Engine capacity	*1,991*	*2,639*
Bore m.m.	*79.4*	
Stroke m.m.	*92*	*89*
Compression ratio :1	*8.5*	*8.25*
No of cylinders	*4*	*6*
B.H.P.	*100*	*102*
@ R.P.M.	*4,800*	*4,600*
No. of carburettors	*2*	*2*

        The Austin Healey has a theoretical advantage in having a six-cylinder engine of over 2.5 litres capacity as against the four-cylinder, 2 litre engine of the T.R.3. In spite of this, however, maximum B.H.P. is almost identical, the Austin Healey having a mere 2 B.H.P. more than the T.R.3.

3.Performance
        Translated into performance, the T.R.3 has a clear lead. In direct top gear the road speed is 20 m.p.h. per 1,000 R.P.M. while for the Austin Healey the road speed in direct top gear is 18.9 m.p.h. per 1,000 R.P.M. The maximum speed of the Austin Healey is said to be 107 m.p.h. while that of the T.R.3 is 110 m.p.h. As far as economy in concerned the advantage is definitely with the T.R.3 whose petrol consumption is 28-32 m.p.g. as compared with 23-24 m.p.g. for the Austin Healey.

4. Chassis
(a) Transmission

	T.R.3	Austin Healey
No. of direct gear speeds	*4*	*4*
Overdrive as optional extra	*YES*	*YES*
No. of overdrive speeds	*3*	*2*
Rear axle ratio direct	*3.7*	*3.91*
" " " with overdrive	*4.1*	*4.1*

        The T.R.3 has the advantage of offering three overdrive speeds compared with two on the Austin Healey and also of offering a lower rear axle ratio when the overdrive is not fitted.

(b) Brakes
        Here the T.R.3 possesses the outstanding advantage of disc brakes fitted to the front wheels as against normal drum-type brakes on the Austin Healey. Disc brakes are much more effective and this makes the T.R.3 safer at very high speeds.

5. Dimensions
        The new Austin Healey has been slightly enlarged compared with the previous model.

	T.R.3		Austin Healey	
	ft.	*ins.*	*ft.*	*ins.*
Wheelbase	*7.*	*4.*	*7.*	*8.*
Overall length	*12.*	*7.*	*13.*	*1 1/2*
Overall width	*4.*	*7 1/2.*	*5.*	*0 1/2.*
Overall height hood up	*4.*	*2.*	*4.*	*1.*
Overall height hood down	*3.*	*10.*	*3.*	*10.*
Ground clearance		*6.*		*5 1/2*
Turning circle	*34.*		*35.*	
Kerb weight	*18 3/4 cwt*		*.21 3/4 cwt.*	

New model comparison (continued):-

	T.R.3	Austin Healey
Tyre size	5.50 x 15	5.90 x 15

The Austin Healey has a longer wheelbase and is overall longer and wider than the T.R.3. However, is has less ground clearance, a larger turning circle and is 3cwt. heavier than the T.R.3. These three items, especially the last, more than outweigh any advantages accruing to the Austin Healey by virtue of its increased dimensions.

6. Sales features

	T.R.3	Austin Healey
Engine & Chassis		
Four speed gearbox	YES	YES
Two carburettors	YES	YES
Telescopic shock absorbers	YES	NO
Overdrive as extra	YES	YES
Electric fuel pump	NO	YES
Disc brakes	YES	NO
Body exterior		
Flush fitting headlamps	NO	YES
Over-riders	YES	YES
Spare wheel in separate compartment	YES	NO
Hard top as optional extra	YES	YES
Two tone exterior colours	NO	YES
Body interior		
Heater	NO	NO
Leather upholster to seat facings	NO	YES
Foam rubber seat cushions	YES	YES
Lockable glove box	YES	NO
Pockets in doors	YES	YES
Passenger grab handle	YES	YES
Occasional seating	Extra	YES
Instruments		
Instruments in front of driver	YES	YES
Rev. counter	YES	YES
Oil gauge	YES	YES
Ammeter	YES	NO
Trip recorder	YES	NO
Temperature gauge	YES	YES
No. of items offered	17	17

The T.R.3 has the same number of sales features as the Austin Healey, but the items specified on the T.R.3 and not offered on the Austin Healey are, in most cases, more important than is so vice versa.

7.Price

	Basic	Purchase Tax	Total
Triumph T.R.3	£680.0. 0.	£341. 7. 0.	£1021. 7. 0.
Austin Healey	£762.0. 0.	£382. 7. 0.	£1144. 7. 0.
Austin Healey + on T.R.3	£ 82. 0. 0.	£ 41. 0. 0.	£ 123. 0. 0.

The T.R.3 is over £120 cheaper than the Austin Healey if Purchase Tax is included, and as the above analysis has shown, yields nothing to it in performance or specification.

Issued by Market and Economic Analysis Dept.
28th September, 1956

100,000 MGA's found homes, but this car was always a step down from the TR/Austin-Healey league, both in terms of cost and performance (though it still used more fuel than the TR!) so no direct comparison is valid.

Moving on to the start of 1960, "Motor Sport" carried an interesting article by Mr J D Hart, who had purchased in 1956 one of the very earliest 1954 TR2s, KNT 888, and used it for racing. Prior to purchasing, he found that many of the early TR's he inspected had poor paintwork, although they were then only 1 or 2 years old! His first impression was of a good ride, but poor wet weather roadholding - "the rear wheels would spin and the front wheels would fail to steer the car unless engine performance was used with great discretion" - the exhaust noise was described as "shattering", but the speed and acceleration were there, the car "somehow asking to be driven hard", he stated. "All this with 34 mpg still seems incredible," Mr Hart continued, "but careful checks were made, and on a 2400 mile return trip to Rome, 40 mpg was recorded!" I should add that this car did not have overdrive, but did have the aluminium bonnet, so must have been amongst the first 500 TRs made.

In racing the TR, Hart found that he did not suffer brake fade, unlike many other TR2 pilots, and he put this down to the extra cooling from the wire wheels. As to troubles, the engine was stripped at 28,000 miles whereupon the bearings were found to be worn, and all four pistons cracked (these were the very early unmodified type) - however, the unit had still been running well, although the advance and retard mechanism was found to be seized in the fully retarded position. Rear axle seals and bearings gave trouble (surprise, surprise!), three cylinder head gaskets were needed, a water pump failed, as did two speedo cables. The front suspension needed frequent lubrication, and tyres lasted but 7,000 miles per set - well, he was racing it! Hart fairly states that most of these problems were teething troubles associated only with the early cars, rectified in later models, but overall he concluded, "It was a great car, and provided a year of real pleasure motoring before it was sold".

Finally, and I make no apology for yet again referring to "Motor Sport" magazine, for it was the most definitive and authoritative periodical of the day, there was in the April 1962 edition an illuminating reader's survey on the TR. This was part of a long-term project surveying many different vehicles, and it is pleasing to report that the TR acquitted itself well overall, 77.8% of those TR owners responding to the survey stating that they would buy a TR again. It was not revealed exactly how many TR2/3/3A owners returned their survey forms, but as the editorial stated that 25% of all the magazine's readers took part in the survey project, and as quite a large number of "Motor Sport" readers would, in the

On the right, the TR Register's Good-wood Sprint Weekends, from the early 1980s, are recalled by this view of Joe Vella sitting in his ex-Works TR2 PKV 693. He is talking to TR Register stalwart Julian Furniss, another regular competitor (Joe Vella).

Below: Mr Hart is seen racing his very early TR2, KNT 888, at Brands Hatch in 1957. Some of his opinions on this car are set out in this Chapter. Note the fitment of front over-riders without the accompanying bumper (LAT Photographic).

nature of things, be TR owners, I would guess that the number of TR owners responding ran into three figures, making the results well worthwhile. Asked whether the factory and dealership service was satisfactory, 53% said yes, 18% said no, 11% did their own servicing and the rest made no comment. As to modifications, 14% had modified the cylinder head and other engine components, 11% had performed suspension modifications and 4.6% had fitted overdrive to a non-overdrive TR.

Quite a few said that they had fitted fibreglass wings to replace rusted steel wings. Engine reliability appeared good, but a number of bearing failures had occurred at between 50,000 and 60,000 miles. One particular engine had covered 163,000 miles with only minor attention, and overall the engine proved very study, as did the clutch, where mileages of up to 85,000 were achieved without attention. 5% of TR3s had had oil on the clutch, but 10% of TR3/3A's had needed

replacement clutch master cylinders. Yet again, the gearbox came in for approval as most reliable, only 5.3% of all cars having needed any serious gearbox work. However, the overdrive solenoid was singled out as a part that regularly failed. Brakes were troublefree, and mileages of up to 30,000 were reported prior to any relining or new pads being required. Short silencer life was reported by 13% of correspondents, but steering reliability was good provided the greasing schedule was adhered to. Many owners complained of hard springing and consequent uncomfortable ride, but the suspension generally suffered few mechanical failures, only 4% suffering broken springs, with 8% having shock absorber problems.

The rear axle itself was excellently reliable, but not so the hubs, oil seals and bearings on the TR2/3 "Lockheed" axle, where 16% reported problems (I'm surprised that it was not 100%!). The later type axle produced no failures at all, and hardly any failures had occurred to the propshafts, but the speedometer and its associated cable was probably the least reliable part of the car, 27% reporting problems. The water temperature gauge also failed quite frequently, invariably due to the sender tube fracturing. Electrical components were not too bad, but dynamos failed on 14%, and starter motors on 7% of cars. As to tyres, more than 70% of all TRs concerned were, by 1962, running on Michelin "X" tyres, Dunlops being the second most popular tyre at 16.5%. Crossply tyres wore very rapidly during hard driving (see Mr J D Hart's statement above), but the Michelin radial lasted at least 20,000 miles, which probably explains why so many TRs were thus fitted. In fact, I have encountered people who have claimed 80,000 miles from a set of these tyres in their original, hard rubber compound form.

A pair of matching seven-inch spotlights grace this TR2 of RF Morrison. The test, part of the Scottish Sports Car Club's Highland Rally, is taking place at Broomhall, Dunfermline ("Autosport").

An Irish-registered TR2 attempts to extricatre itself from mud with the help of "bouncing" from the passenger. The driver is Robin McKinney, but the event is unknown ("Autosport").

As can be seen therefore, the great majority of TR owners were satisfied with the mechanical parts of their cars, but the bodywork proved not so satisfactory. No less than 39% of all owners commented on faded paintwork and excessive rusting, particularly on the wings. Dropped doors, poor chrome, defective locks, rusty floors and water leaks were also cited by many, so it is clear that in service, the TR did not live up cosmetically to its well deserved mechanical reputation. Good value for money was frequently mentioned, and when asked to report any other serious defects not listed on the survey forms, very few people had anything to

remark! Most of the foregoing problems are well known to today's TR owners, particularly those have bought a ruin and attempted to restore it - still, that 78% of owners would have purchased another TR despite the rust and rattles is a real testimony to the soundness of the overall design.

As mentioned briefly earlier "Motor Sport" again carried a series of letters in praise of the TR from the end of 1969 and into the first half of 1970, these being the catalysts that led directly to the formation of the TR Register in January 1970. In fact, so great was the volume of enthusiastic correspondence received from past and present TR owners that the magazine took the unprecedented step in its March 1970 issue of devoting two whole pages to the subject. The very first letter was from a Mr Douglas Thompson in November 1969, and this and the three initial replies printed in December 1969 deserve reproducing here. One of the three replies was from Terry Simpson, who took the plunge and undertook to form a TR club, the TR Register, the first club specifically for TR owners since the demise of the UK Triumph Sports Owners Association some years before. He became the club's first President, serving from 1970 until 1988, when he was replaced by one of the other writers of those three initial replies, Darryl Uprichard, who remained President until 1993. TR enthusiasm is certainly long lasting, and it is thanks to the formation of the Register in 1970, when the fortunes of the sidescreen TRs were probably at their lowest ebb, that so many TRs exist today in such good condition, still giving the pleasure to their owners that they have provided now for the best part of 40 years!

Below are three letters extracted from the December 1969 issue of "Motor Sport"; these led to the calling of the inaugural meeting of the TR Register in January 1970. The first President was Terry Simpson, one of the letter writers.

LETTERS FROM READERS

N.B.—*Opinions expressed are those of our Correspondents and* MOTOR SPORT *does not necessarily associate itself with them.*—ED.

TRIUMPH TR—THE LAST REAL SPORTS CAR?

Sir,

I can explain to Mr. Thomson why the Triumph TR3A is so unloved but, in so doing, will probably unleash more comments from "experts" than MOTOR SPORT can or will be willing to, handle.

The TR3A invokes such uncomplimentary remarks because it is the last of the real sports cars. One must be able to drive to release the potential of 2, 3, 3A. Compared with, say, the MG-B, which is the most forgiving car I have ever driven, the TR is lethal in the wrong hands. Find a wrong line in a bend with a "B" and, within reason, the car will find its way round; while making the same mistake with the TR (unless you know, really know, how to drive) provides one with the academic exercise of working out not, will she go through the hedge, but, in which direction will she go through said greenery.

To me, the TR is the *pons asinorum* of sports cars, the best mechanical sporting machine ever! I derive more pleasure from driving my '58 TR3A than from other, more exotic, machinery. Perhaps I am "old fashioned" though, because I like to have to drive, not just sit back and be taken to my destination.

As to the question of observing the red line, Mr. Thomson is fortunate with his problem of piston rings as I broke the crankshaft, though this was probably assisted by the fact that two weeks prior to the crankshaft developing the "ooh nasties" some goon punted the TR up the boot, while in gear, and knocked it forward 15 yards.

Finally, my advice to Mr. Thomson is, stick to the TR. Try my dodge of taking it up to 2.2-litres—using 87 mm. pistons—and you can blow off *anything* from a standing start—that includes E-types and Elans, although one has to pay *them* the compliment of using 1st gear.

Stewarton.   DAVID A. ADAMS.

Sir,

Like Mr. D. Thomson I, too, am at a loss to see why there is not an enthusiastic following for the Triumph TR. My interest in these cars started in 1964 when I purchased a 1955 TR2 for £210. In the TR I found a car that was exciting to drive, especially with the top down. It was a car that never needed to be driven with the "foot to the floor" but it did like to be put through its paces on an open road, and seemed all the better for a good burst up to about 4,500 in 2nd and 3rd gears in order to obtain the notorious TR "roar" from its straight-through silencer. This car I kept for about three years until my marriage, in that time replacing only the plugs at 10,000-mile intervals, the rear springs (not such a hard job!) and the water pump.

Once bitten by the bug I just had to obtain another TR and so early this year I purchased a 1960 TR3A. This car had done 68,000 miles but still had plenty of power under the bonnet. In my 10,000 miles since then I have replaced only the rear springs and the plugs. Other than that I have had a very enjoyable year's motoring and am looking forward to more to come. If there are any other TR enthusiasts around I would be only too pleased to hear from them. Regrettably, it seems that Mr. Thomson is the only other TR owner who shares my enthusiasm.

Redbourn.   TERRENCE J. SIMPSON.

Sir,

Bravo MOTOR SPORT, at last you have led the field by printing a reader's letter on TR2s-TR3As. In reply to Mr. Thomson's article, I believe that, to their owners, the TR is a much-loved and respected sports car retaining the cameraderie of bygone years.

I have owned TRs since 1966 and my present TR3A has covered 45,000 miles since 1967 without any serious trouble. There is ample torque to keep the revs within the 5,000 limit and I find that with overdrive 4,700 is a very competitive limit. The TR is also good to my pocket: 30-32 m.p.g. and 600+ to the pint plus minimal tyre wear. It is a dynamic machine and although it weighs over a ton my wife has no difficulty in driving it, though on one occasion she drove through our double gates when they were shut. (I had permission to write that!) I can go on ignoring the draughts but not the road-holding in the wet which is the only unloved thing about it; one has to be very careful not to do anything violent! Thereby hang the tales!

Personally I find the TR an exciting car with much character. A "TR" Register perhaps?

Sunbury-on-Thames.   DARRYL K. UPRICHARD.

Morecambe Promenade is the location of this, the final test, in the May 1957 Morecambe National Rally. In brilliant sunshine, J Ashall hurls his wire-wheeled TR3 around a pylon with considerable enthusiasm, though he did not figure highly in the results ("Autosport").

Below is a letter published by "Motor Sport" in November 1969. This brought forth further correspondence (reproduced overleaf) which culminated in a deluge of enthusiastic letters to the magazine in early 1970 .

A TRIUMPH TR ENTHUSIAST

Sir

During the past year I have covered a distance of 12,000 miles in a 1959 Triumph TR3A, which replaced my previous well thrashed 1958 VW. As well as being used every day of the week as transport to and from work, the TR has been used most weekends in some form of motoring sport, namely driving tests, rallies, hill-climbs, sprints, and practice days, under which conditions the car has performed with commendable reliability. The only attention required so far has been a decoke, a new set of bearings, and a new set of piston rings for the engine (the old piston rings had broken up, due mainly I am sure to consistent gross over-revving, which indicates that the red line at 5,000 is meant to be observed), a complete new clutch assembly (the old one wasn't bad, but I have always considered a good clutch a worthwhile investment), and new rear springs, this work being done by myself.

The trouble is that I seem to be the only person who has any faith in the car. Whenever I enter the car for an event, without fail at least one uncomplimentary remark will be passed, usually of the form, "That's a real handful you've got there", or "You're a brave man entering that thing".

Why is this then? I can't say I've had a great deal of success with the car, but I have gained three class wins in driving tests, and a third in class at a recent very wet National hill-climb, when I beat a Porsche and an Elan. It is completely standard, the rear shockers are u/s, because so far new ones have proved unobtainable, and I run it on Cinturato tyres on the front, and Michelin ZX on the rear.

As long as a firm grip is kept on the steering wheel, and an eye on the revs., I don't see why a TR should give anyone any trouble. Furthermore, at a purchase price of £275, I feel it has been a reasonably cheap way of getting 100 m.p.h. performance, and a great deal of fun. So I admit to being rather mystified as to the reason why the TR is so unloved among spectators and fellow competitors alike. Perhaps someone can provide an explanation.

Incidentally, I expect my next car to be one of three: either a Healey 3000, a Sunbeam Tiger, or another TR.

Edinburgh.   DOUGLAS N. THOMSON.

· · · ·

Above: during the 1956 RAC Rally, these TR2s are seen at the Goodwood circuit, the car on the left clearly receiving some "fettling". Both these long-door cars carry the "add-on" rear reflectors, indicating that they have commission numbers below TS1308. However, despite being only two years old, both have also received the later three-piece rear-window hoods, perhaps explaining why the original type of hood is so rare today. An archaic breakdown truck adds to the vitntage scene, but what, one conjectures, is a "buffer depot?".

CHAPTER NINE:
More Sidescreen Miscellany

Continuing from Chapter Five, this Chapter brings to the reader more "miscellany" on the Sidescreen TR. Had it all been placed in a single chapter, I think you would have found it too much in one place. As a result, I've split it quite deliberately into two parts, which I hope will not detract from its interest value. It continues, then, with Item 39 of "Sidescreen TR Miscellany":-

39.   Introducing the TR to the USA - Reproduced in the Colour section is a fascinating early colour photograph showing the official introduction of the TR2 to the Californian market. Unfortunately, the colour faithfulness and reproduction is not perfect, but historical interest calls for its inclusion. The photograph was taken in the Embassy Hall of the Ambassador Hotel in Los Angeles at the beginning of January 1954, the opening of the presentation taking place on the 7th of that month. The display was organised jointly by Cal Sales Inc, the local distributors, and Standard-Triumph's export division, and as can be seen, a spectacular exhibition was mounted, including a replica of the TR2 shield badge six feet high made entirely of flowers! Five TR2s were shown, plus two Swallow Dorettis and a display TR2 chassis. This chassis must have been TS 20, the exhibition chassis originally built for the London Motor Show in October 1953, as it is the only "chassis without body" listed in the early build records. Where did it go, one wonders, and was it ever bodied?

As to the identities of the other TRs, the Olive Yellow car has a Blackberry tonneau fitted, so it must have been TS 43, 44 or 45, all of which had this specification and went to the USA. The Geranium car was TS3L, the White car was TS4L and the Ice Blue car was TS5L. The Black car was drawn from the batch TS53L to TS57L, although its exact identity cannot be ascertained. Two more intriguing things

spring to mind on perusal of the photograph - firstly the Geranium car appears to be fitted with sunvisors - never a listed accessory, at least in the literature I have seen, and secondly, the Black and Ice Blue cars appear not only to have wheel rim embellishers fitted, but also to have what appear to be red wheels or possibly tyres with red lines on them, for red is clearly visible on the wheels of both cars!

This January 1954 display was the official introduction of the TR to what was hoped would become its most important market and, in addition to the cars detailed above, several TR2s had reached California in 1953, including TS7. It is not known whether these were sold during 1953 or whether they were retained by Dealers as demonstration vehicles - I suspect the latter. In fact, I understand that TS5 and TS7 still survive on the West Coast of the USA, and if this is correct, it means that at least five out of the first ten production TR2s still exist, for TS1 is in the USA, TS2 is in the UK and TS9 is in Sweden, where it has been since new. Around 50 TR2s reached the various parts of the USA before the end of 1953, but only in the case of California is the actual state mentioned on the build records.

The East Coast introduction of the car took place after the California show, Standard-Triumph co-promoting this with Fergus Motors Inc. in New York on February 4th 1954, at Fergus Motors' own premises in Park Avenue. On 6th February the International Motor Sports Show started in New York, running until the 14th, and the TR2 display was one of the main attractions, many orders being taken. In fact, one US distributor was said to have been ready to take 100 cars a week for the whole of 1954! This equates to something over five thousand cars, more than were actually produced for all markets, so one feels he was a trifle ambitious! Lawrence

Pomeroy, a very well known motoring journalist of the day, wrote in "The Motor" that the black TR2 placed on a turntable and surrounded by a white pavilion was possibly the most imaginatively presented car at the show. Clearly, and as was proved by subsequent sales, the inauguration of the TR in the USA was a success.

40.   A good example of Standard-Triumph's recognition of the importance of the North American market for TR sales occurred annually between the years 1957 and 1962. Dave Thomas, a Triumph dealer from Long Beach, California, in conjunction with Cal-Sales Incorporated, the USA branch of the TSOA, and the Coventry factory Publicity Department, hit

The New York Motor Show in early 1959 shows a TR3A amid the signs of the Zodiac! Chrome wire wheels are evident on the car.

An aerial view taken at the 1959 New York Motor Show, showing, on the right hand side, the Triumph stand (TR Register Archive).

1

TRIUMPH

SPORTS OWNERS ASSOCIATION

RALLY OF EUROPE

by KEITH HOPKINS
Overseas Public Relations Officer,
The Standard Motor Co. Ltd.
and
Secretary,
T.S.O.A.

Any more for the s.s. *Dinard*? The Triumphs are driven aboard the cross-Channel steamer at Dover.

"Welcome to Belgium!" reads the banner as the rallyists arrive at the Franco-Belgian frontier at Veurne.

No doubt where this is. The Eiffel Tower and the Seine make a fitting Parisian background for the Triumphs arrayed on the right bank after their European trip.

A pause in the Alps for Mr. Leo Villa, the engineer who helped the late Sir Malcom Campbell and his son Donald to success, to photograph his car and his wife.

A study in "horsepower." An older form of transport ambles lazily past the Triumphs standing in Vienna.

A great welcome awaited the cars at Brussels. Here they are seen in the Place Rogier, Brussels' busiest square.

An extract from the "Standard Car Review" of May 1957, giving something of the flavour of the first TSOA Tour of Europe.

The chartered DC7c bringing the participants from the USA for the 1957 TSOA Tour of Europe is seen at London's Heathrow Airport. The lucky owners are encountering their new TRs for the first time.

on the idea of taking a group of US citizens, who were each prepared to order a new TR, over to the UK to take personal delivery of their individual vehicles. They would then lead them on a tour of the UK and parts of the continent of Europe. Naturally a visit to the factory was included, and the resultant photographs were used as excellent publicity to help sell cars. The TRs were given UK (Coventry) registrations under the personal export scheme whereby UK taxes did not need to be paid, the vehicles then being re-registered in the buyer's home state upon conclusion of the tour. The cars were almost all supplied with left hand drive, and it appears that between 30 and 50 TRs were involved on each occasion, most drivers having passengers but some going solo. The cost, including the price of the new car, was around $3,000, with a further $1,000 for a passenger.

For the first tour, in April 1957, it was considered of sufficient publicity value to warrant the company's official photographer, Frank Callaby, accompanying the cars, and he produced some superb photographs, a few of which were in colour. The continental part of the tour took in Brussels, Vienna, Innsbruck and Lucerne, 2,500 miles in all and covered six countries. The whole thing was said to have been well oversubscribed and thoroughly enjoyed, may of the participants evidently viewing the trip and the car purchase as the bargain of a lifetime! On the second day when the tour of the factory was taking place, many of the new owners took the opportunity to have further accessories fitted to their cars, the contemporary report stating that never had so many wing mirrors been fitted in so short a time! One near disas-

ter occurred that day, for one of the drivers forgot to drive on the left as he was leaving the factory and hit one of the factory trucks! The driver was unhurt, but the car suffered considerable frontal damage. However, a team of Triumph mechanics set to and worked throughout their lunch break, soon having the car fully rebuilt and ready to commence the continental part of the tour with the other participants.

The TR3s purchased by these USA buyers were presumably built in the early Spring of 1957 and in several of the photographs, details of the cars can be seen showing that they were fitted with separate rear flashing indicators in the TR3A style. This proves once and for all that overseas market TR3s had these items well before they were incorporated on home market cars. The later tours followed very much the same pattern, and were always heavily oversubscribed. By 1959, the continental mileage had grown to nearly 4,000, the tour taking four weeks and by 1960, ten countries in all were visited. In fact, so popular was the 1959 event that a second tour was run that year which used a different itinerary, this one involving in addition Denmark and parts of Sweden. The tours continued through 1961 and into 1962, when the final trip was promoted, the participants in that year using both TR3Bs and TR4s.

Strangely, I have never seen any record of Jaguar, or the British Motor Corporation with their MGs and Austin-Healeys, being involved in a similar jolly, so clearly it was an example of the enterprising Standard-Triumph Publicity Department stealing a march on their rivals. As an aside, the more one

A further shot taken on the 1957 TSOA Tour shows two TR3s in Switzerland. As can be seen, despite being TR3s and not TR3As, these USA-bound cars were fitted with separate flashing indicators at the rear.

delves into the various aspects of Standard-Triumph's Publicity Department during the 1950s, the more one realises how innovative and enterprising it was. Small wonder that the cars sold so well - for whatever its merits, the best product in the world will not sell if no-one knows about it! Triumph always had an eye to the main chance in the North American market, a policy which certainly paid off handsomely during the TR3A years. The publicity surrounding the six TSOA trips must have sold hundreds, if not thousands, of TRs in the USA.

41.   The 1955 Le Mans TR2s - Much has already been written over the years about these three vehicles the, famous 'PKV' cars - however,with the help of Jan Pearce, who has owned PKV374 for many years, I have been able to gather a little further background information. The technical details of the cars and their performance in the race have been well covered and I do not propose to repeat these aspects - however, what is not so well known is what happened to them afterwards, or that there was in fact a fourth car, PKV373.

Initially only two TRs were accepted for the race by the organisers, the third car (PKV374) being placed on the reserve list - indeed the factory's Competition Department did not expect it to get an entry, and so when a mere week prior to the race they were told that it could run after all as

there had been some withdrawals, it was prepared in a great hurry and the papers necessary for its reimportation back into England after the race were incomplete. This late acceptance explains why PKV 374 ran with the very high race number of 68, whereas PKV375 was number 29 and PKV376 was number 28. Immediately after the race, 375 and 376 came back to the UK but because its documentation was incomplete, 374 had to stay on in France for a long period. In fact it is believed it did not return to the UK until May 1956, virtually a year later. Quite where it was during this time, and whether it was actually impounded, is not certain. However, these circumstances have turned out to be fortuitous in that they allowed PKV 374 to survive unmodified from its race condition. PKV376 upon its arrival back in England was used during that Summer at several competitive events, including Shelsley Walsh hill climb and in the Tourist Trophy race that September; it is also believed to be the car that Ken Richardson used on the road for a period, and the one he took to Prescott Hill climb.

PKV375 upon its arrival home disappeared into the factory and I understand that it was stripped right down by the Works to see what effect 24 hours of racing had had on the various components. It does not seem to have been used again in its 'Le Mans' form but the evidence is (although I'm happy to be proved wrong) that following this stripping process the car was fully rebuilt by the factory and sold off to a private owner, most of the special racing components being removed and standard production ones being substituted. This car eventually came to light in a scrapyard in 1973, and Jan Pearce, by then the owner of 374, inspected it very thoroughly. It did not have the large 22 gallon petrol tank, it had drum brakes all round rather than discs at the front as raced, and nor were the oversized Alfin drums still on the rear axle. The body did not have evidence of holes in the boot floor to accommodate the larger fuel tank, and nor was there evidence of the oversized 'Le Mans' style filler cap. Upon looking underneath, Pearce could find no sign of the "quick lift" type jacking points known to have been fitted to this car's chassis, and thus he had to conclude that the rebuilding by the Works was so thorough as to have obliterated almost all trace of its history.

The only non standard item Pearce could find was the fact that the near side door was skinned in aluminium and not in steel as normal. The scrapyard owner was aware of the car's pedigree , and as Jan recalls wanted something like £250 for it, a not inconsiderable sum 20 years ago for a TR in poor condition, even one with historic connections, so Jan was unable to add it to his stable. As to what happened to PKV 375, it is believed to have been purchased in the mid 1970's by an enthusiast who intended to rebuilt it. By then, the original engine had become separated from the car, the engine being said to have been fitted to a TR2 in the Carlisle area. Nothing certain is known by the TR Register as to 375's fate beyond the late 1970's, but evidently in around 1977, the registration number was transferred from the TR2 to a new car and is now believed to be void.

The greatest puzzle is what happened to PKV376, the TT car. Despite diligent searching by myself and others, no trace of

the car has been found, and nothing is known of its history subsequent to 1955 - was it rebuilt, as was 375, at the end of the season and then sold off? Alternatively, was it sold off still in its Le Mans form? Ken Richardson could not recall its fate, but as the TR3 came out at the end of the 1955 season and the TR2 would have been perceived as an outdated model, it seems highly likely that it was sold off shortly following the TT race. Jan Pearce seems to recall the UK licensing authorities confirmed in the early 1970's that the car was then still in existence, although as is their usual practice, they would not reveal ownership. A recent enquiry of the Driver and Vehicle Licencing Centre has elicited that no car bearing the registration number PKV 376 is currently registered on their computer, so it seems unlikely that 376 has survived, unless of course it was exported from the UK at some time.

At this point, the mystery surrounding the fate of these 'PKV' cars deepens, for I uncovered the following advertisement, printed in "Autosport" of 15th August 1958. I quote the advert verbatim: "Immaculate TR2, late property of King Hussein of Jordan and still bearing his personal emblem. Raced as one of the Triumph Works team cars at the 1955 Le Mans, but not since. Kept in almost concours condition and maintained regardless of cost by fastidious owner. Extras include disc brakes front, Alfin rears, special overdrive (3500 at 100 mph) heater, 'X' tyres, H6 carbs, magnificent radio, 17 gallon tank and a host of extras. Specially upholstered in blue and white leather, special bodywork in blue/white, hardtop and tonneau - only one like it in the country, 21000 genuine miles, never bent or pranged - price £750."

Now assuming the foregoing details are correct, King Hussein must have purchased one of the 'PKV' cars, but which one? PKV 376 had disc brakes all round, rather than

One of the few post-Le Mans public outings for PKV 376 was at Shelsley Walsh Hill Climb in 1955. The car was entered for two drivers, Ken Richardson (seen here in the car) and Mrs Cherry Osborn (Fred Nicklin).

only on the front wheels, so presumably it was 374 or 375. Jan Pearce has not been able to uncover the 1950's history of his car following its re-importation in 1956, so maybe this was the King's car, but equally, because nothing is known of 375 either, it too may have been the Royal vehicle. In fact, it seems to me more likely that it was 375, for this was fully rebuilt by the Works prior to sale, and so may well have been re-upholstered and resprayed. If it was 375 however, how did it come to be in a northern scrapyard 15 years later missing all the special items listed in the advertisement? As the reader can see, there is more to discover about these cars, and the writer is engaged on further research. A letter written to King Hussein brought forth a reply from his office that all the 1950s records had been destroyed. Furthermore, the last surviving member of his 1950s garage staff who would have recalled the car had died but a few months prior to my enquiry.

I asked Jan Pearce how he came by PKV374, which incidentally he has almost finished rebuilding to its Le Mans condition. It was, he told me, advertised for sale in "Motorsport" magazine in November 1972 and stated to be a Le Mans car by its then owner. No price was quoted, so Jan offered a hopeful £100, about as much as he could muster at the time, and the market value in 1972 of a tatty TR2! The owner wanted somewhat somewhat more and a deal was evidently struck at £115, Jan Pearce having the receipt to this day! Due presumably to its sojourn in France referred to above, it still, in 1972, had most of its original racing fittings, and these have been carefully preserved and incorporated in the rebuild. The commission number of this car is TS 5691-0 and that of PKV375 Jan recorded when he saw it as being TS 5582, again with an "0" suffix for overdrive. Jan even has a copy of the original licence application form for his car as made by the Works. The exact commission number of 376 is unknown, but must have been somewhere in the mid 5,000's. The mystery car, PKV373, was numbered TS 5486-0. As to PKV 373, many years ago I received a letter from a TR Register member, Keith Perrett, who had owned this car in the 1966/67 period. It was fitted with disc brakes, overdrive but not wire wheels. Perrett was unaware at the time that his car might be anything unusual, but he confirmed that it was always much faster than the average TR, so much so that he thought that there was something amiss with the other sidescreen TRs he drove subsequently! During his ownership there were no engine problems, so he had no cause to investigate the extent of its modifications, but a genuine 120 mph proved possible in overdrive. I have a poor quality photograph of this vehicle in my collection and the registration number can just be discerned, evidencing its existence beyond doubt. It seems most likely that this was a Works proving or development vehicle for the Le Mans modifications, principally to the cylinder head and brakes, and

was probably used as a track and road-going test bed prior to the race in June 1955. After all, the factory would be most unlikely to want to wear our their three race cars prior to the actual event, so it would make sense to have a development vehicle and I suspect that PKV 373 was it.

42.   Delivery - I have managed to find several photographs indicating how new cars reached their owners, some by road, some by rail, most by ship to the USA and some even by air! The car transporter lorry came into general use in the UK at around the time the TR2 came out, although in those days they generally carried only four cars rather than the 16 or even 20 one sees on a transporter and trailer today! In fact, certain trucks taking TR3As to the docks for shipment to the USA actually carried six cars, these being "crated" in open crates with the windscreens and weather equipment unfitted. These crates were evidently loaded direct into the ship's hold, stacked several rows high so as to maximise the use of space. The crates were collapsible when empty, thus when returning very little space was required. Interestingly, the tractor unit is a Commer, for although Standards did built light commercials, they made nothing sufficiently heavy. This picture dates from 1959, when up to 2,000 TR3As a month were crossing the Atlantic, so clearly new methods of bulk transport such as these crates were required.

A February 1956 photograph shows a privately-owned transporter with a new TR3 on board, together with several Standard saloon cars. This one, with a Seddon tractor unit,

TRs are "boxed" to make them easy to handle and as space-efficient as possible for shipping. A Commer transporter is used here to take six USA-bound cars to the docks. The "boxes" can be collapsed for easy return when empty.

KEEPING PACE . . .

An early purpose-built car transporter with a Seddon tractor unit takes a TR3 and other Company products from the factory to the premises of Somerset Motors Limited in Taunton (TR Register Archive).

A new early TR2 (note the small rear window,) is loaded on to a Silver City Airways Bristol Freighter at Lympne Airport in Kent during March 1954. It was being delivered with others to US Forces personnel stationed in Continental Europe (TR Register Archive).

belonged to an enterprising dealer, Somerset Motors of Taunton, who used it to collect new cars direct from the factory. Cars could of course be collected direct from the works by individual owners by special arrangement, though orders had to be processed by distributors and dealers to ensure that they got their "cut." The more enthusiastically minded owners tended to do this, and could, if they were lucky, be treated to a Works tour and lunch on the Company!

Picking up one's own car from the factory had the ancillary advantage that it would not have been "overdriven" by a delivery driver anxious to get home early, an important point in the days when running-in was a matter of more importance than it appears to be now. Although cars were, as can be seen, increasingly being delivered on transporters, a great many UK supplied vehicles were still delivered on trade plates by individual delivery drivers employed by the company, and thus could have quite a few miles on the clock when handed over to the first owner. On occasions, as can be seen in one photograph, air was used as a stage in delivery, in this case where cars were supplied to Continental Europe. An early TR2 is seen being swallowed by a Bristol Freighter for the journey across the Channel to France. As relatively few cars were supplied to the Continent, it was not usually worth sending them by transporter and in any event this was before the days of roll-on, roll-off ferries carrying large lorries, so cars were still swung onto ships by cranes and slings. Cars for European destinations were therefore sometimes driven on an individual basis to their destination,

and thus could have many hundreds of miles behind them before the purchaser even saw them!

Trains were also used, individual cars sometimes being sent long distances mounted on flat railway trucks marshalled within ordinary goods trains. Bulk carrying by train was also

A TR3 consigned to Continental railway transport shows the method by which many TRs travelled across Europe to meet their owners.

utilised, especially to get vehicles for the USA in large quantities from Coventry to the various docks at Liverpool, London Southampton and Cardiff. One picture showing this was taken in May 1960 at Cardiff Docks, and shows a consignment of TR3As bound for the USA. As can be seen, dummy wooden "bumpers" were fitted, and the brightwork, hoods and windscreens were not fitted, being placed in the footwells of the individual vehicles. The photograph showing TR2s in a ship's hold demonstrates how tightly they were packed, and dates from 5 or 6 years earlier. These cars have bumpers and windscreens fitted, and look much more vulnerable than the TR3As. One imagines that quite a lot of

rectification work was necessary upon arrival in the USA after a rough Atlantic crossing! Cars for the West and South of the USA were usually shipped direct to West Coast and Southern USA ports, but even then they may have still been many hundreds of miles from their new owners' homes. Delivery was completed by rail, truck or, on occasions, by the car itself being driven to the buyer, arriving with many of the all-important running-in miles already completed. At all events, the logistics of transporting many thousands of TRs each year from Central England to all the various states of the USA and Canada must have been complicated, and is an aspect of TR production that I for one had not considered previously!

43   Marathons and Records - In the early days of the TR, quite a number of records were attempted, usually successfully, the Publicity Department at Canley being quick as usual to make the most of the particular effort. I have already written of the duel between the TR3 and the light aircraft, but others have come to light. For instance, in 1954 two gentlemen, R B James and C P Nichols, decided that it would be possible to cover 1,000 miles in 24 hours on Britain's notoriously slow roads. The vehicle involved was ORW 600, one of the very first TR2s. In order to appreciate the difficulty of this feat, one has to think oneself back into the road and traffic conditions obtaining in this country at that time, when motorways did not exist, by-passes were rare and to average more than 30 mph on a cross country journey was considered to be doing well. Messrs James and Nichols managed in their TR to average 41.79 mph throughout the 24 hours, covering in the process 1,003 miles at a fuel consumption of 37.28 miles per gallon.

In the Summer of 1956, a further "24 hour" record was

A rare photograph, taken in the Summer of 1957 at Liverpool Docks, showing TR3s lined up prior to being shipped to the USA. The car in the foreground is red, but the remainder seem all to be White (Brian Pugh).

Shown at the finish of the "Three Peaks" Challenge Run are the three TRs involved. The two TR3s were lent by the Factory's Publicity Department, but TR2 VNW 11 was privately owned. Note the headlamp hoods! (BMIHT).

attempted. This involved the climbing (not in a TR!) of the three highest peaks in England, Scotland and Wales within 24 hours; it had in fact been done before, and the existing record stood at 22 hours 38 minutes. The speed with which the mountaineering participants could be rushed between Snowdon in Wales, Scafell Pike in the English Lakes and Ben Nevis in Scotland was paramount, and fast cars were called for. Not surprisingly, TRs were chosen, three such cars being required to carry the mountaineers and their gear. One car, a TR2 registered VNW 11 was privately owned, but the two TR3s sported Coventry registrations, leading me to believe that the Standard-Triumph publicity department probably lent them. Certainly RKV 335 was a car known to be on the publicity fleet, being a very early, hard top equipped, TR3, and a veteran of the 1956 "Motor" magazine road test. The third car was a TR3 registered RVC 205.

Once the plans of the TR equipped mountain-climbers became known, a second team challenged them and the attempt became a true race. The TR chaps started at the foot of Snowdon on the stroke of midnight, 23rd May 1956, whereas the challengers set off at the same time from Ben Nevis in Scotland. It had been calculated in advance that approximately 12 hours driving and 12 hours climbing ought to be required, but in order actually to beat the existing record, a considerable shortening of these times would be necessary. Almost 500 miles of driving was involved, and the team of TRs proved more than a match for the occasion, reaching 100 mph on several stretches of road. The three peaks were duly climbed, Ben Nevis being the final one, and the mission was accomplished by 4.30 pm the next day, slashing the record by some six hours. The challengers were soundly beaten, the TRs averaging more than 31 mpg and better than 46 mph, good going indeed as each of the three mountains in those days was approached by many

miles of rough and narrow roads.

Another record attempt in a TR at around the same time involved a TR2 registered VHT 911. This car belonged to a publican from Bristol, a Mr Cecil Jay, and he was bet by some of his customers that he could not drive it all around Britain's 3,700 mile coastline in 7 days, a feat that had not been attempted previously. The bet was for a pint of beer for himself and his co-driver Mr Eddie Wood, so clearly the principle rather than the prize was the driving force. Despite the run taking place in mid-Summer, the participants were hampered by snow in Northern Scotland, the average speed dropping at one period to as low as 13 mph. To compensate, over 800 miles were covered on another day, and do remember that this was not a dash down main roads

VHT 911 was the car used for the "Round Britain's Coastline for a Pint" Run, described in the text. Cecil Jay is seen on the left, with Mrs Jay, and co-driver Eddie Wood is on the right.

between cities, but a trip around Britain's notoriously winding coastal routes, keeping as close to the sea as practicable.

The attempt was commenced at 7.00 am one Sunday morning in mid 1956, the plan being to be back in his pub in Bristol prior to "last orders" being called at 10.30 pm the following Saturday evening. In fact, after a hard run including taking no sleep at all on a couple of nights in order to make up time, they arrived back in Bristol at 6.45 pm that Saturday evening to a hero's welcome and not one but several pints of beer. Over the whole journey, the average speed during the time that they were actually driving worked out at 34 mph, and it was still 23 mph taking the week as a whole including all sleeping and stopping time! Fuel consumption, as was by then expected of a TR2, was staggeringly good at 38.9 mpg, something over 92 gallons being used. Mr Jay stated that the car had required no attention of any sort other than petrol, oil and water, and that they had cruised at around 60/65 mph whenever possible, the maximum reached being 108 mph. Asked whether they would do it again, these redoubtable drivers not only confirmed that they would ,but that they thought that they could knock a day and a half off the time "if we went the other way round."

Perhaps an even more staggering feat in a TR was performed in early 1957, when a Mr A T Rajah from Kuala Lumpur drove his hard top equipped TR2 single handedly the 12,000 miles from Singapore to London in 36 days, 12,317 miles to be precise, an average of 342 miles a day! This feat was accomplished with no advanced publicity nor Works support, the first that the company heard of it being when a Standard-Triumph executive in the City of London happened by chance to see the red, dusty and dented TR2 in city traffic! He flagged the driver down because the car had "Singapore-to London - 12,000 miles" written on its black hardtop, and

Mr Rajah, hero of the Singapore-to-London drive in his TR2, poses following the completion of his epic 12,000-mile trip.

Mr Rajah told him the story. He was duly invited up to Coventry and entertained by the company, acquiring a new TR3 for shipment back to Kuala Lumpur! The report does not state whether Mr Rajah had to buy this or was awarded it - maybe he purchased it on favourable terms, for Standard-Triumph's were not known to be **that** generous! Also one wonders whether they held onto his TR2 for mechanical investigation - again the report is unclear.

Some of the trials and tribulations of this trip bear repeating, such as having to light small fires in the TR2's front apron air intake to prevent total freezing of the engine in the Iranian deserts, where he ran into snow and icy winds. He had on other occasions actually to build his own road from brushwood and stones, the worst day being in Iran where he managed to cover only 54 miles in 11 hours. At the foot of Mount Ararat he had an enforced halt for two days for the car was frozen solid, and his fingers were so numb that he couldn't operate the door catch! One wonders whether he was stuck inside or outside the car during this period! Asked at Coventry what he thought about this epic journey in retrospect, he modestly stated that it was "somewhat tougher than I had expected!" Petrol consumption worked out at 26.5 mpg, by no means bad taking into account the many hours of first and second gear work, and mechanical defects were reported to be nil!

The Standard Review magazine refers briefly to two further sidescreen TR marathons; firstly, in the Spring of 1954 a Mr F. Oxley set out in a TR2 to visit all the (then) 48 States in the USA in 21 days. He covered 14181 miles, and completed his run in 20 days 22 hours, which included a 2½ day delay caused by accident repairs. His average speed was just over 50 mph, and fuel consumption was 33 miles per US Gallon. Secondly, a 1955 TR2, registration number SOC 866, was used in 1958 for a successful overland run from London to Capetown. A hardtop was fitted, with an extra fuel tank mounted on the roof, and the two drivers, Mr Power and Mr Wickens endured many hardships. These included having to drive 1200 miles with a broken rear spring, and having to tow a broken down vehicle for nearly 200 miles. This London - Capetown trip was said to be only part of a 'Round the World' trip in the TR, but as to whether this was ever completed, I can find no reference.

TRs were also used to race passengers carried in commercial airlines on occasions, from London to Brussels and London to Paris inter-alia, and I'm sure that there were also many other instances of these rapid and rugged cars performing outstanding feats of endurance.

44.   Economy runs - The extreme fuel efficiency of the early TRs is both well-known and has been referred to in many places in this book. However, officially observed

economy runs put the matter beyond all doubt and speculation, and in 1955 Mobil, the petrol company, inaugurated their "Mobilgas economy run." This event, in its first year, allowed economy tuning to take place, and also allowed coasting with a "dead" engine, a practice of doubtful safety that was outlawed in subsequent years. A TR2 won this first event outright, pitted against various small saloons and tiny "economy" vehicles, for it covered a varied route (including Welsh mountain roads) of some 600 miles at just better than 71 mpg! The winning car was a long-door TR2, registered SYA176, and the driver was Richard Bensted-Smith, as referred to in Chapter 8. As to the tuning involved for this economy run, the Engineering Department at Canley advised Bensted-Smith that the valves be carefully ground in, a special "hot" thermostat be fitted, and that the carburettors be given "weak" needles. Tyres were inflated very hard to reduce rolling resistance (and presumably grip!). Upon giving his analysis after the event as to how a two litre sports car was able to win outright against vehicles designed specifically for economy, Bensted-Smith put it down to the fact that the torque from the engine enabled it to pull the TR up hills in high gear. He also alluded to the "excellent brakes" which enabled long periods of "coasting" to be safely indulged in. As the TR2s always had something of a reputation for brake fade, at least when driven hard and in competitions, this statement leaves one wondering just what the brakes of an average family saloon in the 1950's were like!

In June 1956, the Mobil economy run took place again, this year with somewhat tightened regulations. Again, the winner of the all-comers class was a TR, and significantly a long-

door car was used, by then 2 years old, as the later cars never had quite the same frugality of fuel use. The drivers were Mr G Heaps and Mr A C Slade, and the car was registered JUH3, another TR used in many different types of competition. They covered a 640 mile route using almost exactly ten gallons of fuel, averaging 64.06 m.p.g., slightly down on the previous year due to the ban on "dead engine" coasting, but still pretty good. The car's fuel system was officially sealed, and RAC observers patrolled the route, so these mpg figures cannot have been other than genuine. Rather surprisingly, although the published road tests of sidescreen TRs almost always remarked on their economy, the Company's Publicity Department was uncharacteristically reluctant to use this as a selling point in their UK advertising; maybe they felt that such stress on economy was bad for the sporting image they were otherwise promoting!

45. The "Ferodo" test car - JDB 361 was a 1955 TR2 described as can be seen in the reproduction of the Ferodo advert, as "the car with the built in brain." Ferodo Ltd wanted a high speed vehicle to use as a mobile test bed with which to record and analyse brake performance, and they chose a TR2 as their guinea pig. As the car involved bore not a Coventry registration but one from Stockport, near to the Ferodo Works at Chapel-en-le-Frith, one must presume that they purchased the car themselves rather than that they were lent one by Standard-Triumph's. This vehicle was kitted out with a plethora of special equipment and it was test driven and described by John Bolster for "Autosport" magazine in mid-1956. It had a generator mounted at the rear of the gearbox thus producing an accurate record of speed and

Mr G Heaps and Mr AC Slade display period all-weather gear at the finish of the Mobilgas Economy Run of 1956. They had just won the Allcomers' Class outright in this TR2, JUH 3, averaging 64 miles per gallon!

The car with a Built-in brain

This car of the Ferodo Test Fleet is packed with equipment to record and analyze brake performance. For, when arranging schedules for tests, Ferodo research workers must know what a brake lining is expected to do under practical conditions, and that is what these instruments tell them.

There is a high-speed multi-pen recorder which notes four parameters of brake performance: speed, deceleration, brake drum temperature and rate at which work is done at the brakes.

This information is collected electronically, and used by Ferodo to devise accurate, reliable testing schedules that help to produce brake linings highly resistant to fade and wear.

The electronic calculating unit installed in the boot of the TR.2.

FERODO
ANTI-FADE Brake Linings

The power pack for the electronic apparatus, on the right of which may be seen some of the intricate cable connections.

FERODO LIMITED · CHAPEL-EN-LE-FRITH *A Member of the Turner & Newall Organisation*

distance. Various electronic recording devices were mounted in the boot, these being powered by a supplementary battery in the passenger's footwell.

Four separate pens, one coupled electronically to each brake, recorded continuously on a strip of paper the force and duration of each braking application, the results being minutely analysed at the Ferodo works thereafter. All sorts of different drivers and driving techniques were employed, and wear on the brakes and the heat generated were monitored. Bolster was let loose in this TR on a mountainous circuit in the Derbyshire Peak District, and confessed to "braking deliberately late and hard for corners in an attempt (unsuccessful) to get the brakes to fade." The presence of wire wheels and their aid to cooling must I feel have had something to do with this lack of fade, and even descending the A57 Snake Pass at 100 mph evidently failed to cause the TR to become brakeless - maybe Ferodo Ltd had fitted some top-secret linings for Mr Bolster's drive?

46. "Customising" your TR - this was a very popular sport in the 50's and 60's, although one which is frowned upon today when "originality", whatever that is, is a target to be aimed at in concours competitions. As a representative example of the lengths to which owners would go to make their cars either "different" or more convenient, I feel I can do no better than to reproduce a two page picture article from the Standard Car Review magazine of February 1956. The car involved was a TR2 registered NFH 33, the owner being a Major M G Burges-Short. Many of the items are genuinely useful, as anyone who has covered a reasonable mileage in a sidescreen TR will know, but one or two cause a smile or a raised eyebrow, such as the hinged front number plate "to avoid damage when parking or turning" - one wonders

Above: Ferodo Limited's advertisement features the TR2, JDB 361. The company used this as their brake test car.

Right: John Bolster sits in JDB 361 prior to a test drive to see if he could make the brakes fade. Part of the test equipment is visible between the front seats ("Autosport").

THE STANDARD CAR REVIEW   *February, 1956*

Some alter

64

Above and opposite are seen two pages from the "Standard Car Review" detailing the many modifi-cations to Major Burges-Short's TR2.

ations to a TR2

Major M. G. Burges-Short, who is this month's enthusiast, has obviously had considerable motoring experience. He has very definite ideas about the extras he needs on his car. The various modifications and additions which he has effected on his TR2 to suit his personal requirements are illustrated on these pages. The Major is a member of the Triumph Sports Owners' Association.

1. Switch and light for under-bonnet work, reading dipstick, etc.

2. Lockable tool box bolted to bulkhead platform.

3. Windscreen washer bottle and knob.

4. Plastic quart bottle for multi-grade oil, with spring-retaining loop.

5. Starting handle in clips.

6. Front number plate suspension on brass hinges ; this allows the plate to swing 90° either way and avoids damage from stones or banks when parking or turning. It is difficult to clean the bumper behind the plate when mounted in the usual way.

7. Driving mirror mounted on scuttle which looks neater and is easier to see than the usual position on the wing.

8. Vynide covered sponge rubber pad on door to stop right knee rubbing against sharp corner of side screen socket.

9. Pocket for maps with torch clipped alongside.

10. Extensions to de-mister slots to make hot air cover larger area of screen.

11. Map light.

12. Hinged mirror for passengers.

13. Breather pipe for master cylinder filler. This prevents the top of the cylinder becoming oily and from accumulating dust.

14. Access plate in transmission tunnel for over-drive solenoid, accumulator and pump delivery valve.

15. Access plates for removing and cleaning over-drive valves.

I have also fitted an ex-R.A.F. clock with chrome rim added.

I think that items 14 and 15 are very useful and save a lot of time in the event of trouble with the over-drive.

Item 13, though a little thing, contributes to the ease of keeping the engine room clean.

whether the Major was in the habit of "parking by feel" - or maybe he just drove furiously on night rallies! The car appears to be fitted with a non-standard gear lever knob, which he does not comment upon, and one vital item he omitted is something to stop the dreaded "handbrake-on-left-leg rubbing" that all drivers of right hand drive TRs know so well. Maybe he had a foam pad attached to his left trouser leg by a stout leather strap!

47.   TRs and the famous - The Publicity Department lost no opportunities here, and I have uncovered quite a number of photographs of well-known people, from the Duke of Edinburgh to Santa Claus, posing in or beside sidescreen

TRs. A superb contemporary colour shot, reproduced in the colour section of the book, of a Works Publicity Department TR2 has surfaced, the car being PDU 730 (TS 2090) finished in British Racing Green with brown trim. This car was depicted on the front cover of the June 1955 Standard Car Review, and shows film star Eva Bartok with film producer Michael Carreras. They were filming "Break in the Circle," the TR featuring in the action. It seems a little strange that the factory were loaning out what was an "outdated" model for such a high-profile event, for the short-door TR2 came out in October 1954, yet this car was the earlier model. This colour shot is all the more interesting as it shows the correct shade of BRG (not too dark - always assuming that the colour rendition of the original film was reasonably accurate) and also it shows how the wheels were painted (on TR2s and TR3s) to match the bodywork.

As a complete contrast to film stars, the popular pianist of the 1950's, Semprini, was photographed inspecting under the bonnet of a TR2 in March 1954, and as a further complete contrast, Communist politician Herr Grotewohl, then the President of the East German Republic, was pictured at the Leipzig trade fair in 1955 closely examining a red TR2 with wire wheels. In fact, he did more than this, for he purchased this car after the show for his wife's use, and it must at the time have been the only TR - possibly the only modern British sports car - in that Country.

In view of import and currency restrictions, one can only speculate as to how they got on for spares, and what 70 octane petrol did for the TR's engine - maybe the Party laid on a special supply of high octane spirit! As an aside and an interesting sequel to this, Grotewohl must have liked his TR2, for he later purchased an early TR3A. This was mainly used by his daughter, and it was maintained in a

Above: SWK 772 was a Publicity Department TR3, seen here in the foyer of the Gaumont Cinema in Coventry, helping to advertise "Checkpoint", a motor racing film. The car is made to look like a racer with number discs and an aero screen (TR Register Archive).

TR2 PDU 730 is seen on location during the filimng of "Break in the Circle" in 1954. Actor Forrest Tucker is shown at the wheel, posing in front of a brace of classic petrol pumps.

President of the East German Republic, Herr Grotewohl, inspects a new red TR2 at a Central European Trade Fair in 1955. As related in the text, he later purchased this acrual car for personal use (TR Register Archive).

Government workshop with parts supplied via Switzerland! A correspondent has told me the story of how this TR3A later came to leave East Germany in interesting circumstances, but it cannot be repeated in print! As to the fate of the red TR2 one can only wonder!

Racing drivers and rally drivers of course frequently appeared in TRs, but one lady TR driver who was at the time famous mainly for being the sister of Stirling, Britain's most illustrious driver, was Pat Moss. Pat had started her driving career at the wheel of a TF MG, but this was awfully slow when compared with the new generation of Austin-Healey and Triumph TR sports cars, and thus in late 1954 she acquired a new TR2. This was one of the first short-door cars, TS 4376, registered VFM 377, and a car that still survives today. It was used by her as her road car throughout 1955, and was campaigned successfully during the 1955 season in all manner of competitions. It evidently rejoiced in the nick-

name of "Fruity" an epithet occasioned by its typical TR exhaust note!

Another young lady to pose in a TR, was singing star Petula Clarke, seen in the photograph looking most fetching in a TR2. This picture was evidently taken when she visited "the Manchester Triumph dealers", presumably Hollingdrakes. Another "television personality" was Macdonald Hobley, the well-known BBC announcer and presenter. He was pictured in 1955 with Autosport's John Bolster and Works Publicity Department hardtop TR3 RVC 204. Hobley and Bolster were presenting "The Television Motor Show" from the RAC Country Club in Surrey.

The author has a clear childhood memory of this annual programme which took place just prior to the opening of the London Motor Show, and in which the latest models (in both senses!) were paraded around the grounds of the RAC's establishment for the benefit of TV viewers. Incidentally, the same car was driven by King Hussein of Jordan at Goodwood that year at the Motor Show test day, presumably to compare the latest TR3 with his own TR2. On the subject of the "Television Motor Show" programme, in October 1953 the road test car OHP 771 was used to demonstrate the new TR2 to viewers, although which TR (if any) was used for the 1954 programme I have not been able to discover. The 1953 show came from Kenwood House in Hampstead, North London, and featured actor (Sir) John Mills in the TR.

TRs were also given as prizes on occasions to lucky recipients, one such being the 1955 winner of the "Miss World" contest, Susanna Duijm from Venezuela. She received a brand new TR3 provided by Lex Garages, London Triumph Dealers, and is pictured posing with it, the report also saying that she appeared at the Motor Show on the Standard-Triumph stand. In 1956 a similar prize was given to that year's Miss World, who came from Western Germany. A slightly less glamorous competition to feature a TR as a prize was the 100th edition of one of the earliest of television's game shows, "Take Your Pick". The car was registered as

Pat Moss takes delivery of her new TR2 at the Standard-Triumph factory in November 1954. Although picked up at the Works, the car carris the Chester registration number VFM 377, as it was supplied via Chester-based dealer Denis Done. In this photograph, Pat is seen with Bernard Roberts (left) of the Company's Sales Department, Denis Done and Ken Gregory (right), who was Stirling Moss's manager. Alongside can be seen Stirling's own Standard Eight, fitted with a tuned Standard Ten engine and Borrani wire wheels ("Autosport").

Top left: singing star Petula Clark poses in a new TR2 at Hollingdrakes of Manchester early in 1955 (BMIHT).

Below left: "Miss World 1955", Susanna Duijm from Venezuela, won a new TR3 as part of her prize. She is seen here seated in the car, which was supplied by Lex Garages of London.

Below right: 6 MMK, the 1959 TR3A, now owned by Mike Ellis, is seen here when new, having been given away on the "Take Your Pick" television game show by Michael Miles. Mr EG Atkins, the lucky winner, is seen in the centre. The picture was taken at Standard-Triumph's London depot and shows Michael Miles on the right.

6MMK, a TR3A commission number TS 27538. It was won by a Mr E G Atkins and the lucky fellow can be seen receiving it from the show's host, Michael Miles. This car was later purchased by Mike Ellis, a founder member of the TR Register and one of the club's early Treasurers - he still has it, and had no idea of its history until so informed by the Author!

A further German politician to be seen in a TR was Herr Willy Brandt, at the time (1958) Mayor of West Berlin. He visited Coventry and was entertained at the Standard-Triumph Works; maybe this was a political compensation to counter-act publicity given to East German Herr Grotewohl when he

bought a TR2! In 1957 the first of Britain's old colonies to be given its independence was the Gold Coast, becoming the new country of Ghana. The Publicity Department swung into action, and Miss Ghana was invited to Coventry and given the full Works tour, plus a 100 mph ride in a TR3, this all being part of her prize for winning the Miss Ghana contest. Unfortunately for her, she did not actually win the car! Also in 1957 the Duke of Edinburgh was seen with a TR3, the occasion being his visit to the Motor Industry Research Association Proving Ground near Nuneaton. The report at the time says that the Duke drove himself round the banked track at 100 mph - it doesn't actually say that he was driving the TR rather than something else, but that is the innuendo!

At the end of that year, the Publicity Department lent SKV655, a former road-test TR3, for a tour of Coventry by Father Christmas himself, in full regalia and with the hood down - the car's, not his! As I have said, the Company rarely missed any form of publicity opportunity, however bizarre - this must have been the slowest public appearance by one of the "SKV" Works owned TR3s! Sports personalities were not neglected either, the then world mile record holder Herb Elliott of Australia being invited to the Coventry works by the company, himself ordering a TR3A shortly after that event. Another athletics star of the time to own TRs was Christopher Brasher, as mentioned in paragraph 10 of Chapter 5. Brasher became engaged to Miss Shirley Bloomer, a leading British tennis player of the late 1950's, and the couple were photographed with a TR3A which looked to have been VWK610, a Works rally car.

Leading British golfer of the day Harry Weetman, renowned at the time as having the longest drive in golf, ran a TR3 as personal transport, and is seen posing with it at Palm Springs Golf Course in Florida, and Stirling Moss, who needs no introduction, was also seen in TRs. In particular he was photographed driving OHP 677 at Oulton Park Circuit in early 1954, where he was said to be "advising the Company on any alterations necessary to the TR!" Finally Mike Hawthorn, World motor racing champion in 1958, was photographed many times in various TRs, both in publicity shots and also actually using the cars. In the featured picture Hawthorn is engaged in a bizarre televised indoor driving test competition that took place on 8th November 1958. The TR3A Mike is driving cannot be identified unfortunately, but was almost

Mike Hawthorn accelerates away during the indoor driving tests that took place for the benefit of television in November 1958. His Works TR3A, for some reason, carried rather effete wheel discs! ("Autosport").

Chris Brasher, Olympic Gold Medallist, is seen with his fiancee, Shirley Bloomer, a tennis star of the time. The car is VWK 610, a former Works vehicle, presumably loaned to Brasher for the Monte Carlo Rally of 1959. He personally owned ex-Works TR3 TRW 735, but for some reason used VWK 610 instead (TR Register).

certainly a Works owned vehicle, though the presence of wheel discs seems a strange anomaly.

This event was promoted by the Hagley and District Light Car Club, and took place inside a huge industrial building in Staffordshire, specially lit for television. Mike had at the time just become World Champion, so there was considerable public interest. One of the tests involved a match between Hawthorn in the 3A and Ken Rawlings in his old trials car "Buttercup", which was one of the fore-runners of the TR (see Chapter One). Both cars covered the same course flat out for the benefit of TV, Hawthorn winning by some six seconds! This may well have been Mike Hawthorn's last run in a TR, for within a few weeks, he was dead.

48.   The Army Team - A little-known TR fact is that in 1958 the factory prepared three additional TR3As for the gruelling Liege-Rome-Liege rally, known as the Marathon de la Route, in addition to the four normal Works team rally cars. These extra cars, registered VVC 288, VVC 289 and VVC 290, were factory owned, and were prepared for and lent to the British Army Motoring Association team, based at the Army Mechanical Transport School at Bordon in Hampshire. They were not competing directly with the Works cars, for all three had "normal" 1991 cc engines, whereas the four Works cars were by then running with 2,138 cc engines, hence the Army team cars were in the under 2 litre class.

The Army team met with some success, for VVC 288, driven by Lt Colonel "Bing" Crosby and Major Robin Holmes won

VVC 290 was one of three Army Team TR3As described in the text. Here the team poses at the start of the Liege-Rome-Liege Rally in 1958. Major Holmes and Lieut-Col Crosby (second and fourth from the left) won the 2-Litre Category in VVC 288 (Mike Hazlewood).

the up to 2 litre class, and was in fact the only car to finish at all in that class. Out of a total of 96 starters in the Rally, only 22 cars finished, three of these being TR3As, for two of the Works cars finished fifth and sixth overall respectively. The remaining two Army 3As retired, although the reports do not say from what cause.

Although I have not been able to find further references to this "Army" team in contemporary motoring magazines, I gather from correspondence shown to me by Mike Hazlewood of the TR Register that the cars were used in 1959 as well as 1958, and that the team competed in the Monte Carlo, Tulip, R.A.C., German and Geneva Rallies of the period, although not presumably with any particular success or the Works Publicity Department would have made this known. In overall charge of the team was Lt. Colonel Crosby, and the idea was that suitably qualified Army personnel would drive the cars in rotation, a panel of 9 or 10 drivers being used over the time that the team ran these TR3As. Maintenance was performed at the Bordon depot, and not surprisingly, there was keen competition to get into the team. Of the 3 cars, VVC 290 survives and is being rebuilt to original specification, but neither VVC 288 nor VVC 289 is known still to exist.

49.   I am reprinting a cutting from an unknown magazine which I presume dates from the early to mid-1960's, although I have not been able to identify the source; it deals with the strange story of the shooting of one Peter Alder, driving home late through the London suburbs in his TR3A. As can be seen, the car sports bullet holes, including one in the

hardtop made by a bullet that entered the unfortunate driver's brain. Amazingly, he was able to drive for 200 yards after this had occurred, although he eventually lost control and hit a fence. Even more amazingly, he appears to have survived, for he is described only as "wounded". Unfortunately, I have uncovered no further details of this extraordinary affair - were the culprits apprehended, did Mr Alder make a full recovery and if so, did he drive his TR again? Maybe someone can elucidate?

50.   Finally, two small but interesting points of sidescreen TR lore; firstly, I have heard from two separate sources that TR3As were sometimes supplied when new with a spare ignition key, wrapped up in waxed paper, and secreted within the rear number plate lamp! In both cases, original owners of cars known to be authentic, unrebuilt examples discovered such keys years later, the keys presumably having been placed there when the cars were built, so if you happen to own a really original TR3A, it might just be worth looking to see if such a key has survived hidden for more than thirty years on your particular car!

Secondly, a few TR3As had their front apron "medallion" badges finished differently from the norm. Although the "shield" part of the badge was blue and white enamel as usual, the bottom loop and the surround were in black rather than blue enamel, the badge looking quite distinctive as a result. It is not known how many were made thus, but one at least survives, fitted to a 1959 TR3A registered XLA 1. This car has been owned since it was three months old by Nigel Holmes, and the badge is known to

AMBUSH

Shooting motive a mystery to police in sniper attack.

J.H. Alder, father of wounded man.

Is an organized gang of snipers, out for thrills, behind the mysterious attacks being made on motorists in London suburbs at night?

That's the question Scotland Yard seeks to answer following the senseless shooting of young Peter Alder, mysteriously fired on as he drove home one evening after a date with his girl. The 25 year old youth was wounded by a .22 calibre rifle bullet. Two other shots struck the car. "I know of no reason for the attack," the boy's father said. ●

Photographic reconstruction of shooting. The wounded driver managed to drive about 200 yards before car went out of control.

THEORY SHOT FROM HERE

CAR BELIEVED HIT HERE

VICTORIA RD.

CAR MOUNTED PATH, STOPPED HERE

Car, left, in which Peter Alder was shot. Bullet entered the plexiglass top (circle) and into brain of driver. Police seek four youths.

Above: this press cutting refers to the shooting incident mentioned in the text . Note the bullet hole in the rear wing.

Above right: seated in this TR is Alderman Cuthbert Ackroyd, at the time (1955?) Lord Mayor of London. He is talking to John Warren, Director of Export Sales for Standard-Triumph, possibly at the Earls Court Motor Show. An excellent view is afforded of the narrow full-profile cross-ply tyres then in use ("Autosport").

Bottom right: a TR2 being employed by MR Davis on an unknown rally kicks up the dust. Badges were clearly the order of the day! (Julian Stephens).

be original. XLA 1 was used when new by Castrol Ltd in several advertisements for its oils, and although it was built with Powder Blue paintwork, this proved to be defective and Standard-Triumph resprayed it under warranty. The colour used was metallic silver grey, which the owner was told by the Factory at the time was an "experimental" colour that they were testing on four cars. This is further evidence that metallic paint finishes were indeed used by the Factory on sidescreen TRs, and the one example that the Author has seen so finished looked exceedingly smart.

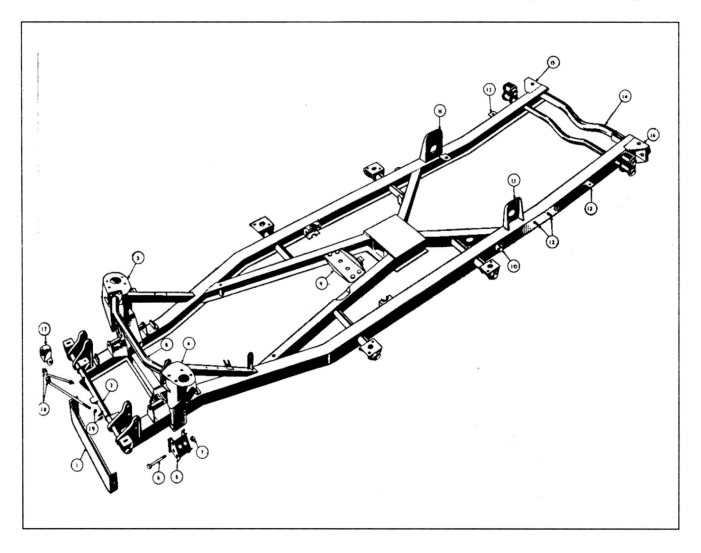

CHAPTER TEN:

Significant Sidescreen TRs

An exercise that I hope will be of interest is a review of those sidescreen TRs that, for want of a better term, I would call "significant" cars, including details (where known) as to their fate and their present status if they still exist. Such records are of necessity not comprehensive, and as I have suggested in several places within this book, there must be a number of undiscovered "interesting" TRs out there awaiting rescue, for some once famous cars have disappeared without trace. Clearly a good number were broken up in the 1960's and 70's when the cars were worth very little, but survival rates of TRs on the whole are pretty good, so I am certain that there are a few more significant cars to yet come to light, both here and abroad.

In the UK, the TR Register can authenticate any historic TRs that re-emerge in the future, and any such authentication would inevitably be more valid if it were performed on a car in "as found" condition rather than after a full rebuild, so if you should be fortunate enough to find what might be a historic sidescreen TR, do call in the experts to verify it before parting with a large bag of gold or submitting it to a "Queen Anne's Axe" type of rebuild - "it's had four new heads and five new shafts, but it's still Queen Anne's Axe!". Incidentally, be aware that the Works were not above doing temporary (or even permanent) registration number "swaps" at times if it proved convenient or expedient!

I shall start by listing all the ex-Works competition cars, citing UK registration number and commission number (if known).

LIST ONE - WORKS COMPETITION CARS

OVC 262 TR2 1954   Gatsonides' car in 1954 Rally Soleil Cannes -no other details available - Fate unknown.

OVC 276 TR2 1954   TS403L built 18/1/54 - the "Mille Miglia" car-survives in the ownership of a prominent TR Register member in the UK - full restoration recently completed.

PDU 20 TR2 1954   TS 1927 LO - 1954 Alpine Rally car - survives in the ownership of a TR Register member in the UK and is currently undergoing long-term restoration.

PDU 21 TR2 1954   1954 Alpine Rally car - fate unknown.

PKV 693 TR2 1955   TS 5202 1955 Tulip Rally Car - survives, and has been seen in various TR Register events in the 1980's - Advertised for sale in the early1990's, now believed to be in Germany.

PKV 697 TR2 1955   TS 5543 1955 Tulip Rally Car - entered onto TR Register in 1977 by an owner who had by then owned it for 13 years - present status unknown.

PKV 698 TR2 1955   TS 5530 1955 Tulip Rally Car. Last licenced in the UK November 1964 in Lancashire, presumed broken up.

PKV 374 TR2 1955   TS 5691-O 1955 Le Mans Car - owned for many years by a TR Register member - car now nearing completion of a long term rebuild - See Chapter 9.

PKV 375 TR2 1955   TS5582-O 1955 Le Mans Car - known to have been in a scrapyard in 1973 in somewhat unoriginalcondition (see Chapter 9) - subsequent fate unknown. Registration number belived to have been transferred to a modern car in about 1977.

Left: PDU 21 was the least used and least photographed of the trio of 1954 Alpine Rally TR2s. Here it is seen on the Lyon-Charbonnieres Rally in 1955, possibly with Gregor Grant at the wheel (NMM Beaulieu).

Below: Few photographs seem to exist showing Works rally TR2 PKV 698. Here, Bobby Dickson is seen in action during the Tulip Rally of 1955 (TR Register Archive).

Above: a well-known car being put to unfamiliar use: PDU 20 is seen in Holland, in the Winter of 1954/55. Driven by Maurice Gatsonides, it is hauling the local lads on their sledges. PDU 20 has clearly been rebuilt following its rally adventures and even sports a front bumper ("Autosport").

Right: Ex-Works TR2 PKV 693 has found a new owner in Mr Hurn, who is seen racing it in the rain at Goodwood in April 1958. Both this car and ULF 5, the white TR following, are listed as existing on the TR Register ("Autosport").

A Works TR2, RHP 557, is seen in action on the London Motor Club "Little Rally". The date is 21st April 1956 and the driver is thought to be Kit Heathcote (NMM Beaulieu).

By June 1959, TR3As were common on the race track: here four such cars are seen powering away from a Le Mans-type start at Goodwood. The front car bears the registration number SRW 991, one of the 1956 Works cars that went to Sebring in 1957. It was then a TR3, but here it is shown with a TR3A front and external door handles. Possibly, it had been fully rebuilt following re-importation? ("Autosport").

TRW 735 still worked hard for its living in the 1970s; it is seen being piloted by owner Jon Laver during a trials event - a real "TR Man" picture (Jon Laver).

PKV 376   TR2 1955   Comm. no. unknown. 1955 Le Mans and TT car -possibly existed in the UK in the early 1970's - fate unknown - (see Chapter 9).

RHP 557   TR2 1955   Comm. no. unknown. 1955 Liege-Rome-Liege rally car - not heard of for many years, fate unknown (was advertised for sale by "Performance Cars" of London in September 1956)

SRW 410   TR3 1956   1956 Works Team car - sent to compete in 1957 Sebring 12 hour race - fate unknown.

SRW 990   TR3 1956   Works team Car for Midnight Sun rally - fate unknown. This TR was used as the support car to SVC 368, the vehicle used to "race" the Auster aircraft - see Chapter 5.

SRW 991   TR3 1956   1956 Works team car - sent to compete in 1957 Sebring race in the USA - originally believed to have remained in USA, but a photograph in "Autosport" shows it racing at Goodwood in 1959, so presumably it returned to the UK. Fate unknown.

SRW 992   TR3 1956   TS10614-O - 1956 works team car - competed in 1957 Sebring 12 hours race in USA, but must have been reimported to UK, as it was licenced in the UK in the 1950's and 1960's, the last time being in Suffolk in 1966 - assumed broken up.

SHP 520 TR3 1956   Works development and rally car - Alpine rally 1956 and 1957 Mille Miglia. Still believed to exist in the UK.

SKV 656 TR3 1957   Works team car - TS13312-O has been owned for many years by former committee member of TR Register.

TRW 735   TR3 1957   TS17064-O 1957 Tulip rally and Liege-Rome-Liege car - this car belonged for many years to a well known TR Register member, and was cam-

paigned in a large variety of events rebuilt in the late 1980's, sold at auction, and believed still to be in the UK.

TRW 736   TR3 1957   Tulip rally and Liege-Rome-Liege car - reported to exist in the 1970's and registration number currently still "live" on DVLC computer. This car presumably exists, although its present whereabouts are unknown.

TRW737 TR3 1957   The third works Tulip rally and Liege-Rome-Liege car - no definite details as to its fate are known, but it is said to have been dismantled and rumoured that the remains were thrown down a Cornish tin mine shaft in the early 1970's! However, a car bearing this registration is still registered with the DVLC, so it may possibly still exist.

VRW 219   TR3A 1958*   TS23854-LO - 1958 Monte Carlo Rally Car - last licenced in UK in September 1964 - believed scrapped.

VRW 220   TR3A 1958   1958 Monte Carlo Rally Car - ultimate fate unknown, presumed scrapped.

VRW 221   TR3A 1958   Monte Carlo Rally Car - comm.no. TS23870-O- This car has been fully rebuilt, and is owned by a TR Register member in the Midlands.

VRW 223   TR3A 1958   TS23864 - O 1958 Monte Carlo Rally Car - last licenced in UK January 1966 - subsequent fate unknown - presumed scrapped. Note: the number VRW 222 was issued to a Standard Ensign.

VWK 610   TR3A 1958   Tulip Rally car in 1958. TS25991-LO - owned in late 1960's by a founder member of the TR Register, but by the early 1970's, it had reached a scrapyard in Lancashire, was rescued and is now owned by a current TR Register member who intends to rebuild it as original.

VHP 529 TR3A 1958   TS23635-O- Works team car, owned for many years by a TR Register member.

The 1957 TR3 Works Team, seen here prior to the 1957 Tulip Rally. John Waddington is seen on the extreme left and Ken Richardson is seen with Willie Cave on the right. Tom and Mrs Gold, centre, managed to overturn TRW 736, fortunately without injury.

Right: VRW 220 being driven in March 1959 by Fred Snaylam on the RAF Motor Sports Association Spring Rally. The car had, by then, been sold off by the Works. Below left: VRW 221 undergoes preparation in the Competitions Department alongside an unknown TR3A, January 1958. Below right: XHP 259 during its Monza record-breaking run. Ken Richardson peers anxiously at the car during a pit stop. Bottom: January 1958 and the new team of Apple Green TR3As is prepared for the Monte Carlo Rally. One wonders what the Triumph Renown in the background was being prepared for? (TR Register Archive).

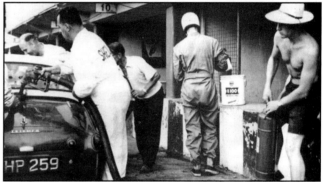

VVC 672 TR3A 1958   Works rally car - Tulip rally 1958 - fate unknown.

VVC 673 TR3A 1958   TS26020-O 1958 Liege-Rome-Liege car - owned and restored by a TR Register member.

WDU 712   TR3A 1958   TS32618;although its continued existence was not known for many years, this car came on to the TR Register in the late 1970's, and is believed now to be owned in good condition by a member in the Midlands.

WVC 247   TR3A 1959   Monte Carlo Rally Car. TS39090-O - Car on TR Register during 1980's - assumed still to exist although whereabouts unknown.

WVC 248   TR3A 1959   Comm.no. unknown - Monte Carlo Rally Car - exported at some stage to USA, where it is believed that some parts at least still exist.

WVC 249   TR3A 1959   TS39022-O - 1959 Monte Carlo Rally Car - on TR Register in 1986 - assumed still to exist.

WVC 250   TR3A 1959   TS39037-O 1958 Monte Carlo Rally Car - believed not licenced in UK since 1958 - possibly exported?. No further details known.

WVC 251   TR3A 1959   believed to have been Ken Richardson's personal road car - also used on 1961 Acropolis Rally, fate thereafter unknown.

XHP 259 TR3A 1959   TS38965-O- "Monza" record car - It was
crashed heavily and badly damaged at some time; the remains of this car still exists in hands of a TR Register member.

XHP 938)   1959 Le Mans TR3'S' cars - dismantled and
some parts
XHP 939)   incorporated into the 1960/61 Le Mans cars
                - Body of at
XHP 940)   least one car still survives.

926 HP) The four TR'S' cars built for the 1960/61 Le Mans -all
927 HP) still believed to exist. All went to North America in
928 HP) the1960's, but one at least has returned to the UK.
929 HP)

LIST TWO:

The next group of 'significant' sidescreen TRs to be reviewed are factory owned publicity, road test or what I might call quasi-Works competition cars, such as the "Army" team cars. That is, cars used in the occasional event by factory or associated personnel, yet which were not part of the works team "fleet" as defined in the first part of this chapter. I cannot claim that this list is exhaustive, and further evidence, usually photographic, comes to light from time to time, indicating further examples of what must have been factory or press demonstrator or development cars. Thus, I have no doubt that there are further additions yet to be made to the

following list. One characteristic that these cars share is that they all carry the coveted Coventry registration marks. Although the possession of an RW, DU, VC, HP, KV or WK registration mark on a particular TR is no guarantee of a 'Works' pedigree, the lack of such a mark **is** almost a sure indication of a "non works" pedigree!

OHP 242 - This was TS14-O - the first publicity as opposed to road test car. The factory record states "to Mr A S Dick, VERY URGENT!". It was much photographed with Ken Richardson at the wheel, and it was eventually sold off to one of the Company's secretaries who ran it for some years. It was advertised for sale in around 1975, but has never appeared on the TR Register. Rumour has it that it has found its way to Germany.

OHP 300 - This was TS28, one of the cars displayed at the 1953 London Motor Show. It was used by Sales Director Lyndon Mills and by rally driver and Motor trader Dennis Done pending the delivery of his own TR2. Subsequent fate unkown.

OHP 676 - This was TS8, used both as a very early demonstrator, development car and rally car, driven on occasions by Richardson/Heathcote - It was not a Works team car however, if only for the reason that the team did not exist when it was first used! It was also used by Gregor Grant, Editor of "Autosport", in the Lyons-Charbonnieres rally in March 1954. Following Company use, the car was overhauled and fitted with "short" doors prior to being sold off. Barrie March bought it in 1955 and used it for severl years. I have traced this car to Scotland, where it was last licenced in 1965, and was stated to have been broken up in 1971.

OHP 677 - This car was TS15, a further publicity and "photographic" car. It is seen in "glorious technicolor" on the dust jacket. Very little further information has turned up however, and nothing is known of its fate.

OHP 771 - The well-known "Motor", "Autocar" and "Autosport" road test car, TS6. It was not built with overdrive, hence no 'O' in the commission number, but overdrive was fitted very shortly thereafter. It appears to have led a very hard and busy early life, including being lent to Tom Blackburn (see chapter 4). It was sold off to Ted Lund, and was almost certainly the so-called "ex-Works" car offered for sale by him. No details as to the eventual fate of this car are known.

NHP 476 - TS774L - left hand drive development car - owned by SMC Canley until late 1955, whereupon it was stated to have been shipped abroad.

Top left: OHP 300 was a very early TR2 Commission Number TS28. It is seen on the Liverpool Motor Club's New Year Rally, which took place on the 23rd/24th January 1954. "Autosport" stated that this was the first appearance of a TR2 in a rally in the UK, the driver being Denis Done ("Autosport"). Above: Proof that there was a TR2 registered OVC 270 in addition to the well-known OVC 272 and OVC 276. Unfortunately, nothing is known about this car, but it probably had a factory connection. Left: OHP 676 photographed whilst in the ownership of Barrie March in 1956. The Factory had sold this very early car (TS8) in late 1955, having converted it to short doors during its rebuild. Barrie March ran the car for several years without being aware of its comparatively illustrious past (Barrie March).

OKV 603 - Believed to have been a development car - no further details known.

OKV 777 - TS1730 - O This was really a privately-owned car (by Bobby Dickson) but it received considerable Works support in connection with its appearance at Le Mans in 1954. For many years now OKV 777 has been in the hands of a well known Register Member in Northern England. The car is restored largely to its "Le Mans" condition.

ORW 600 - A very early TR2 (TS78), possibly used by factory personnel and as a development car for a couple of months. It was purchased in December 1953 by Mr R.B. James, who later used it to cover 1000 miles in 24 hours, as related in

Chapter 9. It was also used by the National Benzole fuel company in its advertising. Nothing is known as to its fate.

OVC 270 - A Sales Department demonstrator - believed still to have existed in the 1970's - subsequent details unknown.

OVC 272 - TS 875 - This car was used and subsequently owned by Dr W H Osborne, the Standard-Triumph company doctor, and his wife Cherry. The car passed through many hands following their ownership, and is now being rebuilt to original specification in Northern England.

OVC 999 - TS1083-O Believed to have been a further press/publicity car. It was in London in the early 1960's, but

On the left: taken at a TR Register meeting in the early 1980s, the car on the left is PHP 727, the original "Motor Sport" road test car from February 1955. This car survives today following rstoration. The other car, RYF 346, was raced extensively by John Wellburn, later being owned by the author. This car achieved notoriety at a Goodwood sprint in 1979, when it performed a spectacular roll at 80mph. John Wellburn had fitted a rollover bar only the day before, which undoubtedly saved him serious injury. On the right is RHP 560, which was built as a TR2, but is shown here wearing a TR3 grille. It looks as if the grille was added by an artist, rather than by a mechanic, a suspicion reinforced by the existence of other pictures oif this same car as a TR2, apparently taken at the same location (TR Register Archive).

was stated to have been shipped to Libya in 1964.

PDU 730 - TS2090 - was a publicity car and was used in a feature film (see Chapter 9), and also as a loan and press car. It survives, and when last heard of was being rebuilt.

PHP 727 - TS3392-O, - "Motorsport" magazine road test car, February 1955 - it survives, and has been rebuilt recently, believed owned by a current TR register member.

PKV 373 - TS5486-O, - This car is registered adjacent to the 1955 Le Mans TR2s, and is thought to have been a spare and development car to PKV374/375 and 376. It survived into the late 1960's, but its subsequent fate is unknown.

PRW 137 - TS3517-O, - The first "second generation" (ie short door) TR2 press car, used for the "Autocar" hardtop TR2 road test in February 1955. The observant will notice that from its commission no, it should have been a long door car, so it must have had prototype 'short' doors! It was last licenced in London in 1965, and is not now known to exist.

PVC 993 - TS5515-O, - Believed to be the second "second generation" press/publicity TR2. This vehicle was on the Register in the late 1970's, but its present status is unknown.

NWK 156 - TS5924 - a mid 1955 TR2 used as a publicity and development car. Photographed (in colour) on the front of

the February 1956 Standard Car Review Magazine, but with a TR3 grille! - further evidence that certain TR2s were "upgraded" to TR3s by the Works. Car existed in the 1970's - present status unknown.

RHP 560 - Another TR2/3 crossbreed. This car is the one used in the earliest TR3 publicity shots showing the new grille, but other photographs exist of it as a TR2. Possibly the grille was added to the older photographs by a stroke of the brush in the design studio? Nothing is known as to the survival of this car.

RHP 564 - This was probably another publicity car, but I have not been able to confirm this. It survived and was on the TR Register in the 1970's.

RKV 335 - Early Press TR3 - TS6415-O, used for "Motor" road test in 1956, amongst others. It carries a TR2 commission number, and was therefore presumably built as a TR2. Last licenced in Hertfordshire in 1961 - believed scrapped.

RKV 352
RVC 204
RVC 205
-All these three were also press/publicity cars used for the launch of the TR3 in the Autumn of 1955 and through the first part of 1956. Somewhat surprisingly, none of the three is known to have survived. I suspect that like RKV 335, they

would also have had commission numbers in the TR2 sequence (ie below TS8637).

SDU 57 - This was a further early drum-braked TR3 publicity department car, commission no. TS9439-O, finished in Salvador Blue. It survives in restored condition, and is pictured in the colour section.

SHP 865 - a publicity car, pictured on the front cover of the September 1956 Standard Car Review - nothing further is known.

SKV 654 - TS13149-O - The first of the trio of "SKV" cars, the "second generation" (ie disc braked) TR3 press fleet. SKV 654 seems to have been a general publicity/development hack. It was on the TR Register in the early 1980's and is presumed to have survived.

SKV 655 - The second "SKV" car, and used as John Bolster's "Autosport" road test car in 1957. This car was re-registered as MCA 305 in May 1960 by Alfred MacAlpine & Co - an early example of a "cherished number?" Nothing regarding its subsequent fate is known.

SKV 656 - TS13312-O - This was the most well-known of the trio, being used for several road tests, and then being taken into the Works competition team, thus becoming the only car to appear in both list one and list two! Restored and owned by a former TR Register committee member.

SRW 411 - It seems that a TR bearing this number did exist but no details are known. As the adjacent number to Works car SRW 410 it probably had some factory connection.
SRW 993 - This last of the quartet of "SRW" TR3s did indeed exist, and is dealt with in Chapter 5. It is not known to have survived beyond the late 1960s.

SVC 368 - A further early disc-braked publicity department

TR3 - this car was used as the "Auster" air race car, details of which are found in Chapter 5. Nothing is known as to its fate.

SWK 772 - TS8902 - O - an early drum braked 1955 TR3, again known to have been on the press/publicity fleet - this car survived on the TR Register in the 1980's, and thus probably still exists.

TWK 84 - A photograph exists of this disc-braked TR3 undergoing water-splash tests at the MIRA test track, so it was presumably an experimental/development car. It's commission number was TS18483-O, and it was listed on the TR Register in the 1980's - present status unknown.

VDU 565 - TS22045-O. One of the very earliest 1957 built TR3As, used as a UK publicity and press car at a time when all TR3A production was going to North America. This car was tested by the UK edition of Sports Cars Illustrated in February 1958, as far as I know the only formal British road test of a TR3A. As with the previous car, it was on the TR Register in the 1980's, but its present status is unknown.

VVC 288
VVC 289
VVC 290
-These were the three 1958 TR3As prepared by the Works for the British Army Motoring Association Crews on the 1958 Liege-Rome-Liege Rally and later events. Their subsequent fate is unclear, but one at least (VVC 290 - TS30373-O) survives in the care of a TR Register member.

VWK 999 - This 1958 TR3A (TS29193-0) was used as a publicity/press TR3A, and was photographed in colour on the cover of the August 1958 issue of the Standard Car Review. It survives, and was listed on the TR Register in 1985.

YDU 212 This was a 1959 Works publicity and press TR3A, seen in several factory photographs, and also in the 1960 feature film "Carry on Constable", when it was lent to the film

YDU 212 looks smart with a white hood and wire wheels, as it poses for an official photograph. This car was added to the publicity fleet in 1959 and was also lent to a film company, appearing in the film"Carry on Constable" (TR Register Archive).

33 DNK was a very rapid and much-raced TR3A, seen here at Goodwood on 25th April 1959, the driver being Bill de Selincourt. The modified front presumably aided air penetration as much as it detracted from the car's appearance. This car has just been rediscovered in France and is being brought back to the UK for restoration as this book closes for press (NMM Beaulieu).

company by Standard-Triumphs. Nothing is known as to its subsequent fate.

46 HP - TS67966-O. This "post TS60000" revised body TR3A was used as a press car and demonstrator in 1960/61, being the car used by "Motorsport" magazine for their trip to Italy in October 1960. The Works sold it off in October 1961, and after many years of storage, it was "rediscovered" in the 1980's in very original condition, and has now been restored.

2242 RW - TS81769-O. This very late TR3A was the final sidescreen TR used by Standard-Triumphs for press work, but only as far as I can see for comparative photography with the then newly-introduced TR4 in 1961. By that time, the 3A series would have held little interest for the Motoring Press. This car is believed to survive in a restored state in the UK.

LIST THREE :

I shall now turn to significant privately owned sidescreen TRs. Most of the following TRs are notable because of competition success, but having had well-known personalities as owners also qualifies cars for inclusion! This list must of necessity be only representative rather than exhaustive, for to be the latter probably upwards of one thousand entries would be required! The whim of the author is at work here, and I apologise in advance for any glaring omissions or unlikely inclusions!

I have arranged cars in registration number sequence, the numerical part of the number being listed in ascending order. Where cars are known or believed still to exist, this is stated. Where nothing is mentioned, please assume that nothing is known of that particular vehicle's fate.

TTF 1 - One of the 6 1954 Tourist Trophy Cars, owned by Tom Blackburn. This car was re-registered 585 BTB upon sale - See Chapter 4 for details of this car.

OOK 2 - Used in 1954 RAC Rally by N. Jarrett.

PYT 2 - The "Wilen Engineering" car - TS3634 - see Chapter 6 - still exists but has been re-registered WPV 72A.

TPP 2 - Believed to have belonged to Earl Howe, the well-known motor sporting personality, and to have been used by him in various competitive events.

2 SMC
3 SMC
- TR3A demonstrators used by the Company's London distribution depot - SMC = Standard Motor Co. Possibility the number 1 SMC was also utilised in this way, but I have seen no evidence that it was ever on a TR.

JBO 3 - TS122 - Monte Seal's very early TR2 - much campaigned by him in competitive events. Broken up early 1970's. See Chapter 4.

SXX 3   TR3 belonging to famous horn-playing musician Dennis Brain, and in which he was killed. (See Chapter 5).

JUH 3 - Winner 1956 Mobilgas Economy Run - see Chapter 9.
SXK 4 - Used on 1956 Alpine Rally by Joseph Kat.

VUG 6 - TR2 used in "Autocar" used car test, March 1958.

6 MMK - TR3A TS27538. This was the car won on the TV game show "Take Your Pick" as related in Chapter 9. It sur-

RON 100 belonged to Ron Dalglish, the well-known and successful rally competitor. He is seen here leaving the Oban control on the 1959 Scottish Rally, which he won outright ("Autosport").

vives and has belonged to Mike Ellis of the TR Register for around 25 years.

SMB 10 - Driven by V Cooper in 1954 RAC Rally.

VNW 11 - One of the "3 Peaks" cars - See chapter 9.

12 EAR - TR3A used in "Autocar" used car test - October 1959 - Subsequently owned by Motoring Journalist Stuart Bladon.

GES 33 - Successful TR3 rally car owned and campaigned by Ron Dalgliesh.

33 DNK - Bill de Selincourt's racing TR3A, a very rapid TR during the 1960's. It has recently been re-discovered in France.

GRN 37 - John Waddington's second TR2, successfully rallied by him in mid 1950's.

46 BHX - TS554-O. This early TR2 appeared on the front cover of "Autosport" magazine, 5th March 1954, posing with film actress Belinda Lee. It was thought to have been a demonstration vehicle used in the London area, and it is believed still to exist in the Midlands.

NHP 49 - A very interesting and early TR2, this was TS10 LO, built 31st August 1953, first registered 14th September 1953 and fitted with engine no. TS18E. The build records state that it was built in Ice Blue with Geranium trim, but the contemporary colour photograph reproduced in this book shows it to have been white! Possibly it was resprayed, or maybe became the subject of a "registration number swap!" Credence is lent to the latter theory as the registration details state the car to have been Ice Blue, and its first owner is

given as B M (Basil) D'Almeida, of 101 Leadenhall Street, London, EC3. This gentleman clearly had influence at Standard-Triumph's to have obtained such an early TR, and he is known to have used it in late 1953/early 1954 in Rallies, principally the Lisbon Rally and Tour of Portgual event, where it received a "first in class", one of the TR's very earliest competition successes. The registration details state that the car was "permanently exported" in 1954, and in fact, the series of numbers from NHP1 to NHP200 was reserved by Coventry Licencing Authority for personal export vehicles according to their own records. My research indicates that many later 'NHP' numbers were also used for personal export cars, in particular 8 out of the 10 TR2s registered NHP 847 to NHP 856 (excluding 851 and 853) were shipped abroad in May 1953 having previously been registered with these "personal export" plates.

OKV 72 - An April 1954 TR2, TS1237 LO - This car was privately owned and campaigned by Leslie Brooke, including use as one of the 1954 "TT" cars and in the 1955 Mille Miglia. It survived until 1962 when the registration records note that it was written off, colliding with a telegraph pole and a tree, and presumably doing no great good to it's driver? Despite the "L" in the commission number, it appears to have been right-hand drive.

KAT 99 - TR2 used in the Liege-Rome-Liege rally (in 1955?). Believed broken up in a Sheffield scrapyard in 1973.

RON 100 - Ron Dalgleish's second rally TR - much used and a very successful car.

NUF 135 - TR2 supplied new to Robert Irving, then the director of Sadler's Wells Ballet Company, and pictured in the Standard Car Review Magazine.

SAH 137 - TR owned and raced by Sid Hurrell of SAH Accessories, the Triumph tuning firm. This number was believed to have been used on more than one TR.

SYA 176 - TR2 - Richard Bensted-Smith's Pomeroy Trophy and Mobil Economy run winning TR2 .

RSC 190 - 1957 TR3 - Jim Clark's competition TR, owned by Border Reivers and campaigned by Clark in 1957/8

MSP 200 - 1954-TR2 supplied to Lord Bruce (now the Earl of Elgin) and used by him in many rallies. Car was supplied new specially finished in the family's colour of "rich yellow".

GJA 205 - John Wallwork's 1954 RAC Rally winning TR2 - extensive research has failed to uncover the fate of this car, which was sold by Wallwork in 1956, or to establish its commission number, though this must have been very early.

OOY 218 - This TR2 belonged to Leo Villa, Sir Malcolm Campbell's mechanic who maintained "Bluebird". Commission number was TS4519, and the car is believed still to exist.

NHP 222 - TS82-O. This was one of the very first UK supplied TR2s, although I have not been able to establish that it was used by the factory, despite its "Coventry" registration number. It survives in Northern England in good condition, and is believed to be the earliest TR in the UK in running order.

UOC 279 - TS14906. Reg Woodcock's very well known racing TR, owned by him since 1960.

OON 292 - `1954 "Tourist Trophy" TR2 - a private entry car much raced in the mid 1950's.

UPE 301 - Very early TR2 used on the 1954 Paris - St Raphael rally.

MUY 334 - Bill Parkes' 1954 TR2 - believed to have been TS428-O - See Chapter 4.

PKF 357 - TS942 - an early rally TR2, significant in that it was one of the very few UK supplied TRs finished in Olive Yellow. Survives today, but not in that colour!

JDB 361 - The "Ferodo" brake testing TR2 - See Chapter 9.

VFM 377 - TS4376 - TR2 supplied new to Pat Moss, Stirling Moss's sister, who became arguably the most successful lady rally driver so far. She rallied this car extensively in 1955/56. It still survives, and was seen at TR Register events in the 1980's.

ONF 378 - This TR2 came 5th overall in the 1954 RAC Rally, owned and driven by Bill Bleakley from Manchester

TFM 400 - A further very early TR2, owned and rallied by Chester based Motor dealer Dennis Done. Used by him on the 1954 RAC Rally.

RTT 417 - This is the TR2 now fully restored and on display in the National Motor Museum. More details of this car can be found in Chapter 5.

VYM 429 - TR3A, TS38141. This car was a Standard Motor Co (London) demonstrator, hence its registration in the Capital rather than in Coventry. It was used in a number of publicity photographs, and is believed still to exist today.

PYU 430 - TR2 owned and raced with great success by Sid Hurrell, of the SAH tuning firm. This car has recently "resurfaced" and is believed to be in running order.

UJO 440 - Very early TR2 owned by J H King and rallied by him, including the 1954 RAC Rally.

OEL 505 - This TR2 was the Stanbourne Motors (Bournemouth) demonstrator, borrowed by Peter Cooper for the 1954 RAC Rally as his own TR2 had not by then been delivered. Cooper came second overall in this important event. He originally recalled that the car was TS69, but this has proved not to be the case, for TS69 was sent new to the USA (where it still exists), was left hand drive and painted Ice Blue, whereas OEL 505 was right hand drive and black! - TS52 seems a more likely candidate to have been OEL 505.

NVC591 - A very late TR2 (TS8627), campaigned in the mid-1950s by Betty Haig.

635 KRE - John Waddington's 3rd TR2 - again much rallied by him - See Chapter 4. - believed broken up in the mid 1960's.

TZ 635 - A further member of the 1954 team of 6 TR2s competing in the Tourist Trophy race.

KAK 656 - Barry Leaven's TR2, competed in 1954 RAC Rally.

UPC 700 - Used in 1954 RAC Rally, driven by R Cookson.

GWH 720 - TR2 campaigned by Fred Snaylam, well known and successful rallyist in the 1950s.

VHP 724 - Used in the Monte Carlo Rally 1958, nothing further known.

Johnny Wallwork was still campaigning his hard-worked TR2 in October 1956, as this photograph, taken on the 27th of that month, demonstrates. The car was nearly three years old by then and has acquired a wood rim steering wheel as well as the later type of rear lights and combined reflectors. A very severe-looking policewoman stands in front of a Vauxhall Velox with period seat covers and the Morris Commercial van adds a nice touch. The event is the Blackpool Rally driving tests ("Autosport").

At Prescott Hill Climb on 9th May 1954, JM Tew forges past a charming period Austin ambulance and an archaic Thames recovery truck. OON 292 later raced in one of the TR teams in the 1954 Ulster TT Race (NMM Beaulieu).

UPE 301 was a very early production TR2, much used competitively in 1954. It is seen here on 10th April that year on the London Motor Club's Little Rally (NMM Beaulieu).

Above: Two TR2s, both showing off their original hoods with the small rear windows, climb the Devil's Staircase in the MCC Rally of October 1954. RTT 417 is the car that is now in the National Motor Musuem. The other car, RUO 511, is also believed still to exist (LAT Photographic).
Above right: ORW 868 (TS191) was Bobby Dickson's own TR2. It was only a few weeks old when, in March 1954, it was put to use on a bumpy and muddy autocross event, clearly a car destined for a hard life. ("Autosport"). Right: LVJ 932 was the TR2 in which Harold Rumsey took second place in the 1955 RAC Rally. Here it is seen on another occasion during a driving test. The bakelite screen heaters can be seen and an imposing Austin Sheerline is visible in the background (LAT Photographic).

VPJ 770 - Vic Derrington's TR2, raced and modified extensively in the 1954 - 1958 period, TS4077-O. This car was "discovered" in 1993 by the Author following the death of the then owner, and it is now being restored by a TR Register member in Southern England.

773 EWO - TS2 - the second production TR - now undergoing restoration in the UK Midlands.

VYD 797 - TR3, used as a private entry by Leslie Griffiths on the 1956 Alpine rally along with SXK 4 and the Works team cars. This car was finished in an unusual two-tone colour scheme.

809 CMF - One of the three TR2s entered privately in the 1955 Mille Miglia, this was the car driven by Dick Steed and Bruce Adams. OKV 72 was driven by Leslie Brooke and Jack Fairman, and the identity of the third car, driven by Tom Haigh and Peter Scott-Russell I have not been able to ascertain.

NHP 850 - TS1711 LO. This Geranium TR2 was used as a private entry in the 1954 Alpine rally by Stewart and Blodgett, racing alongside the Works team cars.

NHP 853 - TS1082 - O. This TR2 was extensively raced during the 1950's by several drivers. Its last recorded owner was racing driver John Quick (later to race 'E' types successfully), who owned it in 1960.

SOC 866 - TR2 driven from London to Capetown, South Africa overland - See Chapter 9.

ORW 868 - TS191, used extensively during 1954 (including the RAC Rally) by Bobby Dickson, the Standard-Triumph dealer from Carlisle. Although Coventry-registered, this was a privately owned TR2. It was last heard of in 1965 in North Wales.

OWK 888 - TS616 - O. Mary Walker's private TR2, used by her to win the Ladies prize in the 1954 RAC rally, and in many subsequent events. (See Chapter 4). This car is stated by the licencing records to have been broken up in Lancashire in 1964.

JDF 888 - TR2 used in the 1954 RAC Rally by E. Elliott.

MCG 909 - Peter Cooper's own TR2 (see OEL 505), finally delivered to him in April 1954, commission no. TS1079-O. Extensively and successfully rallied by him. This car was on the TR Register in the 1980's, and is thought still to exist.

VHT 911 - TR2 driven 3700 miles around Britain's coastline in

7 days! See Chapter 9.

LVJ 932 - TR2 owned by Harold Rumsey, which came second overall in the 1955 RAC Rally.

975 BRF - John Waddington's first TR2 - extensively raced and rallied in 1954/55. (See Chapter 4).

IT 3241 - TR2 owned by Raymond Laird in Ireland. Rallied, and believed to have been used (because of its appropriate registration number?) by Standard-Triumph in their "Here IT is" advertising campaign.

PZ 6400 - TR2 owned by racing driver Desmond Titterington, and widely rallied and raced by him in the mid 1950's.

BI 6600 - A further TR2 that competed in the award winning 1954 Tourist Trophy race team of 6 TRs.

OS 9049 - 1954 RAC Rally TR2, driven by Eric Batte. This car (TS 556) is believed to survive and was listed in the TR Register in the late 1970's.

Finally, and for the sake of completeness, I will briefly list the various factory prototypes that were road-registered, adding a note as to their current status, where known. Fuller details of these cars can be found in Chapter One.

MWK 950 - X508 - owned by a private collector near London - car awaiting restoration.

ORW 666 - X516 - The Registration number is still held as in use on the DVLC computer - this car may exist, but no details are known.

MVC 575 - X519 - "Jabbeke" record breaking TR2 prototype, now owned by a private collector near London - car dismantled, awaiting reassembly.

YDU 208 - X592 - Exists in the UK and believed to be under restoration.

TVC 819 - X598 - Stated to have been broken up by the Works.

WDU 708 - X614 - This car was dismantled some years ago, and what remains is owned by a private collector near London.

XHP 938 - X627 - Dismantled by the factory in 1959/60.

XHP 939 - X628 - Dismantled by the factory in 1959/60, although some parts have survived in the UK.

XHP 940 - X629 - Dismantled by the factory in 1959/60.

926 HP - X654 - Believed to exist in North America.

927 HP - X655 - Believed to exist in North America.

928 HP - X656 - Exists in complete state, owned by a private collector near London.

929 HP - X657 - In UK in 1980's but believed re-exported to the USA late in that decade - exists in a complete state.

AVT 413C - X660 - The "Red" Beta - Exists in a complete state (but with non-original engine) in the ownership of a private collector near London.

917 HP - X693 - The "Black" Beta - Exists in the UK and was seen at a TR Register event in the 1980's - last reported to be undergoing restoration.

3097 VC - X707 - The "Conrero" Triumph. Exists in a complete state in the ownership of a private collector near London.

Although it has never carried a UK registration number, mention must be made of TS1-L0, the first production TR. As mentioned in Chapter One, this car survives in the USA and is currently undergoing a comprehensive restoration.

The late Paul Good, to whom this book is dedicated, seen at Goodwood Circuit in 1980, preparing to compete in the TR Register's sprint meeting. His well-used and fast TR2 was his daily transport at the time (Rosy Good).

Another photograph taken in 1980 shows the author and his long-door TR2 about to fill up at a very old-fashioned garage in Oxfordshire, the left hand petrol pump being of the hand-cranked variety. Sadly, the garage is now demolished, the car is long since sold - and the author has grey hair! (Bob Kemp)

APPENDIX ONE:

Production Figures 1953-1962

T his Appendix lists production numbers for each model, year by year. The accompanying notes are self-explanatory:

	TR2	TR3	TR3A	TR3B	TOTALS
1953	305				305
1954	4897				4897
1955	3434	1029			4463
1956		5333			5333
1957		7015	3619		10634
1958			16035		16035
1959			21186		21186
1960			17054		17054
1961			408		408
1962			7	3334	3341
TOTAL	8636*	13377**	58309	3334	83656

* Possibly a handful fewer than this number were actually built; some sources say 8628, as a few numbers may not have been used.

** Of the 13377 TR3s built, 4409 were drum braked cars, and 8968 were disc braked versions. Thus there were more than twice as many disc as drum-braked TR3s, making the drum braked TR3 considerably the rarer.

Note The totals above include completely knocked down 'kits' sent from Coventry for local assembly, and also include chassis supplied without bodies to Italy for Triumph Italia production. It should be noted that 2045 TR3A numbers between TS47956 and TS50000 inclusive were not used. In addition, as no one has yet had the time to check all 80000 plus production records individually, there may be some further TR3/3A/3B numbers that were not used; thus, the totals quoted above should be considered maximum numbers. TR owners should also be careful not to confuse the date of first registration of their car with the date of building. The latter date can often be much earlier than the former for a variety of reasons. For instance, there are quite a number of TR3As in the UK that were first registered in 1962, but some of these were actually manufactured as early as late 1960 and then stored due to slow sales as a result of economic recession and the imminent arrival of the TR4.

APPENDIX TWO:
Sample Build Records

C learly there is no scope or space for a full listing of extracts from factory build records, but for interest and as examples I have extracted some details from "round number" cars' build records. This information is available for any TR2/3/3A either through the TR Register or the British Motor Industry Heritage Trust provided one is able to furnish the particular commission number concerned. The records usually include more details than are quoted below - just the principal features have been extracted. CKD cars usually have very few details listed. B.M.I.H.T can also usually provide build records for the TR3Bs, but the records available to the TR Register do not include these cars.

TS 1000 L		Built 25th March 1954, Black with Grey leather and Ice Blue hood - dispatched to the USA.
TS2000		Built 1st June 1954, Signal Red with Black vynide and Black hood - delivered to H A Browett & Co, Leicester.
TS3000	L'O'	Built 5th August 1954, Black with Red vynide and Black sidescreens - destination not quoted.
TS4000	'O'	Built 7th October 1954, Signal Red with Brown vynide and Fawn hood - delivered to Standard Motor Co's London depot.
TS5000		Built 7th December 1954, but as a CKD kit of parts, so no further details quoted. Destination not listed.
TS6000	L'O'	Built 20th April 1955, Black - hood and trim colour too indistinct to read on microfilm record - Delivered to W. Germany.
TS7000	L'O'	Built 28th June 1955 - Pearl White - exported to W. Germany - no further details.
TS8000	L	Built 5th September 1955 - Pearl White - exported to USA.
TS9000	L'O'	Built 1st November 1955 - Pearl White with White hard top - exported to USA.
TS10000		Built 2nd February 1956 - CKD kit vehicle for local assembly. No destination details listed.
TS20000 L		Built 9th July 1957, Black - exported to USA.
TS30000 L		Built 17th April 1958 - Primrose Yellow - Exported to USA.
TS40000 L		Built 27th November 1958 - British Racing Green - Exported to USA.
TS50001 L		(TS50000 never built) - Built 16th April 1959 - Black Exported to USA.
TS60000 L		Built 22nd October 1959 - Silverstone Grey - Exported to USA.
TS70000 L		Built 7th March 1960 - Sebring White with Black leather and Black hood, wire wheels and heater. Exported to USA.
TS80000 L		Built 5th September 1960 - Signal Red with Black vynide and Black hood - Exported to France.

From this small sample, it can be seen that the USA figures very prominently in export destinations - by the late 1950's, around 90% of all TRs were finding their way to North America!

APPENDIX THREE: *UK Standard-Triumph*
Distributors as at 1953/54

As a build record certificate for a UK market TR frequently lists the distributor/dealer to whom the car was delivered when new, I feel it is worth incorporating a list of these as they were at the commencement of TR production. Frequently the build record will only quote the distributor's name, not the town or city where they were based, and thus this list could be of use to those seeking to trace the history of their vehicle where only the name is quoted. Very few of these firms are still in business in that same location under that same name, for 40 years of merger and liquidations have supervened - nevertheless, it might prove possible in some cases to obtain further information via the original dealer where records and or personnel have survived the years - don't hold your breath though!

The firms listed were the Standard Triumph main distributors - below them came a chain of smaller retail dealers which are not listed, for it is the main distributorship that crops up as the name on the build records, and almost all UK supplied TRs passed through a main distributor on their way to a customer. I say "almost all" as it **was** possible in some circumstances to order one's car direct from the Works and collect it personally. This seems to have occurred when competition minded owners had special equipment or tuning items fitted to their new TRs, and in such cases, the cars were normally pre-registered by the Works with a Coventry registration plate, thus enabling the owner to drive home legitimately and misleading hopeful purchasers years later into thinking that they had acquired a Works team car! However, it does seem that even in such cases as this, a distributor would get a "rake-off" and credit for selling such a car, even where they had never actually seen it prior to the customer taking possession!

The following list is in alphabetical order of town/city, and the Counties are quoted as they were in 1953 before the Government upset things!

Rossleigh Ltd	Aberdeen,
Station Garages	Amersham, Bucks
Chamberlain and Sons	Aylesbury, Bucks
Quenby Bros	Baldock, Herts
County Garages	Bath, Somerset
Wilson Bros and Humphreys	Bedford
Clarence Engineering	Belfast,
Bexhill Motor Co	Bexhill, Sussex
P J Evans & Co	Birmingham
H R Moore & Co	Bishop's Stortford, Herts
Stanbourne Motor Co	Bournemouth.
Albert Farnell Ltd	Bradford,
Moore of Brighton	Brighton.

College Motors	Bristol
K J Motors	Bromley, Kent
Burton Automobile Co	Burton-on-Trent, Staffs
King and Harper	Cambridge
Nortons of Cardiff	Cardiff. Wales
County Motors	Carlisle, Cumberland
Eastern Automobiles	Chelmsford, Essex
James Edwards	Chester
Wadham Bros	Chichester, Sussex
Kennings	Clay Cross, Derbyshire
Hollingdrakes	Colwyn Bay, Wales
S H Newsome	Coventry
Cookes Garages	Crewe, Cheshire
Cleveland Car Co	Darlington,
J J Wright & Sons	Dereham, Norfolk
Edwards Motors	Doncaster, Yorks
Tilleys	Dorchester, Dorset
F W Mays Ltd	Dorking, Surrey
Dumfries Motor Co	Dumfries, Scotland
Rossleigh Ltd	Dundee, Scotland
Rossleigh Ltd	Edinburgh, Scotland
Motor Macs Ltd	Exeter, Devon
Swain and Jones	Farnham, Surrey
Martin Walter & Co	Folkestone, Kent
Macharg Rennie and Lindsay	Glasgow, Scotland
Westgate Motor House & Co	Gloucester
Jordans Garage	Godalming, Surrey
White's Garage	Grimsby, Lincolnshire
Puttocks of Guildford	Guildford, Surrey
Central Garage	Halifax, Yorks
Glovers of Ripon	Harrogate, Yorks
County Motors	Hereford
A G Boyes & Co	Huddersfield, Yorks
W L Thompson Ltd	Hull, Yorks
James Ferries Ltd	Inverness, Scotland
Botwoods	Ipswich, Suffolk
St. Aubin's Motor Co	Jersey, C. I.
Atkinson and Griffin	Kendal, Westmoreland
Central Motor Co	Kettering, Northants
W H Johnson & Co	King's Lynn, Norfolk
Lankester Engineering Co	Kingston, Surrey
Rossleigh Ltd	Kirkcaldy, Fife.
Midland Autos	Leamington Spa
John Kaye & Co	Leeds, Yorks
H A Browett & Co	Leicester
Wests of Lincoln	Lincoln
C A Brittain & CO	Liverpool
Frank Jones & Son	Llanelli, Wales
Standard Triumph Sales	London, 37 Davies St, Grosvenor Square, W1
Standard Triumph Sales	98A Boundary Road, St.John's Wood London, NW8
Miles of Maidstone	Maidstone, Kent
Portland Motor Co	Mansfield, Nottinghamshire
Northdown Motor Co	Margate, Kent
Metropole Motor Co	Minehead, Somerset
Martin and Chillingworth	Newbury, Berkshire
Rossleigh Ltd	Newcastle-upon-Tyne
Douglas Garages	Northampton
Duff, Morgan and Vermont	Norwich, Norfolk
F Mitchell & Co	Nottingham
Eyles and Eyles	Oxford
Julians	Reading, Berkshire
Reigate Garages	Reigate, Surrey
Kings Road Garages	St. Annes, Lancs
E W Hatfield	Sheffield, Yorks
Arthur Charles Ltd	Shrewsbury
South Bucks Garages	Slough, Bucks
Wadham Brothers	Southampton
Wadham Brothers	Southsea, Hants
Attwoods Garages	Stafford
Rossleigh Ltd	Stirling, Scotland
Hollingdrake Motor Co	Stockport, Cheshire
Tom Byatt Ltd	Stoke on Trent
F Guyver & Sons	Stratford on Avon
Dunn's Garage	Sunderland
Quantock Motors	Swindon, Wiltshire
Somerset Motors	Taunton, Somerset
South Devon Garages	Torquay, Devon
Central Garages	Trowbridge, Wiltshire
S Hicks and Co	Truro, Cornwall
G Stevenson & Co	Tunbridge Wells, Kent
Wadham Brothers	Waterlooville, Hants
Wadham Brothers	Winchester, Hants
Lambs	Woodford Green, Essex
P W Barker	Worcester
Douglas Seaton & Co	Yeovil, Somerset
Myers and Burnell	York

Exactly 100 Standard-Triumph distributors, all happy to sell you a new TR, guaranteed for 6 months and at full list price!

APPENDIX FOUR:
The First Hundred Cars

T his Appendix gives details of the first 100 cars - production details of the first 100 TR2s built between July and November 1953.

I felt it might be of interest to extract from the records brief details of the first 100 cars built, together with their delivery destinations. Space precludes any greater number being listed, unfortunately; I have used a key to refer to paint/trim/hood colour details as follows:-

IB	=	Ice Blue
W	–	Pearl White
B	=	Black
OY	=	Olive Yellow
G	=	Geranium
BY	=	Blackberry
GY	=	Grey

All these first 100 cars were fitted with leather upholstery, and fortunately delivery destinations are listed in each case. However, several cars listed as destined for export actually stayed in the UK, in order to satisfy the clamour from the 100 home market distributors for a demonstrator. Despite this, some of the distributors did not receive their first TR2 until the start of 1954. 'L' of course denotes left hand drive, and 'O' overdrive. Right hand drive cars have no suffix letter.

1953 Date Built	Comm.ission Number	Delivery Dest'n	Paint/trim/ hood colour	Notes
July 22nd	TS1 LO	Canada	W/G/G	Exists in the USA
July 22nd	TS2	Dublin Ireland	W/G/G	Exists in the UK Reg.No. 773EWO
Aug 10th	TS3 L	California USA	G/GY/IB	
Aug 12th	TS4 L	California USA	W/G/G	
Aug 14th	TS5 L	California USA	IB/G/G	Exists in California
Aug 18th	TS6	S/T Publicity Dept	G/GY/GY	OHP771, the first road test car (engine TS9E)
Aug 21st	TS7 L	California USA	W/GY/W	Believed still to exist in USA

1953 Date Built	Commission Number	Delivery Destination	Paint/trim/ hood colour	Notes
Aug 25th	TS8	Works	IB/G/IB	OHP676 - engine TS10E. Works development car.
Aug 27th	TS9 L	Sweden	OY/GY/G	Believed still to exist in Sweden
Aug 31st	TS10 LO	Portugal	B/G/G	This was NHP49,used initially for some publicity shots, presum ably resprayed white, as this is its colour in the photographs.
Sept 4th	TS11 L	France	W/G/G	Paris Motor Show car.
Sept 7th	TS12 L	USA	OY/G/G	
Sept 9th	TS13	Scottish Motor Show	G/GY/IB	
Sept 10th	TS14'O'	Publicity Dept	W/GY/G	"To Mr Alick Dick,Very Urgent". Registered OHP242, believed still to exist, possibly in Germany?
Sept 11th	TS15	Home Market Demonstrator	G/GY/IB	OHP 677
Sept 14th	TS16	"to Berkeley Square "	W/GY/W	1st car built with wire wheels, London Demonstrator
Sept 15th	TS17 L	USA	W/GY/W	
Sept 16th	TS18	Earls Court Motor Show	IB/GY/IB	
Sept 22nd	TS19 L(SP)O	Earls Court Motor Show	W/G/G	The first so-called "speed" model, "Jabbeke" replica.
Sept 23rd	TS20 L	No details	No body	Chassis only built for exhibition purposes.
Sept 23rd	TS21 L	USA	G/GY/IB	
Sept 25th	TS22 L	USA	IB/G/G	Still exists in USA.
Sept 29th	TS23 L	USA	W/G/G	
Sept 29th	TS24 L	USA	W/G/G	
Sept 30th	TS25	"To Standard Triumph London Sales Office"	OY/BY/BY	
Sept 30th	TS26 L	W Germany	IB/G/G	
Oct 1st	TS 27 L	W Germany	W/G/G	
Oct 1st	TS28	"Earls Court Motor Show"	G/BY/BY	"Fit rear wheel spats" . OHP 300
Oct 2nd	TS29 L	USA	W/G/G	
Oct 2nd	TS30 L	Belgium	IB/G/G	
Oct 5th	TS31 L	Canada	IB/BY/BY	
Oct 5th	TS32 L	Hawaii	IB/BY/BY	
Oct 6th	TS33 L	USA	W/G/G	
Oct 6th	TS34 L	Colombia	IB/BY/BY	
Oct 7th	TS35 L	France	IB/GY/IB	
Oct 8th	TS36 L	Holland	IB/GY/IB	
Oct 8th	TS37 L	Portugal	G/GY/IB	
Oct 9th	TS38 L	USA	W/G/G	
Oct 12th	TS39 L	Sweden	G/GY/IB	
Oct 12th	TS40 L	Belgium	G/BY/BY	
Oct 13th	TS41 L	USA	G/BY/BY	
Oct 14th	TS43 L	USA	OY/BY/BY	
Oct 15th	TS44 L	USA	OY/BY/BY	

1953 - Date Built	Commission Number	Delivery Destination	Paint/trim/ hood colour	Notes
Oct 15th	TS45 L	USA	OY/GY/IB	
Oct 16th	TS46	Home Market	IB/BY/BY	Reg.No.STB999 still exists in UK in need of restoration.
Oct 19th	TS47	Home Market	IB/BY/BY	
Oct 19th	TS48	Ceylon	IB/G/G	Reimported to UK where it still exists, registered SXY91.
Oct 20th	TS49	Hong Kong	B/GY/W	First black car built.
Oct 20th	TS50	Singapore	B/BY/G	
Oct 22nd	TS51	Gold Coast	B/G/IB	
Oct 22nd	TS52	Home Market	B/G/IB	
Oct 22nd	TS53L	USA	B/GY/IB	
Oct 23rd	TS54 L	USA	B/GY/W	
Oct 23rd	TS55 L	USA	B/G/G	
Oct 23rd	TS56 L	USA	B/BY/IB	
Oct 23rd	TS57 L	USA	B/G/G	
Oct 27th	TS58 L	Sweden	W/G/G	
Oct 27th	TS59 L	Holland	W/G/G	
Oct 28th	TS60 L	Casablanca	W/G/G	
Oct 29th	TS61 L	Norway	W/G/G	
Oct 29th	TS62 L O	Hawaii	W/G/G	
Oct 29th	TS63 O	Home Market	W/G/G	Believed still to exist in UK- reg.no.6969UA (not original registration).
Oct 30th	TS64 O	Home Market	G/GY/BY	Recently rebuilt in UK, reg. no. unknown.
Oct 30th	TS65 O	New Zealand	W/GY/W	
Nov 2nd	TS66	South Africa	W/GY/W	
Nov 2nd	TS67	Malta	W/G/G	
Nov 3rd	TS68 L	USA	IB/G/G	
Nov 3rd	TS69 L	USA	IB/G/G	Still exists in USA
Nov 3rd	TS70 L	USA	IB/GY/IB	
Nov 4th	TS71 L	USA	IB/GY/IB	
Nov 4th	TS72 L	USA	IB/GY/IB	
Nov 5th	TS73	Home Market	IB/GY/IB	
Nov 5th	TS74	Home Market	IB/BY/BY	
Nov 5th	TS75	Trinidad	W/G/G	
Nov 6th	TS76 L O	Kuwait	W/G/G	
Nov 6th	TS77	Home Market	W/BY/BY	Originally destined for South Africa.
Nov 6th	TS78	Home Market	W/GY/W	Originally destined for West Indies. Registered ORW 600.
Nov 9th	TS79	Home Market	W/GY/W	
Nov 9th	TS80	Home Market	W/G/G	
Nov 9th	TS81	Home Market	W/BY/BY	
Nov 10th	TS82 O	Home Market	W/BY/BY	Originally destined for India, Reg No.NHP222 -still exists in UK.
Nov 10th	TS83	Home Market	W/BY/BY	
Nov 10th	TS84 L	Denmark	W/GY/GY	Still exists in Denmark
Nov 10th	TS85 O	Rhodesia	B/GY/IB	
Nov 11th	TS86 L O	Portugal	B/GY/G	
Nov 11th	TS87 L	Norway	B/G/BY	
Nov 11th	TS88 L O	W.Germany	B/G/BY	
Nov 11th	TS89 L	Holland	B/G/BY	Still exists in Holland
Nov 12th	TS90 L O	USA	IB/G/G	

1953 - Date Built	Commission Number	Delivery Destination	Paint/trim/ hood colour	Notes
Nov 12th	TS91 L O	Canada	IB/G/G	
Nov 12th	TS92 L O	Canada	IB/BY/BY	
Nov 13th	TS93 L	USA	IB/BY/BY	Still exists in USA
Nov 13th	TS94 L	USA	IB/BY/BY	
Nov 13th	TS95 L	USA	IB/BY/BY	
Nov 13th	TS96 L	USA	IB/BY/BY/	
Nov 16th	TS97 L	USA	IB/BY/BY	
Nov 16th	TS98 L	USA	IB/GY/BY	
Nov 16th	TS99 L	USA	IB/GY/BY	
Nov 16th	TS100 L	USA	IB/GY/BY	

One can draw a few conclusions from a brief study of these first 100 cars. By mid November, 5 months after production had started, it had staggered up to 4 cars each working day - just about qualifying the TR2 as a serious production car. Of these first 100, 33 were right hand drive, of which 23 stayed in the UK and 67 (including the chassis TS20) were left hand drive. Of these latter, no fewer than 36 went to the USA, not including the two cars to Hawaii. It seems extraordinary that cars should reach Hawaii, the Gold Coast and Trinidad, for instance, while none apparently went to India, Australia, Spain or Italy! Only 16 were initially equipped with overdrive (although TS6 had it fitted later), and of these, amazingly, only one went to the USA, the remaining 35 cars for the States having standard transmission. Quite why overdrive wasn't specified on USA cars, with that Country's huge distances and long, straight roads, yet it turned up on cars sent to confined places such as Hawaii and Kuwait, defies the imagination! As to colours, White was just more popular than Ice Blue, with 34 as opposed to 33 cars. 14 were black, 12 Geranium, 6 Olive Yellow and one had no bodywork. The most common colour combination was the reasonably tasteful one of Pearl White bodywork with Geranium trim and hood, 21 such cars being built within this first 100. Some of the combinations must have bordered on the outrageous, however, such as TS9 in Olive Yellow with Grey trim and a Geranium hood, or TS37 finished in Geranium Pink with Grey upholstery and an Ice Blue hood! Were such cars to be restored today to these specifications, surely more than just eyebrows would be raised in concours competitions!

Survival rates over the past 40 years have been surprisingly good, with 16 of the 100 known or believed still to exist. I would guess that there are at least another 7 or 8 not known to the TR Register however, probably more. One question that does forever intrigue me is whether any of these first cars survive anywhere in genuinely original condition, that is with original paint and trim, and to unmodified mechanical and bodily specification. Just possibly one such car does exist somwhere in the world - and if it does, the TR Register would be delighted to hear of it!

BIBLIOGRAPHY:

"Motor Sport" Magazine — 1951 - 1970
"Autosport" Magazine — 1953 - 1960
"The Motor" Magazine — 1952 - 1960
"The Autocar" Magazine — 1952 - 1961
"Sports Cars Illustrated" Magazine — 1957 - 1962
"Road and Track" Magazine — 1954 - 1960
"TRaction" - The Magazine of
the TR Register — 1970 - 1994
"Standard Car Review" Magazine — 1953 - 1960
The Triumph Register of America
newsletter — 1980 - 1994
"The Triumph Companion",
K. Ullyett — 1962
"TR for Triumph", C. Harvey — 1983
"The Works Triumphs", G. Robson — 1993
"The Story of Triumph Sports Cars",
G. Robson — 1972
"Triumph TRs", G. Robson — 1991
"Original TR", W. Piggott — 1991
"TR2/3/3A Superprofile", W. Piggott — 1987
"TR2/3/3A Gold Portfolio",
Brooklands Books — 1994
"Country Life" Magazine
"Tatler and Bystander" Magazine
Express Newspapers Ltd

Standard-Triumph Sales Catalogues and literature generally

Other Research Sources:

British Motor Industry Heritage Trust, Gaydon
Archives of the TR Register
Archives of Haymarket Publishing Ltd
National Motor Museum, Beaulieu
Standard Register Archives
Birmingham Central Reference Library
Coventry Public Record Office
Royal Automobile Club Archives
Ian Gibson's TR Archive

Also many private individuals who have given of their time and lent irreplaceable items and photographs, and whose names I hope appear in the "Acknowledgements" at the front of this book. If I have inadvertently omitted any source or individual, then my apologies are profuse.

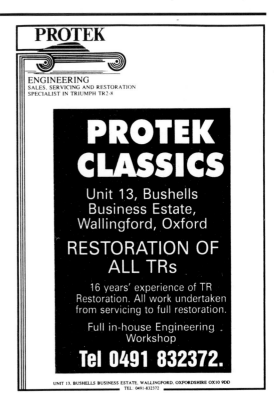

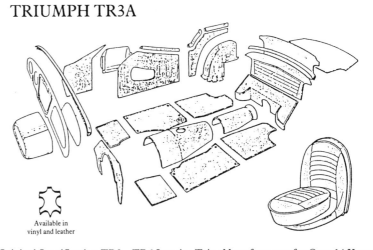

287

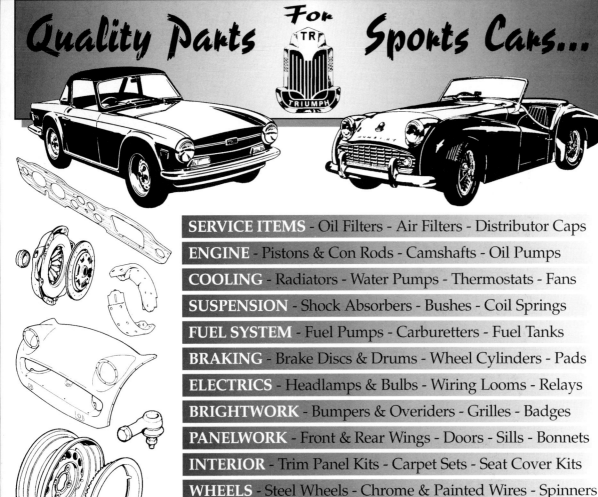

Quality Parts For Sports Cars...

SERVICE ITEMS - Oil Filters - Air Filters - Distributor Caps

ENGINE - Pistons & Con Rods - Camshafts - Oil Pumps

COOLING - Radiators - Water Pumps - Thermostats - Fans

SUSPENSION - Shock Absorbers - Bushes - Coil Springs

FUEL SYSTEM - Fuel Pumps - Carburetters - Fuel Tanks

BRAKING - Brake Discs & Drums - Wheel Cylinders - Pads

ELECTRICS - Headlamps & Bulbs - Wiring Looms - Relays

BRIGHTWORK - Bumpers & Overiders - Grilles - Badges

PANELWORK - Front & Rear Wings - Doors - Sills - Bonnets

INTERIOR - Trim Panel Kits - Carpet Sets - Seat Cover Kits

WHEELS - Steel Wheels - Chrome & Painted Wires - Spinners

ACCESSORIES - Alloy Wheels - Halogen Headlamp Kits

ACCESSORIES - Steering Wheels - Wire Wheel Conversions

ACCESSORIES - Tools - Handbooks - Workshop Manuals

TUNING PARTS - Oil Cooler Kits - Electronic Ignition Kits

TUNING PARTS - Handling Kits - Cylinder Heads - Carbs

TUNING PARTS - Rocker Feed Kits - Uprated Suspension

TUNING PARTS - Lowered Springs - Fast Road Camshafts

To order your copies of the Moss Triumph catalogues please contact your nearest branch listed opposite.

MOSS

Birmingham

991 Wolverhampton Rd
Oldbury, West Midlan
B69 4RJ
Tel. 0121 544 5555
Fax. 0121 544 4340

Darlington

15 Allington Way
Yarm Road Industrial E
Darlington, Co. Durhan
DL1 4QB
Tel. 01325 281 343
Fax. 01325 485 563

Manchester

113-115 Stockport Roa
Cheadle Heath
Stockport, Cheshire
SK3 0JE
Tel. 0161 480 6402
Fax. 0161 429 0349

Bristol

93 Newfoundland Roa
Bristol, Avon
BS2 9LU
Tel. 0272 232 523
Fax. 0272 428 236

Shipley

Regent House
Dockfield Road
Shipley, West Yorkshi
BD17 7SF
Tel. 01274 594 071
Fax. 01274 531 149

London

22-28 Manor Road
Richmond
Surrey
TW9 1YB
Tel. 0181 948 6666
Fax. 0181 940 9268

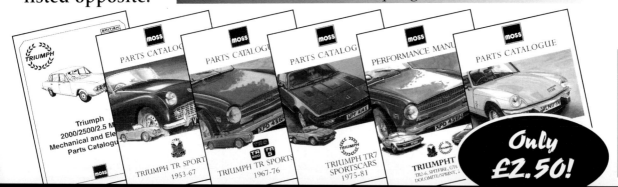

Triumph 2000/2500/2.5 M Mechanical and Ele Parts Catalogu

TRIUMPH TR SPORT 1953-67

TRIUMPH TR SPORTS 1967-76

TRIUMPH TR7 SPORTSCARS 1975-81

TRIUMPHT TR-6, SPITFIRE, GT6 DOLOMITE/SPRINT, 4

Only £2.50!

BRITISH MOTOR
HERITAGE APPROV